Connected Mathematics 2

Thinking With Mathematical Models
Looking for Pythagoras
Growing, Growing, Growing
Frogs, Fleas, and Painted Cubes
Kaleidoscopes, Hubcaps, and Mirrors
Say It With Symbols
The Shapes of Algebra
Samples and Populations

Glenda Lappan
James T. Fey
William M. Fitzgerald
Susan N. Friel
Elizabeth Difanis Phillips

PEARSON

Prentice Hall

Boston, Massachusetts
Upper Saddle River, New Jersey

Connected Mathematics™ was developed at Michigan State University with financial support from the Michigan State University Office of the Provost, Computing and Technology, and the College of Natural Science.

This material is based upon work supported by the National Science Foundation under Grant No. MDR 9150217 and Grant No. ESI 9986372. Opinions expressed are those of the authors and not necessarily those of the Foundation.

The Michigan State University authors and administration have agreed that all MSU royalties arising from this publication will be devoted to purposes supported by the MSU Mathematics Education Enrichment Fund.

All **Acknowledgments** pages constitute an extension of this copyright page.

Acknowledgments for *Thinking With Mathematical Models* appear on page 69 of *Thinking With Mathematical Models*.
Acknowledgments for *Looking for Pythagoras* appear on page 72 of *Looking for Pythagoras*.
Acknowledgments for *Growing, Growing, Growing* appear on page 84 of *Growing, Growing, Growing*.
Acknowledgments for *Frogs, Fleas, and Painted Cubes* appear on page 88 of *Frogs, Fleas, and Painted Cubes*.
Acknowledgments for *Kaleidoscopes, Hubcaps, and Mirrors* appear on page 112 of *Kaleidoscopes, Hubcaps, and Mirrors*.
Acknowledgments for *Say It With Symbols* appear on page 95 of *Say It With Symbols*.
Acknowledgments for *The Shapes of Algebra* appear on page 91 of *The Shapes of Algebra*.
Acknowledgments for *Samples and Populations* appear on page 93 of *Samples and Populations*.

ISBN 0-13-165623-6

4 5 6 7 8 9 10   09 08 07

Authors of Connected Mathematics

(from left to right) Glenda Lappan, Betty Phillips, Susan Friel, Bill Fitzgerald, Jim Fey

Glenda Lappan is a University Distinguished Professor in the Department of Mathematics at Michigan State University. Her research and development interests are in the connected areas of students' learning of mathematics and mathematics teachers' professional growth and change related to the development and enactment of K–12 curriculum materials.

James T. Fey is a Professor of Curriculum and Instruction and Mathematics at the University of Maryland. His consistent professional interest has been development and research focused on curriculum materials that engage middle and high school students in problem-based collaborative investigations of mathematical ideas and their applications.

William M. Fitzgerald *(Deceased)* was a Professor in the Department of Mathematics at Michigan State University. His early research was on the use of concrete materials in supporting student learning and led to the development of teaching materials for laboratory environments. Later he helped develop a teaching model to support student experimentation with mathematics.

Susan N. Friel is a Professor of Mathematics Education in the School of Education at the University of North Carolina at Chapel Hill. Her research interests focus on statistics education for middle-grade students and, more broadly, on teachers' professional development and growth in teaching mathematics K–8.

Elizabeth Difanis Phillips is a Senior Academic Specialist in the Mathematics Department of Michigan State University. She is interested in teaching and learning mathematics for both teachers and students. These interests have led to curriculum and professional development projects at the middle school and high school levels, as well as projects related to the teaching and learning of algebra across the grades.

Field Test Sites for CMP2

During the development of the revised edition of *Connected Mathematics* (CMP2), more than 100 classroom teachers have field-tested materials at 49 school sites in 12 states and the District of Columbia. This classroom testing occurred over three academic years (2001 through 2004), allowing careful study of the effectiveness of each of the 24 units that comprise the program. A special thanks to the students and teachers at these pilot schools.

Arkansas
Magnolia Public Schools
Kittena Bell*, Judith Trowell*; *Central Elementary School:* Maxine Broom, Betty Eddy, Tiffany Fallin, Bonnie Flurry, Carolyn Monk, Elizabeth Tye; *Magnolia Junior High School:* Monique Bryan, Ginger Cook, David Graham, Shelby Lamkin

Colorado
Boulder Public Schools
Nevin Platt Middle School: Judith Koenig
St. Vrain Valley School District, Longmont
Westview Middle School: Colleen Beyer, Kitty Canupp, Ellie Decker*, Peggy McCarthy, Tanya deNobrega, Cindy Payne, Ericka Pilon, Andrew Roberts

District of Columbia
Capitol Hill Day School: Ann Lawrence

Georgia
University of Georgia, Athens
Brad Findell
Madison Public Schools
Morgan County Middle School: Renee Burgdorf, Lynn Harris, Nancy Kurtz, Carolyn Stewart

Maine
Falmouth Public Schools
Falmouth Middle School: Donna Erikson, Joyce Hebert, Paula Hodgkins, Rick Hogan, David Legere, Cynthia Martin, Barbara Stiles, Shawn Towle*

Michigan
Portland Public Schools
Portland Middle School: Mark Braun, Holly DeRosia, Kathy Dole*, Angie Foote, Teri Keusch, Tammi Wardwell
Traverse City Area Public Schools
Bertha Vos Elementary: Kristin Sak; *Central Grade School:* Michelle Clark; Jody Meyers; *Eastern Elementary:* Karrie Tufts; *Interlochen Elementary:* Mary McGee-Cullen; *Long Lake Elementary:* Julie Faulkner*, Charlie Maxbauer, Katherine Sleder; *Norris Elementary:* Hope Slanaker; *Oak Park Elementary:* Jessica Steed; *Traverse Heights Elementary:* Jennifer Wolfert; *Westwoods Elementary:* Nancy Conn; *Old Mission Peninsula School:* Deb Larimer; *Traverse City East Junior High:* Ivanka Berkshire, Ruthanne Kladder, Jan Palkowski, Jane Peterson, Mary Beth Schmitt; *Traverse City West Junior High:* Dan Fouch*, Ray Fouch
Sturgis Public Schools
Sturgis Middle School: Ellen Eisele

Minnesota
Burnsville School District 191
Hidden Valley Elementary: Stephanie Cin, Jane McDevitt
Hopkins School District 270
Alice Smith Elementary: Sandra Cowing, Kathleen Gustafson, Martha Mason, Scott Stillman; *Eisenhower Elementary:* Chad Bellig, Patrick Berger, Nancy Glades, Kye Johnson, Shane Wasserman, Victoria Wilson; *Gatewood Elementary:* Sarah Ham, Julie Kloos, Janine Pung, Larry Wade; *Glen Lake Elementary:* Jacqueline Cramer, Kathy Hering, Cecelia Morris, Robb Trenda; *Katherine Curren Elementary:* Diane Bancroft, Sue DeWit, John Wilson; *L. H. Tanglen Elementary:* Kevin Athmann, Lisa Becker, Mary LaBelle, Kathy Rezac, Roberta Severson; *Meadowbrook Elementary:* Jan Gauger, Hildy Shank, Jessica Zimmerman; *North Junior High:* Laurel Hahn, Kristin Lee, Jodi Markuson, Bruce Mestemacher, Laurel Miller, Bonnie Rinker, Jeannine Salzer, Sarah Shafer, Cam Stottler; *West Junior High:* Alicia Beebe, Kristie Earl, Nobu Fujii, Pam Georgetti, Susan Gilbert, Regina Nelson Johnson, Debra Lindstrom, Michele Luke*, Jon Sorenson
Minneapolis School District 1
Ann Sullivan K-8 School: Bronwyn Collins; Anne Bartel* (Curriculum and Instruction Office)
Wayzata School District 284
Central Middle School: Sarajane Myers, Dan Nielsen, Tanya Ravenholdt
White Bear Lake School District 624
Central Middle School: Amy Jorgenson, Michelle Reich, Brenda Sammon

New York
New York City Public Schools
IS 89: Yelena Aynbinder, Chi-Man Ng, Nina Rapaport, Joel Spengler, Phyllis Tam*, Brent Wyso; *Wagner Middle School:* Jason Appel, Intissar Fernandez, Yee Gee Get, Richard Goldstein, Irving Marcus, Sue Norton, Bernadita Owens, Jennifer Rehn*, Kevin Yuhas

---

* indicates a Field Test Site Coordinator

Ohio

Talawanda School District, Oxford
Talawanda Middle School: Teresa Abrams, Larry Brock, Heather Brosey, Julie Churchman, Monna Even, Karen Fitch, Bob George, Amanda Klee, Pat Meade, Sandy Montgomery, Barbara Sherman, Lauren Steidl

Miami University
Jeffrey Wanko*

Springfield Public Schools
Rockway School: Jim Mamer

Pennsylvania

Pittsburgh Public Schools
Kenneth Labuskes, Marianne O'Connor, Mary Lynn Raith*; *Arthur J. Rooney Middle School:* David Hairston, Stamatina Mousetis, Alfredo Zangaro; *Frick International Studies Academy:* Suzanne Berry, Janet Falkowski, Constance Finseth, Romika Hodge, Frank Machi; *Reizenstein Middle School:* Jeff Baldwin, James Brautigam, Lorena Burnett, Glen Cobbett, Michael Jordan, Margaret Lazur, Melissa Munnell, Holly Neely, Ingrid Reed, Dennis Reft

Texas

Austin Independent School District
Bedichek Middle School: Lisa Brown, Jennifer Glasscock, Vicki Massey

El Paso Independent School District
Cordova Middle School: Armando Aguirre, Anneliesa Durkes, Sylvia Guzman, Pat Holguin*, William Holguin, Nancy Nava, Laura Orozco, Michelle Peña, Roberta Rosen, Patsy Smith, Jeremy Wolf

Plano Independent School District
Patt Henry, James Wohlgehagen*; *Frankford Middle School:* Mandy Baker, Cheryl Butsch, Amy Dudley, Betsy Eshelman, Janet Greene, Cort Haynes, Kathy Letchworth, Kay Marshall, Kelly McCants, Amy Reck, Judy Scott, Syndy Snyder, Lisa Wang; *Wilson Middle School:* Darcie Bane, Amanda Bedenko, Whitney Evans, Tonelli Hatley, Sarah (Becky) Higgs, Kelly Johnston, Rebecca McElligott, Kay Neuse, Cheri Slocum, Kelli Straight

Washington

Evergreen School District
Shahala Middle School: Nicole Abrahamsen, Terry Coon*, Carey Doyle, Sheryl Drechsler, George Gemma, Gina Helland, Amy Hilario, Darla Lidyard, Sean McCarthy, Tilly Meyer, Willow Neuwelt, Todd Parsons, Brian Pederson, Stan Posey, Shawn Scott, Craig Sjoberg, Lynette Sundstrom, Charles Switzer, Luke Youngblood

Wisconsin

Beaver Dam Unified School District
Beaver Dam Middle School: Jim Braemer, Jeanne Frick, Jessica Greatens, Barbara Link, Dennis McCormick, Karen Michels, Nancy Nichols*, Nancy Palm, Shelly Stelsel, Susan Wiggins

---

* indicates a Field Test Site Coordinator

Reviews of CMP to Guide Development of CMP2

Before writing for CMP2 began or field tests were conducted, the first edition of *Connected Mathematics* was submitted to the mathematics faculties of school districts from many parts of the country and to 80 individual reviewers for extensive comments.

School District Survey Reviews of CMP

Arizona
Madison School District #38 (Phoenix)

Arkansas
Cabot School District, Little Rock School District, Magnolia School District

California
Los Angeles Unified School District

Colorado
St. Vrain Valley School District (Longmont)

Florida
Leon County Schools (Tallahassee)

Illinois
School District #21 (Wheeling)

Indiana
Joseph L. Block Junior High (East Chicago)

Kentucky
Fayette County Public Schools (Lexington)

Maine
Selection of Schools

Massachusetts
Selection of Schools

Michigan
Sparta Area Schools

Minnesota
Hopkins School District

Texas
Austin Independent School District, The El Paso Collaborative for Academic Excellence, Plano Independent School District

Wisconsin
Platteville Middle School

Individual Reviewers of CMP

Arkansas
Deborah Cramer; Robby Frizzell *(Taylor)*; Lowell Lynde *(University of Arkansas, Monticello)*; Leigh Manzer *(Norfork)*; Lynne Roberts *(Emerson High School, Emerson)*; Tony Timms *(Cabot Public Schools)*; Judith Trowell *(Arkansas Department of Higher Education)*

California
José Alcantar *(Gilroy)*; Eugenie Belcher *(Gilroy)*; Marian Pasternack *(Lowman M. S. T. Center, North Hollywood)*; Susana Pezoa *(San Jose)*; Todd Rabusin *(Hollister)*; Margaret Siegfried *(Ocala Middle School, San Jose)*; Polly Underwood *(Ocala Middle School, San Jose)*

Colorado
Janeane Golliher *(St. Vrain Valley School District, Longmont)*; Judith Koenig *(Nevin Platt Middle School, Boulder)*

Florida
Paige Loggins *(Swift Creek Middle School, Tallahassee)*

Illinois
Jan Robinson *(School District #21, Wheeling)*

Indiana
Frances Jackson *(Joseph L. Block Junior High, East Chicago)*

Kentucky
Natalee Feese *(Fayette County Public Schools, Lexington)*

Maine
Betsy Berry *(Maine Math & Science Alliance, Augusta)*

Maryland
Joseph Gagnon *(University of Maryland, College Park)*; Paula Maccini *(University of Maryland, College Park)*

Massachusetts
George Cobb *(Mt. Holyoke College, South Hadley)*; Cliff Kanold *(University of Massachusetts, Amherst)*

Michigan
Mary Bouck *(Farwell Area Schools)*; Carol Dorer *(Slauson Middle School, Ann Arbor)*; Carrie Heaney *(Forsythe Middle School, Ann Arbor)*; Ellen Hopkins *(Clague Middle School, Ann Arbor)*; Teri Keusch *(Portland Middle School, Portland)*; Valerie Mills *(Oakland Schools, Waterford)*; Mary Beth Schmitt *(Traverse City East Junior High, Traverse City)*; Jack Smith *(Michigan State University, East Lansing)*; Rebecca Spencer *(Sparta Middle School, Sparta)*; Ann Marie Nicoll Turner *(Tappan Middle School, Ann Arbor)*; Scott Turner *(Scarlett Middle School, Ann Arbor)*

Minnesota
Margarita Alvarez *(Olson Middle School, Minneapolis)*; Jane Amundson *(Nicollet Junior High, Burnsville)*; Anne Bartel *(Minneapolis Public Schools)*; Gwen Ranzau Campbell *(Sunrise Park Middle School, White Bear Lake)*; Stephanie Cin *(Hidden Valley Elementary, Burnsville)*; Joan Garfield *(University of Minnesota, Minneapolis)*; Gretchen Hall *(Richfield Middle School, Richfield)*; Jennifer Larson *(Olson Middle School, Minneapolis)*; Michele Luke *(West Junior High, Minnetonka)*; Jeni Meyer *(Richfield Junior High, Richfield)*; Judy Pfingsten *(Inver Grove Heights Middle School, Inver Grove Heights)*; Sarah Shafer *(North Junior High, Minnetonka)*; Genni Steele *(Central Middle School, White Bear Lake)*; Victoria Wilson *(Eisenhower Elementary, Hopkins)*; Paul Zorn *(St. Olaf College, Northfield)*

New York
Debra Altenau-Bartolino *(Greenwich Village Middle School, New York)*; Doug Clements *(University of Buffalo)*; Francis Curcio *(New York University, New York)*; Christine Dorosh *(Clinton School for Writers, Brooklyn)*; Jennifer Rehn *(East Side Middle School, New York)*; Phyllis Tam *(IS 89 Lab School, New York)*;

Marie Turini *(Louis Armstrong Middle School, New York)*; Lucy West *(Community School District 2, New York)*; Monica Witt *(Simon Baruch Intermediate School 104, New York)*

Pennsylvania
Robert Aglietti *(Pittsburgh)*; Sharon Mihalich *(Pittsburgh)*; Jennifer Plumb *(South Hills Middle School, Pittsburgh)*; Mary Lynn Raith *(Pittsburgh Public Schools)*

Texas
Michelle Bittick *(Austin Independent School District)*; Margaret Cregg *(Plano Independent School District)*; Sheila Cunningham *(Klein Independent School District)*; Judy Hill *(Austin Independent School District)*; Patricia Holguin *(El Paso Independent School District)*; Bonnie McNemar *(Arlington)*; Kay Neuse *(Plano Independent School District)*; Joyce Polanco *(Austin Independent School District)*; Marge Ramirez *(University of Texas at El Paso)*; Pat Rossman *(Baker Campus, Austin)*; Cindy Schimek *(Houston)*; Cynthia Schneider *(Charles A. Dana Center, University of Texas at Austin)*; Uri Treisman *(Charles A. Dana Center, University of Texas at Austin)*; Jacqueline Weilmuenster *(Grapevine-Colleyville Independent School District)*; LuAnn Weynand *(San Antonio)*; Carmen Whitman *(Austin Independent School District)*; James Wohlgehagen *(Plano Independent School District)*

Washington
Ramesh Gangolli *(University of Washington, Seattle)*

Wisconsin
Susan Lamon *(Marquette University, Hales Corner)*; Steve Reinhart *(retired, Chippewa Falls Middle School, Eau Claire)*

Table of Contents

Thinking With Mathematical Models
Linear and Inverse Variation

Table of Contents

Looking for Pythagoras
The Pythagorean Theorem

Table of Contents

Growing, Growing, Growing
Exponential Relationships

Table of Contents

Frogs, Fleas, and Painted Cubes
Quadratic Relationships

Frogs, Fleas, and Painted Cubes

Table of Contents

Kaleidoscopes, Hubcaps, and Mirrors
Symmetry and Transformations

Kaleidoscopes, Hubcaps, and Mirrors

Table of Contents

Say It With Symbols
Making Sense of Symbols

Say It With Symbols

Table of Contents

The Shapes of Algebra
Linear Systems and Inequalities

The Shapes of Algebra

Table of Contents

Samples and Populations
Data and Statistics

Samples and Populations

Connected Mathematics 2

Thinking With Mathematical Models

Linear and Inverse Variation

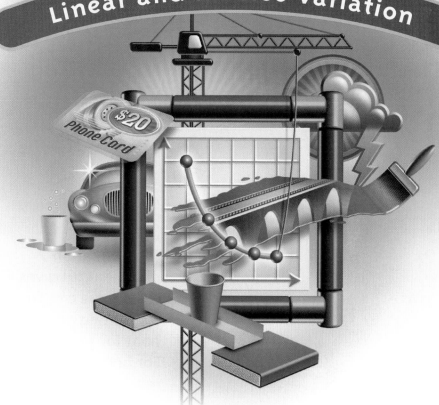

Glenda Lappan

James T. Fey

William M. Fitzgerald

Susan N. Friel

Elizabeth Difanis Phillips

PEARSON

Prentice
Hall

Boston, Massachusetts
Upper Saddle River, New Jersey

Thinking With Mathematical Models

How is the thickness of a steel beam or bridge related to its strength? How is the length of a beam or bridge related to its strength?

The equation $c = 4 + 0.10t$ gives the charge c in dollars for renting a paddle boat for t minutes. For how long can you rent a paddle boat if you have $12?

The cost for a group of students to go on an overnight field trip to a nature center is $750. Describe the shape of a graph relating the number of students to the cost per student.

In earlier *Connected Mathematics* units, you explored relationships between variables. You learned to recognize linear relationships from patterns in tables and graphs and to write equations for such relationships. You then used the equations to help you solve problems. As you work through the investigations in this unit, you will enhance your skill in recognizing and analyzing linear relationships. You will also compare linear patterns with nonlinear patterns, focusing on a special type of nonlinear relationship called an *inverse variation*.

You will conduct experiments, analyze the data, and then write equations that summarize, or model, the data patterns. You will then use your equations to make predictions about values beyond and between the data you collected.

The skills you develop in this unit will help you answer questions like those on the facing page.

Mathematical Highlights

Linear and Inverse Variation

In *Thinking With Mathematical Models,* **you will model relationships with graphs and equations, and then use your models to analyze situations and solve problems.**

You will learn how to:

- Recognize linear and nonlinear patterns in tables and graphs
- Describe data patterns using words and symbols
- Write equations to express patterns appearing in tables, graphs, and problems
- Solve linear equations
- Model situations with inequalities
- Write equations to describe inverse variations
- Use linear and inverse variation equations to solve problems and to make predictions and decisions

As you work on problems in this unit, ask yourself questions about problem situations that involve related variables.

What are the key variables in this situation?

What is the pattern relating the variables?

What kind of equation will express the relationship?

How can I use the equation to answer questions about the relationship?

Exploring Data Patterns

People in many professions use data and mathematical reasoning to solve problems and make predictions. For example, engineers analyze data from laboratory tests to determine how much weight a bridge can hold. Market researchers use customer survey data to predict demand for new products. Stockbrokers use algebraic formulas to forecast how much their investments will earn over time.

In several previous *Connected Mathematics* units, you used tables, graphs, and equations to explore and describe relationships between variables. In this investigation, you will develop your skill in using these tools to organize data from an experiment, find patterns, and make predictions.

1.1 Testing Bridge Thickness

Many bridges are built with frames of steel beams. Steel is very strong, but any beam will bend or break if you put enough weight on it. The amount of weight a beam can support is related to its thickness, length, and design. To design a bridge, engineers need to understand these relationships.

- How do you think the thickness of a beam is related to its strength? Do you think the relationship is linear?

- What other variables might affect the strength of a bridge?

Engineers often use scale models to test their designs. You can do your own experiments to discover mathematical patterns involved in building bridges.

Instructions for the Bridge-Thickness Experiment

Equipment:

- Two books of the same thickness
- A small paper cup
- About 50 pennies
- Several 11-inch-by-$4\frac{1}{4}$-inch strips of paper

Instructions:

- Start with one of the paper strips. Make a "bridge" by folding up 1 inch on each long side.

- Suspend the bridge between the books. The bridge should overlap each book by about 1 inch. Place the cup in the center of the bridge.

- Put pennies into the cup, one at a time, until the bridge collapses. Record the number of pennies you added to the cup. This number is the *breaking weight* of the bridge.

- Put two *new* strips of paper together to make a bridge of double thickness. Find the breaking weight for this bridge.

- Repeat this experiment to find the breaking weights of bridges made from three, four, and five strips of paper.

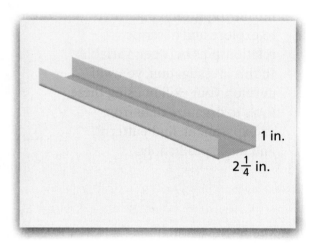

1 in.

$2\frac{1}{4}$ in.

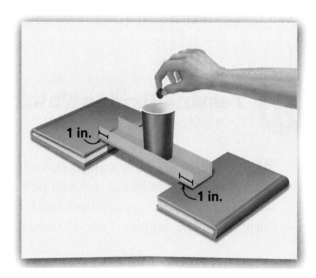

1 in.

1 in.

A. Conduct the bridge-thickness experiment to find breaking weights for bridges 1, 2, 3, 4, and 5 layers thick. Record your data in a table.

B. Make a graph of your (*bridge layers, breaking weight*) data.

C. Does the relationship between bridge thickness and breaking weight seem to be linear or nonlinear? How is this shown in the table and graph?

D. Suppose you could split layers of paper in half. What breaking weight would you predict for a bridge 2.5 layers thick? Explain.

E. 1. Predict the breaking weight for a bridge 6 layers thick. Explain your reasoning.

2. Test your prediction. Explain why results from such tests might not exactly match predictions.

ACE Homework starts on page 12.

For: Virtual Bridge Experiment
Visit: PHSchool.com
Web Code: apd-1101

1.2 Testing Bridge Lengths

In the last problem, you tested paper bridges of various thicknesses. You found that thicker bridges are stronger than thinner bridges. In this problem, you will experiment with paper bridges of various lengths.

How do you think the length of a bridge is related to its strength?

Are longer bridges stronger or weaker than shorter bridges?

You can do an experiment to find out how the length and strength of a bridge are related.

Instructions for the Bridge-Length Experiment

Equipment:

- Two books of the same thickness
- A small paper cup
- About 50 pennies
- $4\frac{1}{4}$-inch-wide strips with lengths 4, 6, 8, 9, and 11 inches

Instructions:

- Make paper bridges from the strips. For each strip, fold up 1 inch on each of the $4\frac{1}{4}$-inch sides.

- Start with the 4-inch bridge. Suspend the bridge between the two books as you did before. The bridge should overlap each book by about 1 inch. Place the paper cup in the center of the bridge.

- Put pennies into the cup, one at a time, until the bridge collapses. Record the number of pennies you added to the cup. As in the first experiment, this number is the breaking weight of the bridge.

- Repeat the experiment to find breaking weights for the other bridges.

A. Conduct the bridge-length experiment to find breaking weights for bridges of lengths 4, 6, 8, 9, and 11 inches. Record your data in a table.

B. Make a graph of your data.

C. Describe the relationship between bridge length and breaking weight. How is that relationship shown by patterns in your table and graph?

D. Use your data to predict the breaking weights for bridges of lengths 3, 5, 10, and 12 inches. Explain how you made your predictions.

E. Compare your data from this experiment with the data from the bridge-thickness experiment. How is the relationship between bridge thickness and breaking weight similar to the relationship between bridge length and breaking weight? How is it different?

ACE **Homework starts on page 12.**

Did You Know?

When designing a bridge, engineers need to consider the *load*, or the amount of weight, the bridge must support. The *dead load* is the weight of the bridge and fixed objects on the bridge. The *live load* is the weight of moving objects on the bridge.

On many city bridges in Europe—such as the famous Ponte Vecchio in Florence, Italy—dead load is very high because tollbooths, apartments, and shops are built right onto the bridge surface. Local ordinances can limit the amount of automobile and rail traffic on a bridge to help control live load.

Custom Construction Parts

Suppose a company called Custom Steel Products (CSP for short) provides construction materials to builders. CSP makes beams and staircase frames by attaching 1-foot-long steel rods in the following patterns. CSP will make these materials in any size a builder needs.

CSP Beams

1-foot steel rod

1-foot beam
made from 3 rods

2-foot beam
made from 7 rods

7-foot beam
made from 27 rods

CSP Staircase Frames

1 step
made from 4 rods

2 steps
made from 10 rods

3 steps
made from 18 rods

The manager at CSP needs to know the number of rods required for each design in any size a customer might order. To figure this out, she decides to study a few simple cases. She hopes to find *trends,* or patterns, she can extend to other cases.

A. 1. Copy and complete the table below to show the number of rods in beams of different lengths. **Hint:** Make drawings of the beams.

CSP Beams

Beam Length (ft)	1	2	3	4	5	6	7	8
Number of Rods	3	7	▦	▦	▦	▦	27	▦

2. Make a graph of the data in your table.

3. Describe the pattern of change in the number of rods as the beam length increases.

4. How is the pattern you described shown in the table? How is it shown in the graph?

5. How many steel rods are in a beam of length 50 feet? Explain.

B. 1. Copy and complete the table below to show the number of rods in staircase frames with different numbers of steps. **Hint:** Make drawings of the staircase frames.

CSP Staircase Frames

Number of Steps	1	2	3	4	5	6	7	8
Number of Rods	4	10	18	▦	▦	▦	▦	▦

2. Make a graph of the data in your table.

3. Describe the pattern of change in the number of rods as the number of steps increases.

4. How is the pattern you described shown in the table? How is it shown in the graph?

5. How many steel rods are in a staircase frame with 12 steps?

C. How is the pattern of change in Question A similar to the pattern in Question B? How is it different? Explain how the similarities and differences are shown in the tables and graphs.

D. Compare the patterns of change in this problem with the patterns of change in Problems 1.1 and 1.2. Describe any similarities and differences you find.

ACE | **Homework starts on page 12.**

Applications

1. A group of students conducts the bridge-thickness experiment with construction paper. Their results are shown in this table.

Bridge-Thickness Experiment

Thickness (layers)	1	2	3	4	5	6
Breaking Weight (pennies)	12	20	29	42	52	61

a. Make a graph of the (*thickness, breaking weight*) data. Describe the relationship between thickness and breaking weight.

b. Suppose it is possible to use half-layers of construction paper. What breaking weight would you predict for a bridge 3.5 layers thick? Explain.

c. Predict the breaking weight for a construction-paper bridge 8 layers thick. Explain how you made your prediction.

2. The table shows the maximum weight a crane arm can lift at various distances from its cab. (See the diagram below.)

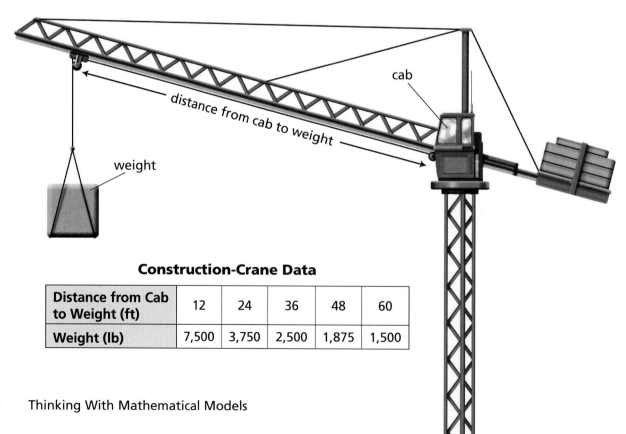

Construction-Crane Data

Distance from Cab to Weight (ft)	12	24	36	48	60
Weight (lb)	7,500	3,750	2,500	1,875	1,500

a. Describe the relationship between distance and weight for the crane.

b. Make a graph of the (*distance, weight*) data. Explain how the graph's shape shows the relationship you described in part (a).

c. Estimate the weight the crane can lift at distances of 18 feet, 30 feet, and 72 feet from the cab.

d. How, if at all, is the crane data similar to the data from the bridge experiments in Problems 1.1 and 1.2?

3. A beam or staircase frame from CSP costs $2.25 for each rod, plus $50 for shipping and handling.

a. Refer to your data for Question A of Problem 1.3. Copy and complete the following table to show the costs for beams of different lengths.

Costs of CSP Beams

Beam Length (ft)	1	2	3	4	5	6	7	8
Number of Rods	3	7	■	■	■	■	27	■
Cost of Beam	■	■	■	■	■	■	■	■

b. Make a graph of the (*beam length, cost*) data.

c. Describe the relationship between beam length and cost.

d. Refer to your data for Question B of Problem 1.3. Copy and complete the following table to show the costs for staircase frames with different numbers of steps.

Costs of CSP Staircase Frames

Number of Steps	1	2	3	4	5	6	7	8
Number of Rods	4	10	18	■	■	■	■	■
Cost of Frame	■	■	■	■	■	■	■	■

e. Make a graph of the (*number of steps, cost*) data.

f. Describe the relationship between the number of steps and the cost.

4. Parts (a)–(f) refer to relationships you have studied in this investigation. Tell whether each relationship is linear.

Homework Help Online
PHSchool.com
For: Help with Exercise 4
Web Code: ape-1104

   a. the relationship between beam length and cost (ACE Exercise 3)

   b. the relationship between the number of steps in a staircase frame and the cost (ACE Exercise 3)

   c. the relationship between bridge thickness and strength (Problem 1.1)

   d. the relationship between bridge length and strength (Problem 1.2)

   e. the relationship between beam length and the number of rods (Problem 1.3)

   f. the relationship between the number of steps in a staircase frame and the number of rods (Problem 1.3)

   g. Compare the patterns of change for all the nonlinear relationships in parts (a)–(f).

5. In many athletic competitions, medals are awarded to top athletes. The medals are often awarded in ceremonies with medal winners standing on special platforms. The sketches show how to make platforms by stacking boxes.

1 medalist
1 box

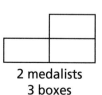
2 medalists
3 boxes

3 medalists
6 boxes

a. Copy and complete the table below.

Medal Platforms

Number of Medalists	1	2	3	4	5	6	7	8
Number of Boxes	1	3	6	■	■	■	■	■

b. Make a graph of the (*number of medalists, number of boxes*) data.

c. Describe the pattern of change shown in the table and graph.

d. Each box is 1 foot high and 2 feet wide. A red carpet starts 10 feet from the base of the platform, and covers all the risers and steps.

2 ft

1 ft

Copy and complete the table below.

Carpet for Platforms

Number of Steps	1	2	3	4	5	6	7	8
Carpet Length (ft)	■	■	■	■	■	■	■	■

e. Make a graph of the (*number of steps, carpet length*) data.

f. Describe the pattern of change in the carpet length as the number of steps increases. Compare this pattern with the pattern in the (*number of medalists, number of boxes*) data.

6. CSP also sells ladder bridges made from 1-foot steel rods arranged to form a row of squares. Below is a 6-foot ladder bridge.

6-foot ladder bridge made from 19 rods

a. Make a table and a graph showing how the number of rods in a ladder bridge is related to length of the bridge.

b. Compare the pattern of change for the ladder bridges with those for the beams and staircase frames in Problem 1.3.

Connections

A survey of one class at Pioneer Middle School finds that
20 out of 30 students would spend $8 for a school T-shirt.
Use this information for Exercises 7 and 8.

7. Multiple Choice Suppose there are 600 students in the
school. Based on the survey, how many students do you
predict would spend $8 for a school T-shirt?

   A. 20   **B.** 200

   C. 300   **D.** 400

8. Multiple Choice Suppose there are 450 students in the
school. Based on the survey, how many students do you
predict would spend $8 for a school T-shirt?

   F. 20   **G.** 200

   H. 300   **J.** 400

9. Below is a drawing of a rectangle with an area of
300 square feet.

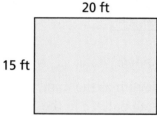

20 ft

15 ft

   a. Make drawings of at least three other rectangles with an area
   of 300 square feet.

   b. What is the width of a rectangle with an area of 300 square feet if
   its length is 1 foot? If its length is 2 feet? If its length is 3 feet?

   c. What is the width of a rectangle with an area of 300 square feet
   and a length of *L* feet?

   d. How does the width of a rectangle change if the length increases,
   but the area remains 300 square feet?

   e. Make a graph of (*width, length*) pairs for a rectangle that give an
   area of 300 square feet. Explain how your graph illustrates your
   answer for part (d).

10. a. The rectangle pictured in Exercise 9 has a perimeter of 70 feet. Make drawings of at least three other rectangles with a perimeter of 70 feet.

b. What is the width of a rectangle with a perimeter of 70 feet if its length is 1 foot? 2 feet? L feet?

c. What is the width of a rectangle with a perimeter of 70 feet if its length is $\frac{1}{2}$ foot? $\frac{3}{2}$ feet?

d. Give the dimensions of rectangles with perimeters of 70 feet and length-to-width ratios of 3 to 4, 4 to 5, and 1 to 1.

e. Suppose the length of a rectangle increases, but the perimeter remains at 70 feet. How does the width change?

f. Make a graph of (*width, length*) pairs that give a perimeter of 70 feet. How does your graph illustrate your answer for part (e)?

11. The 24 students in Ms. Cleary's homeroom are surveyed. They are asked which of several prices they would pay for a ticket to the school fashion show. The results are shown in this table.

Ticket-Price Survey

Ticket Price	$1.00	$1.50	$2.00	$2.50	$3.00	$3.50	$4.00	$4.50
Probable Sales	20	20	18	15	12	10	8	7

a. There are 480 students in the school. Use the data from Ms. Cleary's class to predict ticket sales for the entire school for each price.

b. Use your results from part (a). For each price, find the school's projected income from ticket sales.

c. Which price should the school charge if it wants to earn the maximum possible income?

Tell which graph matches the equation or the set of criteria.

12. $y = 3x + 1$

13. $y = -2x + 2$

14. $y = x - 3$

15. y-intercept = 1; slope = $\frac{1}{2}$

Graph A

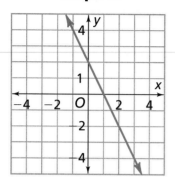

Graph B

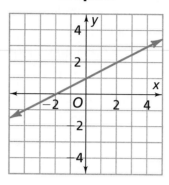

Graph C

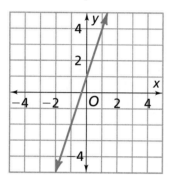

Graph D

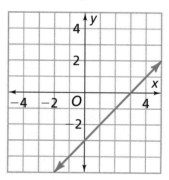

Within each equation, the pouches shown contain the same number of coins. Find the number of coins in each pouch. Explain your method.

16.

17.

18. Refer to Exercises 16 and 17.

   a. For each exercise, write an equation to represent the situation. Let x represent the number of coins in a pouch.

   b. Solve each equation. Explain the steps in your solutions.

   c. Compare your strategies with those you used in Exercises 16 and 17.

Solve each equation for x.

19. $3x + 4 = 10$

20. $6x + 3 = 4x + 11$

21. $6x - 3 = 11$

22. $-3x + 5 = 7$

23. $4x - \frac{1}{2} = 8$

24. $\frac{x}{2} - 4 = -5$

25. $3x + 3 = -2x - 12$

26. $\frac{x}{4} - 4 = \frac{3x}{4} - 6$

Go Online
PHSchool.com

For: Multiple-Choice Skills Practice
Web Code: apa-1154

For Exercises 27–29, tell whether the statement is _true_ or _false_. Explain your reasoning.

27. $6(12 - 5) > 50$

28. $3 \cdot 5 - 4 > 6$

29. $10 - 5 \cdot 4 > 0$

30. You will need two sheets of 8.5- by 11-inch paper and some scrap paper.

   a. Roll one sheet of paper to make a cylinder 11 inches high. Overlap the edges very slightly and tape them together. Make bases for the cylinder by tracing the circles on the ends of the cylinder, cutting out the tracings, and taping them in place.

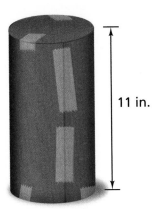
11 in.

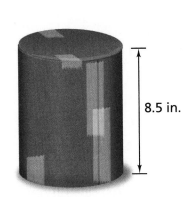
8.5 in.

   b. Roll the other sheet of paper to make a cylinder 8.5 inches high. Make bases as you did in part (a).

   c. Do the cylinders appear to have the same surface area (including the bases)? If not, which has the greater surface area?

   d. Suppose you start with two identical rectangular sheets of paper which are _not_ 8.5 by 11 inches. You make two cylinders as you did before. Which cylinder will have the greater surface area, the taller cylinder or the shorter one? How do you know?

Connections

31. The volume of the cone in the drawing at right is $\frac{1}{3}(28)\pi$. What are some possible radius and height measurements for the cone?

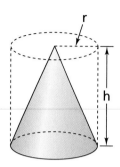

Extensions

32. Study the patterns in this table. Note that the numbers in the x column may not be consecutive after $x = 6$.

x	p	q	y	z
1	1	1	2	1
2	4	8	4	$\frac{1}{2}$
3	9	27	8	$\frac{1}{3}$
4	16	64	16	$\frac{1}{4}$
5	25	125	32	$\frac{1}{5}$
6	▓	▓	▓	▓
▓	▓	▓	1,024	▓
▓	▓	▓	2,048	▓
▓	▓	1,728	▓	▓
n	▓	▓	▓	▓

a. Use the patterns in the first several rows to find the missing values.

b. Are any of the patterns linear? Explain.

33. The table gives data for a group of middle school students.

Data for Middle School Students

Student	Name Length	Height (cm)	Foot Length (cm)
Thomas Petes	11	126	23
Michelle Hughes	14	117	21
Shoshana White	13	112	17
Deborah Locke	12	127	21
Tonya Stewart	12	172	32
Richard Mudd	11	135	22
Tony Tung	8	130	20
Janice Vick	10	134	21
Bobby King	9	156	29
Kathleen Boylan	14	164	28

a. Make a graph of the (*name length, height*) data, a graph of the (*name length, foot length*) data, and a graph of the (*height, foot length*) data.

b. Look at the graphs you made in part (a). Which seem to show linear relationships? Explain.

c. Estimate the average height-to-foot-length ratio. That is, how many "feet" tall is the typical student in the table?

d. Which student has the greatest height-to-foot-length ratio? Which student has the least height-to-foot-length ratio?

34. A staircase is a prism. This is easier to see if the staircase is viewed from a different perspective. In the prism below, the small squares on the top each have an area of 1 square unit.

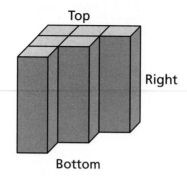

Top

Right

Bottom

a. Sketch the base of the prism. What is the area of the base?

b. Rashid is trying to draw a *net* (flat pattern) that will fold up to form the staircase prism. Below is the start of his drawing. Finish Rashid's drawing and give the surface area of the entire staircase. **Hint:** You may want to draw your net on grid paper and then cut it out and fold it to check.

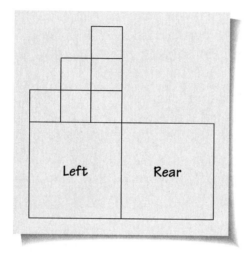

Left   Rear

c. Suppose the prism had six stairs instead of three. Assume each stair is the same width as those in the prism above. Is the surface area of this six-stair prism twice that of the three-stair prism? Explain.

Mathematical Reflections 1

In this investigation, you used tables and graphs to represent relationships between variables and to make predictions. These questions will help you summarize what you have learned.

Think about your answers to these questions. Discuss your ideas with other students and your teacher. Then write a summary of your findings in your notebook.

You can represent a relationship between variables with a table, a graph, or a description in words.

1. What are the advantages and disadvantages of each representation for finding patterns and making predictions?

2. How can you decide from a table whether a relationship is linear?

3. How can you decide from a graph whether a relationship is linear?

Investigation 2

Linear Models and Equations

Organizing and displaying the data from an experiment or survey can help you spot trends and make predictions. When the data show a linear trend, you can find a graph and equation to *model* the relationship between the variables. You can then use the model to make predictions about values between and beyond the data values.

When you make a model to represent a mathematical relationship, examine your model and ask

For what interval of values is the model likely to be reasonably accurate?

2.1 Linear Models

The First State Bridge-Painting Company is often asked to bid on painting projects. It usually gets the contract if it offers the lowest price. However, it needs to make sure the bid is high enough that the company will make a reasonable profit.

First State is preparing a bid for a bridge-painting project. The company looks at its records for previous projects. It finds information about four bridges with similar designs.

First State Bridge-Painting Costs		
Bridge Number	**Length (ft)**	**Painting Cost**
1	100	$18,000
2	200	$37,000
3	300	$48,000
4	400	$66,000

The First State cost estimators plot the data. The points fall in a nearly linear pattern. They draw a line that fits the pattern well. The line is a **mathematical model** for the relationship between bridge length and painting cost. A mathematical model approximates a data pattern.

First State Bridge-Painting Costs

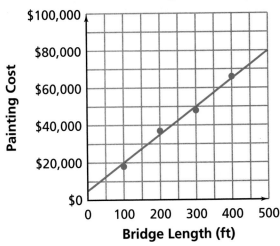

Getting Ready for Problem 2.1

A mathematical model can be used to make predictions about values between and beyond the data points.

- How do you think the cost estimators decided where to draw the line?
- Is the line a reasonable model for these data?
- What information does the model give that the points alone do not?
- What questions could you answer using the model?
- What information do you need to write an equation for the line?

Problem 2.1 Linear Models

A. 1. Write an equation for the line that models the data.

2. Use the line or the equation to estimate painting costs for similar bridges that are

   a. 175 feet long   **b.** 280 feet long

3. Use the line or the equation to estimate lengths of similar bridges for which the painting costs are

   a. $10,000   **b.** $60,000

B. First State is also bidding on a different type of bridge. It has records for three similar bridges.

First State Bridge-Painting Costs

Bridge Number	Length (ft)	Painting Cost
3	150	$50,000
4	300	$80,000
5	500	$140,000

1. Plot these data points. Draw a line that models the pattern in the data points.

2. Write an equation for your line.

3. Use your equation or line to estimate the painting cost for a similar bridge that is 200 feet long.

4. Use your equation or line to estimate the length of a similar bridge that costs $100,000 to paint.

ACE Homework starts on page 33.

Equations for Linear Relationships

Cars and trucks are an important part of American life and culture. There are nearly 200 million licensed drivers and 140 million registered passenger cars in the United States. To help people keep their cars clean, many cities have self-service car washes.

At most self-service car washes, the charge for washing a car and the company's profit depend on the time the customer spends using the car wash. To run such a business efficiently, it helps to have equations relating these key variables.

Getting Ready for Problem 2.2

- Sudzo Wash and Wax charges customers $0.75 per minute to wash a car. Write an equation that relates the total charge c to the amount of time t in minutes.

- Pat's Power Wash charges $2.00 per car to cover the cost of cleaning supplies, plus $0.49 per minute for the use of water sprayers and vacuums. Write an equation for the total charge c for any car-wash time t.

- U-Wash-It charges $10 for each car. The business owners estimate that it costs them $0.60 per minute to provide soap, water, and vacuums for a car. Write an equation for the profit p U-Wash-It earns if a customer spends t minutes washing a car.

- Explain what the numbers and variables in each equation represent.

- What questions can your equations help you answer?

Problem 2.2 Equations for Linear Relationships

A. The Squeaky Clean Car Wash charges by the minute. This table shows the charges for several different times.

Squeaky Clean Car Wash Charges

Time (min)	5	10	15	20	25
Charge	$8	$13	$18	$23	$28

   1. Explain how you know the relationship is linear.

   2. What are the slope and y-intercept of the line that represents the data?

   3. Write an equation relating charge c to time t in minutes.

B. Euclid's Car Wash displays its charges as a graph. Write an equation for the charge plan at Euclid's. Describe what the variables and numbers in your equation tell you about the situation.

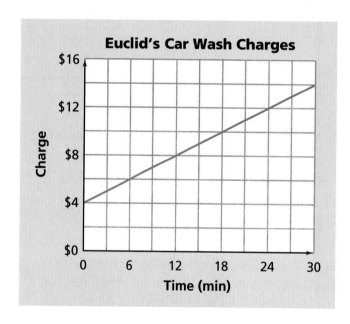

C. Below are two receipts from Super Clean Car Wash. Assume the relationship between charge c and time used t is linear.

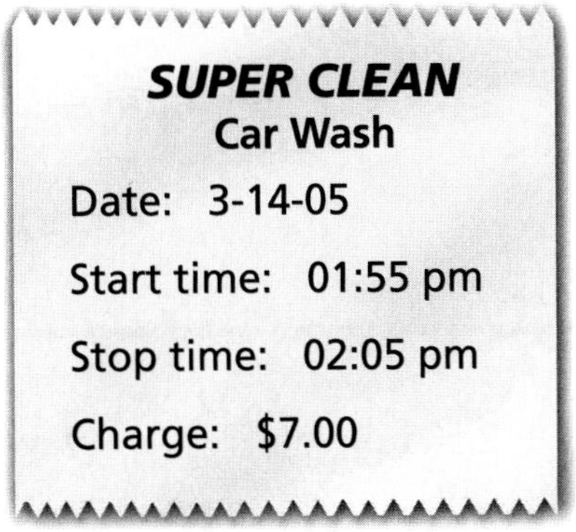

```
vvvvvvvvvvvvvvvvvvvvv

    SUPER CLEAN
      Car Wash

Date:  3-14-05

Start time:  01:55 pm

Stop time:  02:05 pm

Charge:  $7.00
AAAAAAAAAAAAAAAAAAAAA
```

```
vvvvvvvvvvvvvvvvvvvvv

    SUPER CLEAN
      Car Wash

Date:  4-04-05

Start time:  09:30 am

Stop time:  09:50 am

Charge:  $12.00
AAAAAAAAAAAAAAAAAAAAA
```

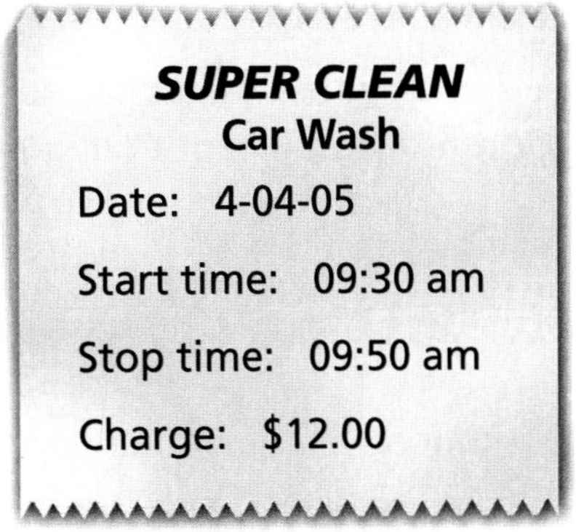

1. Each receipt represents a point (t, c) on the line. Find the coordinates of the two points.

2. What are the slope and y-intercept of the line?

3. Write an equation relating c and t.

D. Write an equation for the line with slope -3 that passes through the point $(4, 3)$.

E. Write an equation for the line with points $(4, 5)$ and $(6, 9)$.

F. Suppose you want to write an equation of the form $y = mx + b$ to represent a linear relationship. What is your strategy if you are given

1. a description of the relationship in words?

2. two or more (x, y) values or a table of (x, y) values?

3. a graph showing points with coordinates?

ACE Homework starts on page 33.

2.3 Solving Linear Equations

Sandy's Boat House rents canoes. The equation $c = 0.15t + 2.50$ gives the charge c in dollars for renting a canoe for t minutes.

Getting Ready for Problem

- Explain what the numbers in the equation $c = 0.15t + 2.50$ tell you about the situation.

- Rashida and Serena apply for jobs at Sandy's. The manager tests them with three questions.

  What is the charge for renting a canoe for 30 minutes?

  A customer is charged $8.50. How long did he use the canoe?

  A customer has $10 to spend. How long can she use a canoe?

  Suppose you were applying for a job at Sandy's. How would you answer these questions?

Problem 2.3 Solving Linear Equations

A. Rashida uses a graph of $c = 0.15t + 2.50$. Explain how to use the graph to estimate the answers to the manager's questions.

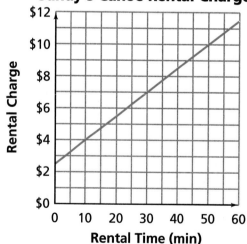

Sandy's Canoe Rental Charges

B. Rashida could use a table instead of a graph. Explain how to use a table to estimate answers to the questions.

C. Serena wants to find exact answers, not estimates. For the second question, she solves the linear equation $0.15t + 2.50 = 8.50$. She reasons as follows:

- If $0.15t + 2.50 = 8.50$, then $0.15t = 6.00$.

- If $0.15t = 6.00$, then $t = 40$.

- I check my answer by substituting 40 for t: $0.15(40) + 2.50 = 8.50$

Is Serena correct? How do you know?

D. For the third question, Rashida says, "She can use the canoe for 50 minutes if she has \$10." Serena says there are other possibilities— for example, 45 minutes or 30 minutes. She says you can answer the question by solving the **inequality** $0.15t + 2.50 \leq 10$. This inequality represents the times for which the rental charge is *at most* \$10.

1. Use a table, a graph, and the equation $0.15t + 2.50 = 10$ to find all of the times for which the inequality is true.

2. Express the solution as an inequality.

E. River Fun Paddle Boats competes with Sandy's. The equation $c = 4 + 0.10t$ gives the charge in dollars c for renting a paddle boat for t minutes.

1. A customer at River Fun is charged \$9. How long did the customer use a paddle boat? Explain.

2. Suppose you want to spend \$12 at most. How long could you use a paddle boat? Explain.

3. What is the charge to rent a paddle boat for 20 minutes? Explain.

ACE Homework starts on page 33.

2.4 Intersecting Linear Models

A resort area has two main attractions—the Big Fun amusement park and the Get Reel movie multiplex. The number of visitors to each attraction on a given day is related to the probability of rain.

This table gives attendance and rain-forecast data for several Saturdays.

Saturday Resort Attendance

Probability of Rain (%)	0	20	40	60	80	100
Big Fun Attendance	1,000	850	700	550	400	250
Get Reel Attendance	300	340	380	420	460	500

The same company owns both businesses. The managers want to be able to predict Saturday attendance at each attraction so they can assign their workers efficiently.

Problem 2.4 Intersecting Linear Models

A. Use the table to find a linear equation relating the probability of rain p to

1. Saturday attendance A_B at Big Fun.

2. Saturday attendance A_G at Get Reel.

B. Use your equations from Question A to answer these questions. Show your calculations and explain your reasoning.

1. Suppose there is a 50% probability of rain this Saturday. What is the expected attendance at each attraction?

2. Suppose 460 people visited Big Fun one Saturday. Estimate the probability of rain on that day.

3. What probability of rain would give a predicted Saturday attendance of at least 360 people at Get Reel?

4. Is there a probability of rain for which the predicted attendance is the same at both attractions? Explain.

ACE **Homework starts on page 33.**

Applications

1. Below are some results from the bridge-thickness experiment.

Bridge-Thickness Experiment

Thickness (layers)	2	4	6	8
Breaking Weight (pennies)	15	30	50	65

   a. Plot the (*thickness, breaking weight*) data. Draw a line that models the pattern in the data.

   b. Find an equation for the line you drew.

   c. Use your equation to predict the breaking weights of paper bridges 3, 5, and 7 layers thick.

2. Which line do you think is a better model for the data? Explain.

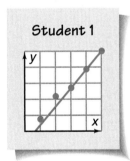

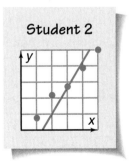

3. Copy each graph onto grid paper. Draw a line that fits each set of data as closely as possible. Describe the strategies you used.

Graph A

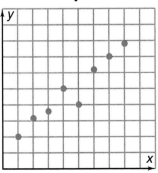

Graph B

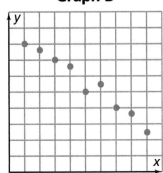

Graph C

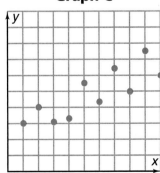

4. This table gives the average weights of purebred Chihuahas from birth to 16 weeks.

Average Weights for Chihuahuas

Age (wk)	0	2	4	6	8	10	12	14	16
Weight (oz)	4	9	13	17.5	21.5	25	30	34	39

SOURCE: *The Complete Chihuahua Encyclopedia*

a. Graph the (*age, weight*) data. Draw a line that models the data pattern.

b. Write an equation of the form $y = mx + b$ for your line. Explain what the values of m and b tell you about this situation.

c. Use your equation to predict the average weight of Chihuahuas for odd-numbered ages from 1 to 15 weeks.

d. What average weight does your linear model predict for a Chihuahua that is 144 weeks old? Explain why this prediction is unlikely to be accurate.

5. U-Wash-It Car Wash did market research to determine how much to charge for a car wash. The company makes this table based on its findings.

For: Help with Exercise 5
Web Code: ape-1205

U-Wash-It Projections

Price per Wash	$0	$5	$10	$15	$20
Customers Expected per Day	100	80	65	45	20

a. Graph the (*price, expected customers*) data. Draw a line that models the data pattern.

b. Write an equation in the form $y = mx + b$ for your graph. Explain what the values of m and b tell you about this situation.

c. Use your equation to estimate the number of customers expected for prices of $2.50, $7.50, and $12.50.

6. Find the slope, *y*-intercept, and equation for each line.

a.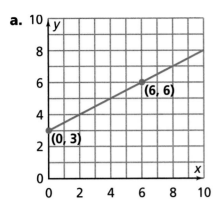

b.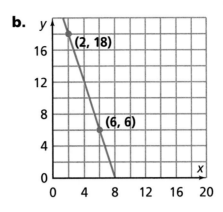

c.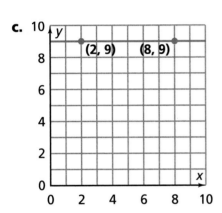

d.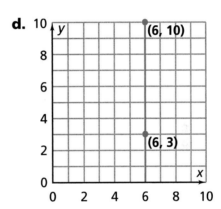

The relationships in Exercises 7–10 are linear.

7. a. A typical American baby weighs about 8 pounds at birth and gains about 1.5 pounds per month for the first year of life. What equation relates weight *w* in pounds to age *a* in months?

   b. Can this model be used to predict weight at age 80? Explain.

8. Kaya buys a $20 phone card. She is charged $0.15 per minute for long-distance calls. What equation gives the value *v* left on her card after she makes *t* minutes of long-distance calls?

9. Dakota lives 1,500 meters from school. She leaves for school, walking at a speed of 60 meters per minute. Write an equation for her distance *d* in meters from school after she walks for *t* minutes.

10. A car can average 140 miles on 5 gallons of gasoline. Write an equation for the distance *d* in miles the car can travel on *g* gallons of gas.

11. Write a linear equation for each table relating x and y.

a.

x	0	3	6	10
y	2	8	14	22

b.

x	0	3	6	10
y	20	8	−4	−20

c.

x	2	4	6	8
y	5	8	11	14

d.

x	0	3	6	9
y	20	11	2	−7

For Exercises 12–17, find an equation for the line that satisfies the conditions.

For: Multiple-Choice Skills Practice
Web Code: apa-1254

12. Slope 4.2; y-intercept $(0, 3.4)$

13. Slope $\frac{2}{3}$; y-intercept $(0, 5)$

14. Slope 2; passes through $(4, 12)$

15. Passes through $(0, 15)$ and $(5, 3)$

16. Passes through $(-2, 2)$ and $(5, -4)$

17. Parallel to the line with equation $y = 15 - 2x$ and passes through $(3, 0)$

18. Write an equation for each line.

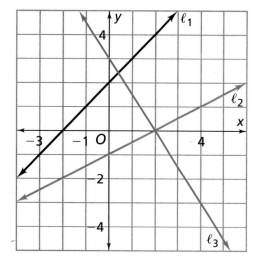

19. Anchee and Jonah earn weekly allowances for doing chores over the summer.

- Anchee's father pays her $5 each week.
- Jonah's mother paid him $20 at the beginning of the summer and now pays him $3 each week.

The relationships between number of weeks worked and dollars earned are shown in this graph.

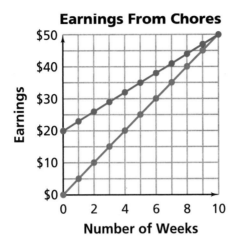

Earnings From Chores

a. Which line represents Jonah's earnings? Which line represents Anchee's earnings? Explain.

b. Write two linear equations in the form $y = mx + b$ to show the relationships between Anchee's earnings and the number of weeks she works and between Jonah's earnings and the number of weeks he works.

c. What do the values of m and b in each equation tell about the relationship between the number of weeks and the dollars earned?

d. What do the values of m and b tell about each line?

For Exercises 20–23, do the following:

    a. Solve the equation. Show your steps.

    b. Graph the associated line (for example, for $5.5x + 32 = 57$, graph $y = 5.5x + 32$). Label the point that shows the solution.

20. $5.5x + 32 = 57$

21. $-24 = 4x - 12$

22. $5x - 51 = 24$

23. $74 = 53 - 7x$

24. At Water Works Amusement Park, the daily profit from the concession stands depends on the number of park visitors. The equation $p = 2.50v - 500$ gives the estimated profit p in dollars if v people visit the park. In parts (a)–(c), use a graph to estimate the answer. Then, find the answer by writing and solving an equation or inequality.

    a. For what number of visitors will the profit be about $2,000?

    b. One day 200 people visit the park. What is the approximate concession-stand profit for that day?

    c. For what number of visitors will the profit be at least $500?

25. The following formulas give the fare f in dollars that two bus companies charge for trips of d miles.

Transcontinental: $f = 0.15d + 12$

Intercity Express: $f = 5 + 0.20d$

In parts (a)–(c), use a graph to estimate the answer. Then, find the answer by writing and solving an equation or inequality.

    a. For Transcontinental, how many miles is a trip that costs $99?

    b. For Intercity Express, how far can a person travel for a fare that is at most $99?

    c. Is there a distance for which the fare for the two bus lines is the same? If so, give the distance and the fare.

Solve each equation. Show the steps in your solutions.

26. $5x + 7 = 3x - 5$ **27.** $7 + 3x = 5x - 5$ **28.** $2.5x - 8 = 5x + 12$

Find at least three values of x for which the inequality is true.

29. $4x \leq 12$

30. $3x < 18$

31. $4x + 5 \leq 13$

32. $3x - 9 \leq 18$

33. Every Friday, the mechanic for Columbus Public Schools records the miles driven and the gallons of gas used for each school bus. One week, the mechanic records these data.

Data for Columbus Bus Fleet

Bus Number	1	2	3	4	5	6	7	8
Gas Used (gal)	5	8	12	15	18	20	22	25
Miles Driven	80	100	180	225	280	290	320	375

a. Write a linear equation that models the relationship between miles driven d and gallons of gas used g.

b. Use your equation to predict the number of miles such a bus could travel on 10 gallons of gas.

c. Use your equation to predict the number of gallons of gas required to drive such a bus 250 miles.

d. What do the values of m and b in your equation $d = mg + b$ tell about the fuel efficiency of the school bus fleet?

34. One of the most popular items at a farmers' market is sweet corn. This table shows relationships among the price for the corn, the demand for the corn (how much corn people want to buy), and the leftovers of corn (how much corn the market has at the end of the day).

Sweet Corn Supply and Demand

Price per Dozen	$1	$1.50	$2.00	$2.50	$3.00	$3.50
Demand (dozens)	200	175	140	120	80	60
Leftovers (dozens)	40	75	125	175	210	260

a. Why do you think the demand for corn decreases as the price goes up?

b. Why do you think the leftovers of corn increases as the price goes up?

c. Write a linear equation that models the relationship between demand d and price p.

d. Write a linear equation that models the relationship between leftovers ℓ and price p.

e. Use graphs to estimate the price for which the leftovers equals the demand. Then, find the price by solving symbolically.

Connections

35. Tell whether each table represents a linear relationship. Explain.

a.

x	2	4	6	8	10	12	14
y	0	1	2	3	4	5	6

b.

x	1	2	3	4	5	6	7
y	0	3	8	15	24	35	48

c.

x	1	4	6	7	10	12	16
y	2	−1	−3	−4	−7	−9	−13

36. For parts (a)–(d), copy the table. Then, use the equation to complete the table. Tell whether the relationship is linear. Explain.

a. $y = -3x - 8$

x	−5	−2	1	4
y	■	■	■	■

b. $y = 4(x - 7) + 6$

x	−3	0	3	6
y	■	■	■	■

c. $y = x(3x + 2)$

x	−3	0	3	6
y	■	■	■	■

d. $y = 4 - 3x$

x	−3	0	3	10
y	■	■	■	■

Copy each pair of numbers in Exercises 37–42. Insert <, >, or = to make a true statement.

37. −5 ■ 3

38. $\frac{2}{3}$ ■ $\frac{1}{2}$

39. $\frac{9}{12}$ ■ $\frac{3}{4}$

40. 3.009 ■ 3.1

41. $\frac{-2}{3}$ ■ $\frac{-1}{2}$

42. −4.25 ■ −2.45

43. Madeline sets a copy machine to enlarge by a factor of 150%. She then uses the machine to copy a polygon. Write an equation that relates the perimeter of the polygon after the enlargement a to the perimeter before the enlargement b.

For Exercises 44–52, evaluate the expression without using a calculator.

44. $-15 + (-7)$ **45.** $-7 - 15$ **46.** $-7 - (-15)$

47. $-15 + 7$ **48.** $-20 \div 5$ **49.** $-20 \div (-5)$

50. $20 \div (-4)$ **51.** $-20 \div (-2.5)$ **52.** $-20 \cdot (-2.5)$

53. You can express the slope of a line in different ways. The slope of the line below is $\frac{6}{10}$, or 0.6. You can also say the slope is 60% because the rise is 60% of the run.

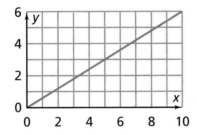

These numbers represent slopes of lines.

$\frac{-4}{-2}$ 60% $\frac{4}{4}$ 1.5 150% 200%

a. Which numbers represent the same slope?

b. Which number represents the greatest slope? Which represents the least slope?

54. Consider the following stories and the graphs.

a. Match each story with a graph. Tell how you would label the axes. Explain how each part of the story is represented in the graph.

Story 1 A parachutist is taken up in a plane. After he jumps, the wind blows him off course. He ends up tangled in the branches of a tree.

Story 2 Ella puts some money in the bank. She leaves it there to earn interest for several years. Then one day, she withdraws half of the money in the account.

Story 3 Gerry has a big pile of gravel to spread on his driveway. On the first day, he moves half of the gravel from the pile to his driveway. The next day he is tired and moves only half of what is left. The third day he again moves half of what is left in the pile. He continues in this way until the pile has almost disappeared.

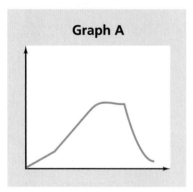

Graph A

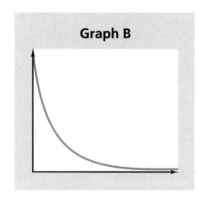

Graph B

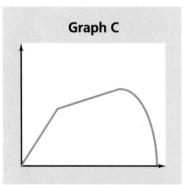

Graph C

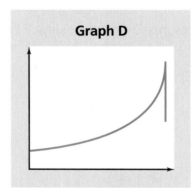

Graph D

b. One of the graphs does not match a story. Make up your own story for that graph.

55. The figures below are similar.

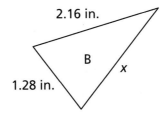
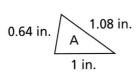

2.16 in.

B

x

1.28 in.

0.64 in. 1.08 in.

A

1 in.

a. Find *x*.

b. What is the scale factor from Triangle A to Triangle B?

c. What is the scale factor from Triangle B to Triangle A?

d. How are the scale factors in parts (b) and (c) related?

Extensions

56. A bridge-painting company uses the formula $C = 5,000 + 150L$ to estimate painting costs. C is the cost in dollars, and L is the length of the bridge in feet. To make a profit, the company increases a cost estimate by 20% to arrive at a bid price. For example, if the cost estimate is $10,000, the bid price will be $12,000.

a. Find bid prices for bridges 100 feet, 200 feet, and 400 feet long.

b. Write a formula relating the final bid price to bridge length.

c. Use your formula to find bid prices for bridges 150 feet, 300 feet, and 450 feet long.

d. How would your formula change if the markup for profit was 15% instead of 20%?

57. Recall that Custom Steel Products builds beams from steel rods. Here is a 7-foot beam.

7-foot beam made from 27 rods

a. Which of these formulas represents the relationship between beam length ℓ and number of rods r?

$r = 3\ell$ $r = \ell + (\ell - 1) + 2\ell$

$r = 4(\ell - 1) + 3$ $r = 4\ell - 1$

b. How might you have reasoned to come up with each formula?

58. Recall that Custom Steel Products uses steel rods to make staircase frames. Here are staircase frames with 1, 2, and 3 steps.

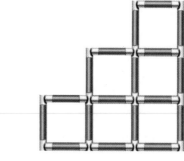

| 1 step
made from 4 rods | 2 steps
made from 10 rods | 3 steps
made from 18 rods |

Which of these formulas represents the relationship between the number of steps n and number of rods r?

$r = n^2 + 3n$ $r = n(n + 3)$

$r = n^2 + 3$ $r = (n + 3)n$

Custom Steel Products builds cubes out of square steel plates measuring 1 foot on a side. At right is a 1-foot cube. Use this information for Exercises 59–61.

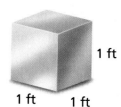

1 ft

1 ft   1 ft

59. How many square plates are needed to make a 1-foot cube?

60. Multiple Choice Suppose CSP wants to triple the dimensions of the cube. How many times the number of plates in the original cube will they need for this larger cube?

A. 2   **B.** 3   **C.** 4   **D.** 9

61. Multiple Choice Suppose CSP triples the dimensions of the original cube. How many times the volume of the original cube is the volume of the new cube?

F. 8   **G.** 9   **H.** 27   **J.** 81

62. At Yvonne's Auto Detailing, car washes cost $5 for any time up to 10 minutes, plus $0.40 per minute after that. The managers at Yvonne's are trying to agree on a formula for calculating the cost c for a t-minute car wash.

a. Sid thinks $c = 0.4t + 5$ is correct. Is he right?

b. Tina proposes the formula $c = 0.4(t - 10) + 5$. Is she right?

c. Jamal told Tina her formula could be simplified to $c = 0.4t + 1$. Is he right?

63. Write an equation for each relationship.

  a. One taxi company charges $1.50 for the first 2 miles of any trip, and then $1.20 for each mile after that. How is the taxi *fare* related to the *distance* of a trip?

  b. An airport offers free parking for 30 minutes and then charges $2.00 for each hour after that. How is the *price* for parking related to the *time* a car is parked?

  c. A local cinema makes $6.50 on each ticket sold. However, it has operating expenses of $750 per day. How is *daily profit* related to *number of tickets* sold?

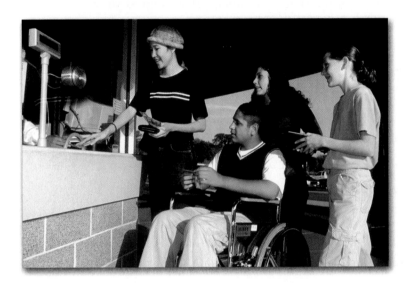

  d. Rush Computer Repair sends technicians to businesses to fix computers. They charge a fixed fee of $50, plus $50 per hour. How is total *cost* for a repair related to *time* the repair takes?

Mathematical Reflections 2

In this investigation, you learned how to find linear models for data patterns. You also developed skill in writing linear equations, practiced translating verbal descriptions into linear equations, and extended your knowledge of solving linear equations.

Think about your answers to these questions. Discuss your ideas with other students and your teacher. Then write a summary of your findings in your notebook.

1. What are the advantages of using a linear model for a set of data?

2. How would you find the equation for a linear relationship
   a. from a verbal description?
   b. from a table of values?
   c. from a graph?

3. What strategies can you use to solve a linear equation such as
   a. $500 = 245 + 5x$?
   b. $500 + 3x = 245 + 5x$?

Investigation 3

Inverse Variation

In Investigation 1, you discovered that the relationship between bridge thickness and bridge strength is approximately linear. You also found that the relationship between bridge length and bridge strength is not linear. In this investigation, you will explore other nonlinear relationships.

3.1 Rectangles With Fixed Area

In recent years, the populations of many small towns have declined as residents move to large cities for jobs. The town of Roseville has developed a plan to attract new residents. The town is offering free lots of land to "homesteaders" who are willing to build houses. Each lot is rectangular and has an area of 21,800 square feet. The lengths and widths of the lots vary.

Getting Ready for Problem

- What are some possible dimensions for a rectangular lot with an area of 21,800 square feet?

In Problem 3.1, you will look at patterns in length and width values for rectangles with fixed area.

Problem 3.1 Relating Length and Width

A. 1. Copy and complete this table.

Rectangles With Area 24 in.²

Length (in.)	1	2	3	4	5	6	7	8
Width (in.)	▪	▪	▪	▪	▪	▪	▪	▪

2. Plot your data on a grid like the one below. Then, draw a line or curve that seems to model the pattern in the data.

Rectangles With Area 24 in.²

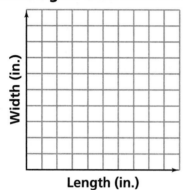

3. Describe the pattern of change in the width as the length increases. Is the relationship between length and width linear?

4. Write an equation that shows how the width w depends on the length ℓ for rectangles with an area of 24 square inches.

B. Now consider rectangles with an area of 32 square inches.

1. Write an equation for the relationship between the length ℓ and the width w.

2. Graph your equation. Show lengths from 1 to 15 inches.

C. Compare your equations. How are they similar? How are they different?

D. Compare your graphs. How are they similar? How are they different?

ACE Homework starts on page 53.

3.2 Bridging the Distance

The relationship between length and width for rectangles with a fixed area is not linear. It is an example of an important type of nonlinear pattern called an **inverse variation.**

The word "inverse" suggests that as one variable increases in value, the other variable decreases in value. However, the meaning of *inverse variation* is more specific than this. The relationship between two non-zero variables, *x* and *y,* is an inverse variation if

$$y = \frac{k}{x}, \text{ or } xy = k$$

where *k* is a constant that is not 0. The value of *k* is determined by the specific relationship.

> *How are the equations* $y = \frac{k}{x}$ *and* $xy = k$ *related?*

> *For the same* x*-value, will the two equations give different* y*-values?*

Inverse variation occurs in many situations. For example, consider the table and graph below. They show the (*bridge length, breaking weight*) data collected by a group of students.

Bridge Experiment Data

Length (in.)	Breaking Weight (pennies)
4	41
6	26
8	19
9	17
10	15

Bridge Experiment Data

Getting Ready for Problem 3.2

- Describe a curve that models the pattern in the data above.

- What value of *k* can you use to model these data with an inverse variation equation? Write the equation.

- In your equation, why does the value of *y* decrease as the value of *x* increases?

- What happens to the value of *y* as the value of *x* gets close to 0? Why is that a reasonable pattern for the bridge experiment?

Mr. Cordova lives in Detroit, Michigan. He often travels to Baltimore, Maryland, to visit his grandfather. The trip is 500 miles each way. Here are his notes for his trips to Baltimore last year.

Date	Notes	Travel Time
February 15	Traveled by plane.	1.5 hours
May 22	Drove.	10 hours
July 3	Drove. Stopped for repairs.	14 hours
November 23	Flew. Flight delayed.	4 hours
December 23	Took overnight train.	18 hours

A. 1. Calculate the average speed in miles per hour for each trip. Record the results in a table like this.

Cordova's Baltimore Trips

Travel Time (hr)	■	■	■	■	■
Average Speed (mph)	■	■	■	■	■

2. Plot the data. Draw a line or curve that models the data pattern. Describe the pattern of change in average speed as travel time increases.

3. Write an equation for the relationship between travel time t and average speed s.

4. Use your equation to find the average speed for 500-mile trips that take 6 hours, 8 hours, 12 hours, and 16 hours.

5. Add the (*travel time, average speed*) data from part (4) to your graph. Do the new points fit the graph model you sketched for the original data?

B. The Cordova family is planning a trip to Mackinac Island (mak uh naw) near the upper peninsula of Michigan. Mr. Cordova does some calculations to see how the travel time will change if the family drives at different average speeds.

Travel Times for Different Speeds

Average Speed (mi/h)	30	40	50	60	70
Travel Time (hr)	10	7.5	6	5	4.3

1. How far is it from Detroit to Mackinac Island?

2. What equation relates travel time t to average speed s?

3. Describe the pattern of change in the travel time as the average speed increases. How would that pattern appear in a graph of the data? How is it shown by your equation?

4. Predict the travel times if the Cordovas drive at average speeds of 45 miles per hour and 65 miles per hour.

C. Suppose Mr. Cordova decides to aim for an average speed of 50 miles per hour for the trip to Mackinac Island.

1. Make a table and graph to show how the distance traveled will increase as time passes. Show times from when the family leaves home to when they reach their destination.

2. Write an equation for the distance d the family travels in t hours.

3. Describe the pattern of change in the distance as time passes.

4. Compare the (*time, distance traveled*) graph and equation with the (*time, average speed*) graphs and equations in Questions A and B.

ACE Homework starts on page 53.

3.3 Average Cost

The science teachers at Everett Middle School want to take their eighth-graders on an overnight field trip to a nature center. It costs $750 to rent the center facilities. The school budget does not provide funds to rent the nature center, so students must pay a fee. The trip will cost $3 per student if all 250 students go. However, the teachers know it is unlikely that all students can go. They want to find the cost per student for any number of students.

Problem 3.3 Inverse Variation Patterns

A. 1. Write an equation relating the cost c per student to the number of students n.

2. Use your equation to make a graph showing how the cost per student changes as the number of students increases.

B. 1. Find the change in the cost per student as the number of students increases from

    a. 10 to 20   **b.** 100 to 110   **c.** 200 to 210

2. How do your results show that the relationship between the number of students and the cost per student is not linear?

C. 1. Find the change in the per-student cost as the number of students increases from

    a. 20 to 40   **b.** 40 to 80   **c.** 80 to 160

2. Describe the pattern in your results. Explain how your equation from Question A shows this pattern.

D. The science teachers decide to charge $5 per student for the trip. They will use any extra money to buy science equipment for the school.

1. Write an equation for the amount a the teachers will collect if n students go on the trip.

2. Sketch a graph of the relationship.

3. Is this a linear relationship or an inverse variation? Explain.

ACE Homework starts on page 53.

Applications

1. Consider rectangles with an area of 16 square inches.

   a. Copy and complete the table.

   Rectangles With an Area of 16 in.²

Length (in.)	1	2	3	4	5	6	7	8
Width (in.)	■	■	■	■	■	■	■	■

   b. Make a graph of the data.

   c. Describe the pattern of change in width as length increases.

   d. Write an equation that shows how the width w depends on the length ℓ. Is the relationship linear?

2. Consider rectangles with an area of 20 square inches.

   a. Make a table of length and width data for at least five rectangles.

   b. Make a graph of your data.

   c. Write an equation that shows how the width w depends on the length ℓ. Is the relationship linear?

   d. Compare and contrast the graphs in this exercise and in Exercise 1.

   e. Compare and contrast the equations in this exercise and in Exercise 1.

3. A student collected these data from the bridge-length experiment.

   Bridge-Length Experiment

Length (in.)	4	6	8	9	10
Breaking Weight (pennies)	24	16	13	11	9

   a. Find an inverse variation equation that models these data.

   b. Explain how your equation shows that breaking weight decreases as length increases. Is this pattern reasonable for this situation? Explain.

For Exercises 4–7, tell whether the relationship between *x* and *y* is an inverse variation. If it is, write an equation for the relationship.

4.

x	1	2	3	4	5	6	7	8	9	10
y	10	9	8	7	6	5	4	3	2	1

5.

x	1	2	3	4	5	6	7	8	9	10
y	48	24	16	12	9.6	8	6.8	6	5.3	4.8

6.

x	2	3	5	8	10	15	20	25	30	40
y	50	33	20	12.5	10	6.7	5	4	3.3	2.5

7.

x	0	1	2	3	4	5	6	7	8	9
y	100	81	64	49	36	25	16	9	4	1

8. A marathon is a 26.2-mile race. The best marathon runners can complete the race in a little more than 2 hours.

   a. Make a table and graph that show how the average running speed for a marathon changes as the time increases. Show times from 2 to 8 hours in 1-hour intervals.

   b. Write an equation for the relationship between time *t* and average running speed *s* for a marathon.

   c. Tell how the average running speed changes as the time increases from 2 hours to 3 hours. From 3 hours to 4 hours. From 4 hours to 5 hours.

   d. How do the answers for part (c) show that the relationship between average running speed and time is not linear?

9. On one day of a charity bike ride, the route covers 50 miles. Individual riders cover this distance at different average speeds.

Homework Help Online
PHSchool.com
For: Help with Exercise 9
Web Code: ape-1309

a. Make a table and a graph that show how the riding time changes as the average speed increases. Show speed values from 4 to 20 miles per hour in intervals of 4 miles per hour.

b. Write an equation for the relationship between the riding time *t* and average speed *s*.

c. Tell how the riding time changes as the average speed increases from 4 to 8 miles per hour. From 8 to 12 miles per hour. From 12 to 16 miles per hour.

d. How do the answers for part (c) show that the relationship between average speed and time is not linear?

10. Students in Mr. Einstein's science class complain about the length of his tests. He argues that a test with more questions is better for students because each question is worth fewer points. All of Mr. Einstein's tests are worth 100 points. Each question is worth the same number of points.

a. Make a table and a graph that show how the number of points per question changes as the number of questions increases. Show point values for 2 to 20 questions in intervals of 2.

b. Write an equation for the relationship between the number of questions *n* and the points per question *p*.

c. Tell how the points per question changes as the number of questions increases from 2 to 4. From 4 to 6. From 6 to 8. From 8 to 10.

d. How do the answers for part (c) show that the relationship between the number of questions and the points per question is not linear?

11. Testers drive eight vehicles 200 miles on a test track at the same speed. The table shows the amount of fuel each vehicle uses.

Fuel-Efficiency Test

Vehicle Type	Fuel Used (gal)
Large Truck	20
Large SUV	18
Limousine	16
Large Sedan	12
Small Truck	10
Sports Car	12
Compact Car	7
Sub-Compact Car	5

a. Find the fuel efficiency in miles per gallon for each vehicle.

b. Make a graph of the (*fuel used, miles per gallon*) data. Describe the pattern of change shown in the graph.

c. Write a formula for calculating the fuel efficiency based on the fuel used for a 200-mile test drive.

d. Tell how the fuel efficiency changes as the amount of fuel used increases from 5 to 10 gallons. From 10 to 15 gallons. From 15 to 20 gallons.

e. How do the answers for part (d) show that the relationship between the fuel used and the fuel efficiency is not linear?

Connections

12. Suppose the town of Roseville is giving away lots with perimeters of 500 feet, rather than with areas of 21,800 square feet.

a. Copy and complete this table.

Rectangles With a Perimeter of 500 Feet

Length (ft)	■	■	■	■	■
Width (ft)	■	■	■	■	■

b. Make a graph of the (*length, width*) data. Draw a line or curve that models the data pattern.

c. Describe the pattern of change in width as length increases.

d. Write an equation for the relationship between length and width. Is this a linear relationship? Explain.

A number *b* is the **additive inverse** of the number *a* if *a* + *b* = 0. For example, −5 is the additive inverse of 5 because 5 + (−5) = 0. For Exercises 13–18, find the additive inverse of each number.

For: Multiple-Choice Skills Practice
Web Code: apa-1354

13. 2

14. $-\dfrac{6}{2}$

15. 2.5

16. −2.11

17. $\dfrac{7}{3}$

18. $\dfrac{3}{7}$

19. On a number line, graph each number in Exercises 13–18 and its additive inverse. Describe any patterns you see.

A number *b* is the **multiplicative inverse** of the number *a* if *ab* = 1. For example, $\dfrac{3}{2}$ is the multiplicative inverse of $\dfrac{2}{3}$ because $\left(\dfrac{2}{3}\right)\left(\dfrac{3}{2}\right) = 1$. For Exercises 20–25, find the multiplicative inverse of each number.

20. 2

21. −2

22. 0.5

23. 4

24. $\dfrac{3}{4}$

25. $\dfrac{5}{3}$

26. On a number line, graph each number in Exercises 20–25 and its multiplicative inverse. Describe any patterns you see.

Jamar takes a 10-point history quiz each week. Here are his scores on the first five quizzes: 8, 9, 6, 7, 10. Use this information for Exercises 27–28.

27. Multiple Choice What is Jamar's average quiz score?

A. 6

B. 7

C. 8

D. 9

28. a. Jamar misses the next quiz and gets a 0. What is his average after six quizzes?

b. After 20 quizzes, Jamar's average is 8. He gets a 0 on the 21st quiz. What is his average after 21 quizzes?

c. Why did a score of 0 have a different effect on the average when it was the sixth score than when it was the 21st score?

29. Suppose a car travels at a speed of 60 miles per hour. The equation $d = 60t$ represents the relationship between the time t in hours and the distance d driven in miles. This relationship is an example of a *direct variation*. A relationship between variables x and y is a direct variation if it can be expressed as $y = kx$, where k is a constant.

  a. Find two relationships in this unit that are direct variations. Give the equation for each relationship.

  b. For each relationship from part (a), find the ratio of the dependent variable to the independent variable. How is the ratio related to k in the general equation?

  c. Suppose the relationship between x and y is a direct variation. How do y-values change as the x-values increase? How does this pattern of change appear in a graph of the relationship?

  d. Compare direct variation and inverse variation. Be sure to discuss the graphs and equations for these types of relationships.

Solve the equation using a symbolic method. Then, describe how the solution can be found by using a graph and a table.

30. $5x - 28 = -3$ **31.** $10 - 3x = 7x - 10$

For Exercises 32–34, find the equation of the line with the given information.

32. slope $-\frac{1}{2}$, y-intercept $(0, 5)$

33. slope 3, passes through the point $(2, 2)$

34. passes through the points $(5, 2)$ and $(1, 10)$

35. Find the equation for the line below.

Al Jabr's Self-Serve Wash

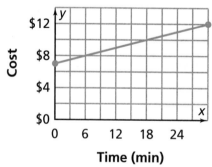

36. Suppose 6 cans of tomato juice cost $3.20. Find the cost for

  a. 1 can   **b.** 10 cans   **c.** n cans

For Exercises 37–39, tell which store offers the better buy. Explain your choice.

37. *Gus's Groceries*: Tomatoes are 6 for $4.00
Super Market: Tomatoes are 8 for $4.60

38. *Gus's Groceries*: Cucumbers are 4 for $1.75
Super Market: Cucumbers are 5 for $2.00

39. *Gus's Groceries*: Apples are 6 for $3.00
Super Market: Apples are 5 for $2.89

Extensions

40. This net folds up to make a rectangular prism.

    a. What is the volume of the prism?

    b. Suppose the dimensions of the shaded face are doubled. The other dimensions are adjusted so that the volume remains the same. What are the dimensions of the new prism?

    c. Which prism has the smaller surface area, the original prism or the prism from part (b)? Explain.

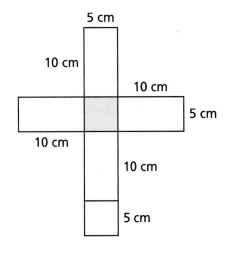

41. Ms. Singh drives 40 miles to her sister's house. Her average speed is 20 miles per hour. On her way home, her average speed is 40 miles per hour. What is her average speed for the round trip?

42. The drama club members at Henson Middle School are planning their spring show. They decide to charge $4.50 per ticket. They estimate their expenses for the show at $150.

  a. Write an equation for the relationship between the number of tickets sold and the club's total profit.

  b. Make a table to show how the profit changes as the ticket sales increase from 0 to 500 in intervals of 50.

  c. Make a graph of the (*tickets sold, total profit*) data.

  d. Add a column (or row) to your table to show the per-ticket profit for each number of tickets sold. For example, for 200 tickets, the total profit is $750, so the per-ticket profit is $750 ÷ 200, or $3.75.

  e. Make a graph of the (*tickets sold, per-ticket profit*) data.

  f. How are the patterns of change for the (*tickets sold, total profit*) data and (*tickets sold, per-ticket profit*) data similar? How are they different? How are the similarities and differences shown in the tables and graphs of each relationship?

For Exercises 43–45, find the value of *c* for which both ordered pairs satisfy the same inverse variation. Then, write an equation for the relationship.

43. $(3, 16), (12, c)$ **44.** $(3, 9), (4, c)$ **45.** $(3, 4), (4, c)$

46. Multiple Choice The force acting on a falling object due to gravity is related to the mass and acceleration of the object. For a fixed force F, the relationship between mass m and acceleration a is an inverse variation. Which equation shows the relationship between F, m, and a?

  A. $F = ma$ **B.** $m = Fa$ **C.** $\frac{m}{F} = a$ **D.** $\frac{m}{a} = F$

47. Multiple Choice Suppose the time t in the equation $d = rt$ is held constant. What happens to the distance d as the rate r increases?

  F. d decreases.   **G.** d increases.

  H. d stays constant.   **J.** There is not enough information.

48. Multiple Choice Suppose the distance d in the equation $d = rt$ is held constant. What happens to the time t as the rate r increases?

  A. t decreases.   **B.** t increases.

  C. t stays constant.   **D.** There is not enough information.

Mathematical Reflections 3

In this investigation, you explored several examples of inverse variations and looked for patterns in the tables, graphs, and equations of these relationships. These questions will help you summarize what you have learned.

Think about your answers to these questions. Discuss your ideas with other students and your teacher. Then, write a summary of your findings in your notebook.

1. Suppose the relationship between variables x and y is an inverse variation.

   a. How do the values of y change as values of x increase?

   b. Describe the pattern in a graph of (x, y) values.

   c. Describe the equation that relates the values of x and y.

2. How is an inverse relationship similar to a linear relationship? How is it different?

Looking Back and Looking Ahead

Unit Review

While working on the problems in this unit, you extended your skill in writing equations to express linear relationships. You also learned about a type of nonlinear relationship called an inverse variation. You used inverse and linear relationships to solve problems and make predictions.

Go Online
PHSchool.com
For: Vocabulary Review Puzzle
Web Code: apj-1051

Use Your Understanding: Linear and Inverse Variation

Test your understanding of linear relationships and inverse variations by solving the following problems about a recreation area that has a playground, hiking trails, amusement rides, and a small farm.

1. This table shows the growth of one pig that was raised on the farm.

Average Growth of Properly-Fed Pig

Age (mo)	0	1	2	3	4	5	6
Weight (lb)	3	48	92	137	182	228	273

SOURCE: Your 4-H Market Hog Project, Iowa State University.

a. Make a graph of the (*age, weight*) data. Draw a line that seems to fit the data pattern.

b. Find a linear equation in the form $y = mx + b$ for your line from part (a).

c. What do the values of m and b in your equation tell you about the growth of the pig?

d. Use your equation to estimate the pig's weight at 3.5 months and at 7 months.

2. One group of students suspects that farm animals eat less when the weather is warmer. They ask the farm staff to keep a record of what an adult goat eats on days with different average temperatures.

Food Consumption for a Goat

Average Daily Temperature (°F)	30	40	45	55	60	75	85	90
Food Eaten (kg)	3.9	3.6	3.4	3.0	2.7	2.5	2.2	1.9

a. Make a graph of the (*temperature, food eaten*) data. Draw a line that seems to fit the data pattern.

b. Find a linear equation in the form $y = mx + b$ for your line from part (a).

c. What do the values of m and b tell you about the relationship between temperature and the goat's food consumption?

d. Use your equation to predict how much the goat would eat on a day with an average temperature of 50°F. On a day with an average temperature of 70°F.

3. A small train gives visitors rides around the park on a 5,000-meter track. The time the trip takes varies. When many people are waiting in line, the drivers go quickly. When there are fewer people waiting, they go more slowly.

a. Sketch a graph showing how the average speed (in meters per minute) changes as the trip time (in minutes) increases.

b. For what parts of your graph are the predicted speeds realistic? Explain.

c. Write an equation relating the average speed s to the trip time t.

d. Write several sentences explaining as accurately as possible how average speed changes as trip time changes. In particular, describe the type of variation involved in this relationship.

Explain Your Reasoning

In this unit, you learned how to use models of linear relationships and inverse variations to solve a variety of problems. When you present work based on these relationships, you should be able to justify your calculations and conclusions.

4. How do you decide when a data pattern can be modeled well by a linear equation in the form $y = mx + b$? How will the values m and b relate to the data pattern?

5. How are the data patterns, graphs, and equations for the inverse variations you studied similar to and different from those modeled by linear equations?

6. How can a graph or equation model for a relationship be used to solve practical problems?

7. What limitations do mathematical models have as problem-solving tools?

Look Ahead

The work you did with linear relationships and inverse variations in this unit will be useful in many upcoming *Connected Mathematics* units and in the algebra and calculus courses you take in the future. As you progress through high school and college, you will see that linear and inverse relationships have applications in science, economics, business, technology, and many other fields of study.

A

additive inverses Two numbers, *a* and *b,* that satisfy the equation $a + b = 0$. For example, 3 and -3 are additive inverses, and $\frac{1}{2}$ and $-\frac{1}{2}$ are additive inverses.

inversos aditivos Dos números, *a* y *b,* que cumplen con la ecuación $a + b = 0$. Por ejemplo, 3 y -3 son inversos aditivos, y $\frac{1}{2}$ y $-\frac{1}{2}$ son inversos aditivos.

I

inequality A statement that two quantities are not equal. The symbols $>$, $<$, $\geq$, and $\leq$ are used to express inequalities. For example, if *a* and *b* are two quantities, then "*a* is greater than *b*" is written as $a > b$, and "*a* is less than *b*" is written as $a < b$. The statement $a \geq b$ means "*a* is greater than or equal to *b*." The statement $a \leq b$ means that "*a* is less than or equal to *b*."

desigualdad Enunciado que dice que dos cantidades no son iguales. Los signos $>$, $<$, $\geq$, y $\leq$ se usan para expresar desigualdades. Por ejemplo, si *a* y *b* son dos cantidades, entonces "*a* es mayor que *b*", se escribe $a > b$, y "*a* es menor que *b*" se escribe $a < b$. El enunciado $a \geq b$ quiere decir "*a* es mayor que o igual a *b*." El enunciado $a \leq b$ quiere decir "*a* es menor que o igual a *b*."

inverse variation A nonlinear relationship in which the product of two variables is constant. An inverse variation can be represented by an equation of the form $y = \frac{k}{x}$, or $xy = k$, where *k* is a constant. In an inverse variation, the values of one variable decrease as the values of the other variable increase. In the bridge-length experiment, the relationship between length and breaking weight was an inverse variation.

variación inversa Una relación no lineal en la que el producto de dos variables es constante. Una variación inversa se puede representar por una ecuación de la forma $y = \frac{k}{x}$, ó $xy = k$, donde *k* es una constante. En una variación inversa, los valores de una variable disminuyen a medida que los valores de la otra variable aumentan. En el experimento de la longitud de los puentes, la relación entre la longitud y el peso de colapso era una variación inversa.

L

linear relationship A relationship in which there is a constant rate of change between two variables. A linear relationship can be represented by a straight-line graph and by an equation of the form $y = mx + b$. In the equation, *m* is the slope of the line, and *b* is the *y*-intercept.

relación líneal Una relación en la que hay una tasa de cambio constante entre dos variables. Una relación lineal se puede representar por una gráfica de línea recta y por una ecuación de la forma $y = mx + b$. En la ecuación, *m* es la pendiente de la recta y *b* es el intercepto *y*.

mathematical model An equation or a graph that describes, at least approximately, the relationship between two variables. In this unit, mathematical models are made by acquiring data, plotting the data points, and, when the points showed a pattern, finding an equation or curve that fits the trend in the data. A mathematical model allows you to make reasonable guesses for values between and sometimes beyond the data points.

modelo matemático Una ecuación o una gráfica que describe, al menos approximadamente, la relación entre dos variables. En esta unidad, los modelos matemáticos se hacen obteniendo datos, trazando los puntos de los datos y, cuando los puntos muestran un patrón, hallando la ecuación o curva que muestra la tendencia de los datos. Un modelo matemático permite hacer estimaciones razonables para los valores entre y, a veces, fuera de los puntos de los datos.

multiplicative inverses Two numbers, a and b, that satisfy the equation $ab = 1$. For example, 3 and $\frac{1}{3}$ are multiplicative inverses, and $-\frac{1}{2}$ and -2 are multiplicative inverses.

inversos multiplicativos Dos números, a y b, que cumplen con la ecuación $ab = 1$. Por ejemplo, 3 y $\frac{1}{3}$ son inversos multiplicativos, y $-\frac{1}{2}$ y -2 son inversos multiplicativos.

Index

Team Credits

The people who made up the **Connected Mathematics 2** team —representing editorial, editorial services, design services, and production services— are listed below. Bold type denotes core team members.

Leora Adler, Judith Buice, Kerry Cashman, Patrick Culleton, Sheila DeFazio, Katie Hallahan, Richard Heater, **Barbara Hollingdale, Jayne Holman,** Karen Holtzman, **Etta Jacobs,** Christine Lee, Carolyn Lock, Catherine Maglio, **Dotti Marshall,** Rich McMahon, Eve Melnechuk, Kristin Mingrone, Terri Mitchell, **Marsha Novak,** Irene Rubin, Donna Russo, Robin Samper, Siri Schwartzman, **Nancy Smith,** Emily Soltanoff, **Mark Tricca,** Paula Vergith, Roberta Warshaw, Helen Young

Additional Credits

Diana Bonfilio, Mairead Reddin, Michael Torocsik, nSight, Inc.

Technical Illustration

WestWords, Inc.

Cover Design:

tom white.images

Photos

2 t, Jay S. Simon/Getty Images, Inc.; **2 b,** Jeff Greenberg/Alamy; **3,** Photodisc/Getty Images, Inc.; **5,** Kaluzny-Thatcher/Getty Images, Inc.; **7,** Javier Larrea/AGE Fotostock; **9,** Simon DesRochers/Masterfile; **14,** Jay S. Simon/Getty Images, Inc.; **16,** Richard Haynes; **21,** Richard Haynes; **26,** Galen Rowell/Corbis; **31,** Jeff Greenberg/Alamy; **34,** Ron Kimball/Ron Kimball Stock; **37,** PictureQuest; **41,** Richard Haynes; **42,** SuperStock, Inc./SuperStock; **45,** Bob Daemmrich/PhotoEdit; **50,** Yellow Dog Productions/Getty Images, Inc.; **51,** Macduff Everton/Corbis; **54,** AP Photo/Keystone/Steffen Schmidt; **55,** Richard Haynes; **57,** Richard Haynes; **59,** Dennis MacDonald/PhotoEdit; **63,** Photodisc/Getty Images, Inc.

Data Sources

The information on the average weights for chihuahuas on page 34 is from The Complete Chihuahua Encyclopedia by Hilary Harmar. Published by Arco Reprints, 1973.
The information on the average growth of pigs on page 62 is from "Your 4H Hog Market Project," Iowa State University, University Extension, January, 1922.

Connected Mathematics 2

Looking for Pythagoras

The Pythagorean Theorem

Glenda Lappan

James T. Fey

William M. Fitzgerald

Susan N. Friel

Elizabeth Difanis Phillips

PEARSON

Prentice
Hall

Boston, Massachusetts
Upper Saddle River, New Jersey

Looking for Pythagoras

The Pythagorean Theorem

Suppose you are planning an airplane trip to several cities in your state. What types of information would you need to give the pilot so he would know where to go?

To mark the square corners of their property, ancient Egyptians used a rope divided by knots into 12 equal segments. How do you think they used this tool?

On a standard baseball diamond, the bases are 90 feet apart. How far must a catcher at home plate throw the ball to get a runner out at second base?

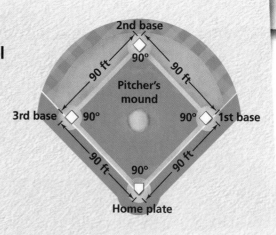

In this unit, you will explore side lengths and areas of right triangles and squares. Your explorations will lead you to discover one of the most important relationships in all of mathematics: the *Pythagorean Theorem*. The Pythagorean Theorem is so important that much of geometry, trigonometry, and calculus would be impossible without it.

In your previous work, you used whole numbers and fractions to describe lengths. In this unit, you will work with lengths that are impossible to describe with whole numbers or fractions. To talk about such lengths, you need to use another type of number, called an *irrational number.*

As you work on this unit, you will use what you are learning to solve problems like those on the previous page.

Mathematical Highlights

The Pythagorean Theorem

In *Looking for Pythagoras,* you will explore an important relationship among the side lengths of a right triangle.

You will learn how to

- Relate the area of a square to its side length
- Develop strategies for finding the distance between two points on a coordinate grid
- Understand and apply the Pythagorean Theorem
- Estimate the values of square roots of whole numbers
- Use the Pythagorean Theorem to solve everyday problems
- Locate irrational numbers on a number line

As you work on problems in this unit, ask yourself questions about problem situations that involve right triangles:

Is it appropriate and useful to use the Pythagorean Theorem in this situation? How do I know this?

Do I need to find the distance between two points?

How are irrational numbers and areas of squares related?

How can I estimate the square root of a number?

How can I find the length of something without directly measuring it?

Coordinate Grids

In this investigation, you will review how to use a coordinate grid to locate points in the plane. You will then explore how to find distances between points and areas of figures on a coordinate grid.

In the first two problems of this investigation, the coordinate grid is in the form of a street map of a fictional city called Euclid. The streets in most cities do not form perfect coordinate grids as they do in Euclid. However, many cities have streets that are at least loosely based on a coordinate system. One well-known example is Washington, D.C.

Did You Know?

The Lincoln Memorial stands at the west end of the National Mall in Washington, D.C. Built between 1914 and 1922, the memorial houses a 99-foot-tall statue of the first Republican president, Abraham Lincoln. The memorial celebrates Lincoln's accomplishments in uniting the divided nation and his quest to end slavery.

People often make speeches at the Lincoln Memorial, using the setting to strengthen their message. Martin Luther King, Jr. gave his famous "I have a Dream" speech at the memorial during the March on Washington in 1963.

Go Online
PHSchool.com

For: Information about the Lincoln Memorial
Web Code: ape-9031

The map on the next page shows the central part of Washington, D.C. The city's street system was designed by Pierre L'Enfant in 1791.

L'Enfant's design is based on a coordinate system. Here are some key features of L'Enfant's system:

- The north-south and east-west streets form grid lines.
- The origin is at the Capitol.
- The vertical axis is formed by North and South Capitol Streets.
- The horizontal axis is the line stretching from the Lincoln Memorial, through the Mall, and down East Capitol Street.
- The axes divide the city into four quadrants known as Northeast (NE), Southeast (SE), Southwest (SW), and Northwest (NW).

Problem 1.1 Locating Points and Finding Distances

A. Give the coordinates of each landmark.

   1. gas station

   2. animal shelter

   3. stadium

B. Euclid's chief of police is planning emergency routes. She needs to find the shortest driving route between the following pairs of locations:

   Pair 1: the police station to City Hall

   Pair 2: the hospital to City Hall

   Pair 3: the hospital to the art museum

   1. Give precise directions for an emergency car route for each pair.

   2. For each pair, find the total distance in blocks a police car following your route would travel.

C. Suppose you know the coordinates of two landmarks in Euclid. How can you determine the shortest driving distance (in blocks) between them?

D. A helicopter can travel directly from one point to another. For each pair in Question B, find the total distance (in blocks) a helicopter would have to travel to get from the starting location to the ending location. You may find it helpful to use a centimeter ruler.

E. Will a direct helicopter route between two locations always be shorter than a car route? Explain your reasoning.

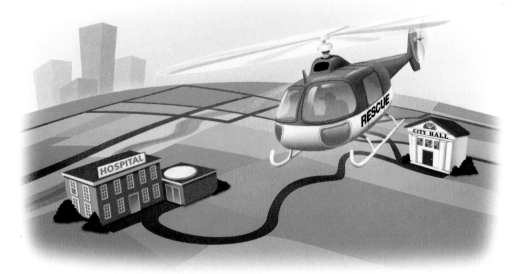

ACE Homework starts on page 12.

- Describe the locations of these landmarks:

   George Washington University

   Dupont Circle

   Benjamin Banneker Park

   The White House

   Union Station

- How can you find the distance from Union Station to Dupont Circle?

- Find the intersection of G Street and 8th Street SE and the intersection of G Street and 8th Street NW. How are these locations related to the Capitol Building?

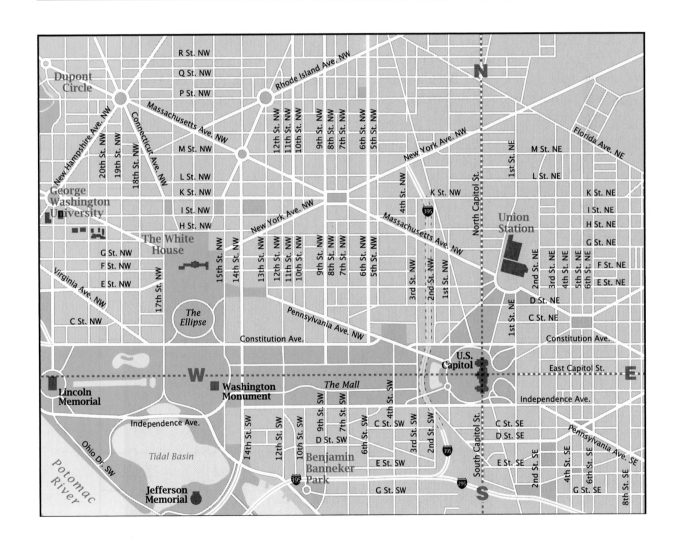

In mathematics, we use a coordinate system to describe the locations of points. Recall that horizontal and vertical number lines, called the *x*- and *y*-axes, divide the plane into four quadrants.

You describe the location of a point by giving its coordinates as an ordered pair of the form (*x*, *y*). On the coordinate grid at the right, four points are labeled with their coordinates.

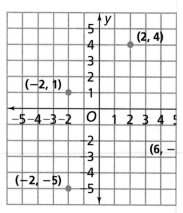

1.1 Driving Around Euclid

The founders of the city of Euclid loved math. They named their city after a famous mathematician, and they designed the street system to look like a coordinate grid. The Euclideans describe the locations of buildings and other landmarks by giving coordinates. For example, the art museum is located at (6, 1).

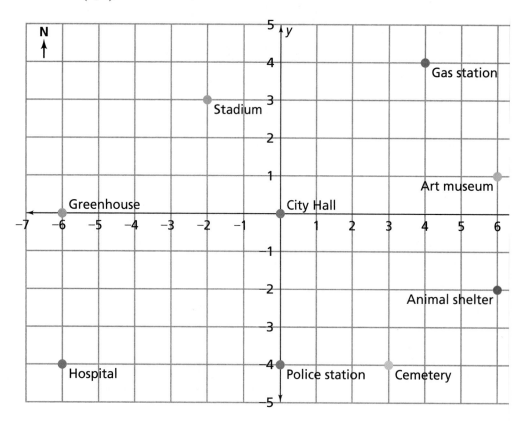

1.2 Planning Parks

The Euclid City Council is developing parks with geometric shapes. For some of the parks, the council gives the park designers constraints. For example, Descartes Park must have a border with vertices (1, 1) and (4, 2).

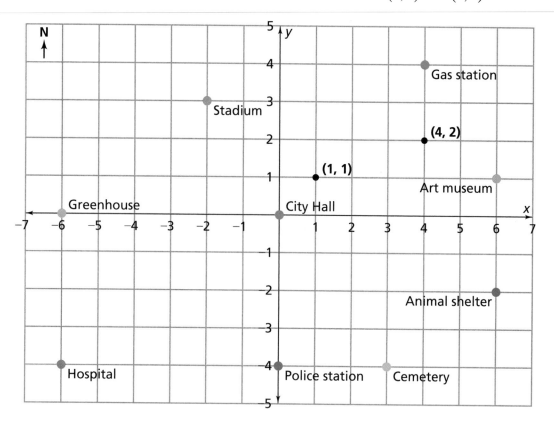

Problem 1.2 Shapes on a Coordinate Grid

Be prepared to explain your answers.

A. Suppose the park is to be a square. What could the coordinates of the other two vertices be? Give two answers.

B. Suppose the park is to be a nonsquare rectangle. What could the coordinates of the other two vertices be?

C. Suppose the park is to be a right triangle. What could the coordinates of the other vertex be?

D. Suppose the park is to be a parallelogram that is not a rectangle. What could the coordinates of the other two vertices be?

ACE Homework starts on page 12.

Below are some park designs submitted to the Euclid City Council. To determine costs, the council needs to know the area of each park.

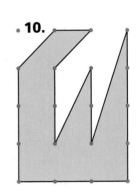

Problem 1.3 Finding Areas

Consider the horizontal or vertical distance between two adjacent dots to be 1 unit.

A. Find the area of each figure.

B. Find the area of one of the square parks you suggested in Problem 1.2.

C. Describe the strategies you used in Questions A and B.

ACE Homework starts on page 12.

active math online

For: Dynamic Geoboard
Visit: PHSchool.com
Web Code: apd-2100

Applications

For Exercises 1–7, use the map of Euclid from Problem 1.1.

1. Give the coordinates of each landmark.

   a. art museum   **b.** hospital   **c.** greenhouse

2. What is the shortest driving distance from the animal shelter to the stadium?

3. What is the shortest driving distance from the hospital to the gas station?

4. What are the coordinates of a point halfway from City Hall to the hospital if you travel by taxi? Is there more than one possibility? Explain.

5. What are the coordinates of a point halfway from City Hall to the hospital if you travel by helicopter? Is there more than one possibility? Explain.

6. a. Which landmarks are 7 blocks from City Hall by car?

   b. Give precise driving directions from City Hall to each landmark you listed in part (a).

7. Euclid Middle School is located at the intersection of two streets. The school is the same driving distance from the gas station as the hospital is from the greenhouse.

   a. List the coordinates of each place on the map where the school might be located.

   b. Find the flying distance, in blocks, from the gas station to each location you listed in part (a).

The points (0, 0) and (3, 2) are two vertices of a polygon with integer coordinates.

Homework
Help **O**nline
PHSchool.com
For: Help with Exercise 8
Web Code: ape-2108

8. What could the other two vertices be if the polygon is a square?

9. Suppose the polygon is a nonrectangular parallelogram. What could the other two vertices be?

10. What could the other vertex be if the polygon is a right triangle?

The points (3, 3) and (2, 6) are two vertices of a right triangle. Use this information for Exercises 11–13.

11. **Multiple Choice** Which point could be the third vertex of the right triangle?

   A. (3, 2)   **B.** (−1, 5)   **C.** (7, 4)   **D.** (0, 3)

12. Give the coordinates of at least two other points that could be the third vertex.

13. How many right triangles with vertices (3, 3) and (2, 6) can you draw? Explain.

14. Can the following points be connected to form a parallelogram? Explain.

   (1, 1)   (2, −2)   (4, 2)   (3, 5)

Find the area of each triangle. Copy the triangles onto dot paper if you need to.

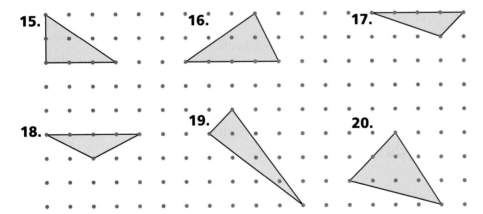

Find the area of each figure, and describe the method you use. Copy the figures onto dot paper if you need to.

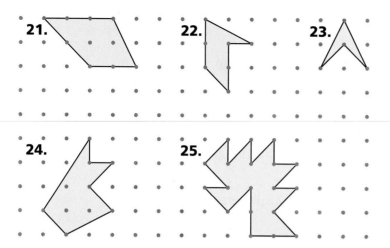

21.
22.
23.
24.
25.

Connections

In the city of Euclid, the length of each block is 150 meters. Use this information and the map from Problem 1.1 for Exercises 26–28.

26. What is the shortest driving distance, in meters, from City Hall to the animal shelter?

27. What is the shortest driving distance, in meters, from the police station to the gas station?

28. Between which two landmarks is the shortest driving distance 750 meters?

29. When she solved Problem 1.2, Fabiola used slopes to help explain her answers.

   a. In Question A, she used slopes to show that adjacent sides of the figure were perpendicular. How might she have done this?

   b. In Question D, she used slopes to show that the figure was a parallelogram. How might she have done this?

30. Refer to the map of Euclid from Problem 1.1.

a. Matsu walks 2 blocks west from the police station and then walks 3 blocks north. Give the coordinates of the place where he stops.

b. Matsu's friend Cassandra is at City Hall. She wants to meet Matsu at his ending location from part (a). What is the shortest route she can take if she walks along city streets? Is there more than one possible shortest route?

c. Lei leaves the stadium and walks 3 blocks east, then 3 blocks south, then 2 blocks west, and finally 4 blocks north. Give the coordinates of the place where she stops.

d. Lei's sister Aida wants to meet her at her ending location from part (c). Aida is now at City Hall. What is the shortest route she can take if she walks along city streets? Is there more than one possible shortest route?

e. In general, how can you find the shortest route, walking along city streets, from City Hall to any point in Euclid?

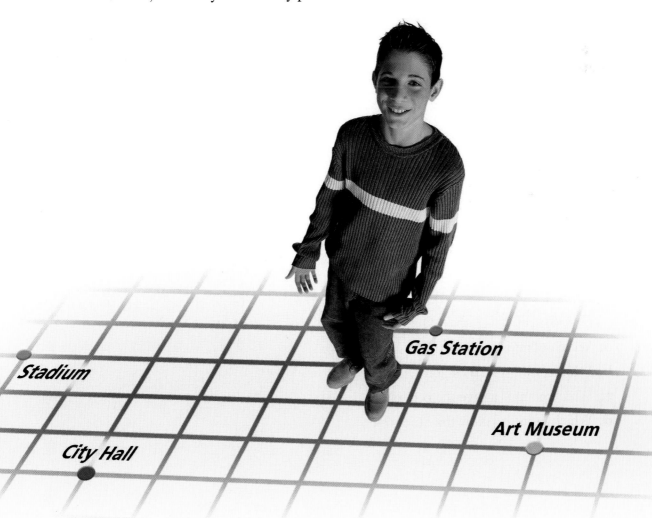

31. Below are equations for eight lines.

line 1: $y = 3x + 5$

line 2: $y = 0.5x + 3$

line 3: $y = 10 - 2x$

line 4: $y = 1 - \frac{1}{3}x$

line 5: $y = 7 + 3x$

line 6: $y = -2x + 1$

line 7: $y = 5 + 6x$

line 8: $y = 3x$

Go Online
PHSchool.com
For: Multiple-Choice Skills Practice
Web Code: apa-2154

a. Which of the lines are parallel to each other?

b. Which of the lines are perpendicular to each other?

32. Marcia finds the area of a figure on dot paper by dividing it into smaller shapes. She finds the area of each smaller shape and writes the sum of the areas as $\frac{1}{2} \cdot 3 + \frac{1}{2} + \frac{1}{2} + 1$.

a. What is the total area of the figure?

b. On dot paper, draw a figure Marcia might have been looking at.

33. In the figure, a circle is inscribed in a square.

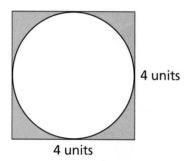

4 units

4 units

a. Find the area of the circle.

b. Find the area of the shaded region.

34. Refer to the ordered pairs to answer the questions. Do *not* plot the points on a grid. Explain each answer.

| $(2, -3)$ | $(3, -4)$ | $(-4, -5)$ | $(4, 5)$ |
| $(-4, 6)$ | $(-5, -5)$ | $(0, -6)$ | $(6, 0)$ |

a. Which point is farthest right?

b. Which point is farthest left?

c. Which point is above the others?

d. Which point is below the others?

Extensions

35. Find a road map of your city or county. Figure out how to use the map's index to locate a city, street, or other landmark. How is finding a landmark by using an index description similar to and different from finding a landmark in Euclid by using its coordinates?

36. Use a map of your state to plan an airplane trip from your city or town to four other locations in your state. Write a set of directions for your trip that you could give to the pilot.

37. On grid paper, draw several parallelograms with diagonals that are perpendicular to each other. What do you observe about these parallelograms?

38. Find the areas of triangles *AST, BST, CST,* and *DST*. How do the areas compare? Why do you think this is true?

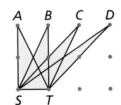

39. Find the areas of triangles *VMN, WMN, XMN, YMN,* and *ZMN*. How do the areas compare? Why do you think this is true?

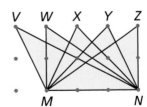

Mathematical Reflections 1

In this investigation, you solved problems involving coordinate grids. You located points, calculated distances and areas, and found vertices of polygons that satisfied given conditions. The following questions will help you summarize what you have learned.

Think about your answers to these questions. Discuss your ideas with other students and your teacher. Then write a summary of your findings in your notebook.

1. In the city of Euclid, how does the driving distance from one place to another compare to the flying distance?

2. Suppose you know the coordinates of two landmarks in Euclid. How can you find the distance between the landmarks?

3. Describe some strategies you can use to find areas of figures drawn on dot paper. Give examples if it helps you explain your thinking.

Investigation 2

Squaring Off

In this investigation, you will explore the relationship between the side lengths and areas of squares and use that relationship to find the lengths of segments on dot grids.

2.1 Looking for Squares

You can draw squares with different areas by connecting the points on a 5 dot-by-5 dot grid. Two simple examples follow.

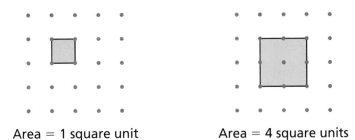

Area = 1 square unit   Area = 4 square units

In this problem, you will explore other possible areas.

Problem 2.1 Looking for Squares

A. On 5 dot-by-5 dot grids, draw squares of various sizes by connecting dots. Draw squares with as many different areas as possible Label each square with its area. Include at least one square whose sides are not horizontal and vertical.

B. Analyze your set of squares and describe the side lengths you found.

ACE Homework starts on page 23.

The area of a square is the length of a side multiplied by itself. This can be expressed by the formula $A = s \cdot s$, or $A = s^2$.

If you know the area of a square, you can work backward to find the length of a side. For example, suppose a square has an area of 4 square units. To find the length of a side, you need to figure out what positive number multiplied by itself equals 4. Because $2 \cdot 2 = 4$, the side length is 2 units. We call 2 a **square root** of 4.

This square has an area of 4 square units. The length of each side is the square root of 4, or 2, units.

In general, if $A = s^2$, then s is a square root of A. Because $2 \cdot 2 = 4$ and $-2 \cdot -2 = 4$, 2 and -2 are both square roots of 4. Every positive number has two square roots. The number 0 has only one square root, 0.

If N is a positive number, then $\sqrt{N}$ indicates the positive square root of N. For example, $\sqrt{4} = 2$. The negative square root of 4 is $-\sqrt{4} = -2$.

If the area of a square is known, then square roots can be used to describe the length of a side of the square.

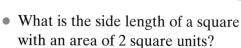

The area of a square is the side length squared.

- What is the side length of a square with an area of 2 square units?

- Is this length greater than 1? Is it greater than 2?

- Is 1.5 a good estimate for $\sqrt{2}$?

- Can you find a better estimate for $\sqrt{2}$?

Problem 2.2 Square Roots

In this problem, use your calculator only when the question directs you to.

A. 1. Find the side lengths of squares with areas of 1, 9, 16, and 25 square units.

   2. Find the values of $\sqrt{1}$, $\sqrt{9}$, $\sqrt{16}$, and $\sqrt{25}$.

B. 1. What is the area of a square with a side length of 12 units? What is the area of a square with a side length of 2.5 units?

   2. Find the missing numbers.

$$\sqrt{\blacksquare} = 12 \qquad \sqrt{\blacksquare} = 2.5$$

C. Refer to the square with an area of 2 square units you drew in Problem 2.1. The exact side length of this square is $\sqrt{2}$ units.

   1. Estimate $\sqrt{2}$ by measuring a side of the square with a centimeter ruler.

   2. Calculate the area of the square, using your measurement from part (1). Is the result exactly equal to 2?

   3. Use the square root key on your calculator to estimate $\sqrt{2}$.

   4. How does your ruler estimate compare to your calculator estimate?

D. 1. Which two whole numbers is $\sqrt{5}$ between? Explain.

   2. Which whole number is closer to $\sqrt{5}$? Explain.

   3. Without using the square root key on your calculator, estimate the value of $\sqrt{5}$ to two decimal places.

E. Give the exact side length of each square you drew in Problem 2.1.

ACE Homework starts on page 23.

2.3 Using Squares to Find Lengths

You can use a square to find the length of a segment connecting dots on a grid. For example, to find the length of the segment on the left, draw a square with the segment as a side. The square has an area of 5 square units, so the segment has length $\sqrt{5}$ units.

Problem 2.3 Using Squares to Find Lengths

A. 1. On 5 dot-by-5 dot grids, draw line segments with as many different lengths as possible by connecting dots. Label each segment with its length. Use the $\sqrt{}$ symbol to express lengths that are not whole numbers. (**Hint:** You will need to draw squares that extend beyond the 5-dot-by-5-dot grids.)

2. List the lengths in increasing order.

3. Estimate each non-whole number length to one decimal place.

B. Ella says the length of the segment at the left below is $\sqrt{8}$ units. Isabel says it is $2\sqrt{2}$ units. Are both students correct? Explain.

C. 1. Question B gives two ways of expressing the exact length of a segment. Express the exact length of the segment at the right above in two ways.

2. Can you find a segment whose length cannot be expressed in two ways as in Question B?

ACE Homework starts on page 23.

Applications

1. Find the area of every square that can be drawn by connecting dots on a 3 dot-by-3 dot grid.

2. On dot paper, draw a hexagon with an area of 16 square units.

3. On dot paper, draw a square with an area of 2 square units. Write an argument to convince a friend that the area is 2 square units.

4. Consider segment *AB* at right.

   a. On dot paper, draw a square with side *AB*. What is the area of the square?

   b. Use a calculator to estimate the length of segment *AB*.

5. Consider segment *CD* at right.

   a. On dot paper, draw a square with side *CD*. What is the area of the square?

   b. Use a calculator to estimate the length of segment *CD*.

6. Find the area and the side length of this square.

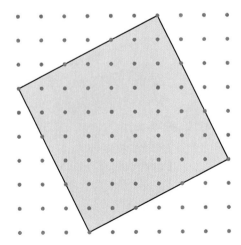

For Exercises 7–34, do not use the $\sqrt{\ }$ key on your calculator.

For Exercises 7–9, estimate each square root to one decimal place.

7. $\sqrt{11}$ **8.** $\sqrt{30}$ **9.** $\sqrt{172}$

Go Online
PHSchool.com

For: Multiple-Choice Skills Practice
Web Code: apa-2254

10. Multiple Choice Choose the pair of numbers $\sqrt{15}$ is between.

     A. 3.7 and 3.8   **B.** 3.8 and 3.9   **C.** 3.9 and 4.0   **D.** 14 and 16

Find exact values for each square root.

11. $\sqrt{144}$ **12.** $\sqrt{0.36}$ **13.** $\sqrt{961}$

Find the two consecutive whole numbers the square root is between. Explain.

14. $\sqrt{27}$ **15.** $\sqrt{1,000}$

Tell whether each statement is true.

16. $6 = \sqrt{36}$ **17.** $1.5 = \sqrt{2.25}$ **18.** $11 = \sqrt{101}$

Find the missing number.

19. $\sqrt{\blacksquare} = 81$ **20.** $14 = \sqrt{\blacksquare}$ **21.** $\blacksquare = \sqrt{28.09}$

22. $\sqrt{\blacksquare} = 3.2$ **23.** $\sqrt{\blacksquare} = \frac{1}{4}$ **24.** $\sqrt{\frac{4}{9}} = \blacksquare$

Find each product.

25. $\sqrt{2} \cdot \sqrt{2}$ **26.** $\sqrt{3} \cdot \sqrt{3}$ **27.** $\sqrt{4} \cdot \sqrt{4}$ **28.** $\sqrt{5} \cdot \sqrt{5}$

Give both the positive and negative square roots of each number.

29. 1   **30.** 4   **31.** 2

32. 16   **33.** 25   **34.** 5

Sorry, you can't use my square root key.

35. Find the length of every line segment that can be drawn by connecting dots on a 3 dot-by-3 dot grid.

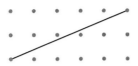
Homework Help nline
PHSchool.com
For: Help with Exercise 35
Web Code: ape-2235

36. Consider this segment.

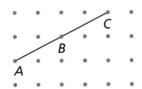

a. Express the exact length of the segment, using the $\sqrt{\ }$ symbol.

b. What two consecutive whole numbers is the length of the segment between?

37. Show that $2\sqrt{5}$ is equal to $\sqrt{20}$ by finding the length of line segment AC in two ways:

- Find the length of AB. Use the result to find the length of AC.
- Find the length of AC directly, as you did in Problem 2.3.

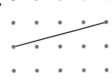

38. Multiple Choice Which line segment has a length of $\sqrt{17}$ units?

F.

G.

H.

J.

For Exercises 39 and 40, find the length of each side of the figure.

39.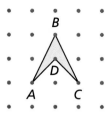

40.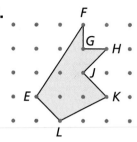

41. Put the following set of numbers in order on a number line.

2.3	$2\frac{1}{4}$	$\sqrt{5}$	$\sqrt{2}$	$\frac{5}{2}$	$\sqrt{4}$
4	-2.3	$-2\frac{1}{4}$	$\frac{4}{2}$	$-\frac{4}{2}$	2.09

Connections

42. a. Which of the triangles below are right triangles? Explain.

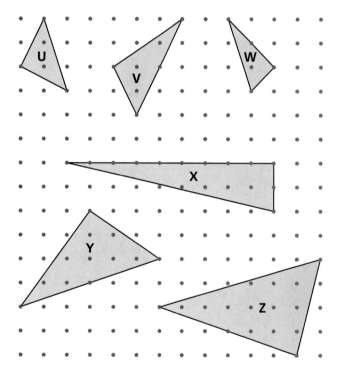

b. Find the area of each right triangle.

43. Refer to the squares you drew in Problem 2.1.

    a. Give the perimeter of each square to the nearest hundredth of a unit.

    b. What rule can you use to calculate the perimeter of a square if you know the length of a side?

44. On grid paper, draw coordinate axes like the ones below. Plot point P at $(1, -2)$.

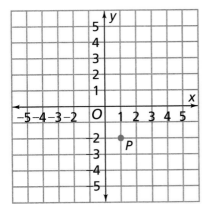

    a. Draw a square $PQRS$ with an area of 10 square units.

    b. Name a vertex of your square that is $\sqrt{10}$ units from point P.

    c. Give the coordinates of at least two other points that are $\sqrt{10}$ units from point P.

P needs to be a vertex of the square.

45. In Problem 2.3, you drew segments of length 1 unit, $\sqrt{2}$ units, 4 units, and so on. On a copy of the number line below, locate and label each length you drew. On the number line, $\sqrt{1}$ and $\sqrt{2}$ have been marked as examples.

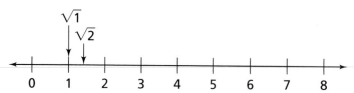

46. In Problem 2.1, it was easier to find the "upright" squares. Two of these squares are represented on the coordinate grid.

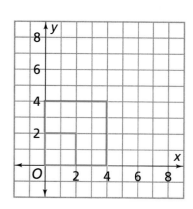

   a. Are these squares similar? Explain.

   b. How are the coordinates of the corresponding vertices related?

   c. How are the areas of the squares related?

   d. Copy the drawing. Add two more "upright" squares with a vertex at $(0, 0)$. How are the coordinates of the vertices of these new squares related to the 2×2 square? How are their areas related?

Extensions

47. On dot paper, draw a non-rectangular parallelogram with an area of 6 square units.

48. On dot paper, draw a triangle with an area of 5 square units.

49. Dalida claims that $\sqrt{8} + \sqrt{8}$ is equal to $\sqrt{16}$ because 8 plus 8 is 16. Is she right? Explain.

50. The drawing shows three right triangles with a common side.

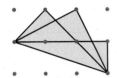

    a. Find the length of the common side.

    b. Do the three triangles have the same area? Explain.

We know that $\sqrt{5} \cdot \sqrt{5} = \sqrt{5 \cdot 5} = \sqrt{25} = 5$. Tell whether each product is a whole number. Explain.

51. $\sqrt{2} \cdot \sqrt{50}$

52. $\sqrt{4} \cdot \sqrt{16}$

53. $\sqrt{4} \cdot \sqrt{6}$

Mathematical Reflections 2

In this investigation, you explored squares and segments drawn on dot paper. You learned that the side length of a square is the positive square root of the square's area. You also discovered that, in many cases, a square root is not a whole number. These questions will help you summarize what you have learned.

Think about your answers to these questions. Discuss your ideas with other students and your teacher. Then write a summary of your findings in your notebook.

1. Describe how you would find the length of a line segment connecting two dots on dot paper. Be sure to consider horizontal, vertical, and tilted segments.

2. Explain what it means to find the square root of a number.

Investigation 3

The Pythagorean Theorem

Recall that a right triangle is a triangle with a right, or 90°, angle. The longest side of a right triangle is the side opposite the right angle. We call this side the **hypotenuse** of the triangle. The other two sides are called the **legs.** The right angle of a right triangle is often marked with a square.

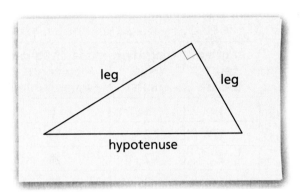

3.1 The Pythagorean Theorem

Each leg of the right triangle on the left below has a length of 1 unit. Suppose you draw squares on the hypotenuse and legs of the triangle, as shown on the right.

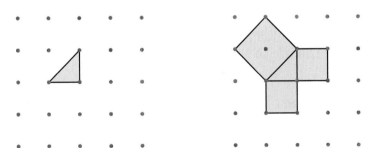

How are the areas of the three squares related?

In this problem, you will look for a relationship among the areas of squares drawn on the sides of right triangles.

A. Copy the table below. For each row of the table:

- Draw a right triangle with the given leg lengths on dot paper.
- Draw a square on each side of the triangle.
- Find the areas of the squares and record the results in the table.

Length of Leg 1 (units)	Length of Leg 2 (units)	Area of Square on Leg 1 (square units)	Area of Square on Leg 2 (square units)	Area of Square on Hypotenuse (square units)
1	1	1	1	2
1	2	■	■	■
2	2	■	■	■
1	3	■	■	■
2	3	■	■	■
3	3	■	■	■
3	4	■	■	■

B. Recall that a **conjecture** is your best guess about a mathematical relationship. It is usually a generalization about a pattern you think might be true, but that you do not yet know for sure is true.

For each triangle, look for a relationship among the areas of the three squares. Make a conjecture about the areas of squares drawn on the sides of any right triangle.

C. Draw a right triangle with side lengths that are different than those given in the table. Use your triangle to test your conjecture from Question B.

ACE Homework starts on page 38.

active math online

For: Interactive Pythagoras
Visit: PHSchool.com
Web Code: apd-2300

The pattern you discovered in Problem 3.1 is a famous theorem named after the Greek mathematician Pythagoras. A *theorem* is a general mathematical statement that has been proven true. The Pythagorean Theorem is one of the most famous theorems in mathematics.

Over 300 different proofs have been given for the Pythagorean Theorem. One of these proofs is based on the geometric argument you will explore in this problem.

Did You Know?

Pythagoras lived in the sixth century B.C. He had a devoted group of followers known as the Pythagoreans.

The Pythagoreans were a powerful group. Their power and influence became so strong that some people feared they threatened the local political structure, and they were forced to disband. However, many Pythagoreans continued to meet in secret and to teach Pythagoras's ideas.

I had help!

PYTHAGORAS

Because they held Pythagoras in such high regard, the Pythagoreans gave him credit for all of their discoveries. Much of what we now attribute to Pythagoras, including the Pythagorean Theorem, may actually be the work of one or several of his followers.

Go Online
PHSchool.com **For:** Information about Pythagoras
Web Code: ape-9031

Use the puzzles your teacher gives you.

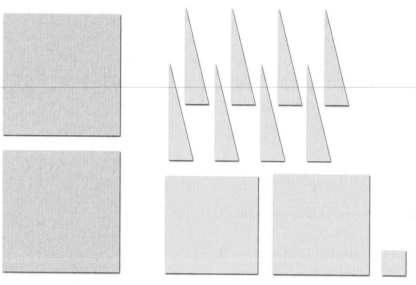

Puzzle frames   **Puzzle pieces**

A. Study a triangle piece and the three square pieces. How do the side lengths of the squares compare to the side lengths of the triangle?

B. 1. Arrange the 11 puzzle pieces to fit exactly into the two puzzle frames. Use four triangles in each frame.

2. What conclusion can you draw about the relationship among the areas of the three squares?

3. What does the conclusion you reached in part (2) mean in terms of the side lengths of the triangles?

4. Compare your results with those of another group. Did that group come to the same conclusion your group did? Is this conclusion true for all right triangles? Explain.

C. Suppose a right triangle has legs of length 3 centimeters and 5 centimeters.

1. Use your conclusion from Question B to find the area of a square drawn on the hypotenuse of the triangle.

2. What is the length of the hypotenuse?

D. In this Problem and Problem 3.1, you explored the Pythagorean Theorem, a relationship among the side lengths of a right triangle. State this theorem as a rule for any right triangle with leg lengths a and b and hypotenuse length c.

ACE Homework starts on page 38.

Finding Distances

In Investigation 2, you found the lengths of tilted segments by drawing
squares and finding their areas. You can also find these lengths using the
Pythagorean Theorem.

Problem 3.3 Finding Distances

In Questions A–D, refer to the grid below.

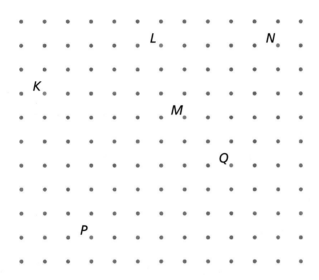

A. 1. Copy the points above onto dot paper. Draw a right triangle with
segment *KL* as its hypotenuse.

   2. Find the lengths of the legs of the triangle.

   3. Use the Pythagorean Theorem to find the length of segment *KL*.

B. Find the distance between points *M* and *N* by connecting them with
a segment and using the method in Question A.

C. Find the distance between points *P* and *Q*.

D. Find two points that are $\sqrt{13}$ units apart. Label the points *X* and *Y*.
Explain how you know the distance between the points is $\sqrt{13}$ units.

ACE Homework starts on page 38.

You will now explore these questions about the Pythagorean Theorem:

- Is any triangle whose side lengths a, b, and c, satisfy the relationship $a^2 + b^2 = c^2$ a right triangle?

- Suppose the side lengths of a triangle do *not* satisfy the relationship $a^2 + b^2 = c^2$. Does this mean the triangle is *not* a right triangle?

Getting Ready for Problem **3.4**

In ancient Egypt, the Nile River overflowed every year, flooding the surrounding lands and destroying property boundaries. As a result, the Egyptians had to remeasure their land every year.

Because many plots of land were rectangular, the Egyptians needed a reliable way to mark right angles. They devised a clever method involving a rope with equally spaced knots that formed 12 equal intervals.

To understand the Egyptians' method, mark off 12 segments of the same length on a piece of rope or string. Tape the ends of the string together to form a closed loop. Form a right triangle with side lengths that are whole numbers of segments.

- What are the side lengths of the right triangle you formed?
- Do the side lengths satisfy the relationship $a^2 + b^2 = c^2$?
- How do you think the Egyptians used the knotted rope?

Problem 3.4 Lengths That Form a Right Triangle

A. Copy the table below. Each row gives three side lengths. Use string, straws, or polystrips to build a triangle with the given side lengths. Then, complete the second and third columns of the table.

Side Lengths (units)	Do the side lengths satisfy $a^2 + b^2 = c^2$?	Is the triangle a right triangle?
3, 4, 5		
5, 12, 13		
5, 6, 10		
6, 8, 10		
4, 4, 4		
1, 2, 2		

B. 1. Make a conjecture about triangles whose side lengths satisfy the relationship $a^2 + b^2 = c^2$.

2. Make a conjecture about triangles whose side lengths do not satisfy the relationship $a^2 + b^2 = c^2$.

3. Check your conjecture with two other triangles. Explain why your conjecture will always be true.

C. Determine whether the triangle with the given side lengths is a right triangle.

1. 12 units, 16 units, 20 units

2. 8 units, 15 units, 17 units

3. 12 units, 9 units, 16 units

D. Which of these triangles are right triangles? Explain.

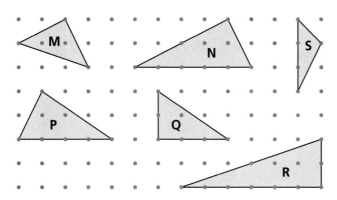

ACE Homework starts on page 38.

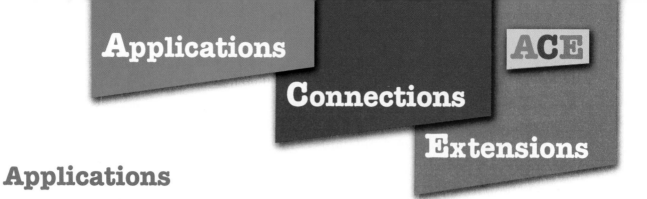

Applications

1. A right triangle has legs of length 5 inches and 12 inches.

   a. Find the area of a square drawn on the hypotenuse of the triangle.

   b. What is the length of the hypotenuse?

2. Use the Pythagorean Theorem to find the length of the hypotenuse of this triangle.

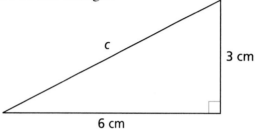

Homework
Help Online
PHSchool.com
For: Help with Exercise 2
Web Code: ape-2302

3. On dot paper, find two points that are $\sqrt{17}$ units apart. Label the points W and X. Explain how you know the distance between the points is $\sqrt{17}$ units.

4. On dot paper, find two points that are $\sqrt{20}$ units apart. Label the points Y and Z. Explain how you know the distance between the points is $\sqrt{20}$ units.

Find the missing length(s).

5.
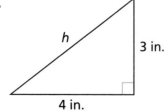

6.
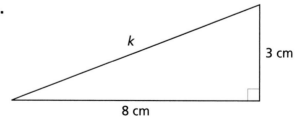

7.
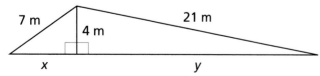

For Exercises 8–11, use the map of Euclid. Find the flying distance in blocks between the two landmarks without using a ruler. Explain.

8. greenhouse and stadium

9. police station and art museum

10. greenhouse and hospital

11. City Hall and gas station

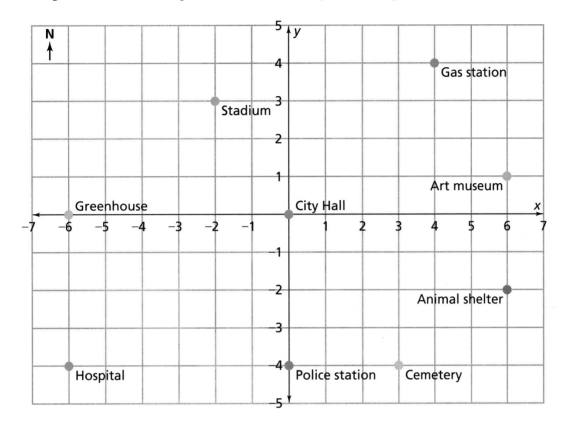

12. Multiple Choice Refer to the map above. Which landmarks are $\sqrt{40}$ blocks apart?

A. greenhouse and stadium

B. City Hall and art museum

C. hospital and art museum

D. animal shelter and police station

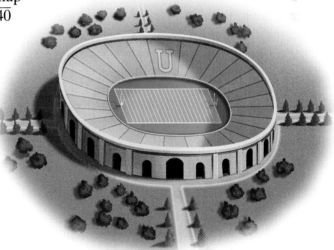

13. The diagram at the right shows a right triangle with a square on each side.

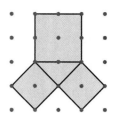

   a. Find the areas of the three squares.

   b. Use the areas from part (a) to show that this triangle satisfies the Pythagorean Theorem.

14. Show that this triangle satisfies the Pythagorean Theorem.

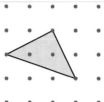

15. Multiple Choice Choose the set of side lengths that could make a right triangle.

   F. 10 cm, 24 cm, 26 cm   **G.** 4 cm, 6 cm, 10 cm

   H. 5 cm, 10 cm, $\sqrt{50}$ cm   **J.** 8 cm, 9 cm, 15 cm

Tell whether the triangle with the given side lengths is a right triangle.

16. 10 cm, 10 cm, $\sqrt{200}$ cm   **17.** 9 in., 16 in., 25 in.

For: Multiple-Choice Skills Practice
Web Code: apa-2354

Connections

18. The prism at the right has a base that is a right triangle.

   a. What is the length of *a*?

   b. Do you need to know the length of *a* to find the volume of the prism? Do you need to know it to find the surface area? Explain.

   c. What is the volume?

   d. What is the surface area?

   e. Sketch a net for the prism.

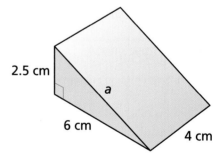

For Exercises 19–22, refer to the figures below.

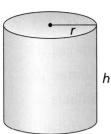

Cylinder

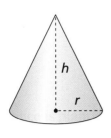

Cone

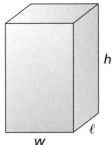

Prism

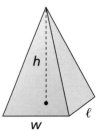

Pyramid

19. Multiple Choice Which expression represents the volume of the cylinder?

A. $2\pi r^2 + 2\pi rh$　　**B.** $\pi r^2 h$　　**C.** $\frac{1}{3}\pi r^2 h$　　**D.** $\frac{1}{2}\pi r^2 h$

20. Multiple Choice Which expression represents the volume of the cone?

F. $2\pi r^2 + 2\pi rh$　　**G.** $\pi r^2 h$　　**H.** $\frac{1}{3}\pi r^2 h$　　**J.** $\frac{1}{2}\pi r^2 h$

21. Multiple Choice Which expression represents the volume of the prism?

A. $2(\ell w + \ell h + wh)$　　　　**B.** ℓwh

C. $\frac{1}{3}\ell wh$　　　　　　　　　**D.** $\frac{1}{2}\ell wh$

22. Multiple Choice Which expression represents the volume of the pyramid?

F. $2(\ell w + \ell h + wh)$　　　　**G.** ℓwh

H. $\frac{1}{3}\ell wh$　　　　　　　　　**J.** $\frac{1}{2}\ell wh$

23. In the city of Euclid, Hilary's house is located at $(5, -3)$, and Jamilla's house is located at $(2, -4)$.

  a. Without plotting points, find the shortest driving distance in blocks between the two houses.

  b. What is the exact flying distance between the two houses?

24. Which labeled point is the same distance from point A as point B is from point A? Explain.

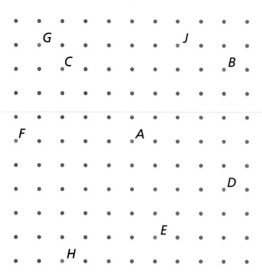

25. In the drawing at right, the cone and the cylinder have the same height and radius. Suppose the radius r of the cone is 2 units and the slant height d is $\sqrt{29}$ units.

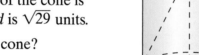

a. What is the height of the cone?

b. What is the volume of the cone?

26. In the drawing below, the pyramid and the cube have the same height and base.

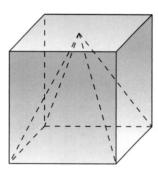

a. Suppose the edge length of the cube is 6 units. What is the volume of the pyramid?

b. Suppose the edge length of the cube is x units. What is the volume of the pyramid?

Extensions

27. Any tilted segment that connects two dots on dot paper can be the hypotenuse of a right triangle. You can use this idea to draw segments of a given length. The key is finding two square numbers with a sum equal to the square of the length you want to draw.

For example, suppose you want to draw a segment with length $\sqrt{5}$ units. You can draw a right triangle in which the sum of the areas of the squares on the legs is 5. The area of the square on the hypotenuse will be 5 square units, so the length of the hypotenuse will be $\sqrt{5}$ units. Because 1 and 4 are square numbers, and $1 + 4 = 5$, you can draw a right triangle with legs of lengths 1 and 2.

a. To use this method, it helps to be familiar with sums of square numbers. Copy and complete the addition table to show the sums of pairs of square numbers.

+	1	4	9	16	25	36	49	64
1	2	5						
4	5							
9								
16								
25								
36								
49								
64								

For parts (b)–(d) find two square numbers with the given sum.

b. 10　　　　　　**c.** 25　　　　　　**d.** 89

For parts (e)–(h), draw tilted segments with the given lengths on dot paper. Use the addition table to help you. Explain your work.

e. $\sqrt{26}$ units　　　　　　**f.** 10 units

g. $\sqrt{10}$ units　　　　　　**h.** $\sqrt{50}$ units

For Exercises 28–33, tell whether it is possible to draw a segment of the given length by connecting dots on dot paper. Explain.

28. $\sqrt{2}$ units   **29.** $\sqrt{3}$ units   **30.** $\sqrt{4}$ units

31. $\sqrt{5}$ units   **32.** $\sqrt{6}$ units   **33.** $\sqrt{7}$ units

34. Ryan looks at the diagram below. He says, "If the center of this circle is at the origin, then I can figure out the radius."

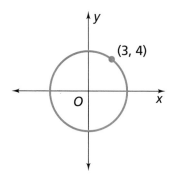

a. Explain how Ryan can find the radius.

b. What is the radius?

35. Use the graph to answer parts (a)–(c).

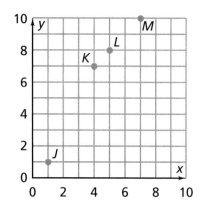

a. Find the coordinates of J and K.

b. Use the coordinates to find the distance from J to K. Explain your method.

c. Use your method from part (b) to find the distance from L to M.

Mathematical Reflections 3

In this investigation, you worked with a very important mathematical relationship called the Pythagorean Theorem. These questions will help you summarize what you have learned.

Think about your answers to these questions. Discuss your ideas with other students and your teacher. Then write a summary of your findings in your notebook.

1. Suppose you are given the lengths of two sides of a right triangle. Describe how you can find the length of the third side.

2. Suppose two points on a grid are not on the same horizontal or vertical line. Describe how you can use the Pythagorean Theorem to find the distance between the points without measuring.

3. How can you determine whether a triangle is a right triangle if you know only the lengths of its sides?

Using the Pythagorean Theorem

In Investigation 3, you studied the Pythagorean Theorem, which states:

> The area of the square on the hypotenuse of a right triangle is equal to the sum of the areas of the squares on the legs.

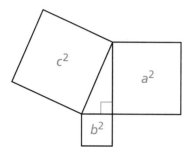

$$a^2 + b^2 = c^2$$

In this investigation, you will explore some interesting applications of the Pythagorean Theorem.

4.1 Analyzing The Wheel of Theodorus

The diagram on the next page is named for its creator, Theodorus of Cyrene (sy ree nee), a former Greek colony. Theodorus was a Pythagorean.

The Wheel of Theodorus begins with a triangle with legs 1 unit long and winds around counterclockwise. Each triangle is drawn using the hypotenuse of the previous triangle as one leg and a segment of length 1 unit as the other leg. To make the Wheel of Theodorus, you need only know how to draw right angles and segments 1 unit long.

Wheel of Theodorus

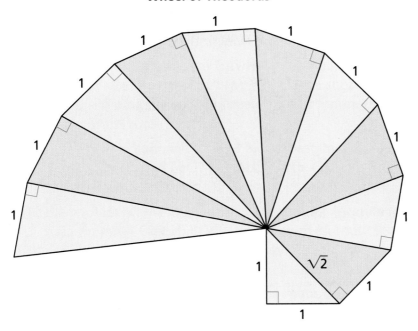

Problem 4.1 Analyzing the Wheel of Theodorus

A. Use the Pythagorean Theorem to find the length of each hypotenuse in the Wheel of Theodorus. On a copy of the wheel, label each hypotenuse with its length. Use the $\sqrt{}$ symbol to express lengths that are not whole numbers.

B. Use a cut-out copy of the ruler below to measure each hypotenuse on the wheel. Label the place on the ruler that represents the length of each hypotenuse. For example, the first hypotenuse length would be marked like this:

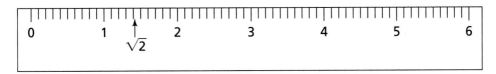

C. For each hypotenuse length that is not a whole number:

  1. Give the two consecutive whole numbers the length is between. For example, $\sqrt{2}$ is between 1 and 2.

  2. Use your ruler to find two decimal numbers (to the tenths place) the length is between. For example $\sqrt{2}$ is between 1.4 and 1.5.

  3. Use your calculator to estimate the value of each length and compare the result to the approximations you found in part (2).

D. Odakota uses his calculator to find $\sqrt{3}$. He gets 1.732050808. Geeta says this must be wrong because when she multiplies 1.732050808 by 1.732050808, she gets 3.000000001. Why do these students disagree?

ACE **Homework starts on page 53.**

Did You Know?

Some decimals, such as 0.5 and 0.3125, *terminate*. They have a limited number of digits. Other decimals, such as 0.3333 . . . and 0.181818 . . . , have a repeating pattern of digits that never ends.

Terminating or repeating decimals are called **rational numbers** because they can be expressed as *ratios* of integers.

$$0.5 = \frac{1}{2} \qquad 0.3125 = \frac{5}{16} \qquad 0.3333\ldots = \frac{1}{3} \qquad 0.181818\ldots = \frac{2}{11}.$$

Some decimals neither terminate nor repeat. The decimal representation of the number π starts with the digits 3.14159265 . . . and goes forever without any repeating sequence of digits. Numbers with non-terminating and non-repeating decimal representations are called **irrational numbers.** They cannot be expressed as ratios of integers.

The number $\sqrt{2}$ is an irrational number. You had trouble finding an exact terminating or repeating decimal representation for $\sqrt{2}$ because such a representation does not exist. Other irrational numbers are $\sqrt{3}$, $\sqrt{5}$, and $\sqrt{11}$. In fact, $\sqrt{n}$ is an irrational number for any value of n that is not a square number.

The set of irrational and rational numbers is called the set of **real numbers.** An amazing fact about irrational numbers is that there is an infinite number of them between any two fractions!

4.2 Stopping Sneaky Sally

You can use the Pythagorean Theorem to solve problems in which you need to find the length of a side of a right triangle.

Problem 4.2 Finding Unknown Side Lengths

Horace Hanson is the catcher for the Humboldt Bees baseball team. Sneaky Sally Smith, the star of the Canfield Cats, is on first base. Sally is known for stealing bases, so Horace is keeping an eye on her.

The pitcher throws a fastball, and the batter swings and misses. Horace catches the pitch and, out of the corner of his eye, he sees Sally take off for second base.

Use the diagram to answer Questions A and B.

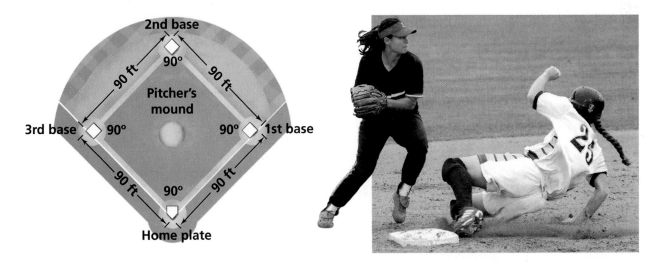

A. How far must Horace throw the baseball to get Sally out at second base? Explain.

B. The shortstop is standing on the baseline, halfway between second base and third base. How far is the shortstop from Horace?

C. The pitcher's mound is 60 feet 6 inches from home plate. Use this information and your answer to Question A to find the distance from the pitcher's mound to each base.

ACE | Homework starts on page 53.

Did You Know?

Although most people consider baseball an American invention, a similar game, called *rounders*, was played in England as early as the 1600s. Like baseball, rounders involved hitting a ball and running around bases. However, in rounders, the fielders actually threw the ball at the base runners. If a ball hit a runner while he was off base, he was out.

Alexander Cartwright was a founding member of the Knickerbockers Base Ball Club of New York City, baseball's first organized club. Cartwright played a key role in writing the first set of formal rules for baseball in 1845.

According to Cartwright's rules, a batter was out if a fielder caught the ball either on the fly or on the first bounce. Today, balls caught on the first bounce are not outs. Cartwright's rules also stated that the first team to have 21 runs at the end of an inning was the winner. Today, the team with the highest score after nine innings wins the game.

Go Online
PHSchool.com   **For:** Information about Alexander Cartwright
Web Code: ape-9031

4.3 Analyzing Triangles

All equilateral triangles have reflection symmetries. This property and the Pythagorean Theorem can be used to investigate some interesting properties of other equilateral triangles.

Getting Ready for Problem 4.3

Triangle *ABC* is an equilateral triangle.

- What is true about the angle measures in an equilateral triangle?
- What is true about the side lengths of an equilateral triangle?

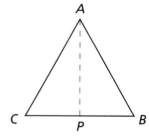

Line AP is a reflection line for triangle ABC.

- What can you say about the measures of the following angles? Explain.

  Angle CAP Angle BAP

  Angle CPA Angle BPA

- What can you say about line segments CP and PB? Explain.
- What can you say about triangles ACP and ABP?

Problem 4.3 Analyzing Triangles

A. Copy triangle ABC on the facing page. If the lengths of the sides of this equilateral triangle are 4 units, label the following measures:

1. angle CAP **2.** angle BAP

3. angle CPA **4.** angle BPA

5. length of CP **6.** length of PB

7. length of AP

B. Suppose the lengths of the sides of ABC triangles are s units. Find the measures of the following:

1. angle CAP **2.** angle BAP

3. angle CPA **4.** angle BPA

5. length of CP **6.** length of PB

7. length of AP

C. A right triangle with a 60° angle is called a 30-60-90 triangle. This 30-60-90 triangle has a hypotenuse of length 6 units.

1. What are the lengths of the other two sides? Explain how you found your answers.

2. What relationships among the side lengths do you observe for this 30-60-90 triangle? Is this relationship true for all 30-60-90 triangles? Explain.

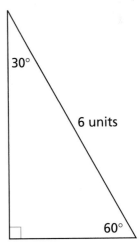

ACE Homework starts on page 53.

In this problem, you will apply many of the strategies you have developed in this unit, especially what you found in Problem 4.3.

Problem 4.4 Finding the Perimeter

Use the diagram for Questions A–C. Explain your work.

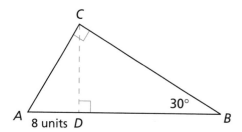

A. Find the perimeter of triangle *ABC*.

B. Find the area of triangle *ABC*.

C. Find the areas of triangle *ACD* and triangle *BCD*.

ACE Homework starts on page 53.

Did You Know?

In the movie *The Wizard of Oz,* the scarecrow celebrates his new brain by reciting the following:

"The sum of the square roots of any two sides of an isosceles triangle is equal to the square root of the remaining side."

Now you know what the scarecrow meant to say, even though his still imperfect brain got it wrong!

Applications

1. The hypotenuse of a right triangle is 15 centimeters long. One leg is 9 centimeters long. How long is the other leg?

2. The Wheel of Theodorus in Problem 4.1 includes only the first 11 triangles in the wheel. The wheel can go on forever.

   a. Find the side lengths of the next three triangles.

   b. Find the areas of the first five triangles in the wheel. Do you observe any pattern?

   c. Suppose you continue adding triangles to the wheel. Which triangle will have a hypotenuse of length 5 units?

In Exercises 3 and 4, find the missing length.

3. 30 in.

   10 in.

   d

4. 4 ft

   j

   12 ft

5. Moesha, a college student, needs to walk from her dorm room in Wilson Hall to her math class in Wells Hall. Normally, she walks 500 meters east and 600 meters north along the sidewalks, but today she is running late. She decides to take the shortcut through the Tundra.

   a. How many meters long is Moesha's shortcut?

   b. How much shorter is the shortcut than Moesha's usual route?

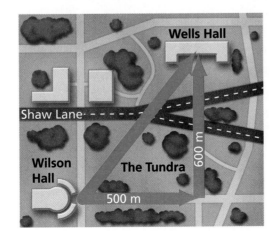

Wells Hall

Shaw Lane

Wilson Hall   The Tundra

600 m

500 m

6. Square *ABCD* has sides of length 1 unit. The diagonal *BD* is a line of reflection.

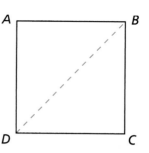

   a. How do the triangles *ABD* and *BDC* compare?

   b. Find the angle measures for one of the triangles. Explain how you found each measure.

   c. What is the length of the diagonal? Explain.

   d. Suppose square *ABCD* had sides of length 5 units instead of 1 unit. How would this change your answers to parts (b) and (c)?

7. A right triangle with a 45° angle is called a 45-45-90 triangle.

   a. Are all 45-45-90 triangles similar to each other? Explain.

   b. Suppose one leg of a 45-45-90 triangle is 5 units long. Find the perimeter of the triangle.

8. The diagram shows an amusement park ride in which tram cars glide along a cable. How long, to the nearest tenth of a meter, is the cable for the ride?

Not drawn to scale

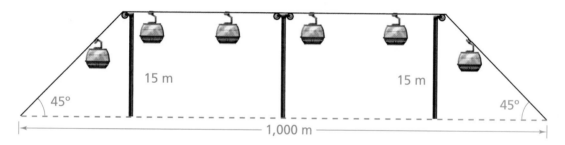

9. At Emmit's Evergreen Farm, the taller trees are braced by wires. A wire extends from 2 feet below the top of a tree to a stake in the ground. What is the tallest tree that can be braced with a 25-foot wire staked 15 feet from the base of the tree?

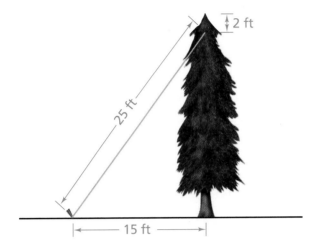

10. As part of his math assignment, Denzel has to estimate the height of a tower. He decides to use what he knows about 30-60-90 triangles.

Denzel makes the measurements shown below. About how tall is the tower? Explain.

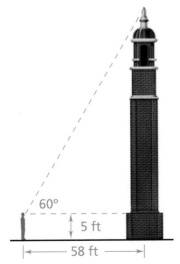

Not drawn to scale

11. a. Name all the 30-60-90 triangles in the figure below. Are all of these triangles similar to each other? Explain.

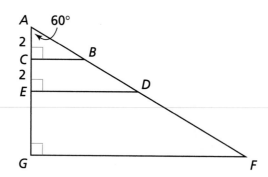

b. Find the ratio of the length of segment *BA* to the length of segment *AC*. What can you say about the corresponding ratio in the other 30-60-90 triangles?

c. Find the ratio of the length of segment *BC* to the length of segment *AC*. What can you say about the corresponding ratios in the other 30-60-90 triangles?

d. Find the ratio of the length of segment *BC* to the length of segment *AB*. What can you say about the corresponding ratios in the other 30-60-90 triangles?

e. Suppose the shortest side of a 30-60-90 triangle is 12 units long. Find the lengths of its other sides.

12. Find the perimeter of triangle *KLM*.

For: Help with Exercise 12
Web Code: ape-2412

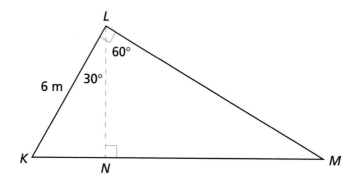

Connections

For: Multiple-Choice Skills Practice
Web Code: apa-2454

Estimate the square root to one decimal place *without* using the $\sqrt{}$ key on your calculator. Then, tell whether the number is rational or irrational.

13. $\sqrt{121}$ **14.** $\sqrt{0.49}$ **15.** $\sqrt{15}$ **16.** $\sqrt{1,000}$

Two cars leave the city of Walleroo at noon. One car travels north and the other travels east. Use this information for Exercises 17 and 18.

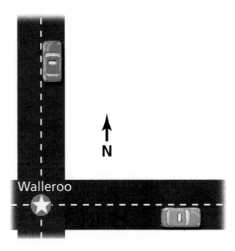

17. Suppose the northbound car is traveling at 60 miles per hour and the eastbound car is traveling at 50 miles per hour. Make a table that shows the distance each car has traveled and the distance between the two cars after 1 hour, 2 hours, 3 hours, and so on. Describe how the distances are changing.

18. Suppose the northbound car is traveling at 40 miles per hour. After 2 hours, the cars are 100 miles apart. How fast is the other car going? Explain.

Write each fraction as a decimal and tell whether the decimal is terminating or repeating. If the decimal is repeating, tell which digits repeat.

19. $\frac{2}{5}$ **20.** $\frac{3}{8}$ **21.** $\frac{5}{6}$ **22.** $\frac{35}{10}$ **23.** $\frac{8}{99}$

Tell whether a triangle with the given side lengths is a right triangle. Explain how you know.

24. 5 cm, 7 cm, $\sqrt{74}$ cm   **25.** $\sqrt{2}$ ft, $\sqrt{7}$ ft, 3 ft

26. The figure at the right is a net for a pyramid.

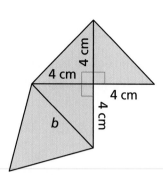

    a. What is the length of side b?

    b. Sketch the pyramid.

    c. What is the surface area of the pyramid?

27. **Multiple Choice** Which set of irrational numbers is in order from least to greatest?

    A. $\sqrt{2}, \sqrt{5}, \sqrt{11}, \pi$ **B.** $\sqrt{2}, \sqrt{5}, \pi, \sqrt{11}$

    C. $\sqrt{2}, \pi, \sqrt{5}, \sqrt{11}$ **D.** $\pi, \sqrt{2}, \sqrt{5}, \sqrt{11}$

28. In Problem 4.3, you found the side lengths of the triangle on the left.

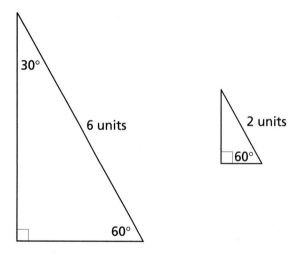

    a. Explain how you know the triangle on the right is similar to the triangle on the left.

    b. Use the side lengths of the larger triangle to find the side lengths of the smaller triangle. Explain.

    c. How are the areas of the triangles related?

Find a fraction equivalent to the terminating decimal.

29. 0.35   **30.** 2.1456   **31.** 89.050

For Exercises 32–34, tell whether the statement is *true* or *false*.

32. $0.06 = \sqrt{0.36}$ **33.** $1.1 = \sqrt{1.21}$ **34.** $20 = \sqrt{40}$

35. In Problem 4.4, you worked with this triangle.

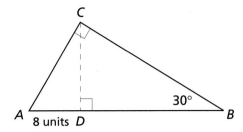

a. Find the perimeter of triangle ACD.

b. How is the perimeter of triangle ACD related to the perimeter of triangle ABC?

c. How is the area of triangle ACD related to the area of triangle ABC?

Find the two consecutive whole numbers the square root is between. Explain.

36. $\sqrt{39}$ **37.** $\sqrt{600}$

Extensions

38. a. Copy the table at the right. Write each fraction as a decimal.

b. Describe a pattern you see in your table.

c. Use the pattern to write decimal representations for $\frac{9}{9}$, $\frac{10}{9}$, and $\frac{15}{9}$. Use your calculator to check your answers.

d. Find fractions equivalent to $1.\overline{2}$ and $2.\overline{7}$, where the bar means the number under the bar repeats forever. (**Hint:** $1.\overline{2}$ can be written as $1 + 0.22222\dots$ The bar on the 2 means the 2 repeats forever.)

Fraction	Decimal
$\frac{1}{9}$	
$\frac{2}{9}$	
$\frac{3}{9}$	
$\frac{4}{9}$	
$\frac{5}{9}$	
$\frac{6}{9}$	
$\frac{7}{9}$	
$\frac{8}{9}$	

39. Explore decimal representations of fractions with a denominator of 99. Look at fractions less than one, $\frac{1}{99}, \frac{2}{99}, \frac{3}{99}$, and so on. What patterns do you see?

40. Explore decimal representations of fractions with a denominator of 999. Look at fractions less than one, $\frac{1}{999}, \frac{2}{999}, \frac{3}{999}$, and so on. What patterns do you see?

Use the patterns you discovered in Exercises 38–40 to find a fraction or mixed number equivalent to each decimal.

41. 0.3333 . . .   **42.** 0.050505 . . .   **43.** 0.454545 . . .

44. 0.045045 . . .   **45.** 10.121212 . . .   **46.** 3.9999 . . .

For Exercises 47 and 48, find the length of the diagonal *d*.

47.

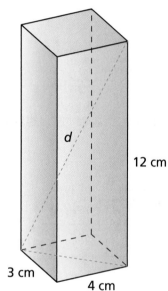

48.

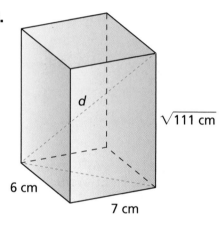

49. Segment *AB* below makes a 45° angle with the *x*-axis. The length of segment *AB* is 5 units.

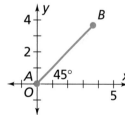

   a. Find the coordinates of point *B* to two decimal places.

   b. What is the slope of line *AB*?

In Exercises 50–52, you will look for relationships among the areas of similar shapes other than squares drawn on the sides of a right triangle.

50. Half-circles have been drawn on the sides of this right triangle.

    a. Find the area of each half-circle.

    b. How are the areas of the half-circles related?

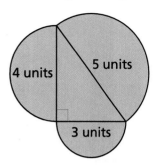

51. Equilateral triangles have been drawn on the sides of this right triangle.

    a. Find the area of each equilateral triangle.

    b. How are the areas of the equilateral triangles related?

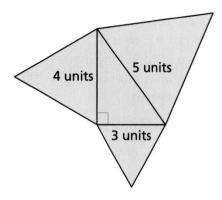

52. Regular hexagons have been drawn on the sides of this right triangle.

    a. Find the area of each hexagon.

    b. How are the areas of the hexagons related?

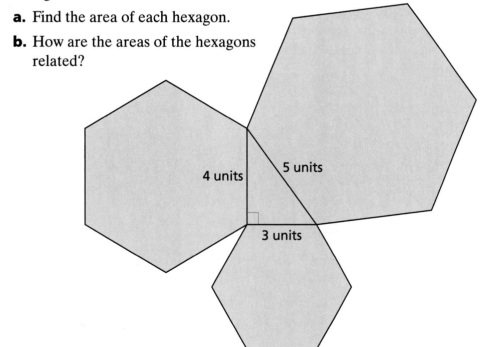

53. Find an irrational number between 6.23 and 6.35.

54. You can use algebra to help you write a repeating decimal as a fraction. For example, suppose you want to write 0.12121212 . . . as a fraction.

Let $x = 0.12121212 . . . .$

$100x = 12.12121212 . . .$ Multiply both sides by 100.

$\underline{- \quad x = 0.12121212 . . .}$ Subtract the first equation from the second.

$99x = 12$

Divide both sides of the resulting equation, $99x = 12$, by 99 to get $x = \frac{12}{99}$. So, $0.12121212 . . . = \frac{12}{99}$.

The key to this method is to multiply each side of the original equation by a power of 10 (such, as 10, 100, or 1,000) that shifts one group of repeating digits to the left of the decimal point. In the example above, multiplying by 100 shifted one "12" to the left of the decimal point.

Use the method described above to write each decimal as a fraction.

a. $0.15151515 . . .$ **b.** $0.7777 . . .$ **c.** $0.123123123123 . . .$

55. When building a barn, a farmer must make sure the sides are perpendicular to the ground.

a. One method for checking whether a wall is perpendicular to the ground involves using a 10-foot pole. The farmer makes a mark exactly 6 feet high on the wall. She then places one end of the pole on the mark and the other end on the ground.

How far from the base of the wall will the pole touch the ground if the wall is perpendicular to the ground? Explain.

b. You may have heard the saying, "I wouldn't touch that with a 10-foot pole!" What would this saying mean to a farmer who had just built a barn?

c. Suppose a farmer uses a 15-foot pole and makes a mark 12 feet high on the wall. How far from the base of the wall will the pole touch the ground if the wall is perpendicular to the ground?

d. Name another pole length a farmer could use. For this length how high should the mark on the wall be? How far from the base of the wall will the pole touch the ground?

56. Find the perimeter of triangle *ABC*.

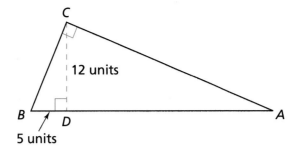

57. Below is the net for a square pyramid and a sketch of the pyramid.

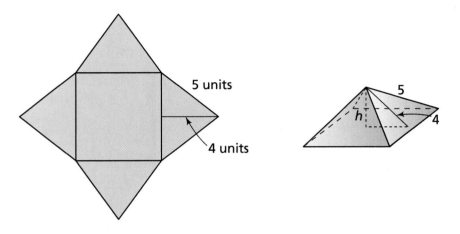

a. What is the area of the base of the pyramid?

b. What is the surface area of the pyramid?

c. What is the height of the pyramid?

d. What is the volume of the pyramid?

58. The managers of Izzie's Ice Cream Shop are trying to decide on the best size for their cones.

a. Izzie thinks the cone should have a diameter of 4.5 inches and a height of 6 inches. What is the volume of the cone Izzie suggests?

b. Izzie's sister Becky thinks the cone should have a height of 6 inches and a slant height of 7 inches. (The slant height is labeled *s* in the diagram at the right.) What is the volume of the cone Becky suggests?

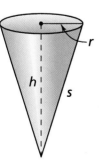

Mathematical Reflections 4

In this investigation, you applied the ideas from the first three investigations. The following questions will help you summarize what you have learned.

Think about your answers to these questions. Discuss your ideas with other students and your teacher. Then write a summary of your findings in your notebook.

1. In what ways is the Pythagorean Theorem useful? Give at least two examples.

2. Describe the special properties of a 30-60-90 triangle.

Looking Back and Looking Ahead

While working on problems in this unit, you extended your skill in using a coordinate system to locate points and figures. Then, by studying patterns in the side lengths and areas of squares on dot grids, you learned the Pythagorean Theorem. You used this property of right triangles to solve a variety of practical problems, some of which involved irrational numbers.

For: Vocabulary Review Puzzle
Web Code: apj-2051

Use Your Understanding:
The Pythagorean Theorem

Test your understanding of the Pythagorean Theorem and its relationship to area, lengths of line segments, and irrational numbers by solving the following problems.

1. The diagram shows a Chinese tangram puzzle on a 10-by-10 grid.

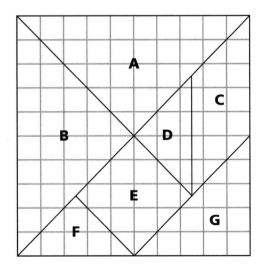

   a. What is the area of shape E?

   b. What is the length of each side of shape E?

   c. What are the lengths of the sides of triangle A?

   d. Name all the triangles that are similar to triangle A. In each case, give a scale factor for the similarity relationship.

2. A 60-foot piece of wire is strung between the top of a tower and the ground, making a 30-60-90 triangle.

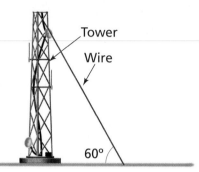

a. How far from the center of the base of the tower is the wire attached to the ground?

b. How high is the tower?

Explain Your Reasoning

When you present work based on the Pythagorean relationship, you should be able to justify your calculations and conclusions.

3. How can you find the side length of a square if you know its area?

4. How can you find the length of a segment joining two points on a coordinate grid?

5. The diagrams below show squares drawn on the sides of triangles.

Figure 1   **Figure 2**

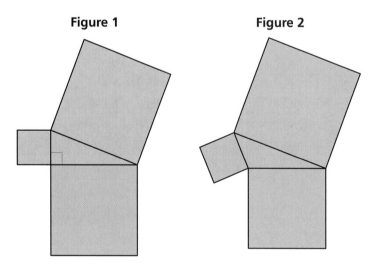

a. In Figure 1, what is the relationship among the areas of the squares?

b. Explain why the relationship you describe in part (a) is not true for Figure 2.

6. Explain with words and symbols how to use the Pythagorean Theorem to find the

    a. length of a diagonal of a square with side length s.

    b. length of a diagonal of a rectangle with side lengths s and t.

    c. length of the hypotenuse of a right triangle with legs of lengths s and t.

    d. height of an equilateral triangle with side length s.

    e. length of one leg of a triangle when the lengths of the hypotenuse and the other leg are h and t, respectively.

Look Ahead

You will use the properties of right triangles you discovered in this unit, including the Pythagorean Theorem, in many future *Connected Mathematics* units, and in the math, science, and technology courses you take in high school and college.

English / Spanish Glossary

C

conjecture A guess about a pattern or relationship based on observations.

conjetura Suposición acerca de un patron o relación, basada en observaciones.

H

hypotenuse The side of a right triangle that is opposite the right angle. The hypotenuse is the longest side of a right triangle. In the triangle below, the side labeled c is the hypotenuse.

hipotenusa El lado de un triángulo rectángulo que está opuesto al ángulo recto. La hipotenusa es el lado más largo de un triángulo rectángulo. En el triángulo de abajo, el lado rotulado c es la hipotenusa.

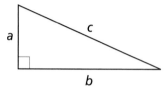

I

irrational number A number that cannot be written as a fraction with a numerator and a denominator that are integers. The decimal representation of an irrational number never ends and never shows a repeating pattern of a fixed number of digits. The numbers $\sqrt{2}$, $\sqrt{3}$, $\sqrt{5}$, and π are examples of irrational numbers.

número irracional Un número que no puede escribirse como una fracción con un numerador y un denominador que sean enteros. La representación decimal de un número irracional nunca termina y nunca muestra un patrón de dígitos que se repite. Los números $\sqrt{2}$, $\sqrt{3}$, $\sqrt{5}$, y π son ejemplos de números irracionales.

L

legs The sides of a right triangle that are adjacent to the right angle. In the triangle above, the sides labeled a and b are the legs.

catetos Los lados de un triángulo rectángulo que son adyacentes al ángulo recto. En el triángulo de arriba, los lados a y b son los catetos.

P

perpendicular Forming a right angle. For example, the sides of a right triangle that form the right angle are perpendicular.

perpendicular Que forma un ángulo recto. Por ejemplo, los lados de un triángulo rectángulo que forman el ángulo recto son perpendiculares.

Pythagorean Theorem A statement about the relationship among the lengths of the sides of a right triangle. The theorem states that if a and b are the lengths of the legs of a right triangle and c is the length of the hypotenuse, then $a^2 + b^2 = c^2$.

Teorema de Pitágoras Un enunciado acerca de la relación que existe entre las longitudes de los lados de un triángulo rectángulo. El teorema enuncia que si a y b son las longitudes de los catetos de un triángulo rectángulo y c es la longitud de la hipotenusa, entonces $a^2 + b^2 = c^2$.

rational number A number that can be written as a fraction with a numerator and a denominator that are integers. The decimal representation of a rational number either ends or repeats. Examples of rational numbers are $\frac{1}{2}$, $\frac{78}{91}$, 7, 0.2, and 0.191919. . . .

número racional Un número que puede escribirse como una fracción con un numerador y un denominador que son enteros. La representación decimal de un número racional termina o bien se repite. Ejemplos de números racionales son $\frac{1}{2}$, $\frac{78}{91}$, 7, 0.2 y 0.191919. . . .

real numbers The set of all rational numbers and all irrational numbers. The number line represents the set of real numbers.

números reales El conjunto de todos los números racionales y todos los números irracionales. La recta numérica representa el conjunto de los números reales.

repeating decimal A decimal with a pattern of a fixed number of digits that repeats forever, such as 0.3333333. . . and 0.73737373. . . . Repeating decimals are rational numbers.

decimal periódico Un decimal con un patrón de dígitos que se repite indefinidamente, como 0.3333333. . . y 0.73737373. . . . Los decimales que se repiten son números racionales.

square root If $A = s^2$, then s is the square root of A. For example, -3 and 3 are square roots of 9 because $3 \cdot 3 = 9$ and $-3 \cdot -3 = 9$. The $\sqrt{\ }$ symbol is used to denote the positive square root. So, we write $\sqrt{9} = 3$. The positive square root of a number is the side length of a square that has that number as its area. So, you can draw a segment of length $\sqrt{5}$ by drawing a square with an area of 5, and the side length of the square will be $\sqrt{5}$.

raíz cuadrada Si $A = s^2$, entonces s es la raíz cuadrada de A. Por ejemplo, -3 y 3 son raíces cuadradas de 9 porque $3 \cdot 3 = 9$ y $-3 \cdot -3 = 9$. El símbolo $\sqrt{\ }$ se usa para indicar la raíz cuadrada positiva. Por eso, escribimos $\sqrt{9} = 3$. La raíz cuadrada positiva de un número es la longitud del lado de un cuadrado que tiene dicho número como su área. Entonces, puedes dibujar un segmento de longitud $\sqrt{5}$ dibujando un cuadrado con un área de 5 y la longitud del lado del cuadrado será $\sqrt{5}$.

T

terminating decimal A decimal that ends, or terminates, such as 0.5 or 0.125. Terminating decimals are rational numbers.

decimal finito Un decimal que se acaba o termina, como 0.5 ó 0.125. Los decimales finitos son números racionales.

Index

Index

Acknowledgments

Team Credits

The people who made up the **Connected Mathematics 2** team—representing editorial, editorial services, design services, and production services—are listed below. Bold type denotes core team members.

Leora Adler, Judith Buice, Kerry Cashman, Patrick Culleton, Sheila DeFazio, Katie Hallahan, Richard Heater, **Barbara Hollingdale, Jayne Holman,** Karen Holtzman, **Etta Jacobs,** Christine Lee, Carolyn Lock, Catherine Maglio, **Dotti Marshall,** Rich McMahon, Eve Melnechuk, Kristin Mingrone, Terri Mitchell, **Marsha Novak,** Irene Rubin, Donna Russo, Robin Samper, Siri Schwartzman, **Nancy Smith,** Emily Soltanoff, **Mark Tricca,** Paula Vergith, Roberta Warshaw, Helen Young

Additional Credits

Diana Bonfilio, Mairead Reddin, Michael Torocsik, nSight, Inc.

Technical Illustration

WestWords, Inc.

Cover Design

tom white.images

Photos

2, Erich Lessing/Art Resource, NY; **3,** Yellow Dog Productions/Getty Images, Inc.; **5,** Francis Miller/Time Life Pictures; **6,** Richard T Nowitz/Getty Images, Inc.; **15,** Comstock Images/Getty Images, Inc.; **20,** Richard Haynes; **27,** Richard Haynes; **28,** Catherine Ledner/Getty Images, Inc.; **33,** The Art Archive/Museo Capitolino Rome/Dagli Orti (A); **36,** Erich Lessing/Art Resource, NY; **41 both,** Richard Haynes; **44,** Richard Haynes; **46,** Patrick Ben Luke Syder/Lonely Planet Images; **49,** AP Photo/Jerry Laizure; **50,** Library of Congress, Prints and Photographs Division, LOT 13163-09, no. 1; **52,** Courtesy Everett Collection/ Everett Collection; **54,** Dennis MacDonald/Photo Edit

Data Sources

Did You Know quote on page 52 is from *The Wizard of Oz* Copyright © 1939, 2005, Turner Entertainment Co. and Warner Bros. Entertainment Inc. All Rights Reserved.

Connected Mathematics 2™

Growing, Growing, Growing

Exponential Relationships

2.7×10^{12}

Glenda Lappan
James T. Fey
William M. Fitzgerald
Susan N. Friel
Elizabeth Difanis Phillips

PEARSON

Prentice
Hall

Boston, Massachusetts
Upper Saddle River, New Jersey

Growing, Growing, Growing

Exponential Relationships

When the water hyacinth was introduced to Lake Victoria, it spread quickly over the lake's surface. At one point, the plant covered 769 square miles, and its area was doubling every 15 days. What equation models this growth?

When Sam was in seventh grade, his aunt gave him a stamp collection worth $2,500. The value of the collection increased by 6% each year for several years in a row. What was the value of Sam's collection after four years?

What pattern of change would you expect to find in the temperature of a hot drink as time passes? What would a graph of the (time, drink temperature) data look like?

One of the most important uses of algebra is to model patterns of change. You are already familiar with linear patterns of change. Linear patterns have constant differences and straight-line graphs. In a linear relationship, the *y*-value increases by a constant amount each time the *x*-value increases by 1.

In this unit, you will study exponential patterns of change.

Exponential growth patterns are fascinating because, although the values may change gradually at first, they eventually increase very rapidly. Patterns that decrease, or decay, exponentially may decrease quickly at first, but eventually they decrease very slowly.

As you work through the investigations in this unit, you will encounter problems like those the on the facing page.

Exponential Relationships

In *Growing, Growing, Growing,* you will explore exponential relationships, one of the most important types of nonlinear relationships.

You will learn how to

- Identify situations in which a quantity grows or decays exponentially
- Recognize the connections between exponential equations and the growth patterns in tables and graphs of those equations
- Construct equations to express exponential patterns in data tables, graphs, and problem situations
- Solve problems about exponential growth and decay from a variety of different areas, including science and business
- Compare exponential and linear relationships
- Understand the rules for working with exponents

As you work on the problems in this unit, ask yourself questions about situations that involve nonlinear relationships:

What are the variables?

Is the relationship between variables an example of exponential growth or decay?

How can the relationship be detected in a table, graph, or equation?

What is the growth or decay factor?

What equation models the data in the table?

What equation models the pattern in the graph?

What can I learn about this situation by studying a table, graph, or equation of the exponential relationship?

How does the relationship compare to other types of relationships that I have studied?

Exponential Growth

In this investigation, you will explore *exponential growth* as you cut paper in half over and over and read about a very smart peasant from the ancient kingdom of Montarek. You will compare exponential growth with linear growth. You will also explore exponential patterns in tables, graphs, and equations.

1.1 Making Ballots

Chen, the secretary of the Student Government Association, is making ballots for tonight's meeting. He starts by cutting a sheet of paper in half. He then stacks the two pieces and cuts them in half. He stacks the resulting four pieces and cuts them in half. He repeats this process, creating smaller and smaller pieces of paper.

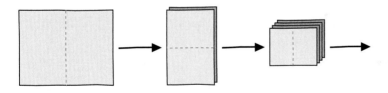

After each cut, Chen counts the ballots and records the results in a table.

Number of Cuts	Number of Ballots
1	2
2	4
3	
4	

Chen wants to predict the number of ballots after any number of cuts.

Problem 1.1 Introducing Exponential Relationships

A. Make a table to show the number of ballots after each of the first five cuts.

B. Look for a pattern in the way the number of ballots changes with each cut. Use your observations to extend your table to show the number of ballots for up to 10 cuts.

C. Suppose Chen could make 20 cuts. How many ballots would he have? How many ballots would he have if he could make 30 cuts?

D. How many cuts would it take to make enough ballots for all 500 students at Chen's school?

ACE Homework starts on page 11.

1.2 Requesting a Reward

When you found the number of ballots after 10, 20, and 30 cuts, you may have multiplied long strings of 2s. Instead of writing long product strings of the same factor, you can use **exponential form.** For example, you can write $2 \times 2 \times 2 \times 2 \times 2$ as 2^5, which is read "2 to the fifth power."

In the expression 2^5, 5 is the **exponent** and 2 is the **base.** When you evaluate 2^5, you get $2^5 = 2 \times 2 \times 2 \times 2 \times 2 = 32$. We say that 32 is the **standard form** for 2^5.

Getting Ready for Problem 1.2

- Write each expression in exponential form.

    a. $2 \times 2 \times 2$ **b.** $5 \times 5 \times 5 \times 5$

    c. $1.5 \cdot 1.5 \cdot 1.5 \cdot 1.5 \cdot 1.5 \cdot 1.5 \cdot 1.5$

- Write each expression in standard form.

    a. 2^7 **b.** 3^3 **c.** 4.2^3

- Most calculators have a or ⌨ key for evaluating exponents. Use your calculator to find the standard form for each expression.

    a. 2^{15} **b.** 3^{10} **c.** 1.5^{20}

- Explain how the meanings of 5^2, 2^5, and 5×2 differ.

One day in the ancient kingdom of Montarek, a peasant saved the life of the king's daughter. The king was so grateful he told the peasant she could have any reward she desired. The peasant—who was also the kingdom's chess champion—made an unusual request:

"I would like you to place 1 ruba on the first square of my chessboard, 2 rubas on the second square, 4 on the third square, 8 on the fourth square, and so on, until you have covered all 64 squares. Each square should have twice as many rubas as the previous square."

The king replied, "Rubas are the least valuable coin in the kingdom. Surely you can think of a better reward." But the peasant insisted, so the king agreed to her request. *Did the peasant make a wise choice?*

Problem 1.2 Representing Exponential Relationships

A. 1. Make a table showing the number of rubas the king will place on squares 1 through 10 of the chessboard.

   2. How does the number of rubas change from one square to the next?

B. Graph the (*number of the square, number of rubas*) data for squares 1 to 10.

C. Write an equation for the relationship between the number of the square n and the number of rubas r.

D. How does the pattern of change you observed in the table show up in the graph? How does it show up in the equation?

E. Which square will have 2^{30} rubas? Explain.

F. What is the first square on which the king will place at least one million rubas? How many rubas will be on this square?

ACE Homework starts on page 11.

The patterns of change in the number of ballots in Problem 1.1 and in the number of rubas in Problem 1.2 show **exponential growth.** These relationships are called **exponential relationships.** In each case, you can find the value for any square or cut by multiplying the value for the previous square or cut by a fixed number. This fixed number is called the **growth factor.**

● What are the growth factors for the situations in Problems 1.1 and 1.2?

The king told the queen about the reward he had promised the peasant. The queen said, "You have promised her more money than we have in the entire royal treasury! You must convince her to accept a different reward."

After much thought, the king came up with Plan 2. He would make a new board with only 16 squares. He would place 1 ruba on the first square and 3 rubas on the second. He drew a graph to show the number of rubas on the first five squares. He would continue this pattern until all 16 squares were filled.

Plan 2

Number of Rubas (vertical axis: 0, 18, 36, 54, 72, 90, 108)

Square Number (horizontal axis: 0, 1, 2, 3, 4, 5)

The queen wasn't convinced about the king's new plan, so she devised a third plan. Under Plan 3, the king would make a board with 12 squares. He would place 1 ruba on the first square. He would use the equation $r = 4^{n-1}$ to figure out how many rubas to put on each of the other squares. In the equation, r is the number of rubas on square n.

A. In the table below, Plan 1 is the reward requested by the peasant. Plan 2 is the king's new plan. Plan 3 is the queen's plan. Copy and extend the table to show the number of rubas on squares 1 to 10 for each plan.

Reward Plans

Square Number	Number of Rubas		
	Plan 1	Plan 2	Plan 3
1	1	1	1
2	2	3	4
3	4	▦	▦
4	▦	▦	▦

B. 1. How are the patterns of change in the number of rubas under Plans 2 and 3 similar to and different from the pattern of change for Plan 1?

2. Are the growth patterns for Plans 2 and 3 exponential relationships? If so, what is the growth factor for each?

C. Write an equation for the relationship between the number of the square n and the number of rubas r for Plan 2.

D. Make a graph of Plan 3 for $n = 1$ to 10. How does your graph compare to the graphs for Plans 1 and 2?

E. The queen's assistant wrote the equation $r = \frac{1}{4}(4^n)$ for Plan 3. This equation is different from the one the queen wrote. Did the assistant make a mistake? Explain.

F. For each plan, how many rubas would be on the final square?

ACE | **Homework starts on page 11.**

1.4 Getting Costs in Line

Before presenting Plans 2 and 3 to the peasant, the king consulted with his financial advisors. They told him that either plan would devastate the royal treasury.

The advisors proposed a fourth plan. Under Plan 4, the king would put 20 rubas on the first square of a chessboard, 25 on the second, 30 on the third, and so on. He would increase the number of rubas by 5 for each square, until all 64 squares were covered.

To help persuade the peasant to accept their plan, the advisors prepared the following table for the first six squares. The king presented the plan to the peasant and gave her a day to consider the offer.

Reward Plans

Square Number	Number of Rubas	
	Plan 1	Plan 4
1	1	20
2	2	25
3	4	30
4	8	35
5	16	40
6	32	45

Do you think the peasant should accept the new plan? Explain.

Problem 1.4 Comparing Growth Patterns

A. Is the growth pattern in Plan 4 an exponential relationship? Explain.

B. Describe the graph of Plan 4 and compare it to the graph of Plan 1.

C. 1. Write an equation for the relationship between the number of the square n and the number of rubas r for Plan 4.

2. Compare this equation to the equation for Plan 1.

3. How is the change in the number of rubas from one square to the next shown in the equations for Plan 1 and Plan 4?

D. For Plans 1 and 4, how many rubas would be on square 20? How many rubas would be on square 21?

ACE Homework starts on page 11.

Applications

1. Cut a sheet of paper into thirds. Stack the three pieces and cut the stack into thirds. Stack all the pieces and cut the stack into thirds again.

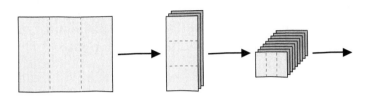

   a. Copy and complete this table to show the number of ballots after each of the first five cuts.

Number of Cuts	Number of Ballots
1	3
2	▦
3	▦
4	▦
5	▦

   b. Suppose you continued this process. How many ballots would you have after 10 cuts? How many would you have after n cuts?

   c. How many cuts would it take to make at least one million ballots?

Write each expression in exponential form.

2. $2 \times 2 \times 2 \times 2$

3. $10 \cdot 10 \cdot 10 \cdot 10 \cdot 10 \cdot 10 \cdot 10$

4. $2.5 \times 2.5 \times 2.5 \times 2.5 \times 2.5$

Write each expression in standard form.

5. 2^{10} **6.** 10^2 **7.** 3^9

8. You know that $5^2 = 25$. Use this fact to evaluate 5^4.

9. The standard form for 5^{14} is 6,103,515,625. Use this fact to evaluate 5^{15}.

10. **Multiple Choice** Which expression is equal to one million?

    A. 10^6 **B.** 6^{10} **C.** 100^2 **D.** 2^{100}

11. Use exponents to write an expression for one billion (1,000,000,000).

Decide whether each number is greater or less than one million *without using a calculator*. Try to decide without actually multiplying. Explain how you found your answer. Use a calculator to check whether you are right.

12. 9^6 **13.** 3^{10} **14.** 11^6

For Exercises 15–20, write the number in exponential form using 2, 3, 4, or 5 as the base.

15. 125   **16.** 64   **17.** 81

18. 3,125   **19.** 1,024   **20.** 4,096

Go Online
PHSchool.com
For: Multiple-Choice Skills Practice
Web Code: apa-3154

21. While studying her family's history, Angie discovers records of ancestors 12 generations back. She wonders how many ancestors she has had in the past 12 generations. She starts to make a diagram to help her figure this out. The diagram soon becomes very complex.

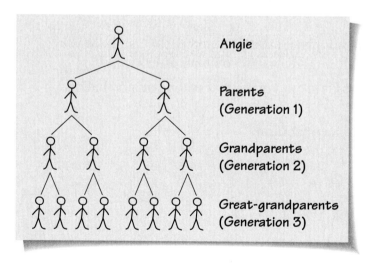

    a. Make a table and a graph showing the number of ancestors in each of the 12 generations.

    b. Write an equation for the number of ancestors a in a given generation n.

    c. What is the total number of ancestors in all 12 generations?

22. Many single-celled organisms reproduce by dividing into two identical cells. Suppose an amoeba (uh MEE buh) splits into two amoebas every half hour.

    a. An experiment starts with one amoeba. Make a table showing the number of amoebas at the end of each hour over an 8-hour period.

    b. Write an equation for the number of amoebas a after t hours.

    c. After how many hours will the number of amoebas reach one million?

    d. Make a graph of the (*time, amoebas*) data from part (a).

    e. What similarities do you notice in the pattern of change for the number of amoebas and the patterns of change for other problems in this investigation? What differences do you notice?

23. Zak's wealthy uncle wants to donate money to Zak's school for new computers. He suggests three possible plans for his donations.

Homework Help Online
PHSchool.com

For: Help with Exercise 23
Web Code: ape-3123

Plan 1: He will continue the pattern in this table until day 12.

Day	1	2	3	4
Donation	$1	$2	$4	$8

Plan 2: He will continue the pattern in this table until day 10.

Day	1	2	3	4
Donation	$1	$3	$9	$27

Plan 3: He will continue the pattern in this table until day 7.

Day	1	2	3	4
Donation	$1	$4	$16	$64

    a. Copy and extend each table to show how much money the school would receive each day.

    b. For each plan, write an equation for the relationship between the day number n and the number of dollars donated d.

    c. Which plan would give the school the greatest total amount of money?

    d. Zak says there is more than one equation for the relationship in Plan 1. He says that $d = 2^{n-1}$ and $d = \frac{1}{2}(2^n)$ both work. Is he correct? Are there two equations for each of the other plans?

24. Jenna is planning to swim in a charity swim-a-thon. Several relatives said they would sponsor her. Each of their donations is explained.

Grandmother: I will give you $1 if you swim 1 lap, $3 if you swim 2 laps, $5 if you swim 3 laps, $7 if you swim 4 laps, and so on.

Mother: I will give you $1 if you swim 1 lap, $3 if you swim 2 laps, $9 if you swim 3 laps, $27 if you swim 4 laps, and so on.

Aunt Lori: I will give you $2 if you swim 1 lap, $3.50 if you swim 2 laps, $5 if you swim 3 laps, $6.50 for 4 laps, and so on.

Uncle Jack: I will give you $1 if you swim 1 lap, $2 if you swim 2 laps, $4 if you swim 3 laps, $8 if you swim 4 laps, and so on.

a. Decide whether each donation pattern is *exponential*, *linear*, or *neither*.

b. For each relative, write an equation for the total donation d if Jenna swims n laps.

c. For each plan, tell how much money Jenna will raise if she swims 20 laps.

25. The graphs below represent $y = 2^x$ and $y = 2x + 1$.

   a. Tell which equation each graph represents. Explain your reasoning.

   b. The dashed segments show the vertical and horizontal change between points at equal x intervals. For each graph, compare the vertical and horizontal changes between pairs of points. What do you notice?

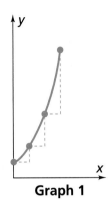

Graph 1

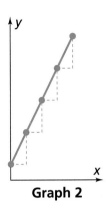

Graph 2

Study the pattern in each table.

   a. Tell whether the relationship between x and y is *linear, exponential,* or *neither*. Explain your reasoning.

   b. If the relationship is linear or exponential, give its equation.

26.

x	0	1	2	3	4	5
y	10	12.5	15	17.5	20	22.5

27.

x	0	1	2	3	4
y	1	6	36	216	1,296

28.

x	0	1	2	3	4	5	6	7	8
y	1	5	3	7	5	8	6	10	8

29.

x	0	1	2	3	4	5	6	7	8
y	2	4	8	16	32	64	128	256	512

30.

x	0	1	2	3	4	5
y	0	1	4	9	16	25

Connections

31. Refer to Problem 1.1. Suppose a stack of 250 sheets of paper is 1 inch high.

    a. How high would the stack of ballots be after 20 cuts? How high would it be after 30 cuts?

    b. How many cuts would it take to make a stack 1 foot high?

32. In Problem 1.2, suppose a Montarek ruba had the value of a modern U.S. penny. What would be the dollar values of the rubas on squares 10, 20, 30, 40, 50, and 60?

33. A ruba had the same thickness as a modern U.S. penny (about 0.06 inch). Suppose the king had been able to reward the peasant by using Plan 1 (doubling the number of rubas in each square).

    a. What would have been the height of the stack of rubas on square 64?

    b. The average distance from Earth to the moon is about 240,000 miles. Which (if any) of the stacks would have reached the moon?

34. One of the king's advisors suggested this plan: Put 100 rubas on the first square of a chessboard, 125 on the second square, 150 on the third square, and so on, increasing the number of rubas by 25 for each square.

    a. Write an equation for the numbers of rubas r on square n for this plan. Explain the meanings of the numbers and variables in your equation.

    b. Describe the graph of this plan.

    c. What is the total number of rubas on the first 10 squares? What is the total number on the first 20 squares?

For Exercises 35–37, find the slope and y-intercept of the graph of each equation.

35. $y = 3x - 10$ **36.** $y = 1.5 - 5.6x$ **37.** $y = 15 + \frac{2}{5}x$

38. Write an equation whose line is less steep than the line represented by $y = 15 + \frac{2}{5}x$.

39. Sarah used her calculator to keep track of the number of rubas in Problem 1.2. She found that there will be 2,147,483,648 rubas on square 32.

 a. How many rubas will be on square 33? How many will be on square 34? How many will be on square 35?

 b. Which square would have the number of rubas shown here?

   $2{,}147{,}483{,}648 \cdot 2 \cdot 2 \cdot 2 \cdot 2 \cdot 2 \cdot 2 \cdot 2 \cdot 2 \cdot 2$

 c. Use your calculator to do the multiplication in part (b). Do you notice anything strange about the answer your calculator gives? Explain.

 d. Calculators use shorthand notation for showing very large numbers. For example, if you enter 10^12 on your calculator, you may get the result 1E12. This is shorthand for the number 1.0×10^{12}. The number 1.0×10^{12} is written in **scientific notation.** For a number to be in scientific notation, it must be in the form:

   (*a number greater than or equal to 1 but less than 10*) $\times$ (*a power of 10*)

   Write $2{,}147{,}483{,}648 \cdot 2 \cdot 2 \cdot 2 \cdot 2 \cdot 2 \cdot 2 \cdot 2 \cdot 2 \cdot 2$ in scientific notation.

 e. Write the numbers $2^{10}, 2^{20}, 2^{30}$, and 2^{35} in both standard and scientific notation.

 f. Explain how to write a large number in scientific notation.

Write each number in scientific notation.

40. 100,000,000 **41.** 29,678,900,500 **42.** 11,950,500,000,000

Find the largest whole-number value of *n* for which your calculator will display the result in standard notation.

43. 3^n **44.** π^n **45.** 12^n **46.** 237^n

Extensions

47. Consider these two equations:

   Equation 1: $r = 3^n - 1$ **Equation 2:** $r = 3^{n-1}$

 a. For each equation, find *r* when *n* is 2.

 b. For each equation, find *r* when *n* is 10.

 c. Explain why the equations give different values of *r* for the same value of *n*.

48. This table represents the number of ballots made by repeatedly cutting a sheet of paper in half four times. Assume the pattern continues.

Number of Cuts	Number of Ballots
1	2
2	4
3	8
4	16

  a. Write an equation for the pattern in the table.

  b. Use your equation and the table to determine the value of 2^0.

  c. What do you think b^0 should equal for any number b? For example, what do you think 6^0 and 23^0 should equal? Explain.

49. When the king of Montarek tried to figure out the total number of rubas the peasant would receive under Plan 1, he noticed an interesting pattern.

  a. Extend and complete this table for the first 10 squares.

Reward Plan 1

Square	Number of Rubas on Square	Total Number of Rubas
1	1	1
2	2	3
3	4	7
4	▪	▪

  b. Describe the pattern of growth in the total number of rubas as the number of the square increases.

  c. Write an equation for the relationship between the number of the square n and the total number of rubas t on the board.

  d. When the total number of rubas reaches 1,000,000, how many squares will have been covered?

  e. Suppose the king had been able to give the peasant the reward she requested. How many rubas would she have received?

50. Refer to Plans 1–4 in Problems 1.2 through 1.4.

  a. Which plan should the king choose? Explain.

  b. Which plan should the peasant choose? Explain.

  c. Write an ending to the story of the king and the peasant.

Mathematical Reflections 1

In this investigation, you explored situations involving exponential growth. You saw how you could recognize patterns of exponential growth in tables, graphs, and equations.

Think about your answers to these questions. Discuss your ideas with other students and your teacher. Then write a summary of your findings in your notebook.

1. Describe an exponential growth pattern. Include key properties such as growth factors.

2. How are exponential growth patterns similar to and different from the linear growth patterns you worked with in earlier units?

Investigation 2

Examining Growth Patterns

Now that you have learned to recognize exponential growth, you are ready to take a closer look at the tables, graphs, and equations of exponential relationships. You will explore this question:

How are the starting value and growth factor for an exponential relationship reflected in the table, graph, and equation?

Getting Ready for Problem 2.1

Students at West Junior High came up with two equations to represent the reward in Plan 1 of Investigation 1. Some students wrote $r = 2^{n-1}$ and others wrote $r = \frac{1}{2}(2^n)$. In both equations, r represents the number of rubas on square n.

- Are both equations correct? Explain.
- What is the value of r if $n = 1$? Does this make sense?
- What is the y-intercept for this relationship?

2.1 Killer Plant Strikes Lake Victoria

Exponential growth occurs in many real-life situations. For example, consider this story from 1998:

> **Water hyacinths, which experts say double in area every 5 to 15 days, are expanding across Africa's giant Lake Victoria. The foreign plant has taken over more than 769 square miles of the lake and is growing exponentially.**

"Killer Weed Strikes Lake Victoria" from *Christian Science Monitor*. January 12, 1998, Vol. 90, No. 32, p. 1.

Plants like the water hyacinth that grow and spread rapidly can affect native plants and fish. This in turn can affect the livelihood of fishermen. To understand how such plants grow, you will look at a similar situation.

Problem 2.1 y-Intercepts Other Than 1

Ghost Lake is a popular site for fishermen, campers, and boaters. In recent years, a certain water plant has been growing on the lake at an alarming rate. The surface area of Ghost Lake is 25,000,000 square feet. At present, 1,000 square feet are covered by the plant. The Department of Natural Resources estimates that the area is doubling every month.

A. 1. Write an equation that represents the growth pattern of the plant on Ghost Lake.

2. Explain what information the variables and numbers in your equation represent.

3. Compare this equation with the equations in Investigation 1.

B. 1. Make a graph of the equation.

2. How does this graph compare with the graphs of the exponential relationships in Investigation 1?

C. How much of the lake's surface will be covered with the water plant by the end of a year?

D. In how many months will the plant completely cover the surface of the lake?

ACE Homework starts on page 24.

Mold can spread rapidly. For example, the area covered by mold on a loaf of bread left out in warm weather grows exponentially.

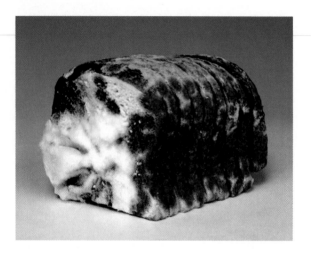

Problem 2.2 Interpreting Exponential Equations

Students at Magnolia Middle School conducted an experiment. They set out a shallow pan containing a mixture of chicken bouillon (BOOL yahn), gelatin, and water. Each day, the students recorded the area of the mold in square millimeters.

The students wrote the exponential equation $m = 50(3^d)$ to model the growth of the mold. In this equation, m is the area of the mold in square millimeters after d days.

A. What is the area of the mold at the start of the experiment?

B. What is the growth factor?

C. What is the area of the mold after 5 days?

D. On which day will the area of the mold reach 6,400 mm^2?

E. An exponential equation can be written in the form $y = a(b^x)$, where a and b are constant values.

   1. What value does b have in the mold equation? What does this value represent?

   2. What value does a have in the mold equation? What does this value represent?

ACE Homework starts on page 24.

2.3 Studying Snake Populations

The graph shows the growth of a garter snake population after it was introduced to a new area. The population is growing exponentially.

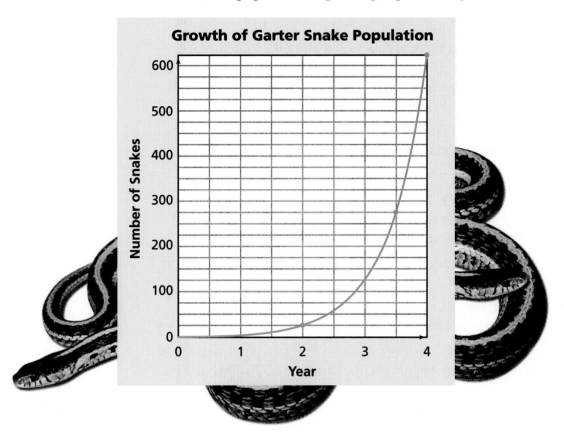

Growth of Garter Snake Population

Problem 2.3 Interpreting Exponential Graphs

A. Explain how to find the growth factor for the population.

B. 1. Find the snake population for years 2, 3, and 4.

    2. Use the pattern in your answers from part (1) to estimate the population in year 1. Explain.

    3. Explain how you can find the *y*-intercept for the graph.

C. Write an equation relating time *t* in years and population *p*. Explain what information the numbers in the equation represent.

D. In what year is the population likely to reach 1,500?

ACE | Homework starts on page 24.

Investigation 2 Examining Growth Patterns　**23**

Applications

1. If you don't brush your teeth regularly, it won't take long for large colonies of bacteria to grow in your mouth. Suppose a single bacterium lands on your tooth and starts multiplying by a factor of 4 every hour.

   a. Write an equation that describes the number of bacteria b in the new colony after n hours.

   b. How many bacteria will be in the colony after 7 hours?

   c. How many bacteria will be in the colony after 8 hours? Explain how you can find this answer by using the answer from part (b) instead of the equation.

   d. After how many hours will there be at least 1,000,000 bacteria in the colony?

   e. Suppose that, instead of 1 bacterium, 50 bacteria land in your mouth. Write an equation that describes the number of bacteria b in this colony after n hours.

   f. Under the conditions of part (e), there will be 3,276,800 bacteria in this new colony after 8 hours. How many bacteria will there be after 9 hours and after 10 hours? Explain how you can find these answers without using the equation from part (e).

2. Loon Lake has a "killer plant" problem similar to Ghost Lake in Problem 2.1. Currently, 5,000 square feet of the lake is covered with the plant. The area covered is growing by a factor of 1.5 each year.

   a. Copy and complete the table to show the area covered by the plant for the next 5 years.

   b. The surface area of the lake is approximately 200,000 square feet. How long will it take before the lake is completely covered?

   Growth of Loon Lake Plant

Year	Area Covered (sq. ft)
0	5,000
1	■
2	■
3	■
4	■
5	■

3. Leaping Leonora just signed a contract with a women's basketball team. The contract guarantees her $20,000 the first year, $40,000 the second year, $80,000 the third year, $160,000 the fourth year, and so on, for 10 years.

a. Make a table showing Leonora's salary each year of this contract.

b. What total amount will Leonora earn over the 10 years?

c. Describe the growth pattern in Leonora's salary.

d. Write an equation for Leonora's salary *s* for any year *n* of her contract.

4. As a biology project, Talisha is studying the growth of a beetle population. She starts her experiment with 5 beetles. The next month she counts 15 beetles.

Homework Help Online
PHSchool.com
For: Help with Exercise 4
Web Code: ape-3204

a. Suppose the beetle population is growing linearly. How many beetles can Talisha expect to find after 2, 3, and 4 months?

b. Suppose the beetle population is growing exponentially. How many beetles can Talisha expect to find after 2, 3, and 4 months?

c. Write an equation for the number of beetles *b* after *m* months if the beetle population is growing linearly. Explain what information the variables and numbers represent.

d. Write an equation for the number of beetles *b* after *m* months if the beetle population is growing exponentially. Explain what information the variables and numbers represent.

e. How long will it take the beetle population to reach 200 if it is growing linearly?

f. How long will it take the beetle population to reach 200 if it is growing exponentially?

5. Fruit flies are often used in genetic experiments because they reproduce very quickly. In 12 days, a pair of fruit flies can mature and produce a new generation. The table below shows the number of fruit flies in three generations of a laboratory colony.

   a. What is the growth factor for this fruit-fly population? Explain how you found your answer.

Growth of Fruit-Fly Population

Generations	0	1	2	3
Number of Fruit Flies	2	120	7,200	432,000

   b. Suppose this growth pattern continues. How many fruit flies will be in the fifth generation?

   c. Write an equation for the population p of generation g.

   d. After how many generations will the population exceed one billion?

6. A population of mice has a growth factor of 3. After 1 month, there are 36 mice. After 2 months, there are 108 mice.

   a. How many mice were in the population initially (at 0 months)?

   b. Write an equation for the population after any number of months. Explain what information the numbers and variables in your equation represent.

7. Fido did not have fleas when his owners took him to the kennel. The number of fleas on Fido after he returned from the kennel grew according to the equation $f = 8(3^n)$, where f is the number of fleas and n is the number of weeks since he returned from the kennel. (Fido left the kennel at week 0.)

   a. How many fleas did Fido pick up at the kennel?

   b. What is the growth factor for the number of fleas?

   c. How many fleas will Fido have after 10 weeks if he is not treated?

8. Consider the equation $y = 150(2^x)$.

   a. Make a table of x and y-values for whole-number x-values from 0 to 5.

   b. What do the numbers 150 and 2 in the equation tell you about the relationship?

For Exercises 9–12, find the growth factor and the y-intercept of the equation's graph.

Go Online
PHSchool.com

For: Multiple-Choice Skills Practice
Web Code: apa-3254

   9. $y = 300(3^x)$

   10. $y = 300(3)^x$

   11. $y = 6,500(2)^x$

   12. $y = 2(7)^x$

13. The following graph represents the population growth of a certain kind of lizard.

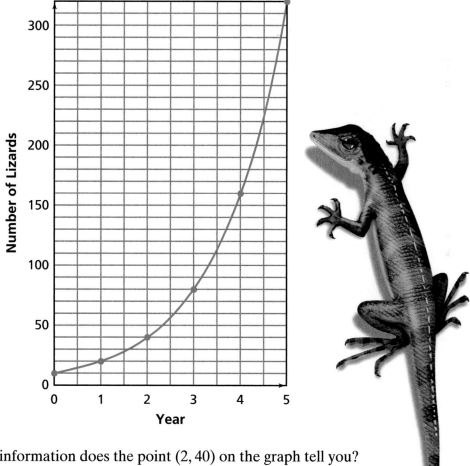

Growth of Lizard Population

   a. What information does the point $(2, 40)$ on the graph tell you?

   b. What information does the point $(1, 20)$ on the graph tell you?

   c. When will the population exceed 100 lizards?

   d. Explain how you can use the graph to find the growth factor for the population.

14. The following graphs show the population growth for two species.

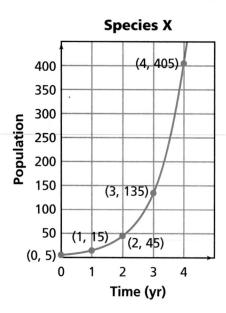

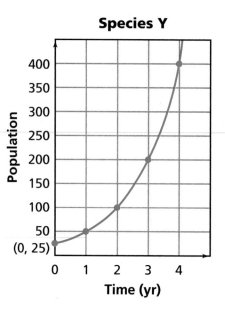

a. Find the growth factors for the two species. Which species is growing faster? Explain.

b. What are the *y*-intercepts for the graphs of Species X and Species Y? Explain what these *y*-intercepts tell you about the populations.

c. Write an equation that describes the growth of Species X.

d. Write an equation that describes the growth of Species Y.

e. For which equation is (5, 1215) a solution?

Connections

15. Multiple Choice Choose the answer that best approximates 3^{20} in scientific notation.

A. 3.5×10^{-9} **B.** 8×10^{3} **C.** 3×10^{9} **D.** 3.5×10^{9}

16. Multiple Choice Choose the answer that is closest to 2.575×10^{6}.

F. 2^{18} **G.** 12^{6} **H.** 6^{12} **J.** 11^{9}

17. Approximate 5^{11} in scientific notation.

For Exercises 18–20, decide whether each number is less than or greater than one million *without using a calculator*. Explain your reasoning.

18. 3^{6} **19.** 9^{5} **20.** 12^{6}

21. The prime factorization of 54 is $3 \times 3 \times 3 \times 2$. This can be written using exponents as $3^3 \times 2$. Write the prime factorization of each number using exponents.

a. 45   **b.** 144   **c.** 2,024

22. Consider these equations.

Equation 1: $y = 10 - 5x$ **Equation 2:** $y = (10)5^x$

a. What is the y-intercept of each equation?

b. For each equation, explain how you could use a table to find how the y-values change as the x-values increase. Describe the change.

c. Explain how you could use the equations to find how the y-values change as the x-values increase.

d. For each equation, explain how you could use a graph to find how the y-values change as the x-values increase.

23. Maria enlarges a 2-cm-by-3-cm rectangle by a factor of 2 to get a 4-cm-by-6-cm rectangle. She then enlarges the 4-cm-by-6-cm rectangle by a factor of 2. She continues this process, enlarging each new rectangle by a factor of 2.

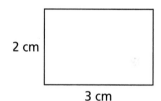

2 cm

3 cm

a. Copy and complete the table to show the dimensions, perimeter, and area of the rectangle after each enlargement.

Rectangle Changes

Enlargement	Dimensions (cm)	Perimeter (cm)	Area (cm²)
0 (original)	2 by 3	▦	▦
1	4 by 6	▦	▦
2	▦	▦	▦
3	▦	▦	▦
4	▦	▦	▦
5	▦	▦	▦

b. Is the pattern of growth for the perimeter *linear, exponential,* or *neither*? Explain.

c. Is the pattern of growth for the area *linear, exponential,* or *neither*? Explain.

d. Write an equation for the perimeter P after n enlargements.

e. Write an equation for the area A after n enlargements.

f. How would your answers to parts (a)–(e) change if the copier were set to enlarge by a factor of 3?

Write an equation for each line. Identify the slope and *y*-intercept.

24.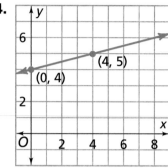

25.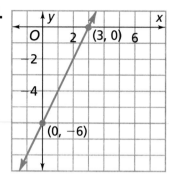

26.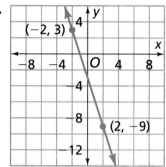

27.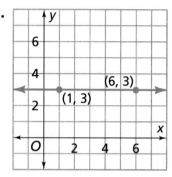

Kele enlarged the figure below by a scale factor of 2. Ahmad enlarged the figure 250%. Use this information for Exercises 28 and 29.

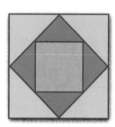

28. Who made the larger image?

29. **Multiple Choice** Which scale factor would give an image whose size is between those of Ahmad's image and Kele's image?

A. $\frac{2}{5}$ **B.** $\frac{3}{5}$ **C.** $\frac{9}{4}$ **D.** $\frac{10}{4}$

30. Companies sometimes describe part-time jobs by comparing them to full-time jobs. For example, a job that requires working half the number of hours of a full-time job is described as a $\frac{1}{2}$-time job or a 50%-time job. ACME, Inc. has three part-time job openings:

- A $\frac{5}{6}$-time job as a gadget inspector

- A 75%-time job as a widget designer

- A 0.875-time job as a gizmo seller

Order these jobs from the one requiring the most time to the one requiring the least time.

Connections Extensions

Extensions

31. a. Make a table and a graph for the exponential equation $y = 1^x$.

b. How are the patterns in the table and the graph of $y = 1^x$ similar to patterns you have observed for other exponential relationships? How are they different?

32. You can find the equation for an exponential relationship if you know two points on its graph. Find the equation of the exponential relationship whose graph passes through each pair of points. Explain.

a. (1, 6) and (2, 12)   **b.** (2, 90) and (4, 810)

33. Leaping Leonora from Exercise 3 also considered an offer from another team. They promised her $1 million a year for the next 25 years. The same team offered Dribbling Dawn $1 the first year, $2 the second year, $4 the third year, $8 the fourth year, and so on for 25 years.

a. Suppose Leonora and Dawn had both accepted the offers and played for 20 years. At the end of 20 years, who would have received more money?

b. Tell which player would have received more after 21 years, 22 years, 23 years, and 25 years.

Mathematical Reflections 2

In this investigation, you studied quantities that grew exponentially. You looked at how the values changed from one stage to the next, and you wrote equations to find the value at any stage.

Think about your answers to these questions. Discuss your ideas with other students and your teacher. Then write a summary of your findings in your notebook.

1. a. Explain how you can use a table, a graph, and an equation to find the y-intercept and growth factor for an exponential relationship.

   b. Explain how you can use the y-intercept and growth factor to write an equation for an exponential relationship.

2. a. In the equation $y = a(b^x)$, explain what the values of a and b represent in the exponential relationship.

   b. How is a represented in a graph of $y = a(b^x)$?

   c. How is b represented in a graph of $y = a(b^x)$?

Growth Factors and Growth Rates

In the previous investigation, you studied exponential growth of plants, mold, and a snake population. In each case, once you knew the growth factor and the starting value, you could make predictions. The growth factors in these examples were whole numbers. In this investigation, you will study examples of exponential growth with fractional growth factors.

3.1 Reproducing Rabbits

In 1859, a small number of rabbits were introduced to Australia by English settlers. The rabbits had no natural predators in Australia, so they reproduced rapidly and became a serious problem, eating grasses intended for sheep and cattle.

Did You Know?

In the mid-1990s, there were more than 300 million rabbits in Australia. The damage they caused cost Australian agriculture $600 million per year. There have been many attempts to curb Australia's rabbit population. In 1995, a deadly rabbit disease was deliberately spread, reducing the rabbit population by about half. However, because rabbits are developing immunity to the disease, the effects of this measure may not last.

Problem 3.1 Fractional Growth Factors

If biologists had counted the rabbits in Australia in the years after they were introduced, they might have collected data like these:

Growth of Rabbit Population

Time (yr)	Population
0	100
1	180
2	325
3	583
4	1,050

A. The table shows the rabbit population growing exponentially.

  1. What is the growth factor? Explain how you found your answer.

  2. Assume this growth pattern continued. Write an equation for the rabbit population p for any year n after the rabbits are first counted. Explain what the numbers in your equation represent.

  3. How many rabbits will there be after 10 years? How many will there be after 25 years? After 50 years?

  4. In how many years will the rabbit population exceed one million?

B. Suppose that, during a different time period, the rabbit population could be predicted by the equation $p = 15(1.2^n)$, where p is the population in millions, and n is the number of years.

  1. What is the growth factor?

  2. What was the initial population?

  3. In how many years will the population double from the initial population?

  4. What will the population be after 3 years? After how many more years will the population at 3 years double?

  5. What will the population be after 10 years? After how many more years will the population at 10 years double?

  6. How do the doubling times for parts (3)–(5) compare? Do you think the doubling time will be the same for this relationship no matter where you start to count?

ACE Homework starts on page 38.

3.2 Investing for the Future

The yearly growth factor for one of the rabbit populations in Problem 3.1 is about 1.8. Suppose the population data fit the equation $P = 100(1.8)^n$ exactly. Then its table would look like the one below.

Rabbit Population Growth

n	P
0	100
1	$100 \times 1.8 =$ 180
2	$180 \times 1.8 =$ 324
3	$324 \times 1.8 =$ 583.2
4	$583.2 \times 1.8 =$ 1049.76

The growth factor of 1.8 is the number by which the population for year n is multiplied to get the population for the next year, $n + 1$.

You can think of the growth factor in terms of a percent change. To find the percent change, compare the difference in population for two consecutive years, n and $n + 1$, with the population of year n.

- From year 0 to year 1, the percent change is $\frac{180 - 100}{100} = \frac{80}{100} = 80\%$. The population of 100 rabbits in year 0 *increased* by 80%, resulting in 100 rabbits $\times$ 80% = 80 additional rabbits.

- From year 1 to year 2 the percent change is $\frac{324 - 180}{180} = \frac{144}{180} = 80\%$. The population of 180 rabbits in year 1 *increased* by 80%, resulting in 180 rabbits $\times$ 80% = 144 additional rabbits.

The percent increase is called the **growth rate.** In some growth situations, the growth rate is given instead of the growth factor. For example, changes in the value of investments are often expressed as percents.

Did You Know?

Some investors use a rule of thumb called the "Rule of 72" to approximate how long it will take the value of an investment to double. To use this rule, simply divide 72 by the annual interest rate. For example, an investment at an 8% interest rate will take approximately 72 ÷ 8, or 9, years to double. At a 10% interest rate, the value of an investment will double approximately every 7.2 years. This rule doesn't give you exact doubling times, only approximations.

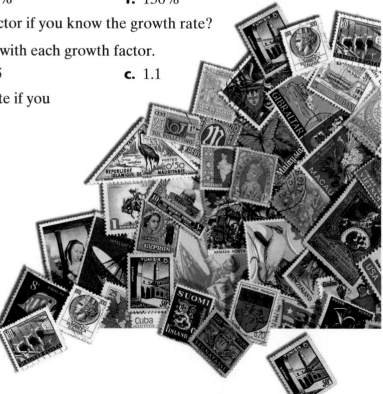

Problem 3.2 Growth Rates

When Sam was in seventh grade, his aunt gave him a stamp collection worth $2,500. Sam considered selling the collection, but his aunt told him that, if he saved it, it would increase in value.

A. Sam saved the collection, and its value increased by 6% each year for several years in a row.

1. Make a table showing the value of the collection each year for the five years after Sam's aunt gave it to him.

2. Look at the pattern of growth from one year to the next. Is the value growing exponentially?

3. Write an equation for the value v of the collection after n years.

B. Suppose the value of the stamps increased by 4% each year instead of by 6%.

1. Make a table showing the value of the collection each year for the five years after Sam's aunt gave it to him.

2. What is the growth factor from one year to the next?

3. Write an equation that represents the value of the stamp collection for any year.

C. 1. Find the growth factor associated with each growth rate.

a. 5%	**b.** 15%	**c.** 30%
d. 75%	**e.** 100%	**f.** 150%

2. How you can find the growth factor if you know the growth rate?

D. 1. Find the growth rate associated with each growth factor.

a. 1.5	**b.** 1.25	**c.** 1.1

2. How can you find the growth rate if you know the growth factor?

ACE Homework starts on page 38.

3.3 Making a Difference

In Problem 3.2, the value of Sam's stamp collection increased by the same percent each year. However, each year, this percent was applied to the previous year's value. So, for example, the increase from year 1 to year 2 is 6% of $2,650, not 6% of the original $2,500. This type of change is called **compound growth.**

In the next problem, you will continue to explore compound growth. You will consider the effects of both the initial value and the growth factor on the value of an investment.

Problem 3.3 Connecting Growth Rate and Growth Factor

Cassie's grandmother started college funds for her two granddaughters. She gave $1,250 to Cassie and $2,500 to Cassie's older sister, Kayle. Each fund was invested in a 10-year bond that pays 4% interest a year.

A. For each fund, write an equation to show the relationship between the number of years and the amount of money in the fund.

B. Make a table to show the amount in each fund for 0 to 10 years.

C. 1. How does the initial value of the fund affect the yearly value increases?

2. How does the initial value affect the growth factor?

3. How does the initial value affect the final value?

D. A year later, Cassie's grandmother started a fund for Cassie's younger brother, Matt. Cassie made this calculation to predict the value of Matt's fund several years from now:

$$\text{Value} = \$2,000 \times 1.05 \times 1.05 \times 1.05 \times 1.05$$

1. What initial value, growth rate, growth factor, and number of years is Cassie assuming?

2. If the value continues to increase at this rate, how much would the fund be worth in one more year?

ACE Homework starts on page 38.

Applications

1. In parts of the United States, wolves are being reintroduced to wilderness areas where they had become extinct. Suppose 20 wolves are released in northern Michigan, and the yearly growth factor for this population is expected to be 1.2.

   a. Make a table showing the projected number of wolves at the end of each of the first 6 years.

   b. Write an equation that models the growth of the wolf population.

   c. How long will it take for the new wolf population to exceed 100?

2. **a.** The table shows that the elk population in a state forest is growing exponentially. What is the growth factor? Explain.

**Growth of
Elk Population**

Time (yr)	Population
0	30
1	57
2	108
3	206
4	391
5	743

   b. Suppose this growth pattern continues. How many elk will there be after 10 years? How many elk will there be after 15 years?

   c. Write an equation you could use to predict the elk population p for any year n after the elk were first counted.

   d. In how many years will the population exceed one million?

3. Suppose there are 100 trout in a lake and the yearly growth factor for the population is 1.5. How long will it take for the number of trout to double?

4. Suppose there are 500,000 squirrels in a forest and the growth factor for the population is 1.6 per year. Write an equation you could use to find the squirrel population p in n years.

5. **Multiple Choice** The equation $p = 200(1.1)^t$ models the growth of a population. The variable p is the population in millions and t is the time in years. How long will it take this population to double?

A. 4 to 5 years   **B.** 5 to 6 years   **C.** 6 to 7 years   **D.** 7 to 8 years

In Exercises 6 and 7, the equation models the growth of a population, where p is the population in millions and t is the time in years. Tell how much time it would take the population to double.

6. $p = 135(1.7)^t$ **7.** $p = 1,000(1.2)^t$

8. a. Fill in the table for each equation.

$y = 50(2.2)^x$

x	0	1	2	3	4	5
y						

$y = 350(1.7)^x$

x	0	1	2	3	4	5
y						

    b. What is the growth factor for each equation?

    c. Predict whether the graphs of these equations will ever cross.

    d. Estimate any points at which you think the graphs will cross.

9. Maya's grandfather opened a savings account for her when she was born. He opened the account with $100 and did not add or take out any money after that. The money in the account grows at a rate of 4% per year.

    a. Make a table to show the amount in the account from the time Maya was born until she turned 10.

    b. What is the growth factor for the account?

    c. Write an equation for the value of the account after any number of years.

Homework Help **O**nline
PHSchool.com

For: Help with Exercise 9
Web Code: ape-3309

Find the growth rate associated with the given growth factor.

10. 1.4   **11.** 1.9   **12.** 1.75

Go Online
PHSchool.com

For: Multiple-Choice Skills
Practice
Web Code: apa-3354

For Exercises 13–15, find the growth factor associated with the given growth rate.

13. 45%   **14.** 90%   **15.** 31%

16. Suppose the price of an item increases by 25% per year. What is the growth factor for the price from year to year?

17. Currently, 1,000 students attend Greenville Middle School. The school can accommodate 1,300 students. The school board estimates that the student population will grow by 5% per year for the next several years.

  a. In how many years will the population outgrow the present building?

  b. Suppose the school limits its growth to 50 students per year. How many years will it take for the population to outgrow the school?

18. Suppose that, for several years, the number of radios sold in the United States increased by 3% each year.

  a. Suppose one million radios sold in the first year of this time period. About how many radios sold in each of the next 6 years?

  b. Suppose only 100,000 radios sold in the first year. About how many radios sold in each of the next 6 years?

19. Suppose a movie ticket costs about $7, and inflation causes ticket prices to increase by 4.5% a year for the next several years.

  a. At this rate, how much will a ticket cost 5 years from now?

  b. How much will a ticket cost 10 years from now?

  c. How much will a ticket cost 30 years from now?

20. Find the growth rate (percent growth) for a relationship with the equation $y = 30(2^x)$.

21. Multiple Choice Ms. Diaz wants to invest $500 in a savings bond. At which bank would her investment grow the most over 8 years?

F. Bank 1: 7% interest for 8 years.

G. Bank 2: 2% interest for the first 4 years and 12% interest for the next four years.

H. Bank 3: 12% interest for the first 4 years and 2% interest for the next four years.

J. All three result in the same growth.

22. Oscar made the following calculation to predict the value of his baseball card collection several years from now:

$$\text{Value} = \$130 \times 1.07 \times 1.07 \times 1.07 \times 1.07 \times 1.07$$

a. What initial value, growth rate, growth factor, and number of years is Oscar assuming?

b. If the value continues to increase at this rate, how much would the collection be worth in three more years?

23. Carlos, Latanya, and Mila work in a biology laboratory. Each of them is responsible for a population of mice.

- The growth factor for Carlos's population of mice is $\frac{8}{7}$.

- The growth factor for Latanya's population of mice is 3.

- The growth factor for Mila's population of mice is 125%.

a. Whose mice are reproducing fastest?

b. Whose mice are reproducing slowest?

Connections

Calculate each percent.

24. 120% of $3,000   **25.** 150% of $200   **26.** 133% of $2,500

For Exercises 27–30, tell whether the sequence of numbers could represent an exponential growth pattern. Explain your reasoning. If the pattern is exponential, give the growth factor.

27. 1   1.1   1.21   1.331   1.4641   1.61051   1.771561

28. 3   5 $8\frac{1}{3}$ $13\frac{8}{9}$ $23\frac{4}{27}$

29. 3 $4\frac{2}{3}$ $6\frac{1}{3}$ 8 $9\frac{2}{3}$ $11\frac{1}{3}$

30. 2   6.4   20.5   66   210

31. The graph shows the growth in the number of wireless subscribers in the United States from 1994 to 2004.

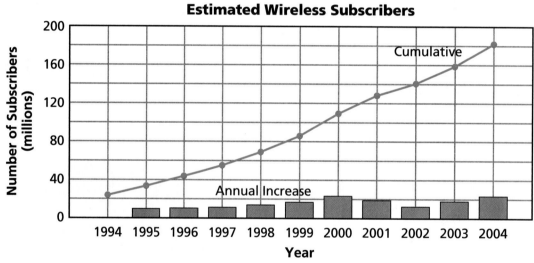

Estimated Wireless Subscribers

SOURCE: CTIA-The Wireless Association™

a. What do the bars in the graph represent?

b. What does the curve represent?

c. Describe the pattern of change in the total number of subscribers from 1994 to 2004. Could the pattern be exponential? Explain.

d. The number of subscribers in 2001 was 128,375,000 and in 2002 the number was 140,455,000. Do these numbers fit the pattern you described in part (c)? Explain.

32. A worker currently receives a yearly salary of $20,000.

   a. Find the dollar values of a 3%, 4%, and 6% raise for this worker.

   b. Find the worker's new annual salary for each raise in part (a).

   c. You can find the new salary after a 3% raise in two ways:

   $20,000 + 3% of ($20,000) *or* 103% of $20,000

   Explain why these two methods give the same result.

33. Arturo enlarges this drawing to 110% of this size. Make a copy of the drawing on grid paper and use it as you answer the following questions.

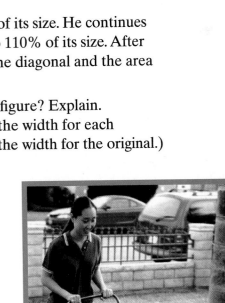

   a. What is the length of the diagonal in the original drawing? What is the area of the shaded region?

   b. What is the length of the diagonal in the enlarged drawing? What is the area of the shaded region?

   c. Arturo enlarges the enlargement to 110% of its size. He continues this process, enlarging each new drawing to 110% of its size. After five enlargements, what will the length of the diagonal and the area of the shaded region be?

   d. Is each enlargement similar to the original figure? Explain. (**Hint:** Compare the ratio of the length to the width for each enlargement with the ratio of the length to the width for the original.)

34. Kwan cuts lawns every summer to make money. One of her customers offers to give her a 3% raise next summer and a 4% raise the summer after that.

Kwan says she would prefer to get a 4% raise next summer and a 3% raise the summer after that. She claims she will earn more money this way. Is she correct? Explain.

35. After graduating from high school, Kim accepts a job with a package delivery service, earning $9 per hour.

    a. How much will Kim earn in a year if she works 40 hours per week for 50 weeks and gets 2 weeks of paid vacation time?

    b. Write an equation showing the relationship between the number of weeks Kim works w and the amount she earns a.

    c. Kim writes the following equation: $9,000 = 360w$. What question is she trying to answer? What is the answer to that question?

    d. Suppose Kim works for the company for 10 years, receiving a 3% raise each year. Make a table showing how her annual income grows over this time period.

    e. When Kim was hired, her manager told her that instead of a 3% annual raise, she could choose to receive a $600 raise each year. How do the two raise plans compare over a 10-year period? Which plan do you think is better? Explain your answer.

36. Which represents faster growth, a growth factor of 2.5 or a growth rate of 25%?

37. Order these scale factors from least to greatest.

    130% $\frac{3}{2}$ 2   1.475

38. Christopher made a drawing that measures $8\frac{1}{2}$ by 11 inches. He needs to reduce it so it will fit into a space that measures $7\frac{1}{2}$ by 10 inches. What scale factor should he use to get a similar drawing that is small enough to fit? (Do not worry about getting it to fit perfectly.)

39. a. Match each growth rate from List 1 with the equivalent growth factor in List 2 if possible.

    List 1: 20%, 120%, 50%, 200%, 400%, 2%

    List 2: 1.5, 5, 1.2, 2.2, 4, 2, 1.02

    b. Order the growth rates from List 1 from least to greatest.

    c. Order the growth factors from List 2 from least to greatest.

Extensions

40. In Russia, shortly after the breakup of the Soviet Union, the yearly growth factor for inflation was 26. What growth rate (percent increase) is associated with this growth factor? We call this percent increase the *inflation rate*.

41. In 1990, the population of the United States was about 250 million and was growing exponentially at a rate of about 1% per year.

   a. At this growth rate, what will the population of the United States be in the year 2010?

   b. At this rate, how long will it take the population to double?

   c. Do you think the predictions in parts (a) and (b) are accurate? Explain.

   d. The population in 2000 was about 282 million. How accurate was the growth rate?

42. Use the table to answer parts (a)–(d).

   a. One model of world population growth assumes the population grows exponentially. Based on the data in this table, what would be a reasonable growth factor for this model?

   b. Use your growth factor from part (a) to write an equation for the growth of the population at 5-year intervals beginning in 1955.

   c. Use your equation from part (b) to estimate the year in which the population was double the 1955 population.

   d. Use your equation to predict when the population will be double the 2000 population.

World Population Growth

Year	Population (billions)
1955	2.76
1960	3.02
1965	3.33
1970	3.69
1975	4.07
1980	4.43
1985	4.83
1990	5.26
1995	5.67
2000	6.07

Write an exponential growth equation that matches each description.

43. A population is initially 300. After 1 year, the population is 360.

44. A population has a yearly growth factor of 1.2. After 3 years, the population is 1,000.

45. The growth rate for an investment is 3% per year. After 2 years, the value of the investment is $2,560.

46. Suppose your calculator did not have an exponent key. You could find 1.5^{12} by entering:

$1.5 \times 1.5 \times 1.5 \times 1.5 \times 1.5 \times 1.5 \times 1.5 \times 1.5 \times 1.5 \times 1.5 \times 1.5 \times 1.5$

   a. How could you evaluate 1.5^{12} with fewer keystrokes?

   b. What is the fewest number of times you could press ❌ to evaluate 1.5^{12}?

47. Mr. Watson sold his boat for $10,000. He wants to invest the money.

   a. How much money will he have after 1 year if he invests the $10,000 in an account that pays 4% interest per year?

   b. Mr. Watson sees an advertisement for another type of savings account:

   "4% interest per year compounded quarterly."

   He asks the bank teller what "compounded quarterly" means. She explains that instead of giving him 4% of $10,000 at the end of one year, the bank will give him 1% at the end of each 3-month period (each quarter of a year).

**Growth of $10,000
Investment at 4% Interest
Compounded Quarterly**

Time (mo)	Money in Account
0	$10,000
3	$10,100
6	$10,201
9	$10,303.01

   If Mr. Watson invests his money at this bank, how much will be in his account at the end of one year?

   c. Mr. Watson sees an advertisement for a different bank that offers 4% interest per year *compounded monthly*. (This means he will get $\frac{1}{12}$ of 4% interest every month.) How much money will he have at the end of the year if he invests his money at this bank?

   d. Which account would have the most money at the end of one year? Explain.

Mathematical Reflections 3

In this investigation, you explored exponential growth situations in which the growth factor was not a whole number. In some of these situations, the growth was described by giving the percent growth, or growth rate.

Think about your answers to these questions. Discuss your ideas with other students and your teacher. Then write a summary of your findings in your notebook.

1. Suppose you know the initial value for a population and the yearly growth rate.

   a. How can you determine the population several years from now?

   b. How is a growth rate related to the growth factor for the population?

2. Suppose you know the initial value for a population and the yearly growth factor.

   a. How can you determine the population several years from now?

   b. How can you determine the yearly growth rate?

3. Suppose you know the equation that represents the exponential relationship between the population size p and the number of years n. How can you determine the doubling time for the population?

Investigation 4

Exponential Decay

The exponential patterns you have studied so far have all involved quantities that increase. In this investigation, you will explore quantities that decrease, or *decay*, exponentially as time passes.

4.1 Making Smaller Ballots

In Problem 1.1, you read about the ballots Chen, the secretary of the Student Government Association, is making for a meeting. Recall that Chen cuts a sheet of paper in half, stacks the two pieces and cuts them in half, stacks the resulting four pieces and cuts them in half, and so on.

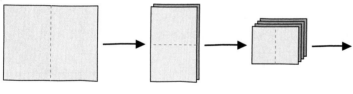

You investigated the pattern in the number of ballots created by each cut. In this problem, you will look at the pattern in the areas of the ballots.

BALLOTS

Problem 4.1 Introducing Exponential Decay

A. The paper Chen starts with has an area of 64 square inches. Copy and complete the table to show the area of a ballot after each of the first 10 cuts.

Number of Cuts	Area (in.^{2})
0	64
1	32
2	16
3	▪
4	▪
5	▪
6	▪
7	▪
8	▪
9	▪
10	▪

B. How does the area of a ballot change with each cut?

C. Write an equation for the area A of a ballot after any cut n.

D. Make a graph of the data.

E. How is the pattern of change in the area different from the exponential growth patterns you studied? How is it similar?

ACE Homework starts on page 53.

4.2 Fighting Fleas

Exponential patterns like the one in Problem 4.1, in which a quantity decreases at each stage, show **exponential decay.** The factor the quantity is multiplied by at each stage is called the **decay factor.** A decay factor is always less than 1 but greater than 0. In Problem 4.1, the decay factor is $\frac{1}{2}$.

After an animal receives a preventive flea medicine, the medicine breaks down in the animal's bloodstream. With each hour, there is less medicine in the blood. The table and graph show the amount of medicine in a dog's bloodstream each hour for 6 hours after receiving a 400-milligram dose.

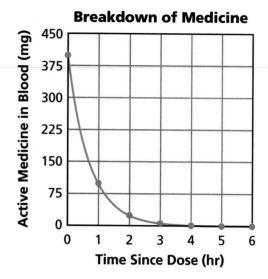

Breakdown of Medicine

Time Since Dose (hr)	Active Medicine in Blood (mg)
0	400
1	100
2	25
3	6.25
4	1.5625
5	0.3907
6	0.0977

Problem 4.2 Representing Exponential Decay

A. Study the pattern of change in the graph and the table.

1. How does the amount of active medicine in the dog's blood change from one hour to the next?

2. Write an equation to model the relationship between the number of hours h since the dose is given and the milligrams of active medicine m.

3. How is the graph for this problem similar to the graph you made in Problem 4.1? How is it different?

B. 1. A different flea medicine breaks down at a rate of 20% per hour. This means that as each hour passes, 20% of the active medicine is used. The initial dose is 60 milligrams. Extend and complete this table to show the amount of active medicine in an animal's blood at the end of each hour for 6 hours.

Breakdown of Medicine

Time Since Dose (hr)	Active Medicine in Blood (mg)
0	60
1	▪
2	▪
⋮	⋮
6	▪

2. For the medicine in part (1), Janelle wrote the equation $m = 60(0.8)^h$ to show the amount of active medicine m after h hours. Compare the quantities of active medicine in your table with the quantities given by Janelle's equation. Explain any similarities or differences.

3. Dwayne was confused by the terms **decay rate** and *decay factor*. He said that because the rate of decay is 20%, the decay factor should be 0.2, and the equation should be $m = 60(0.2^h)$. How would you explain to Dwayne why a rate of decay of 20% is equivalent to a decay factor of 0.8?

ACE **Homework starts on page 53.**

4.3 Cooling Water

Sometimes a cup of hot cocoa or tea is too hot to drink at first, so you must wait for it to cool.

What pattern of change would you expect to find in the temperature of a hot drink as time passes?

What shape would you expect for a graph of (time, drink temperature) data?

This experiment will help you explore these questions.

Equipment:

- very hot water, a thermometer, a cup or mug for hot drinks, and a watch or clock

Directions:

- Record the air temperature.
- Fill the cup with the hot water.
- In a table, record the water temperature and the room temperature in 5-minute intervals throughout your class period.

Hot Water Cooling

Time (min)	Water Temperature	Room Temperature
0	■	■
5	■	■
10	■	■
■	■	■
■	■	■

A. 1. Make a graph of your (*time, water temperature*) data.

   2. Describe the pattern of change in the data. When did the water temperature change most rapidly? When did it change most slowly?

B. 1. Add a column to your table. In this column, record the difference between the water temperature and the air temperature for each time value.

   2. Make a graph of the (*time, temperature difference*) data. Compare this graph with the graph you made in Question A.

   3. Describe the pattern of change in the (*time, temperature difference*) data. When did the temperature difference change most rapidly? When did it change most slowly?

   4. Estimate the decay factor for the relationship between temperature difference and time in this experiment.

   5. Find an equation for the (*time, temperature difference*) data. Your equation should allow you to predict the temperature difference at the end of any 5-minute interval.

C. 1. What do you think the graph of the (*time, temperature difference*) data would look like if you had continued the experiment for several more hours?

   2. What factors might affect the rate at which a cup of hot liquid cools?

   3. What factors might introduce errors in the data you collect?

D. Compare the two graphs in Questions A and B with the graphs in Problems 4.1 and 4.2. What similarities and differences do you observe?

ACE Homework starts on page 53.

Applications

1. Latisha has a 24-inch string of licorice (LIK uh rish) to share with her friends. As each friend asks her for a piece, Latisha gives him or her half of what she has left. She doesn't eat any of the licorice herself.

   a. Make a table showing the length of licorice Latisha has left each time she gives a piece away.

   b. Make a graph of the data from part (a).

   c. Suppose that, instead of half the licorice that is left each time, Latisha gives each friend 4 inches of licorice. Make a table and a graph for this situation.

   d. Compare the tables and the graphs for the two situations. Explain the similarities and the differences.

2. Chen, from Problem 4.1, finds that his ballots are very small after only a few cuts. He decides to start with a larger sheet of paper. The new paper has an area of 324 in^2. Copy and complete this table to show the area of each ballot after each of the first 10 cuts.

   a. Write an equation for the area A of a ballot after any cut n.

   b. With the smaller sheet of paper, the area of a ballot is 1 in^2 after 6 cuts. How many cuts does it take to get ballots this small, starting with the larger sheet?

   c. Chen wants to be able to make 12 cuts before getting ballots with an area of 1 in^2. How large does his starting piece of paper need to be?

Number of Cuts	Area (in.^{2})
0	324
1	162
2	81
3	■
4	■
5	■
6	■
7	■
8	■
9	■
10	■

Investigation 4 Exponential Decay **53**

3. Penicillin decays exponentially in the human body. Suppose you receive a 300-milligram dose of penicillin to combat strep throat. About 180 milligrams will remain active in your blood after 1 day.

For: Help with Exercise 3
Web Code: ape-3403

a. Assume the amount of penicillin active in your blood decreases exponentially. Make a table showing the amount of active penicillin in your blood for 7 days after a 300-milligram dose.

b. Write an equation for the relationship between the number of days d since you took the penicillin and the amount of the medicine m remaining active in your blood.

c. What would be the equation if you had taken a 400-milligram dose?

In Exercises 4 and 5, tell whether the equation represents exponential decay or exponential growth. Explain your reasoning.

4. $y = 0.8(2.1)^x$

5. $y = 20(0.5)^x$

Go **O**nline
PHSchool.com

For: Multiple-Choice Skills Practice
Web Code: apa-3454

6. The graph below shows an exponential decay relationship.

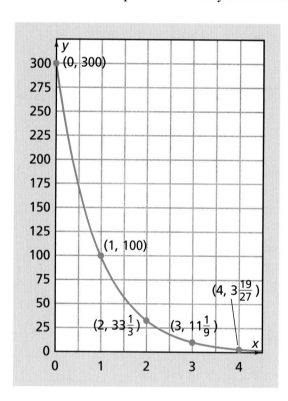

a. Find the decay factor and the y-intercept.

b. What is the equation for the graph?

7. Hot coffee is poured into a cup and allowed to cool. The difference between coffee temperature and room temperature is recorded every minute for 10 minutes.

Cooling Coffee

Time (min)	0	1	2	3	4	5	6	7	8	9	10
Temperature Difference (°C)	80	72	65	58	52	47	43	38	34	31	28

a. Plot the (*time, temperature difference*) data. Explain what the patterns in the table and the graph tell you about the rate at which the coffee cools.

b. Approximate the decay factor for this relationship.

c. Write an equation for the relationship between time and temperature difference.

d. About how long will it take the coffee to cool to room temperature? Explain.

Connections

8. Scientific notation is useful for writing very large numbers. Write each of the following numbers in scientific notation.

a. There are about 33,400,000,000,000,000,000,000 molecules in 1 gram of water.

b. There are about 25,000,000,000,000 red blood cells in the human body.

c. Earth is about 93,000,000 miles (150,000,000 km) from the sun.

d. According to the Big Bang Theory, our universe began with an explosion 18,000,000,000 years ago, generating temperatures of 100,000,000,000° Celsius.

9. Consider these equations:

$$y = 0.75^x \qquad y = 0.25^x \qquad y = -0.5x + 1$$

a. Sketch graphs of all three equations on one set of axes.

b. What points, if any, do the three graphs have in common?

c. In which graph does y decrease the fastest as x increases?

d. How can you use your graphs to figure out which of the equations is not an example of exponential decay?

e. How can you use the equations to figure out which is not an example of exponential decay?

10. A cricket is on the 0 point of a number line, hopping toward 1. She covers half the distance from her current location to 1 with each hop. So, she will be at $\frac{1}{2}$ after one hop, $\frac{3}{4}$ after two hops, and so on.

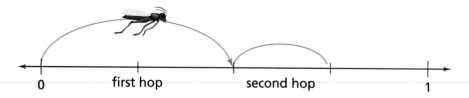

0   first hop   second hop   1

a. Make a table showing the cricket's location for the first 10 hops.

b. Where will the cricket be after *n* hops?

c. Will the cricket ever get to 1? Explain.

11. The pizza in the ad for Mr. Costa's restaurant has a diameter of 5 inches.

a. What are the circumference and area of the pizza?

b. Mr. Costa reduces his ad to 90% of its original size. He then reduces the reduced ad to 90% of its size. He repeats this process five times. Extend and complete the table to show the diameter, circumference, and area of the pizza after each reduction.

Advertisement Pizza Sizes

Reduction Number	Diameter (in.)	Circumference (in.)	Area (in.²)
0	5	▪	▪
1	▪	▪	▪

c. Write equations for the diameter, circumference, and area of the pizza after *n* reductions.

d. How would your equations change if Mr. Costa had used a reduction setting of 75%?

e. Express the decay factors from part (d) as fractions.

f. Mr. Costa claims that when he uses the 90% reduction setting on the copier, he is reducing the size of the drawing by 10%. Is Mr. Costa correct? Explain.

12. Answer parts (a) and (b) without using your calculator.

   a. Which decay factor represents faster decay, 0.8 or 0.9?

   b. Order the following from least to greatest:

   0.9^4 $\qquad$ 0.9^2 $\qquad$ 90% $\qquad$ $\dfrac{2}{10}$ $\qquad$ $\dfrac{2}{9}$ $\qquad$ 0.8^4 $\qquad$ 0.84

Extensions

13. Freshly cut lumber, known as *green lumber,* contains water. If green lumber is used to build a house, it may crack, shrink, and warp as it dries. To avoid these problems, lumber is dried in a kiln that circulates air to remove moisture from the wood. Suppose that, in 1 week, a kiln removes $\frac{1}{3}$ of the moisture from a stack of lumber.

   a. What fraction of the moisture remains in the lumber after 5 weeks in a kiln?

   b. What fraction of the moisture has been removed from the lumber after 5 weeks?

   c. Write an equation for the fraction of moisture m remaining in the lumber after w weeks.

   d. Write an equation for the fraction of moisture m that has been removed from the lumber after w weeks.

   e. Graph your equations from parts (c) and (d) on the same set of axes. Describe how the graphs are related.

   f. A different kiln removes $\frac{1}{4}$ of the moisture from a stack of lumber each week. Write equations for the fraction of moisture remaining and the fraction of moisture removed after w weeks.

   g. Graph your two equations from part (f) on the same set of axes. Describe how the graphs are related. How do they compare to the graphs from part (e)?

   h. Green lumber is about 40% water by weight. The moisture content of lumber used to build houses is typically 10% or less. For each of the two kilns described above, how long should lumber be dried before it is used to build a house?

Mathematical Reflections 4

In this investigation, you explored situations that showed patterns of exponential decay.

Think about your answers to these questions. Discuss your ideas with other students and your teacher. Then, write a summary of your findings in your notebook.

1. How can you recognize an exponential decay pattern from a table of data?

2. How can you recognize an exponential decay pattern from a graph?

3. How can you tell that an equation represents exponential decay?

4. How are exponential growth relationships and exponential decay relationships similar? How are they different?

5. How are exponential decay relationships and decreasing linear relationships similar? How are they different?

Patterns With Exponents

As you explored exponential relationships in previous investigations, you made tables of exponential growth. This table shows some values for $y = 2^x$. The y-values are given in both exponential and standard form.

x	y
1	2^1 or 2
2	2^2 or 4
3	2^3 or 8
4	2^4 or 16
5	2^5 or 32
6	2^6 or 64
7	2^7 or 128
8	2^8 or 256

There are many interesting patterns in the table.

Getting Ready for Problem

- Look at the column of y-values in the table. What pattern do you see in how the ones digits of the standard forms change?
- Can you predict the ones digit for 2^{15}? What about 2^{50}?
- What other patterns do you see in the table?
- Find an x-value and values for the missing digits that will make this a true number sentence.

    $2^x = _____6$

5.1 Predicting the Ones Digit

The values of a^x for a given number a are called *powers of a*. You just looked at powers of 2. In this problem, you will explore patterns in other powers.

Problem 5.1 Predicting the Ones Digit

A. Copy and complete this table.

Powers Table

x	1^x	2^x	3^x	4^x	5^x	6^x	7^x	8^x	9^x	10^x
1	1	2								
2	1	4								
3	1	8								
4	1	16								
5	1	32								
6	1	64								
7	1	128								
8	1	256								
Ones Digits of the Powers	1	2, 4, 8, 6								

B. Describe patterns you see in the ones digits of the powers.

C. Predict the ones digit in the standard form of each number.

    1. 4^{12} **2.** 9^{20} **3.** 3^{17} **4.** 5^{100} **5.** 10^{500}

D. Predict the ones digit in the standard form of each number.

    1. 31^{10} **2.** 12^{10} **3.** 17^{21} **4.** 29^{10}

E. Find the value of a that makes each number sentence true.

1. $a^{12} = 531{,}441$ **2.** $a^9 = 387{,}420{,}489$ **3.** $a^6 = 11{,}390{,}625$

F. Find a value for a and values for the missing digits to make each number sentence true. Explain your reasoning.

1. $a^7 = \underline{\ }\,\underline{\ }\,\underline{\ }\,\underline{\ }\,\underline{\ }\,3$ **2.** $a^8 = \underline{\ }\,\underline{\ }\,\underline{\ }\,\underline{\ }\,\underline{\ }\,\underline{\ }\,1$

ACE Homework starts on page 64.

5.2 Operating With Exponents

In the last problem, you explored patterns in the values of a^x for different values of a. You used the patterns you discovered to make predictions. For example, you predicted the ones digit in the standard form of 4^{12}. In this problem, you will look at other interesting patterns that lead to some important properties of exponents.

Getting Ready for Problem 5.2

- Federico noticed that 16 appears twice in the powers table. It is in the column for 2^x, for $x = 4$. It is also in the column for 4^x, for $x = 2$. He said this means that $2^4 = 4^2$. Write 2^4 as a product of 2's. Then, show that the product is equal to 4^2.

- Are there other numbers that appear more than once in the table? If so, write equations to show the equivalent exponential forms of the numbers.

Use properties of real numbers and your table from Problem 5.1 to help you answer these questions.

A. 1. Explain why each of the following statements is true.

    a. $2^3 \times 2^2 = 2^5$ **b.** $3^4 \times 3^3 = 3^7$ **c.** $6^3 \times 6^5 = 6^8$

  2. Give another example that fits the pattern in part (1).

  3. Complete the following equation to show how you can find the exponent of the product when you multiply two powers with the same base. Explain your reasoning.

$$a^m \times a^n = a^{\blacksquare}$$

B. 1. Explain why each of the following statements is true.

    a. $2^3 \times 3^3 = 6^3$ **b.** $5^3 \times 6^3 = 30^3$ **c.** $10^4 \times 4^4 = 40^4$

  2. Give another example that fits the pattern in part (1).

  3. Complete the following equation to show how you can find the base and exponent of the product when you multiply two powers with the same exponent. Explain your reasoning.

$$a^m \times b^m = \underline{\ ?\ }$$

C. 1. Explain why each of the following statements is true.

    a. $4^2 = (2^2)^2 = 2^4$

    b. $9^2 = (3^2)^2 = 3^4$

    c. $125^2 = (5^3)^2 = 5^6$

  2. Give another example that fits the pattern in part (1).

  3. Complete the following equation to show how you can find the base and exponent when a power is raised to a power. Explain.

$$(a^m)^n = \underline{\ ?\ }$$

D. 1. Explain why each of the following statements is true.

    a. $\dfrac{3^5}{3^2} = 3^3$ **b.** $\dfrac{4^6}{4^5} = 4^1$ **c.** $\dfrac{5^{10}}{5^{10}} = 5^0$

  2. Tom says $\dfrac{4^5}{4^6} = 4^{-1}$. Mary says $\dfrac{4^5}{4^6} = \dfrac{1}{4^1}$. Who is correct and why?

  3. Complete the following equation to show how you can find the base and exponent of the quotient when you divide two powers with the same base. (Assume a is not 0.) Explain your reasoning.

$$\dfrac{a^m}{a^n} = \underline{\ ?\ }$$

E. Use the pattern from Question D to explain why $a^0 = 1$ for any nonzero number a.

ACE Homework starts on page 64.

5.3 Exploring Exponential Equations

In this unit, you have studied situations that show patterns of exponential growth or exponential decay. All of these situations are modeled by equations of the form $y = a(b^x)$, where a is the starting value and b is the growth or decay factor.

Problem 5.3 Exploring Exponential Equations

You can use your graphing calculator to explore how the values of a and b affect the graph of $y = a(b^x)$.

A. First, let $a = 1$ and explore how the value of b affects the graph of $y = b^x$.

   1. Graph these four equations in the same window. Use window settings that show x-values from -5 to 5 and y-values from -5 to 20. Record your observations.

   $y = 1.25^x$ $\qquad$ $y = 1.5^x$ $\qquad$ $y = 1.75^x$ $\qquad$ $y = 2^x$

   2. Next, graph these three equations in the same window. Use window settings that show $-5 \leq x \leq 5$ and $-1 \leq y \leq 2$. Record your observations.

   $y = 0.25^x$ $\qquad$ $y = 0.5^x$ $\qquad$ $y = 0.75^x$

   3. Describe how you could predict the general shape of the graph of $y = b^x$ for a specific value of b.

B. Next, you will look at how the value of a affects the graph of $y = a(b^x)$. You will need to adjust the window settings as you work. Graph each set of equations in the same window. Record your observations for each set.

   1. $y = 2(2^x)$ $\qquad$ $y = 3(2^x)$ $\qquad$ $y = 4(2^x)$

   2. $y = 2(1.5^x)$ $\qquad$ $y = 3(1.5^x)$ $\qquad$ $y = 4(1.5^x)$

   3. $y = 2(0.5^x)$ $\qquad$ $y = 3(0.5^x)$ $\qquad$ $y = 4(0.5^x)$

   4. Describe how the value of a affects the graph of an equation of the form $y = a(b^x)$.

ACE Homework starts on page 64.

Applications

Predict the ones digit for the standard form of the number.

1. 7^{100} **2.** 6^{200} **3.** 17^{100} **4.** 31^{10} **5.** 12^{100}

For Exercises 6 and 7, find the value of a that makes the number sentence true.

6. $a^7 = 823{,}543$ **7.** $a^6 = 1{,}771{,}561$

8. Explain how you can use your calculator to find the ones digit of the standard form of 3^{30}.

9. Multiple Choice In the powers table you completed in Problem 5.1, look for patterns in the ones digit of square numbers. Which number is *not* a square number? Explain.

   A. 289   **B.** 784   **C.** 1,392   **D.** 10,000

Tell how many zeros are in the standard form of the number.

10. 10^{10} **11.** 10^{50} **12.** 10^{100}

Find the least value of x that will make the statement true.

13. $9^6 < 10^x$ **14.** $3^{14} < 10^x$

For Exercises 15–17, identify the greater number in each pair.

15. 6^{10} or 7^{10} **16.** 8^{10} or 10^8 **17.** 6^9 or 9^6

18. Multiple Choice Which expression is equivalent to $2^9 \times 2^{10}$?

   F. 2^{90} **G.** 2^{19} **H.** 4^{19} **J.** 2^{18}

Use the properties of exponents to write each expression as a single power. Check your answers.

19. $5^6 \times 8^6$ **20.** $(7^5)^3$ **21.** $\dfrac{8^{15}}{8^{10}}$

For Exercises 22–27, tell whether the statement is *true* or *false*. Explain.

For: Multiple-Choice Skills Practice
Web Code: apa-3554

22. $6^3 \times 6^5 = 6^8$

23. $2^3 \times 3^2 = 6^5$

24. $3^8 = 9^4$

25. $4^3 + 5^3 = 9^3$

26. $2^3 + 2^5 = 2^3(1 + 2^2)$

27. $\dfrac{5^{12}}{5^4} = 5^3$

28. Multiple Choice Which number is the ones digit of $2^{10} \times 3^{10}$?

A. 2   **B.** 4   **C.** 6   **D.** 8

For Exercises 29 and 30, find the ones digit of the product.

29. $4^{15} \times 3^{15}$

30. $7^{15} \times 4^{20}$

31. Manuela said it must be true that $2^{10} = 2^4 \cdot 2^6$ because she can group $2 \cdot 2 \cdot 2 \cdot 2 \cdot 2 \cdot 2 \cdot 2 \cdot 2 \cdot 2 \cdot 2$ as $(2 \cdot 2 \cdot 2 \cdot 2) \cdot (2 \cdot 2 \cdot 2 \cdot 2 \cdot 2 \cdot 2)$.

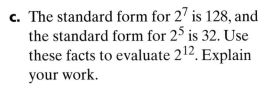

$2 \cdot 2 \cdot 2 \cdot 2 = 2^4$

a. Verify that Manuela is correct by evaluating both sides of the equation $2^{10} = 2^4 \cdot 2^6$.

b. Use Manuela's idea of grouping factors to write three other expressions that are equivalent to 2^{10}. Evaluate each expression you find to verify that it is equivalent to 2^{10}.

c. The standard form for 2^7 is 128, and the standard form for 2^5 is 32. Use these facts to evaluate 2^{12}. Explain your work.

d. Test Manuela's idea to see if it works for exponential expressions with other bases, such as 3^8 or $(1.5)^{11}$. Test several cases. Give an argument supporting your conclusion.

Tell whether the expression is equivalent to 1.25^{10}. Explain your reasoning.

32. $(1.25)^5 \cdot (1.25)^5$

33. $(1.25)^3 \times (1.25)^7$

34. $(1.25) \times 10$

35. $(1.25) + 10$

36. $(1.25^5)^2$

37. $(1.25)^5 \cdot (1.25)^2$

For Exercises 38–41, tell whether the expression is equivalent to $(1.5)^7$. Explain your reasoning.

38. $1.5^5 \times 1.5^2$

39. $1.5^3 \times 1.5^4$

40. 1.5×7

41. $(1.5) + 7$

42. Without actually graphing these equations, describe and compare their graphs. Be as specific as you can.

$y = 4^x \qquad y = 0.25^x \qquad y = 10(4^x) \qquad y = 10(0.25^x)$

Homework
Help Online
PHSchool.com
For: Help with Exercise 42
Web Code: ape-3542

43. Each graph below represents an exponential equation of the form $y = ab^x$.

  a. For which of the three functions is the value of a greatest?

  b. For which of the three functions is the value of b greatest?

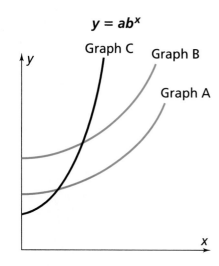

Connections

For Exercises 44 and 45, tell whether the statement is *true* or *false*. Do not do an exact calculation. Explain your reasoning.

44. $(1.56892 \times 10^5) - (2.3456 \times 10^4) < 0$

45. $\dfrac{3.96395 \times 10^5}{2.888211 \times 10^7} > 1$

46. Suppose you start with a unit cube (a cube with edges of length 1 unit). In parts (a)–(c), give the volume and surface area of the cube that results from the given transformation.

   a. Each edge length is doubled.

   b. Each edge length is tripled.

   c. Each edge is enlarged by a scale factor of 100.

47. Suppose you start with a cylinder with a radius of 1 unit and a height of 1 unit. In parts (a)–(c), give the volume of the cylinder that results from the given transformation.

   a. The radius and height are doubled.

   b. The radius and height are tripled.

   c. The radius and height are enlarged by a scale factor of 100.

48. a. Tell which of the following numbers are prime. (There may be more than one.)

   $2^2 - 1$ $2^3 - 1$ $2^4 - 1$ $2^5 - 1$ $2^6 - 1$

   b. Find another prime number that can be written in the form $2^n - 1$.

49. In parts (a)–(d), find the sum of the proper factors for the number.

   a. 2^2 **b.** 2^3 **c.** 2^4 **d.** 2^5

   e. What do you notice about the sums in parts (a)–(d)?

50. Grandville has a population of 1,000. Its population is expected to decrease by 4% a year for the next several years. Tinytown has a population of 100. Its population is expected to increase by 4% a year for the next several years. Will the populations of the two towns ever be the same? Explain.

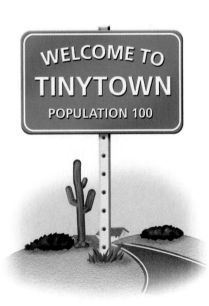

51. The expression $\frac{20}{10^2}$ can be written in equivalent forms, including $\frac{2}{10}$, $\frac{1}{5}$, 0.2, and $\frac{2(10^2)}{10^3}$. In parts (a) and (b), write two equivalent forms for the expression.

a. $\dfrac{3(10)^5}{10^7}$

b. $\dfrac{5(10)^5}{2.5(10)^7}$

Extensions

52. a. Find the sum for each row.

Row 1: $\frac{1}{2}$

Row 2: $\frac{1}{2} + \left(\frac{1}{2}\right)^2$

Row 3: $\frac{1}{2} + \left(\frac{1}{2}\right)^2 + \left(\frac{1}{2}\right)^3$

Row 4: $\frac{1}{2} + \left(\frac{1}{2}\right)^2 + \left(\frac{1}{2}\right)^3 + \left(\frac{1}{2}\right)^4$

b. Study the pattern. Suppose the pattern continues. Write the expression that would be in row 5, and find its sum.

c. What would be the sum of the expression in row 10? What would be the sum for row 20?

d. Describe the pattern of sums in words and with a symbolic expression.

e. For which row does the sum first exceed 0.9?

f. As the row number increases, the sum gets closer and closer to what number?

g. Celeste claims the pattern is related to the pattern of the areas of the ballots cut in Problem 4.1. She drew this picture to explain her thinking. What relationship do you think she has observed?

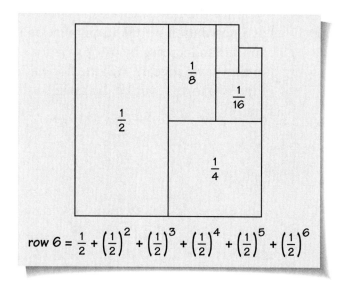

$$\text{row } 6 = \frac{1}{2} + \left(\frac{1}{2}\right)^2 + \left(\frac{1}{2}\right)^3 + \left(\frac{1}{2}\right)^4 + \left(\frac{1}{2}\right)^5 + \left(\frac{1}{2}\right)^6$$

53. a. Find the sum for each row.

Row 1: $\frac{1}{3}$

Row 2: $\frac{1}{3} + \left(\frac{1}{3}\right)^2$

Row 3: $\frac{1}{3} + \left(\frac{1}{3}\right)^2 + \left(\frac{1}{3}\right)^3$

Row 4: $\frac{1}{3} + \left(\frac{1}{3}\right)^2 + \left(\frac{1}{3}\right)^3 + \left(\frac{1}{3}\right)^4$

b. Study the pattern. Suppose the pattern continues. Write the expression that would be in row 5, and find its sum.

c. What would be the sum of the expression in row 10? What would be the sum for row 20?

d. Describe the pattern of sums in words and with an equation.

e. As the row number increases, the sum gets closer and closer to what number?

54. Negative numbers can be used as exponents. Parts (a) and (b) will help you understand negative exponents.

a. Use your calculator to find the value of 2^x for x-values $-1, -2,$ and -3.

b. Use your calculator to find the value of $\left(\frac{1}{2}\right)^x$ for x-values $1, 2,$ and 3.

c. What observation can you make from your computations in parts (a) and (b)?

d. Write each number as a power with a positive exponent.

3^{-1} $\qquad\qquad$ 4^{-2} $\qquad\qquad$ 5^{-3}

55. a. Copy and complete this table.

Standard Form	Exponential Form
10,000	10^4
1,000	10^3
100	10^2
10	10^1
1	10^0
$\frac{1}{10} = 0.1$	10^{-1}
$\frac{1}{100} = 0.01$	10^{-2}
$\frac{1}{1,000} = 0.001$	■
$\frac{1}{10,000} = 0.0001$	■
■	10^{-5}
■	10^{-6}

b. Write each number in standard form as a decimal.

3×10^{-1} 1.5×10^{-2} 1.5×10^{-3}

56. If you use your calculator to compute $2 \div 2^{12}$, the display will probably show one of the following:

Ч.8828125ᴇ ⁻Ч   or   Ч.8828125 ⁻Ч

Both displays mean 4.8828125×10^{-4}. This number is in scientific notation because it is a number greater than or equal to 1, but less than 10 (in this case, 4.8828125), times a power of 10 (in this case, 10^{-4}). You can convert 4.8828125×10^{-4} to standard form as shown:

$4.8828125 \times 10^{-4} = 4.8828125 \times \dfrac{1}{10,000} = 0.00048828125$

a. Write each number in standard notation.

1.2×10^{-1} 1.2×10^{-2} 1.2×10^{-3} 1.2×10^{-8}

b. Using what you discovered in part (a), explain how you would write 1.2×10^{-n} in standard notation where n is any whole number greater than or equal to 1.

c. Write each number in scientific notation.

2,000,000	28,000,000	19,900,000,000
0.12489	0.0058421998	0.0010201

57. When Tia found $0.0000015 \div 1{,}000{,}000$ on her calculator, she got 1.5E ‾12, which means 1.5×10^{-12}.

   a. Write a different division problem that will give the result 1.5E ‾12 on your calculator.

   b. Write a multiplication problem that will give the result 1.5E ‾12 on your calculator.

58. The average radius of the moon is 1.74×10^6 meters.

   a. Express the average radius of the moon in standard notation.

   b. The largest circle that will fit on this page has a radius of 10.795 cm. Express this radius in meters, using scientific notation.

   c. Suppose a circle has the same radius as the moon. By what scale factor would the circle have to be reduced to fit on this page?

59. The number 2^7 is written in standard form as 128 and in scientific notation as 1.28×10^2. The number $\left(\frac{1}{2}\right)^7$ is written in standard form as 0.0078125 and in scientific notation as 7.812×10^{-3}. Write each number in scientific notation.

   a. 2^8 **b.** $\left(\frac{1}{2}\right)^8$ **c.** 20^8 **d.** $\left(\frac{1}{20}\right)^8$

60. a. The y-values in the table below are decreasing by a factor of $\frac{1}{3}$. Copy and complete the table.

x	0	1	2	3	4	5	6	7	8
y	30	10	▦	▦	▦	▦	▦	▦	▦

   b. Using a calculator to find the y-value when x is 12 gives the result 5.645029269E ‾5. What does this mean?

   c. Write the y-values for $x = 8, 9, 10,$ and 11 in scientific notation.

61. Chen, from Problem 4.1, decides to make his ballots starting with a sheet of paper with an area of 1 square foot.

a. Copy and complete this table to show the area of each ballot after each of the first 8 cuts.

b. Write an equation for the area A of a ballot after any cut n.

c. Use your equation to find the area of a ballot after 20 cuts. Write your answer in scientific notation.

Number of Cuts	Area (ft^2)
0	1
1	$\frac{1}{2}$
2	$\frac{1}{4}$
3	■
4	■
5	■
6	■
7	■
8	■

62. In 1803, the U.S. bought the 828,000-square-mile Louisiana Purchase for $15,000,000. Suppose one of your ancestors was given 1 acre of the Louisiana Purchase. Assuming an annual inflation rate of 4%, what is the value of this acre in 2006? (640 acres = 1 square mile)

63. Use the properties of exponents to show that each statement is true.

a. $\frac{1}{2}(2^n) = 2^{n-1}$ **b.** $4^{n-1} = \frac{1}{4}(4)^n$ **c.** $25(5^{n-2}) = 5^n$

Mathematical Reflections 5

In this investigation, you explored properties of exponents and you looked at how the values of *a* and *b* affect the graph of $y = a(b^x)$.

Think about your answers to these questions. Discuss your ideas with other students and your teacher. Then, write a summary of your findings in your notebook.

1. Describe some of the rules for operating with exponents.

2. Assume *a* is a fixed positive number. Describe the graph of $y = a(b^x)$ if

   a. *b* is greater than 1.

   b. *b* is equal to 1.

   c. *b* is between 0 and 1.

3. Assume *b* is a fixed number greater than 1. Describe the graph of $y = a(b^x)$ if

   a. *a* is greater than 1.

   b. *a* is equal to 1.

   c. *a* is between 0 and 1.

Unit Project

Half-Life

Most things around you are composed of atoms that are stable. However, the atoms that make up *radioactive* substances are unstable—they break down in a process known as *radioactive decay*. As these substances decay, they emit radiation. At high levels, radiation can be dangerous.

The rate of decay varies from substance to substance. The term *half-life* describes the time it takes for half of the atoms in a radioactive sample to decay. For example, the half-life of carbon-11 is 20 minutes. This means that 2,000 carbon-11 atoms will be reduced to 1,000 carbon-11 atoms in 20 minutes, and to 500 carbon-11 atoms in 40 minutes.

Half-lives vary from a fraction of a second to billions of years. For example, the half-life of polonium-214 is 0.00016 seconds. The half-life of rubidium-87 is 49 billion years.

In this experiment, you will model the decay of a radioactive substance known as iodine-124. About $\frac{1}{6}$ of the atoms in a sample of iodine-124 decay each day. This experiment will help you determine the half-life of this substance.

Follow these steps to conduct your experiment:

- Use 100 cubes to represent 100 iodine-124 atoms. Mark one face of each cube.

- Place all 100 cubes in a container, shake the container, and pour the cubes onto the table.

- The cubes for which the mark is facing up represent atoms that have decayed on the first day. Remove these cubes, and record the number of cubes that remain. Place the remaining cubes in the container.

- Repeat this process to find the number of atoms that remain after the second day.

- Repeat this process until one cube or no cubes remain.

When you complete your experiment, answer the questions on the next page.

1. **a.** In your experiment, how many days did it take to reduce the 100 iodine-124 atoms to 50 atoms? In other words, how many times did you have to roll the cubes until about 50 cubes remained?

   b. How many days did it take to reduce 50 iodine-124 atoms to 25 atoms?

   c. Based on your answers to parts (a) and (b), what do you think the half-life of iodine-124 is?

2. **a.** In a sample of real iodine-124, $\frac{1}{6}$ of the atoms decay after 1 day. What fraction of the atoms remain after 1 day?

   b. Suppose a sample contains 100 iodine-124 atoms. Use your answer from part (a) to write an equation for the number of atoms n remaining in the sample after d days.

   c. Use your equation to find the half-life of iodine-124.

   d. How does the half-life you found based on your equation compare to the half-life you found from your experiment?

3. **a.** Make up a problem involving a radioactive substance with a different rate of decay that can be modeled by an experiment involving cubes or other common objects. Describe the situation and your experiment.

   b. Conduct your experiment and record your results.

   c. Use the results of your experiment to predict the half-life of your substance.

   d. Use what you know about the rate of decay to write an equation that models the decay of your substance.

   e. Use your equation to find the half-life of your substance.

Write a report summarizing your findings about decay rates and half-lives. Your report should include tables and graphs justifying your answers to the questions above.

Looking Back and Looking Ahead

Go Online
PHSchool.com

For: Vocabulary Review
Puzzle
Web Code: apj-3051

Working on the problems in this unit developed your skills in recognizing and applying *exponential relationships* between variables.

You wrote equations of the form $y = a(b^x)$ to describe *exponential growth* of populations and investments and *exponential decay* of medicines and radioactive materials. You used equations to produce tables and graphs of the relationships. You used those tables and graphs to make predictions and solve equations.

Use Your Understanding: Algebraic Reasoning

To test your understanding and skill in finding and applying exponential models, solve these problems that arise as the student council at Lincoln Middle School plans a fundraising event.

The students want to have a quiz show called *Who Wants to Be Rich?* Contestants will be asked a series of questions. A contestant will play until he or she misses a question. The total prize money will grow with each question answered correctly.

1. Lucy proposes that a contestant receive $5 for answering the first question correctly. For each additional correct answer, the total prize would increase by $10.

   a. For Lucy's proposal, what equation gives the total prize p for correctly answering n questions?

   b. How many questions would a contestant need to answer correctly to win at least $50? To win at least $75? To win at least $100?

   c. Sketch a graph of the (n, p) data for $n = 1$ to 10.

2. Pedro also thinks the first question should be worth $5. However, he thinks a contestant's winnings should double with each subsequent correct answer.

    a. For Pedro's proposal, what equation gives the total prize p for correctly answering n questions?

    b. How many questions will a contestant need to answer correctly to win at least $50? To win at least $75? To win at least $100?

    c. Sketch a graph of the (n, p) data for $n = 1$ to 10.

    d. Compare Pedro's proposal with Lucy's proposal in Exercise 1.

3. The council decides that contestants for *Who Wants to Be Rich?* will be chosen by a random drawing. Students and guests at the fundraiser will buy tickets like the one at right. The purchaser will keep half of the ticket and add the other half to the entries for the drawing.

    a. To make the tickets, council members will take a large piece of paper and fold it in half many times to make a grid of small rectangles. How many rectangles will there be after n folds?

    b. The initial piece of paper will be a square with sides measuring 60 centimeters. What will be the area of each rectangle after n folds?

Decide whether each statement is *true* or *false*. Explain.

    4. $3^5 \times 6^5 = 9^5$ **5.** $8^5 \times 4^6 = 2^{27}$ **6.** $\dfrac{2^0 \times 6^7}{3^7} = 2^7$

Explain Your Reasoning

To answer Questions 1–3, you had to use algebraic knowledge about number patterns, graphs, and equations. You had to recognize linear and exponential patterns from verbal descriptions and represent those patterns with equations and graphs.

7. How can you decide whether a data pattern can be modeled by an exponential equation of the form $y = a(b^x)$? How will the values of a and b relate to the data pattern?

8. Describe the possible shapes for graphs of exponential relationships. How can the shape of an exponential graph be predicted from the values of a and b in the equation?

9. How are the data patterns, graphs, and equations for exponential relationships similar to and different from those for linear relationships?

10. Describe the rules for exponents that you used in Questions 4–6. Choose one of the rules and explain why it works.

Look Ahead

The algebraic ideas and techniques you developed and used in this unit will be applied and extended in future units of *Connected Mathematics* and in problems of science and business. In upcoming units, you will study other important families of algebraic models and you will learn strategies for finding and using those models to solve problems.

B

base The number that is raised to a power in an exponential expression. In the expression 3^5, read "3 to the fifth power", 5 is the exponent and 3 is the base.

base El número que se eleva a una potencia en una expresión exponencial. En la expresión 3^5, que se lee "3 elevado a la quinta potencia", 3 es la base y 5 es el exponente.

C

compound growth Another term for exponential growth, usually used when talking about the monetary value of an investment. The change in the balance of a savings account shows compound growth because the bank pays interest not only on the original investment, but on the interest earned.

crecimiento compuesto Otro término para crecimiento exponencial, normalmente usado para referirse al valor monetario de una inversión. El cambio en el saldo de una cuenta de ahorros muestra un crecimiento compuesto, ya que el banco paga intereses no sólo sobre la inversión original, sino sobre los intereses ganados.

D

decay factor The constant factor that each value in an exponential decay pattern is multiplied by to get the next value. The decay factor is the base in an exponential decay equation. For example, in the equation $A = 64(0.5)n$, where A is the area of a ballot and n is the number of cuts, the decay factor is 0.5. It indicates that the area of a ballot after any number of cuts is 0.5 times the area after the previous number of cuts. In a table of (x, y) values for an exponential decay relationship (with x-values increasing by 1), the decay factor is the ratio of any y-value to the previous y-value.

factor de disminución El factor constante por el cual se multiplica cada valor en un patrón de disminución exponencial para obtener el valor siguiente. El factor de disminución es la base en una ecuación de disminución exponencial. Por ejemplo, en la ecuación $A = 64(0.5)n$, donde A es el área de una papeleta y n es el número de cortes, el factor de disminución es 0.5. Esto indica que el área de una papeleta después de un número cualquiera de cortes es 0.5 veces el área después del número anterior de cortes. En una tabla de valores (x, y) para una relación de disminución exponencial (donde el valor x crece de a 1), el factor de disminución es la razón entre cualquier valor de y y su valor anterior.

decay rate The percent decrease in an exponential decay pattern. A discount, expressed as a percent, is a decay rate. In general, for an exponential pattern with decay factor b, the decay rate is $1 - b$.

tasa de disminución El porcentaje de reducción en un patrón de disminución exponencial. Un descuento, expresado como porcentaje, es una tasa de disminución. En general, para un patrón exponencial con factor de disminución b, la tasa de disminución es $1 - b$.

exponent A number that indicates how many times another number (the base) is to be used as a factor. Exponents are written as raised numbers to the right of the base. In the expression 3^5, read "3 to the fifth power", 5 is the exponent and 3 is the base, so 3^5 means $3 \cdot 3 \cdot 3 \cdot 3 \cdot 3$. In the formula for the area of a square, $A = s^2$, the 2 is an exponent. This formula can also be written as $A = s \cdot s$.

exponente Es un número que indica la cantidad de veces que otro número (la base) se va a usar como factor. Los exponentes se escriben como números elevados a la derecha de la base. En la expresión 3^5, que se lee como "3 elevado a la quinta potencia", 5 es el exponente y 3 es la base. Así, 3^5 significa $3 \cdot 3 \cdot 3 \cdot 3 \cdot 3$. En la fórmula para calcular el área de un cuadrado, $A = s^2$, el 2 es un exponente. Esta fórmula también se puede escribir como $A = s \cdot s$.

exponential decay A pattern of decrease in which each value is found by multiplying the previous value by a constant factor greater than 0 and less than 1. For example, the pattern $27, 9, 3, 1, \frac{1}{3}, \frac{1}{9}, \ldots$ shows exponential decay in which each value is $\frac{1}{3}$ times the previous value.

disminución exponencial Un patrón de disminución en el cual cada valor se calcula multiplicando el valor anterior por un factor constante mayor que 0 y menor que 1. Por ejemplo, el patrón $27, 9, 3, 1, \frac{1}{3}, \frac{1}{9}, \ldots$ muestra una disminución exponencial en la que cada valor es $\frac{1}{3}$ del valor anterior.

exponential form A quantity expressed as a number raised to a power. In exponential form, 32 can be written as 2^5.

forma exponencial Una cantidad que se expresa como un número elevado a una potencia. En forma exponencial, 32 puede escribirse como 2^5.

exponential growth A pattern of increase in which each value is found by multiplying the previous value by a constant factor greater than 1. For example, the doubling pattern $1, 2, 4, 8, 16, 32, \ldots$ shows exponential growth in which each value is 2 times the previous value.

crecimiento exponencial Un patrón de crecimiento en el cual cada valor se calcula multiplicando el valor anterior por un factor constante mayor que 1. Por ejemplo, el patrón $1, 2, 4, 8, 16, 32, \ldots$ muestra un crecimiento exponencial en el que cada valor es el doble del valor anterior.

exponential relationship A relationship that shows exponential growth or decay.

relación exponencial Una relación que muestra crecimiento o disminución exponencial.

growth factor The constant factor that each value in an exponential growth pattern is multiplied by to get the next value. The growth factor is the base in an exponential growth equation. For example, in the equation $A = 25(3)^d$, where A is the area of a patch of mold and d is the number of days, the growth factor is 3. It indicates that the area of the mold for any day is 3 times the area for the previous day. In a table of (x, y) values for an exponential growth relationship (with x-values increasing by 1), the growth factor is the ratio of any y-value to the previous y-value.

factor de crecimiento El factor constante por el cual se multiplica cada valor en un patrón de crecimiento exponencial para obtener el valor siguiente. El factor de crecimiento es la base en una ecuación de crecimiento exponencial. Por ejemplo, en la ecuación $A = 25(3)^d$, donde A es el área enmohecida y d es el número de días, el factor de crecimiento es 3. Esto indica que el área enmohecida en un día cualquiera es 3 veces el área del día anterior. En una tabla de valores (x, y) para una relación de crecimiento exponencial (donde el valor de x aumenta de a 1), el factor exponencial es la razón entre cualquier valor de y y su valor anterior.

growth rate The percent increase in an exponential growth pattern. For example, in Problem 3.1, the number of rabbits increased from 100 to 180 from year 0 to year 1, an 80% increase. From year 1 to year 2, the number of rabbits increased from 180 to 324, an 80% increase. The growth rate for this rabbit population is 80%. Interest, expressed as a percent, is a growth rate. For an exponential growth pattern with a growth factor of b, the growth rate is $b - 1$.

tasa de crecimiento El porcentaje de crecimiento en un patrón de crecimiento exponencial. Por ejemplo, en el Problema 3.1, el número de conejos aumentó de 100 a 180 del año 0 al año 1, un aumento del 80%. Del año 1 al año 2, el número de conejos aumentó de 180 a 324, un aumento del 80%. La tasa de crecimiento para esta población de conejos es del 80%. El interés, expresado como porcentaje, es una tasa de crecimiento. Para un patrón de crecimiento exponencial con un factor de crecimiento b, la tasa de crecimiento es $b - 1$.

scientific notation A short way to write very large or very small numbers. A number is in scientific notation if it is of the form $a \times 10^n$, where n is an integer and $1 \le a < 10$.

notación científica Una manera corta de escribir números muy grandes o muy pequeños. Un número está e notación científica si está en la forma $a \times 10^n$, donde n es un entero y $1 \le a < 10$.

standard form The most common way we express quantities. For example, 27 is the standard form of 3^3.

forma normal La manera más común de expresar una cantidad. Por ejemplo, 27 es la forma normal de 3^3.

Index

Area model, 5, 11, 29–30, 43, 48, 68

Base
definition, 6, 79
two as a, 6–7, 59–60, 65

Calculator
evaluating exponential expressions with, 6, 46
graphing exponential equations, 63
scientific notation and, 17, 70–71
using, 6, 17, 46, 63, 64, 69–71

Check for reasonableness, 20, 64

Compare
equations, 21, 25, 37, 51, 63, 78
graphs, 9–10, 15, 21, 39, 50, 52, 53, 57, 63, 66, 73, 78
tables, 53

Compound growth, 35–37
ACE, 39–41, 43–46, 72
definition, 37, 79
equation for, 36–37, 39, 45, 72
inflation rate, 40, 45, 72
investing, 35–37, 39, 41, 45–46

Concrete model, *see* **Model**

Decay factor, 49–52
ACE, 54–57
decay rate and, 51
definition, 49, 51, 79

Decay pattern, 48–52, 58, 74–75
ACE, 53–57
area and cuts, 48–49, 53, 77, 79
breakdown of medicine, 50–51, 54
cooling water, 51–52, 55
linear, 53
population, 67
radioactive decay, 74–75

Decay rate, definition, 51, 79

Diagram, 5, 11–12, 29–30, 43, 48, 68

Equation
ACE, 11–18, 24–31, 38–46, 53–57, 64–72

comparing, 21, 25, 37, 51, 63, 78
for compound growth, 36–37, 39, 45, 72
for exponential decay, 49–52, 53–69, 72, 73, 75, 78
for exponential growth, 6–10, 11–46, 59–64, 66, 73, 77–78
graphing exponential, 7–9, 12–13, 15–16, 20–21, 23, 27–29, 31–32, 42, 49–55, 57–58, 63, 66, 73, 75, 77–78
writing, 7, 9–10, 12–16, 18, 21, 23, 24–26, 28–31, 32, 34, 36–37, 38–39, 44–45, 49–50, 52, 53–57, 59, 61–62, 68–69, 71–72, 75, 76–77

Experiment
cooling water, 51–52
cutting ballots, 11
half-life, 74–75

Exponent
definition, 6, 80
calculator key for, 6, 46
negative, 69

Exponential decay, 48–52, 58, 74–75
ACE, 53–57
definition, 49, 80
equation for, 49–52, 53–69, 72, 73, 75, 78
graph of, 50, 54
halving, 48–49, 53
rate, 50–52, 79

Exponential form, definition, 6, 80

Exponential growth, 5–47, 59–73, 76–78
ACE, 11–18, 24–31, 38–46, 64–72
definition, 8, 80
doubling, 5–7, 12–13, 20–21, 77
equation for, 6–10, 11–46, 59–64, 66, 73, 77–78
fractional growth factors and, 33–37, 38–46, 47
graph of, 8, 15, 23, 27–28, 30, 42, 66
starting value and, 10, 47

two as a base, 6–7, 59–60, 65
whole number growth factors and, 5–32

Exponential relationship, definition, 8, 80

Glossary, 79–81

Graph, 7–10, 21, 23, 32, 42, 49–50, 52, 63, 73, 75–78
ACE, 12–13, 15, 27–31, 53–55, 57, 66
comparing, 9–10, 15, 21, 39, 50, 52, 53, 57, 63, 66, 73, 78
of exponential decay, 50, 54
of exponential equations on a graphing calculator, 63
of exponential growth, 8, 15, 23, 27–28, 30, 42, 66
making, 7, 9, 12–13, 21, 31, 49, 52, 53, 55, 57, 63, 75, 76–77

Growth factor, 8–9, 20–23, 33–37, 47
ACE, 11–18, 24–31, 38–46
definition, 8, 81
percent change and, 35–37, 40–41, 43–46, 47
whole number, 5–32

Growth pattern, 4–47, 59–78
ACE, 11–18, 24–31, 38–46, 64–72
bread mold, 22
cutting paper in half, 16
doubling money, 25, 31, 77
fractional growth factors and, 33–37, 38–46, 47
investment, 35–37, 39, 41, 45–46
linear, 10, 14–15, 19, 29, 44, 78
plant spread, 20–21, 24
population, 23, 25–28, 33–35, 39–41, 45, 47
starting value and, 10, 47
whole number growth factors and, 5–32

Growth rate, 33, 35–37, 47
ACE, 40–41, 44–46
definition, 35, 81

Half-life, 74–75

Acknowledgments

Team Credits

The people who made up the **Connected Mathematics 2** team—representing editorial, editorial services, design services, and production services—are listed below. Bold type denotes core team members.

Leora Adler, Judith Buice, Kerry Cashman, Patrick Culleton, Sheila DeFazio, Katie Hallahan, Richard Heater, **Barbara Hollingdale, Jayne Holman,** Karen Holtzman, **Etta Jacobs,** Christine Lee, Carolyn Lock, Catherine Maglio, **Dotti Marshall,** Rich McMahon, Eve Melnechuk, Kristin Mingrone, Terri Mitchell, **Marsha Novak,** Irene Rubin, Donna Russo, Robin Samper, Siri Schwartzman, **Nancy Smith,** Emily Soltanoff, **Mark Tricca,** Paula Vergith, Roberta Warshaw, Helen Young

Additional Credits

Diana Bonfilio, Mairead Reddin, Michael Torocsik, nSight, Inc.

Technical Illustration

WestWords, Inc.

Cover Design

tom white.images

Photos

2 t, Jacques Jangoux/Alamy; **2 b,** (ZF) Virgo/Corbis; **3 t,** Inga Spence/Visuals Unlimited; **3 b,** AP Photo/Chuck Burton; **13,** Dr. Stanley Flegler/Visuals Unlimited; **14,** Tim Pannell/Masterfile; **21,** Nicolas Granier/Peter Arnold, Inc.; **21 inset,** Jacques Jangoux/Alamy; **22,** Photodisc/Getty Images, Inc.; **23,** Sheldon, Allen Blake/Animals Animals-Earth Scenes; **25,** Wolfgang Kaehler/Corbis; **26,** David Young-Wolff/PhotoEdit; **33,** Steve Maslowski/Visuals Unlimited; **34,** Geoff Dann/Dorling Kindersley; **35,** Topham/The Image Works; **36 t,** (ZF) Virgo/Corbis; **36 b,** Steve Allen/AGE Fotostock; **38,** Michael Wickes/The Image Works; **40,** Creatas/AGE Fotostock; **41,** DK Limited/Corbis; **43,** David Young-Wolff/PhotoEdit; **44,** George Disario/Corbis; **48,** Tony Freeman/PhotoEdit; **52,** Richard Smith/Masterfile; **57,** Saxpix.com/AGE Fotostock; **61,** Richard Haynes; **65,** Richard Haynes; **69,** Tony Freeman/PhotoEdit; **71,** Design Pics Inc./Alamy

Connected Mathematics 2

Frogs, Fleas, and Painted Cubes

Quadratic Relationships

Glenda Lappan

James T. Fey

William M. Fitzgerald

Susan N. Friel

Elizabeth Difanis Phillips

PEARSON

Prentice
Hall

Boston, Massachusetts
Upper Saddle River, New Jersey

Frogs, Fleas, and Painted Cubes

Quadratic Relationships

Suppose you travel to Mars to prospect a precious metal. You can claim any rectangular piece of land you can surround by 20 meters of laser fencing. How should you arrange your fencing to enclose the maximum area?

After a victory, team members exchange high fives. How many high fives are exchanged among a team with 5 players? With 6 players? With *n* players?

A ball is thrown into the air. Its height *h* in feet after *t* seconds is modeled by the equation $h = -16t^2 + 64t$. What is the maximum height the ball reaches? When does it reach this height?

Mathematics is useful for solving practical problems in science, business, engineering, and economics. In earlier units, you studied problems that could be modeled with linear or exponential relationships. In this unit, you will explore quadratic relationships. Quadratic relationships are found in many interesting situations, such as the path of flares and rockets launched from the ground as well as the situations on the previous page.

Mathematical Highlights

Quadratic Relationships

In *Frogs, Fleas, and Painted Cubes,* you will explore quadratic functions, an important type of nonlinear relationship.

You will learn how to

- Recognize patterns of change for quadratic relationships

- Write equations for quadratic relationships represented in tables, graphs, and problem situations

- Connect quadratic equations to the patterns in tables and graphs of quadratic relationships

- Use a quadratic equation to identify the maximum or minimum value, the *x*- and *y*-intercepts, and other important features of the graph of the equation

- Recognize equivalent quadratic expressions

- Use the Distributive Property to write equivalent quadratic expressions in factored and expanded form

- Use tables, graphs, and equations of quadratic relationships to solve problems in a variety of situations from geometry, science, and business

- Compare properties of quadratic, linear, and exponential relationships

As you work on problems in this unit, ask yourself questions about problem situations that involve nonlinear relationships:

What are the variables?

How can I recognize whether the relationship between the variables is quadratic?

What equation models a quadratic relationship in a table, graph, or problem context?

How can I answer questions about the situation by studying a table, graph, or equation of the quadratic relationship?

Investigation 1

Introduction to Quadratic Relationships

In January of 1848, gold was discovered near Sacramento, California. By the spring of that year, a great gold rush had begun, bringing 250,000 new residents to California.

Throughout history, people have moved to particular areas of the world with hopes of improving their lives.

- In 1867, prospectors headed to South Africa in search of diamonds.
- From 1860 to 1900, farmers headed to the American prairie where land was free.
- The 1901 Spindletop oil gusher brought drillers by the thousands to eastern Texas.

Prospectors and farmers had to stake claims on the land they wanted to work.

1.1 Staking a Claim

Suppose it is the year 2100, and a rare and precious metal has just been discovered on Mars. You and hundreds of other adventurers travel to the planet to stake your claim. You are allowed to claim any rectangular piece of land that can be surrounded by 20 meters of laser fencing. You want to arrange your fencing to enclose the maximum area possible.

Problem 1.1 Maximizing Area

A. Sketch several rectangles with a fixed perimeter of 20 meters. Include some with small areas and some with large areas. Label the dimensions of each rectangle.

B. Make a table showing the length, width, and area for every rectangle with a perimeter of 20 meters and whole-number side lengths. Describe some patterns that you observe in the table.

C. Make a graph of the (*length, area*) data. Describe the shape of the graph.

D. 1. What rectangle dimensions give the greatest possible area? Explain.

    2. Suppose the dimensions were not restricted to whole numbers. Would this change your answer? Explain.

For: Stat Tools
Visit: PHSchool.com
Web Code: apd-4101

ACE Homework starts on page 11.

1.2 Reading Graphs and Tables

The relationship between length and area in Problem 1.1 is a **quadratic relationship.** Quadratic relationships are characterized by their U-shaped graphs, which are called **parabolas.**

In Problem 1.1, the area depends on, or is a *function* of, the length. Recall that a relationship in which one variable depends on another is a **function.** In this case, the relationship is a quadratic function. A more precise definition of functions will be discussed in later mathematics courses.

Many of the relationships you studied in earlier units are functions. For example,

- The distance covered by a van traveling at a constant speed is a function of time. The relationship between time and distance is a linear function.

- The value of an investment that grows at 4% per year is a function of the number of years. The relationship between the number of years and the value is an exponential function.

You have learned about the characteristics of the tables, graphs, and equations of linear and exponential functions. As you explore quadratic functions in this unit, look for common patterns in the tables, graphs, and equations.

The graph and table show length and area data for rectangles with a certain fixed perimeter.

A. 1. Describe the shape of the graph and any special features you see.

2. What is the greatest area possible for a rectangle with this perimeter? What are the dimensions of this rectangle?

3. What is the area of the rectangle whose length is 10 meters? What is the area of the rectangle whose length is 30 meters? How are these rectangles related?

4. What are the dimensions of the rectangle with an area of 175 square meters?

5. What is the fixed perimeter for the rectangles represented by the graph? Explain how you found the perimeter.

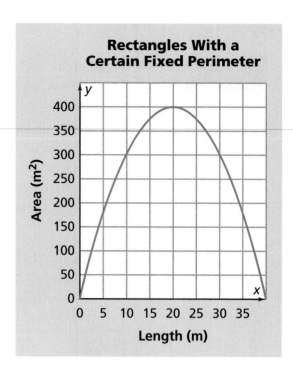

Rectangles With a Certain Fixed Perimeter

B. Use the table to answer parts (1)–(5).

1. What patterns do you observe in the table? Compare these patterns with those you observed in the graph in Question A.

2. What is the fixed perimeter for the rectangles represented by this table? Explain.

3. What is the greatest area possible for a rectangle with this perimeter? What are the dimensions of this rectangle?

4. Estimate the dimensions of a rectangle with this fixed perimeter and an area of 16 square meters.

5. Suppose a rectangle with this perimeter has an area of 35.5 square meters. What are its dimensions?

ACE Homework starts on page 11.

Rectangles With a Certain Fixed Perimeter

Length (m)	Area (m²)
0	0
1	11
2	20
3	27
4	32
5	35
6	36
7	35
8	32
9	27
10	20
11	11
12	0

1.3 Writing an Equation

$\mathbf{Y}$ou used tables and graphs to represent relationships between length and area for rectangles with fixed perimeters. In this problem, you will write equations for these relationships.

Getting Ready for Problem 1.3

You know that the formula for the area A of a rectangle with length ℓ and width w is $A = \ell w$ and the formula for perimeter P is $P = 2\ell + 2w$.

The rectangle below has a perimeter of 20 meters and a length of ℓ meters.

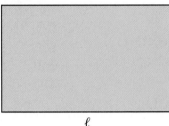

- Use the fixed perimeter to express the width of this rectangle in terms of ℓ.
- Write an equation for the area using A and ℓ as the only variables.

A. Consider rectangles with a perimeter of 60 meters.

    1. Sketch a rectangle to represent this situation. Label one side ℓ. Express the width in terms of ℓ.

    2. Write an equation for the area A in terms of ℓ.

    3. Use a calculator to make a table for your equation. Use your table to estimate the maximum area. What dimensions correspond to this area?

    4. Use a calculator or data from your table to help you sketch a graph of the relationship between length and area.

    5. How can you use your graph to find the maximum area possible? How does your graph show the length that corresponds to the maximum area?

B. The equation for the areas of rectangles with a certain fixed perimeter is $A = \ell(35 - \ell)$, where ℓ is the length in meters.

    1. Draw a rectangle to represent this situation. Label one side ℓ. Label the other sides in terms of ℓ.

    2. Make a table showing the length, width, and area for lengths of 0, 5, 10, 15, 20, 25, 30, and 35 meters. What patterns do you see?

    3. Describe the graph of this equation.

    4. What is the maximum area? What dimensions correspond to this maximum area? Explain.

    5. Describe two ways you could find the fixed perimeter. What is the perimeter?

C. Suppose you know the perimeter of a rectangle. How can you write an equation for the area in terms of the length of a side?

D. Study the graphs, tables, and equations for areas of rectangles with fixed perimeters. Which representation is most useful for finding the maximum area? Which is most useful for finding the fixed perimeter?

active math **online**

For: Algebra Tools
Visit: PHSchool.com
Web Code: apd-4103

ACE Homework starts on page 11.

Applications

1. Find the maximum area for a rectangle with a perimeter of 120 meters. Make your answer convincing by including these things:

   - Sketches of rectangles with a perimeter of 120 meters (Include rectangles that do not have the maximum area and the rectangle you think does have the maximum area.)

   - A table of lengths and areas for rectangles with a perimeter of 120 meters (Use increments of 5 meters for the lengths.)

   - A graph of the relationship between length and area

   Explain how each piece of evidence supports your answer.

2. What is the maximum area for a rectangle with a perimeter of 130 meters? As in Exercise 1, support your answer with sketches, a table, and a graph.

3. The graph shows the length and area of rectangles with a fixed perimeter. Use the graph for parts (a)–(e).

   a. Describe the shape of the graph and any special features.

   b. What is the maximum area for a rectangle with this fixed perimeter? What are the dimensions of this rectangle?

   c. Is there a rectangle with the least possible area? Explain.

   d. What is the area of a rectangle with a length of 3 centimeters?

   e. Describe two ways to find the fixed perimeter for the rectangles represented by the graph.

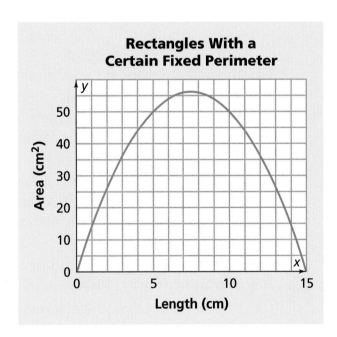

Rectangles With a Certain Fixed Perimeter

4. A farm wants to add a small, rectangular petting zoo for the public. They have a fixed amount of fencing to use for the zoo. This graph shows the lengths and areas of the rectangles they can make.

Rectangular Petting Zoos

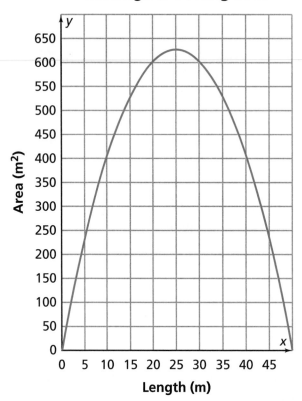

a. Describe the shape of the graph and any special features you observe.

b. What is the greatest area possible for a rectangle with this perimeter? What are the dimensions of this rectangle?

c. What is the area of the rectangle with a length of 10 meters? What is the area of the rectangle with a length of 40 meters? How are these rectangles related?

d. What are the dimensions of the rectangle with an area of 600 square meters?

e. What is the fixed amount of fencing available for the petting zoo? Explain.

5. The lifeguards at a beach want to place a rectangular boundary around the swimming area that can be used for water basketball. They have a fixed amount of rope to make the boundary. They use the table at the right to look at possible arrangements.

a. What patterns do you observe in the table?

b. What is the fixed perimeter for the possible swimming areas?

c. Sketch a graph of the (*length, area*) data. Describe the shape of the graph.

d. Suppose the lifeguards make a rectangle with an area of 11.5 square meters. What are the dimensions of the rectangle?

e. The lifeguards want to enclose the greatest area possible. What should be the dimensions of the swimming area?

Rectangular Swimming Area

Length (m)	Area (m²)
1	15
2	28
3	39
4	48
5	55
6	60
7	63
8	64
9	63
10	60
11	55
12	48
13	39
14	28
15	15

6. a. A rectangle has a perimeter of 30 meters and a side length of ℓ. Express the lengths of the other sides of the rectangle in terms of ℓ.

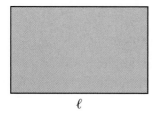

ℓ

b. Write an equation for the area A in terms of ℓ.

c. Make a graph of your equation and describe its shape.

d. Use your equation to find the area of the rectangle with a length of 10 meters.

e. How could you find the area in part (d) by using your graph?

f. How could you find the area in part (d) by using a table?

g. What is the maximum area possible for a rectangle with a perimeter of 30 meters? What are the dimensions of this rectangle?

7. a. A rectangle has a perimeter of 50 meters and a side length of ℓ. Express the lengths of the other sides of the rectangle in terms of ℓ.

b. Write an equation for the area A in terms of ℓ.

c. Sketch a graph of your equation and describe its shape.

d. Use your equation to find the area of the rectangle with a length of 10 meters.

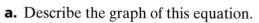

e. How could you find the area in part (d) by using your graph?

f. How could you find the area in part (d) by using a table?

g. What is the maximum area possible for a rectangle with a perimeter of 50 meters? What are the dimensions of this rectangle?

8. The equation for the areas of rectangles with a certain fixed perimeter is $A = \ell(20 - \ell)$, where ℓ is the length in meters.

Homework Help Online
PHSchool.com

For: Help with Exercise 8
Web Code: ape-4108

a. Describe the graph of this equation.

b. What is the maximum area for a rectangle with this perimeter? What dimensions correspond to this area? Explain.

c. A rectangle with this perimeter has a length of 15 meters. What is its area?

d. Describe two ways you can find the perimeter. What is the perimeter?

9. a. Copy and complete the graph to show areas for rectangles with a certain fixed perimeter and lengths greater than 3 meters.

b. Make a table of data for this situation.

c. What is the maximum area for a rectangle with this perimeter? What are the dimensions of this rectangle?

10. Multiple Choice Which equation describes the graph in Exercise 9?

A. $A = \ell(\ell - 6)$ **B.** $A = \ell(12 - \ell)$

C. $A = \ell(6 - \ell)$ **D.** $A = \ell(3 - \ell)$

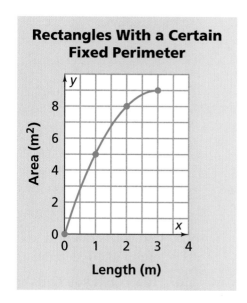

Rectangles With a Certain Fixed Perimeter

11. a. Copy and complete the table to show areas for rectangles with a certain fixed perimeter and lengths greater than 4 m.

b. Make a graph of the relationship between length and area.

c. What are the dimensions of the rectangle with the maximum area?

12. Multiple Choice Which equation describes the table in Exercise 11?

F. $A = \ell(8 - \ell)$ **G.** $A = \ell(16 - \ell)$

H. $A = \ell(4 - \ell)$ **J.** $A = \ell(\ell - 8)$

Rectangles With a Certain Fixed Perimeter

Length (m)	Area (m²)
0	0
1	7
2	12
3	15
4	16
5	▨
6	▨
7	▨
8	▨

13. The equation $p = d(100 - d)$ gives the monthly profit p a photographer will earn if she charges d dollars for each print.

a. Make a table and a graph for this equation.

b. Estimate the price that will produce the maximum profit. Explain.

c. How are the table and graph for this situation similar to those you made in Problem 1.1? How are they different?

Connections

14. Of all the rectangles with whole-number side lengths and an area of 20 square centimeters, which has the least perimeter? Explain.

15. **Multiple Choice** What does $2(-3 + 5) + 7 \times -4 + -1$ equal?

    A. -45 **B.** -31 **C.** -55 **D.** -25

16. Eduardo's neighborhood association subdivided a large rectangular field into two playing fields as shown in the diagram.

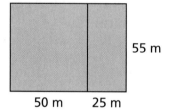

    a. Write expressions showing two ways you could calculate the area of the large field.

    b. Use the diagram and your expressions in part (a) to explain the Distributive Property.

For Exercises 17–20, use the Distributive Property to write the expression in expanded form. Then, simplify.

17. $21(5 + 6)$ **18.** $2(35 + 1)$ **19.** $12(10 - 2)$ **20.** $9(3 + 5)$

For Exercises 21–23, use the Distributive Property to write the expression in factored form.

21. $15 + 6$ **22.** $42 + 27$ **23.** $12 + 120$

Go Online
PHSchool.com

For: Multiple-Choice Skills Practice
Web Code: apa-4154

For Exercises 24 and 25, solve each equation for x.

24. $5x - 30 = 95$ **25.** $22 + 4x = 152 - 9x$

For Exercises 26 and 27,

- **Describe the pattern of change for the relationship.**
- **Describe how the pattern of change would look in a graph and in a table. Give as many details as you can without making a graph or table.**

26. $y = 5x + 12$ **27.** $y = 10 - 3x$

28. A rectangular field has a perimeter of 300 yards. The equation $\ell = 150 - w$ represents the relationship between the length ℓ and width w of the field.

    a. Explain why the equation is correct.

    b. Is the relationship between length and width quadratic? Explain.

c. Suppose a field is a nonrectangular parallelogram with a perimeter of 300 yards. Is the relationship between the lengths of adjacent sides the same as it is for the rectangular field?

d. Suppose a field is a quadrilateral that is not a parallelogram. The perimeter of the field is 300 yards. Is the relationship between the lengths of adjacent sides the same as it is for the rectangular field?

29. Mr. DeAngelo is designing a school building. The music room floor will be a rectangle with an area of 1,200 square feet.

a. Make a table with ten rows showing a range of possible lengths and widths for the music room floor.

b. Add a column to your table for the perimeter of each rectangle.

c. What patterns do you see in the perimeter column? What kinds of rectangles have large perimeters? What kinds have smaller perimeters?

d. Write an equation you can use to calculate the length of the floor for any given width.

Extensions

30. A beach has a rectangular swimming area for toddlers. One side of the swimming area is the shore. Buoys and a rope with a length of 20 meters are used to form the other three sides.

a. How should the rope be arranged to create a rectangle with the maximum area?

b. In Problem 1.1, a fixed perimeter of 20 meters is also used to form a rectangle. Compare the rectangle with maximum area in that problem to the rectangle with maximum area in part (a). Are the shapes and areas of the rectangles the same? Explain.

c. Make a graph relating the length and area for the possible rectangular swimming areas. How does the graph compare with the graph from Problem 1.1?

Mathematical Reflections 1

In this investigation, you looked at the relationship between length and area for rectangles with a fixed perimeter. You learned that this relationship is a quadratic function. The following questions will help you summarize what you have learned.

Think about your answers to these questions. Discuss your ideas with other students and your teacher. Then, write a summary of your findings in your notebook.

1. **a.** Describe the characteristics of graphs and tables of quadratic functions you have observed so far.

   b. How do the patterns in a graph of a quadratic function appear in the table of values for the function?

2. Describe two ways to find the maximum area for rectangles with a fixed perimeter.

3. How are tables, graphs, and equations for quadratic functions different from those for linear and exponential functions?

Investigation **2**

Quadratic Expressions

Suppose you give a friend two $1 bills, and your friend gives you eight quarters. You would consider this a fair trade. Sometimes it is not this easy to determine whether a trade is fair.

 Trading Land

Getting Ready for Problem

- A developer has purchased all of the land on a mall site except for one square lot. The lot measures 125 meters on each side. In exchange for the lot, the developer offers its owner a lot on another site. The plan for this lot is shown below. Do you think this is a fair trade?

125 m

125 m

225 m

25 m

lot offered by the developer

lot on mall site

In this problem, you will look at a trade situation. See if you can find a pattern that will help you make predictions about more complex situations.

Problem 2.1 Representing Areas of Rectangles

Suppose you trade a square lot for a rectangular lot. The length of the rectangular lot is 2 meters greater than the side length of the square lot, and the width is 2 meters less.

A. 1. Copy and complete the table.

Original Square		New Rectangle			Difference in Areas (m²)
Side Length (m)	Area (m²)	Length (m)	Width (m)	Area (m²)	
2	4	4	0	0	4
3	9	5	1	5	4
4	▦	▦	▦	▦	▦
5	▦	▦	▦	▦	▦
6	▦	▦	▦	▦	▦
n	▦	▦	▦	▦	▦

2. Explain why the table starts with a side length of 2 meters, rather than 0 meters or 1 meter.

3. For each side length, tell how the areas of the new and original lots compare. For which side lengths, if any, is the trade fair?

B. 1. Write an equation for the relationship between the side length n and the area A_1 of the original lot.

2. Write an equation for the relationship between the side length n of the original lot and the area A_2 of the new lot.

3. Carl claims there are two different expressions for the area of the new lot. Is this possible? Explain.

C. 1. On the same axes, sketch graphs of the area equations for both lots. For the independent variable, show values from -10 to 10. For the dependent variable, show values from -10 to 30.

2. For each graph, tell which part of the graph makes sense for the situation.

3. Describe any similarities and differences in the two graphs.

D. Are either of the relationships quadratic relationships? Explain.

ACE **Homework starts on page 30.**

Changing One Dimension

The expression $(n - 2)(n + 2)$ is in **factored form** because it is written as a product of factors. The expression $n^2 - 4$ is in **expanded form** because it is written as the sum or difference of terms. A **term** is an expression that consists of variables and/or numbers multiplied together. Specifically, $n^2 - 4$ is the difference of the terms n^2 and 4.

The expressions $(n - 2)(n + 2)$ and $n^2 - 4$ are *equivalent*. This means $(n - 2)(n + 2) = n^2 - 4$ is true for every value of n.

Getting Ready for Problem 2.2

A square has sides of lengths x centimeters. One dimension of the square is increased by 3 centimeters to create a new rectangle.

- How do the areas of the square and the new rectangle compare?

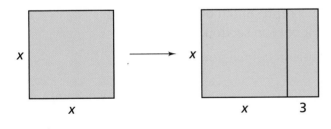

- Write two expressions for the area of the new rectangle. How do you know that the expressions are equivalent?

The expressions $x(x + 3)$ and $x^2 + 3x$ are examples of quadratic expressions. An expression in factored form is quadratic if it has exactly two linear factors, each with the variable raised to the first power. An expression in expanded form is quadratic if the highest power of the variable is 2.

Problem 2.2 Quadratic Expressions

A. Each diagram shows a large rectangle divided into two smaller rectangles. Write two expressions, one in factored form and one in expanded form, for the area of the rectangle outlined in red.

1.

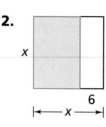

x

x   6

2.

x

6

|← *x* →|

B. Complete the steps in bullets for each of the factored expressions in parts (1)–(3).

- Draw a divided rectangle whose area is represented by the expression. Label the lengths and area of each section.

- Write an equivalent expression in expanded form.

   1. $x(x + 4)$ **2.** $x(x - 4)$ **3.** $x(5 + 2)$

C. Complete the steps in bullets for each of the factored expressions in parts (1)–(3).

- Draw a divided rectangle whose area is represented by the expression. Label the lengths and area of each section.

- Tell what clues in the expanded expression helped you draw the divided rectangle.

- Write an equivalent expression in factored form.

   1. $x^2 + 5x$ **2.** $x^2 - 5x$ **3.** $5x + 4x$

ACE Homework starts on page 30.

2.3 Changing Both Dimensions

You can write the area of the larger rectangle below as $x(x + 3)$ or $x^2 + 3x$.

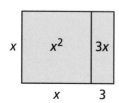

x x^2 $3x$

x   3

The equation $x(x + 3) = x^2 + 3x$ is an example of the **Distributive Property,** which you studied in earlier units.

The Distributive Property says that, for any three numbers a, b, and c,

$a(b + c) = ab + ac$.

	b	c	
a	ab	ac	Area: $a(b + c)$ or $ab + ac$

When you write $a(b + c)$ as $ab + ac$, you are *multiplying*, or writing the expression in expanded form. When you write $ab + ac$ as $a(b + c)$, you are *factoring*, or writing the expression in factored form.

The terms $2x$ and $3x$ are *like terms*. The Distributive Property can be used to add like terms. For example, $2x + 3x = (2 + 3)x = 5x$.

In Problem 2.3, you will explore what happens to the area of a square when both dimensions are changed. You will see how the Distributive Property can be used to change the expression for area from factored form to expanded form.

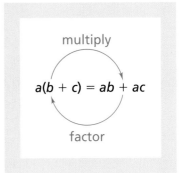

multiply

$a(b + c) = ab + ac$

factor

Getting Ready for Problem 2.3

A new rectangle is made by increasing one side of a square with sides of length x by 2 centimeters and increasing the other side by 3 centimeters.

- How do the areas of the square and the new rectangle compare?
- How can you represent the area of the new rectangle?

A. Each rectangle has been subdivided into four smaller rectangles. Write two expressions for the area of the rectangle outlined in red, one in factored form and one in expanded form.

1.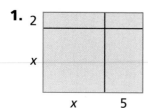

2.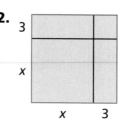

3.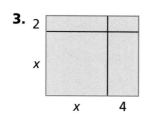

4.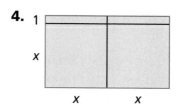

B. A square has sides of length x centimeters. One dimension is doubled and then increased by 2 centimeters. The other dimension is increased by 3 centimeters.

   1. Make a sketch of the new rectangle. Label the area of each section.

   2. Write two expressions, one in factored form and one in expanded form, for the area of the new rectangle.

C. Use a rectangle model to help write each expression in expanded form.

   1. $(x + 3)(x + 5)$ **2.** $(4 + x)(4 + x)$ **3.** $3x(x + 1)$

D. Carminda says she doesn't need a rectangle model to multiply $(x + 3)$ by $(x + 2)$. She uses the Distributive Property.

$$
\begin{aligned}
(x + 3)(x + 2) &= (x + 3)x + (x + 3)2 & (1)\\
&= x^2 + 3x + 2x + 6 & (2)\\
&= x^2 + 5x + 6 & (3)
\end{aligned}
$$

   1. Is Carminda correct? Explain what she did at each step.

   2. Show how using the Distributive Property to multiply $(x + 3)$ and $(x + 5)$ is the same as using a rectangle model.

E. Use the Distributive Property to write each expression in expanded form.

1. $(x + 5)(x + 5)$ 2. $(x + 3)(x - 4)$ 3. $2x(5 - x)$

4. $(x - 3)(x - 4)$ 5. $(x + 2)(x - 2)$

ACE Homework starts on page 30.

2.4 Factoring Quadratic Expressions

You know two ways to change a factored expression, such as $(x + 2)(x + 6)$, to expanded form.

Rectangle Model

Subdivide.

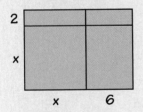

Label areas.

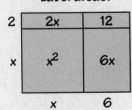

Add the areas of the sections:

$(x + 2)(x + 6) = x^2 + 2x + 6x + 12$
$\qquad\qquad\quad = x^2 + 8x + 12$

Distributive Property

$(x + 2)(x + 6) = (x + 2)x + (x + 2)6$

$= x^2 + 2x + 6x + 12$

$= x^2 + 8x + 12$

How can you write an expanded expression, such as $x^2 + 8x + 12$, in factored form?

In the next problem, we will use the distributive property to write expressions in factored form.

Problem 2.4 Factoring Quadratic Expressions

A. 1. Copy the diagram. Replace each question mark with the correct length or area.

2. Write two expressions for the area of the rectangle outlined in red.

		?	
?		?	9
x	x^2		?
	x		?

B. Consider this expression.

$$x^2 + bx + 8$$

1. Choose a value for b that gives an expression you can factor. Then, write the expression in factored form.

2. Compare your work with your classmates. Did everyone write the same expressions? Explain.

C. In parts (1)–(4), find values of r and s that make the equations true.

1. $x^2 + 10x + 24 = (x + 6)(x + r)$

2. $x^2 + 11x + 24 = (x + s)(x + r)$

3. $x^2 + 25x + 24 = (x + r)(x + s)$

4. Describe the strategies you used to factor the expressions in parts (1)–(3).

D. Alyse says she can use the Distributive Property to factor the expression $x^2 + 10x + 16$. She writes:

$$x^2 + 10x + 16 = x^2 + 2x + 8x + 16 \qquad (1)$$
$$= x(x + 2) + 8(x + 2) \qquad (2)$$
$$= (x + 2)(x + 8) \qquad (3)$$

Is Alyse correct? Explain what she did at each step.

E. Use the Distributive Property to factor each expression.

1. $x^2 + 5x + 2x + 10$ **2.** $x^2 + 11x + 10$ **3.** $x^2 + 3x - 10$

4. $x^2 + 16x + 15$ **5.** $x^2 - 8x + 15$ **6.** $x^2 - 12x + 36$

ACE Homework starts on page 30.

In Investigation 1, you saw that graphs of quadratic equations of the form $y = x(a - x)$ are parabolas. A vertical line drawn through the maximum point of a parabola is called a **line of symmetry.** If you were to fold along this line, the two halves of the parabola would exactly match.

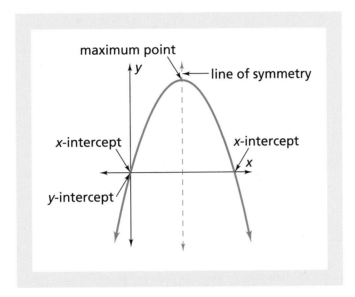

In the last four problems, you worked with expanded and factored forms of quadratic expressions. Next, you will examine graphs of the equations associated with these expressions.

Getting Ready for Problem 2.5

- Sketch the graph of $y = (x + 3)(x - 2)$.
- Describe the features of the graph. Include the x- and y-intercepts, the maximum or minimum point, and the line of symmetry.
- Sketch a graph of $y = x^2 + x - 6$. How does this graph compare with the graph of $y = (x + 3)(x - 2)$? Explain.

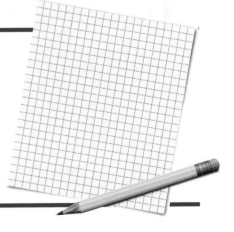

In this problem, you will explore these questions:

What can you learn about a quadratic function from its graph?

How are the features of a parabola related to its equation?

Problem 2.5 A Closer Look at Parabolas

These equations, all in factored form, were graphed using the window settings shown at the right. The graphs are shown below.

$$y_1 = x^2$$
$$y_3 = (x + 2)(x + 3)$$
$$y_5 = x(4 - x)$$
$$y_7 = x(x + 4)$$

$$y_2 = 2x(x + 4)$$
$$y_4 = (x + 3)(x + 3)$$
$$y_6 = x(x - 4)$$
$$y_8 = (x + 3)(x - 3)$$

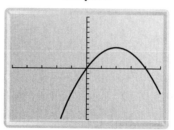

WINDOW FORMAT
Xmin=−5
Xmax=5
Xscl=1
Ymin=−10
Ymax=10
Yscl=1
Xres=1

Graph A

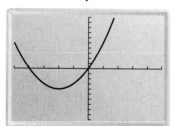

Graph B

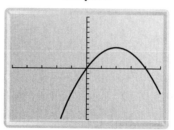

Graph C

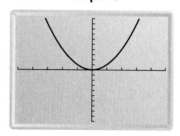

Graph D

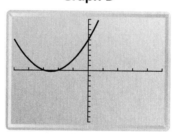

Graph E

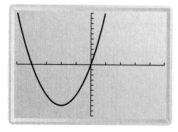

Graph F

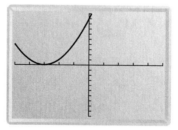

Graph G

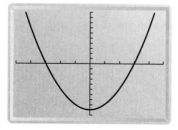

Graph H

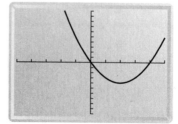

A. Do parts (1)–(5) for each equation.

   1. Match the equation to its graph.

   2. Label the coordinates of the x- and y-intercepts of the graph. Describe how you can predict the x- and y-intercepts from the equation.

   3. Draw the line of symmetry of the graph. Can you predict the location of the line of symmetry from the equation? Explain.

   4. Label the coordinates of the maximum or minimum point. Can you predict the maximum or minimum point from the equation? Explain.

   5. Describe the shape of the graph.

B. **1.** Write each of the equations in expanded form.

   2. What features of the graph can you predict from the expanded form of the equation? What features can you predict from the factored form? Explain.

C. *Without* graphing, describe the graph of each equation. Give as many details as possible.

   1. $y = x^2 + 6x + 5$ **2.** $y = -x^2 + 4x$ **3.** $y = (x - 2)(x + 3)$

D. How can you tell whether an equation represents a quadratic relationship if it is in expanded form? If it is in factored form?

ACE **Homework starts on page 30.**

Applications

1. A square has sides of length x centimeters. One dimension increases by 4 centimeters and the other decreases by 4 centimeters, forming a new rectangle.

   a. Make a table showing the side length and area of the square and the area of the new rectangle. Include whole-number x-values from 4 to 16.

   b. On the same axes, graph the (x, *area*) data for both the square and the rectangle.

   c. Suppose you want to compare the area of a square with the area of the corresponding new rectangle. Is it easier to use the table or the graph?

   d. Write equations for the area of the original square and the area of the new rectangle in terms of x.

   e. Use your calculator to graph both equations. Show values of x from -10 to 10. Copy the graphs onto your paper. Describe the relationship between the two graphs.

2. A square has sides of length x centimeters. One dimension increases by 5 centimeters, forming a new rectangle.

   a. Make a sketch to show the new rectangle.

   b. Write two equations, one in factored form and one in expanded form, for the area of the new rectangle.

   c. Graph the equations in part (b).

For Exercises 3 and 4, draw a divided rectangle whose area is represented by each expression. Label the lengths and area of each section. Then, write an equivalent expression in expanded form.

   3. $x(x + 7)$

   4. $x(x - 3)$

For Exercises 5–7, draw a divided rectangle whose area is represented by each expression. Label the lengths and area of each section. Then, write an equivalent expression in factored form.

5. $x^2 + 6x$ **6.** $x^2 - 8x$ **7.** $x^2 - x$

For Exercises 8–11, write the expression in factored form.

Go Online
PHSchool.com
For: Multiple-Choice Skills Practice
Web Code: apa-4254

8. $x^2 + 10x$ **9.** $x^2 - 6x$

10. $x^2 + 11x$ **11.** $x^2 - 2x$

For Exercises 12–15, write the expression in expanded form.

12. $x(x + 1)$ **13.** $x(x - 10)$

14. $x(x + 6)$ **15.** $x(x - 15)$

For Exercises 16–20, write two expressions, one in factored form and one in expanded form, for the area of the rectangle outlined in red.

16.
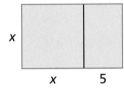

17.
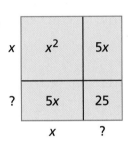

18.
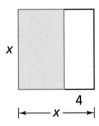

19.
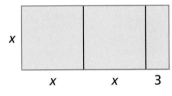

20.
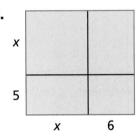

21. A square has sides of length x meters. Both dimensions increase by 5 meters, forming a new square.

   a. Make a sketch to show the new square.

   b. Write two equations, one in factored form and one in expanded form, for the area of the new square in terms of x.

   c. Graph the equations in part (b).

22. A square has sides of length x centimeters. One dimension increases by 4 centimeters and the other increases by 5 centimeters, forming a new rectangle.

    a. Make a sketch to show the new rectangle.

    b. Write two equations, one in factored form and one in expanded form, for the area of the new rectangle.

    c. Graph the equations in part (b).

For Exercises 23–28, use the Distributive Property to write each expression in expanded form.

23. $(x - 3)(x + 4)$ **24.** $(x + 3)(x + 5)$ **25.** $x(x + 5)$

26. $(x - 2)(x - 6)$ **27.** $(x - 3)(x + 3)$ **28.** $(x - 3)(x + 5)$

29. a. Draw and label a rectangle whose area is represented by each expression.

$$x^2 + 3x + 4x + 12 \qquad\qquad x^2 + 7x + 10$$

    b. For each expression in part (a), write an equivalent expression in factored form.

30. Write each expression in factored form.

    a. $x^2 + 13x + 12$ **b.** $x^2 - 13x + 12$ **c.** $x^2 + 8x + 12$

    d. $x^2 - 8x + 12$ **e.** $x^2 + 7x + 12$ **f.** $x^2 - 7x + 12$

    g. $x^2 + 11x - 12$ **h.** $x^2 - 11x - 12$ **i.** $x^2 + 4x - 12$

    j. $x^2 - 4x - 12$ **k.** $x^2 + x - 12$ **l.** $x^2 - x - 12$

Homework Help Online
PHSchool.com
For: Help with Exercise 30
Web Code: ape-4230

For Exercises 31–39, determine whether the equation represents a quadratic relationship *without* making a table or a graph. Explain.

31. $y = 5x + x^2$ **32.** $y = 2x + 8$ **33.** $y = (9 - x)x$

34. $y = 4x(3 + x)$ **35.** $y = 3^x$ **36.** $y = x^2 + 10x$

37. $y = x(x + 4)$ **38.** $y = 2(x + 4)$ **39.** $y = 7x + 10 + x^2$

40. Give the line of symmetry, the x- and y-intercepts, and the maximum or minimum point for the graph of each equation.

    a. $y = (x - 3)(x + 3)$ **b.** $y = x(x + 5)$

    c. $y = (x + 3)(x + 5)$ **d.** $y = (x - 3)(x + 5)$

    e. $y = (x + 3)(x - 5)$

For Exercises 41 and 42, complete parts (a)–(e) for each equation.

41. $y = x^2 + 5x + 6$ **42.** $y = x^2 - 25$

    a. Find an equivalent factored form of the equation.

    b. Identify the x- and y-intercepts for the graph of the equation.

    c. Find the coordinates of the maximum or minimum point.

    d. Find the line of symmetry.

    e. Tell which form of the equation can be used to predict the features in parts (b)–(d) without making a graph.

43. Darnell makes a rectangle from a square by doubling one dimension and adding 3 centimeters. He leaves the other dimension unchanged.

    a. Write an equation for the area A of the new rectangle in terms of the side length x of the original square.

    b. Graph your area equation.

    c. What are the x-intercepts of the graph? How can you find the x-intercepts from the graph? How can you find them from the equation?

For Exercises 44–47, match the equation with its graph. Then, explain how to locate the line of symmetry for the graph.

44. $y = (x + 7)(x + 2)$

45. $y = x(x + 3)$

46. $y = (x - 4)(x + 6)$

47. $y = (x - 5)(x + 5)$

Graph A

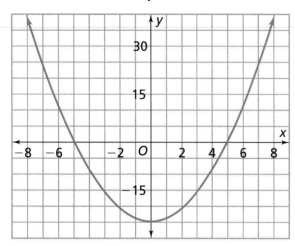

Graph B

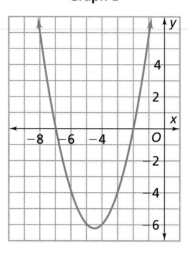

Graph C

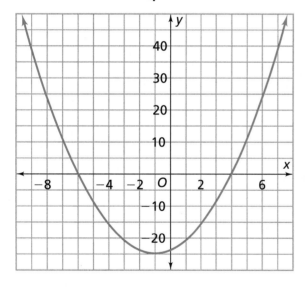

Graph D

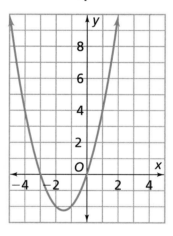

48. a. How are the graphs at the right similar?

b. How are the graphs different?

c. The maximum value for $y = x(10 - x)$ occurs when $x = 5$. How can you find the y-coordinate of the maximum value?

d. The minimum value for $y = x(x - 10)$ occurs when $x = 5$. How can you find the y-coordinate of the minimum value?

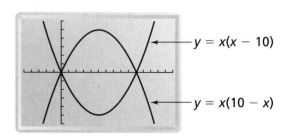

$y = x(x - 10)$

$y = x(10 - x)$

49. Multiple Choice Which quadratic equation has x-intercepts at $(3, 0)$ and $(-1, 0)$?

A. $y = x^2 - 1x + 3$

B. $y = x^2 - 2x + 3$

C. $y = 3x^2 - 1x$

D. $y = x^2 - 2x - 3$

Connections

50. The Stellar International Cellular long-distance company charges $13.95 per month plus $0.39 per minute of calling time. The Call Anytime company charges no monthly service fee but charges $0.95 per minute.

    a. Represent each charge plan with an equation, a table, and a graph.

    b. For each plan, tell whether the relationship between calling time and monthly cost is quadratic, linear, exponential, or inverse. How do your equation, table, and graph support your answer?

    c. For what number of minutes are the costs for the two plans equal?

51. The winner of the Jammin' Jelly jingle contest will receive $500. Antonia and her friends are writing a jingle. They plan to divide the prize money equally if they win.

    a. Suppose n friends write the winning jingle. Write an equation to show how much prize money p each of the friends receive.

    b. Describe the relationship between the number of friends and the prize money each friend receives.

    c. Write a question about this relationship that is easier to answer by using a graph. Write a question that is easier to answer by using a table. Write a question that is easier to answer by using an equation.

    d. Is this relationship quadratic, linear, exponential, or inverse? Explain.

52. Suppose the circumference of a cross section of a nearly circular tree is *x* feet.

a. What is the diameter in terms of *x*?

b. What is the radius in terms of *x*?

c. What is the area of the cross section in terms of *x*?

d. Is the relationship between the circumference *x* and the area of the cross section linear, quadratic, exponential, or none of these?

e. Suppose the circumference of the cross section is 10 feet. What are the diameter, radius, and area of the cross section?

53. A square has sides of length *x* centimeters.

a. The square is enlarged by a scale factor of 2. What is the area of the enlarged square?

b. How does the area of the original square compare with the area of the enlarged square?

c. Is the new square similar to the original square? Explain.

54. A rectangle has dimensions of *x* centimeters and $(x + 1)$ centimeters.

a. The rectangle is enlarged by a scale factor of 2. What is the area of the enlarged rectangle?

b. How does the area of the original rectangle compare with the area of the enlarged rectangle?

c. Is the new rectangle similar to the original rectangle? Explain.

55. For each polygon, write formulas for the perimeter P and area A in terms of ℓ, if it is possible. If it is not possible to write a formula, explain why.

Rectangle

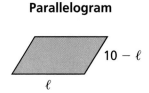

$10 - \ell$

ℓ

Parallelogram

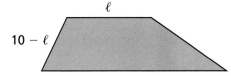

$10 - \ell$

ℓ

Kite

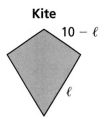

$10 - \ell$

ℓ

Non-isosceles Trapezoid

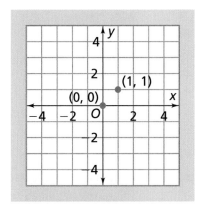

ℓ

$10 - \ell$

Isosceles Right Triangle

ℓ

$10 - \ell$

56. a. Write the equation of the line that passes through the two points shown.

b. Is there a different line that can be drawn through these points? Explain.

For Exercises 57–60, evaluate the expression for the given values of x.

57. $x(x - 5)$ for $x = 5$ and $x = -5$

58. $3x^2 - x$ for $x = 1$ and $x = \frac{1}{3}$

59. $x^2 + 5x + 4$ for $x = 2$ and $x = -4$

60. $(x - 7)(x + 2)$ for $x = -2$ and $x = 2$

61. Refer to Graphs A, E, and G in Problem 2.5. Without using your calculator, answer the following questions.

   a. Suppose parabola A is shifted 1 unit left. Write an equation for this new parabola.

   b. Suppose parabola E is shifted 4 units right. Write an equation for this new parabola.

   c. Can parabola E be transformed into parabola G by a shift to the right only? Explain.

Extensions

62. Multiple Choice Which expression is equivalent to $(2n + 3)(4n + 2)$?

   F. $8n + 5$ **G.** $6n^2 + 7n + 4n + 5$

   H. $8n^2 + 16n + 6$ **J.** $8n^2 + 6$

For Exercises 63–64, write each expression in factored form. You may want to draw a rectangle model.

63. $2x^2 + 3x + 1$ **64.** $4x^2 + 10x + 6$

65. Sketch graphs of the equations $y = x^2 + 2x$ and $y = x^2 + 2$.

   a. How are the graphs similar?

   b. How are the graphs different?

   c. Find the y-intercept for each graph.

   d. Find the x-intercepts for each graph if they exist. If there are no x-intercepts, explain why.

   e. Do all quadratic relationships have y-intercepts? Explain.

Mathematical Reflections 2

In this investigation, you wrote quadratic expressions to represent areas of rectangles formed by transforming a square. You converted expressions to different forms by using rectangular models and by using the Distributive Property. These questions will help you summarize what you have learned.

Think about your answers to these questions. Discuss your ideas with other students and your teacher. Then, write a summary of your findings in your notebook.

1. Show how the area of a rectangle can illustrate the Distributive Property.

2. Explain how you can use the Distributive Property to answer each question. Use examples to help with your explanations.

   a. Suppose a quadratic expression is in factored form. How can you find an equivalent expression in expanded form?

   b. Suppose a quadratic expression is in expanded form. How can you find an equivalent expression in factored form?

3. How can you recognize a quadratic function from its equation?

4. Describe what you know about the shape of the graph of a quadratic function. Include important features of the graph and describe how you can predict these features from its equation.

Quadratic Patterns of Change

In previous units, you studied patterns in linear and exponential relationships. In this investigation, you will look for patterns in quadratic relationships as you solve some interesting counting problems.

What patterns of change characterize linear and exponential relationships?

What patterns of change did you notice in the quadratic relationships in Investigations 1 and 2?

3.1 Exploring Triangular Numbers

Study the pattern of dots.

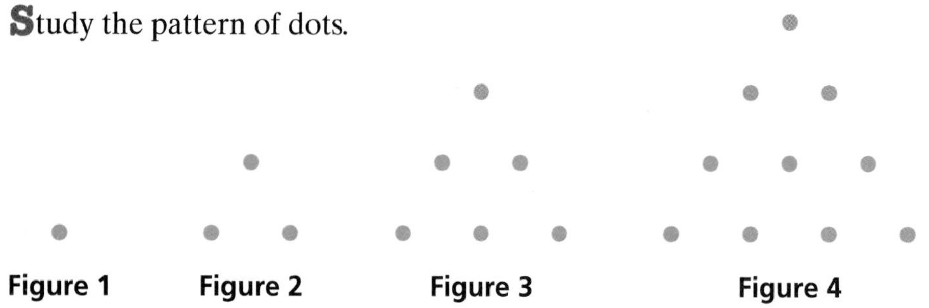

| Figure 1 | Figure 2 | Figure 3 | Figure 4 |

How many dots do you predict will be in Figure 5? In Figure n?

The numbers that represent the number of dots in each triangle above are called **triangular numbers.** The first triangular number is 1, the second triangular number is 3, the third is 6, the fourth is 10, and so on.

Problem 3.1 Exploring Triangular Numbers

You can also represent triangular numbers with patterns of squares.
The number of squares in Figure *n* is the *n*th triangular number.

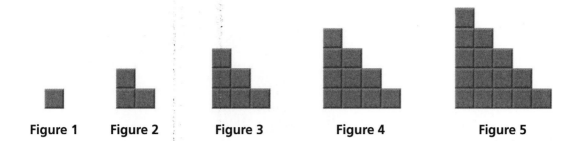

Figure 1   Figure 2   Figure 3   Figure 4   Figure 5

A. 1. What is the sixth triangular number? What is the tenth triangular number?

  2. Make a table of (*figure number, triangular number*) values for the first ten triangular numbers.

  3. Describe the pattern of change from one triangular number to the next.

  4. Describe how you can use the pattern in the table to find the 11th and 12th triangular numbers.

B. 1. Write an equation for the *n*th triangular number *t*. In other words, write an equation for the number of squares *t* in Figure *n*. Explain your reasoning.

  2. Use your equation to find the 11th and 12th triangular numbers.

C. 1. Use a calculator to graph your equation. Show *n* values from −5 to 5. Make a sketch of your graph.

  2. Does your graph represent the relationship you observed in the table? Explain.

  3. Does your equation represent a quadratic relationship? Explain.

  4. Compare this equation with the equations in Investigations 1 and 2.

ACE Homework starts on page 44.

3.2 Counting Handshakes

After a sporting event, the opposing teams often line up and shake hands. To celebrate their victory, members of the winning team may congratulate each other with a round of high fives.

Problem 3.2 Another Quadratic Relationship

Consider three cases of handshaking:

Case 1 Two teams have the same number of players. Each player on one team shakes hands with each player on the other team.

Case 2 One team has one more player than the other. Each player on one team shakes hands with each player on the other team.

Case 3 Each member of a team gives a high five to each teammate.

A. Consider Case 1.

  1. How many handshakes will take place between two 5-player teams? Between two 10-player teams?

  2. Write an equation for the number of handshakes h between two n-player teams.

B. Consider Case 2.

  1. How many handshakes will take place between a 6-player team and a 7-player team? Between an 8-player team and a 9-player team?

  2. Write an equation for the number of handshakes h between an n-player team and an $(n - 1)$-player team.

C. Consider Case 3.

    1. How many high fives will take place among a team with 4 members? Among a team with 8 members?

    2. Write an equation for the number of high fives h among a team with n members.

ACE **Homework starts on page 44.**

3.3 Examining Patterns of Change

In this problem, you will examine the patterns of change that characterize quadratic relationships.

Problem 3.3 Examining Patterns of Change

A. Complete parts (1)–(2) for each case in Problem 3.2.

    1. Make a table showing the number of players on each team and the number of handshakes or high fives. Include data for teams with 1 to 10 members.

    2. Describe a pattern of change that can help you predict the numbers of handshakes or high fives for larger teams.

B. Compare the patterns in the three tables you made in Question A. How are the patterns similar? How are they different?

C. 1. Use your calculator to graph the equations you wrote for the three cases in Problem 3.2. Show n values from -10 to 10. Make a sketch of the graph.

    2. Compare the three graphs.

D. For each case, compare the table and its graph. Describe how the tables and graphs show the same pattern of change.

E. Are any of the three relationships quadratic? Explain.

F. Compare the patterns of change for the three cases with the patterns of change you observed in Investigations 1 and 2.

ACE **Homework starts on page 44.**

Applications

1. These dot patterns represent the first four *square numbers,* 1, 4, 9, and 16.

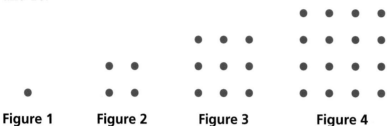

Figure 1   Figure 2   Figure 3   Figure 4

    a. What are the next two square numbers?

    b. Write an equation for the nth square number s.

    c. Make a table and a graph of (n, s) values for the first ten square numbers. Describe the pattern of change from one square number to the next.

2. The numbers of dots in the figures below are the first four *rectangular numbers.*

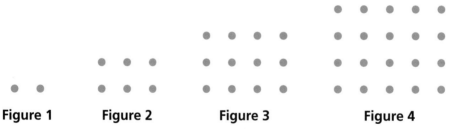

Figure 1   Figure 2   Figure 3   Figure 4

    a. What are the first four rectangular numbers?

    b. Find the next two rectangular numbers.

    c. Describe the pattern of change from one rectangular number to the next.

    d. Predict the 7th and 8th rectangular numbers.

    e. Write an equation for the nth rectangular number r.

3. In Problem 3.1, you looked at triangular numbers.

    a. What is the 18th triangular number?

    b. Is 210 a triangular number? Explain.

4. a. In Problem 3.1, you found an equation for the nth triangular number. Sam claims he can use this equation to find the sum of the first 10 counting numbers. Explain why Sam is correct.

   b. What is the sum of the first 10 counting numbers?

   c. What is the sum of the first 15 counting numbers?

   d. What is the sum of the first n counting numbers?

Did You Know?

Carl Friedrich Gauss (1777–1855) was a German mathematician and astronomer. When Gauss was about eight years old, his teacher asked his class to find the sum of the first 100 counting numbers. Gauss had the answer almost immediately!

Gauss realized that he could pair up the numbers as shown. Each pair has a sum of 101.

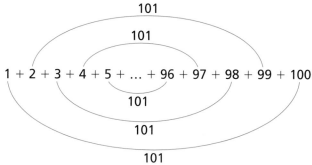

There are 100 numbers, so there are 50 pairs. This means the sum is $50 \times 101 = 5{,}050$ [or $\frac{100}{2}(101)$ or $\frac{100}{2}$ (first number plus last number)].

For: Information about Gauss
Web Code: ape-9031

For Exercises 5–8, tell whether the number is a triangular number, a square number, a rectangular number, or none of these. Explain.

5. 110   **6.** 66   **7.** 121   **8.** 60

9. In a middle school math league, each team has six student members and two coaches.

Johnson Middle School

Hillsdale Middle School

   a. At the start of a match, the coaches and student members of one team exchange handshakes with the coaches and student members of the other team. How many handshakes occur?

   b. At the end of the match, the members and coaches of the winning team exchange handshakes. How many handshakes occur?

   c. The members of one team exchange handshakes with their coaches. How many handshakes occur?

10. In a 100-meter race, five runners are from the United States and three runners are from Canada.

Homework Help Online
PHSchool.com
For: Help with Exercise 10
Web Code: ape-4310

   a. How many handshakes occur if the runners from one country exchange handshakes with the runners from the other country?

   b. How many high fives occur if the runners from the United States exchange high fives?

11. A company rents five offices in a building. There is a cable connecting each pair of offices.

   a. How many cables are there in all?

   b. Suppose the company rents two more offices. How many cables will they need in all?

   c. Compare this situation with Case 3 in Problem 3.2.

For Exercises 12–15, describe a situation that can be represented by the equation. Tell what the variables p and n represent in that situation.

12. $p = n(n - 1)$ **13.** $p = 2n$

14. $p = n(n - 2)$ **15.** $p = n(16 - n)$

16. The graphs below represent equations for situations you have looked at in this unit.

Graph I

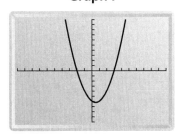

Graph II

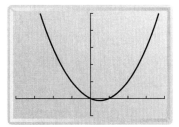

Graph III

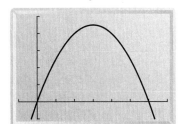

Graph IV

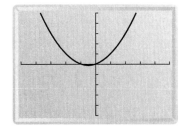

a. Which graph might represent the equation for the number of high fives exchanged among a team with n players? Explain.

b. Which graph might represent the equation for the areas of rectangles with a fixed perimeter?

c. Which graph might represent the equation for the areas of a rectangle formed by increasing one dimension of a square by 2 centimeters and decreasing the other dimension by 3 centimeters?

d. Which graph might represent the equation for a triangular-number pattern?

For Exercises 17–19, the tables represent quadratic relationships. Copy and complete each table.

17.

x	y
0	0
1	1
2	3
3	6
4	▨
5	▨
6	▨

18.

x	y
0	0
1	3
2	8
3	15
4	▨
5	▨
6	▨

19.

x	y
0	0
1	4
2	6
3	6
4	▨
5	▨
6	▨

Connections

20. a. Make sketches that show two ways of completing the rectangle model at the right using whole numbers. For each sketch, express the area of the largest rectangle in both expanded form and factored form.

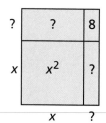

b. Is there more than one way to complete the rectangle model below using whole numbers? Explain.

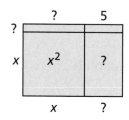

21. Write two equivalent expressions for the area of the rectangle outlined in red below.

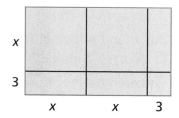

22. Consider these quadratic expressions.

$$2x^2 + 7x + 6 \qquad x^2 + 6x + 8$$

a. For each expression, sketch a rectangle whose area the expression represents.

b. Write each expression in factored form. Which expression is easier to factor? Why?

For Exercises 23–28, write the expression in expanded form.

29 $x(5 - x)$ **24.** $(x + 1)(x + 3)$ **25.** $(x - 1)(x + 3)$

26. $3x(x + 5)$ **27.** $(2x + 1)(x + 3)$ **28.** $(2x - 1)(x + 3)$

For Exercises 29–35, write the expression in factored form.

29. $x^2 - 9x + 8$ **30.** $4x^2 - 6x$ **31.** $x^2 - 2x - 3$

32. $3x^2 + 14x + 8$ **33.** $4x^2 + 6x$ **34.** $4x^2 - x - 3$

35. $x^3 - 2x^2 - 3x$

Go Online
PHSchool.com

For: Multiple-Choice Skills Practice
Web Code: apa-4354

36. Min was having trouble factoring the expression in Exercise 32.
Ricardo suggested that she use a rectangle model.

    a. Explain how a rectangle model can help Min factor the expression.
Make a sketch to illustrate your explanation.

    b. How can you factor this expression without drawing a rectangle?

37. A diagonal of a polygon is a line segment connecting any two
nonadjacent vertices. A quadrilateral has two diagonals like
the one at the right.

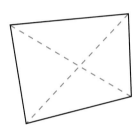

    a. How many diagonals does a pentagon have? How many
does a hexagon have? A heptagon? An octagon?

    b. How many diagonals does an *n*-sided polygon have?

38. These "trains" are formed by joining identical squares.

   Train 1   **Train 2**   **Train 3**   **Train 4**   **Train 5**

    a. How many rectangles are in each of the first five trains? For
example, the drawing below shows the six rectangles in Train 3.
(Remember, a square is a rectangle.)

    b. Make a table showing the number of rectangles in each of the first
ten trains.

    c. How can you use the pattern of change in your table to find the
number of rectangles in Train 15?

    d. Write an equation for the number of rectangles in Train *n*.

    e. Use your equation to find the number of rectangles in Train 15.

39. a. What is the area of the base of the can?

b. How many centimeter cubes or parts of cubes can fit in a single layer on the bottom of the can?

c. How many layers of this size would fill the can?

d. Use your answers to parts (a)–(c) to find the volume of the can.

e. The label on the lateral surface of the can is a rectangle with a height of 10 cm. What is the other dimension of the label?

f. What is the area of the label?

g. Use your answers to parts (a) and (f) to find the surface area of the can.

10 cm

10 cm

40. A company is trying to choose a box shape for a new product. It has narrowed the choices to the triangular prism and the cylinder shown below.

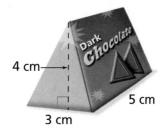
4 cm
5 cm
3 cm

4.24 cm
2.12 cm

a. Sketch a net for each box.

b. Find the surface area of each box.

c. Which box will require more cardboard to construct?

For Exercise 41–44, tell whether the pattern in the table is linear, quadratic, exponential, or none of these.

41.

x	y
0	2
3	4
5	5
6	6
7	7
8	8
10	10

42.

x	y
−3	12
−2	7
−1	4
0	3
1	4
2	7
3	12

43.

x	y
0	1
2	9
5	243
6	729
7	2,187
8	6,561
10	59,049

44.

x	y
1	−2
2	0
3	3
4	8
5	15
6	24
7	14

45. Multiple Choice Which equation represents a quadratic relationship?

A. $y = (x - 1)(6 - 2)$ **B.** $y = 2x(3 - 2)$

C. $y = 2^x$ **D.** $y = x(x + 2)$

46. Multiple Choice Which equation has a graph with a minimum point at $(1, 4)$?

F. $y = -x^2 + 5$ **G.** $y = -x^2 + 5x$

H. $y = x^2 - 2x + 5$ **J.** $y = -x^2 + 7x - 10$

Extensions

47. You can use Gauss's method to find the sum of the whole numbers from 1 to 10 by writing the sum twice as shown and adding vertically.

$$1 + 2 + 3 + 4 + 5 + 6 + 7 + 8 + 9 + 10$$
$$10 + 9 + 8 + 7 + 6 + 5 + 4 + 3 + 2 + 1$$
$$\overline{11 + 11 + 11 + 11 + 11 + 11 + 11 + 11 + 11 + 11}$$

Each vertical sum of 11 occurs 10 times, or $10(11) = 110$. This result is twice the sum of the numbers from 1 to 10, so we divide by 2 to get $\frac{10(11)}{2} = \frac{110}{2} = 55$.

a. How can you use this idea to find $1 + 2 + 3 + \ldots + 99 + 100$?

b. How could you use this idea to find $1 + 2 + 3 + \ldots + n$ for any whole number n?

c. How is this method related to Gauss's method?

48. The patterns of dots below represent the first three *star numbers.*

Figure 1   **Figure 2**   **Figure 3**

a. What are the first three star numbers?

b. Find the next three star numbers.

c. Write an equation you could use to calculate the *n*th star number.

49. In parts (a) and (b), explain your answers by drawing pictures or writing a convincing argument.

a. Ten former classmates attend their class reunion. They all shake hands with each other. How many handshakes occur?

b. A little later, two more classmates arrive. Suppose these two people shake hands with each other and the ten other classmates. How many new handshakes occur?

50. The pattern of dots below represents the first three *hexagonal numbers*.

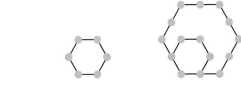

Figure 1   **Figure 2**   **Figure 3**

a. What are the first three hexagonal numbers?

b. Find the next two hexagonal numbers.

c. Write an equation you can use to calculate the nth hexagonal number.

51. There are 30 squares of various sizes in this 4-by-4 grid.

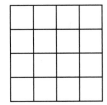

a. Sixteen of the squares are the identical small squares that make up the grid. Find the other 14 squares. Draw pictures or give a description.

b. How many squares are in an n-by-n grid? (**Hint:** Start with some simple cases and search for a pattern.)

Mathematical Reflections 3

In this investigation, you counted handshakes and studied geometric patterns. You found that these situations can be represented by quadratic functions. These questions will help you summarize what you have learned.

Think about your answers to these questions. Discuss your ideas with other students and your teacher. Then, write a summary of your findings in your notebook.

1. **a.** In what ways is the triangle-number relationship similar to the relationships in the handshake problems? In what ways are these relationships different?

   b. In what ways are the quadratic functions in this investigation similar to the quadratic functions in Investigations 1 and 2? In what ways are they different?

2. **a.** In a table of values for a quadratic function, how can you use the pattern of change to predict the next value?

   b. How can you use a table of values to decide if a function is quadratic?

What Is a Quadratic Function?

When you jump from a diving board, gravity pulls you toward Earth. When you throw or kick a ball into the air, gravity brings it back down. For several hundred years, scientists have used mathematical models to describe and predict the effect of gravity on the position, velocity, and acceleration of falling objects.

Did You Know?

Aristotle, the ancient Greek philosopher and scientist, believed that heavier objects fall faster than lighter objects. In the late 1500s, the great Italian scientist Galileo challenged this idea.

It is said that, while observing a hailstorm, Galileo noticed that large and small hailstones hit the ground at the same time. If Aristotle were correct, this would happen only if the larger stones dropped from a higher point or if the smaller stones started falling first. Galileo didn't think either of these explanations was probable.

A famous story claims that Galileo proved that heavy and light objects fall at the same rate by climbing to the highest point he could find—the top of the Tower of Pisa—and dropping two objects simultaneously. Although they had different weights, the objects hit the ground at the same time.

 **Go Online**
PHSchool.com **For:** Information about Galileo
Web Code: ape-9031

4.1 Tracking a Ball

No matter how hard you throw or kick a ball into the air, gravity returns it to Earth. In this problem, you will explore how the height of a thrown ball changes over time.

Problem 4.1 Interpreting a Table and an Equation

Suppose you throw a ball straight up in the air. This table shows how the height of the ball might change as it goes up and then returns to the ground.

A. 1. Describe how the height of the ball changes over this 4-second time period.

   2. Without actually making the graph, describe what the graph of these data would look like. Include as many important features as you can.

   3. Do you think these data represent a quadratic function? Explain.

B. The height h of the ball in feet after t seconds can be described by the equation $h = -16t^2 + 64t$.

   1. Graph this equation on your calculator.

   2. Does the graph match the description you gave in Question A? Explain.

   3. When does the ball reach a height of about 58 feet? Explain.

   4. Use the equation to find the height of the ball after 1.6 seconds.

   5. When will the ball reach the ground? Explain.

ACE Homework starts on page 64.

Height of Thrown Ball

Time (seconds)	Height (feet)
0.00	0
0.25	15
0.50	28
0.75	39
1.00	48
1.25	55
1.50	60
1.75	63
2.00	64
2.25	63
2.50	60
2.75	55
3.00	48
3.25	39
3.50	28
3.75	15
4.00	0

4.2 Measuring Jumps

Many animals are known for their jumping abilities. Most frogs can jump several times their body length. Fleas are tiny, but they can easily leap onto a dog or a cat. Some humans have amazing jumping ability as well. Many professional basketball players have vertical leaps of more than 3 feet!

Getting Ready for Problem 4.2

In Problem 4.1, the initial height of the ball is 0 feet. This is not very realistic because it means you would have to lie on the ground and release the ball without extending your arm. A more realistic equation for the height of the ball is $h = -16t^2 + 64t + 6$.

- Compare this equation with the equation in Problem 4.1.

- Use your calculator to make a table and a graph of this quadratic function.

- Compare your graph with the graph of the equation in Problem 4.1. Consider the following:
  - the maximum height reached by the ball
  - the x-intercepts
  - the y-intercepts
  - the patterns of change in the height of the ball over time

Problem 4.2 Comparing Quadratic Relationships

A. Suppose a frog, a flea, and a basketball player jump straight up. Their heights in feet after *t* seconds are modeled by these equations.

Frog: $h = -16t^2 + 12t + 0.2$

Flea: $h = -16t^2 + 8t$

Basketball player: $h = -16t^2 + 16t + 6.5$

1. Use your calculator to make tables and graphs of these three equations. Look at heights for time values between 0 seconds and 1 second. In your tables, use time intervals of 0.1 second.

2. What is the maximum height reached by each jumper? When is the maximum height reached?

3. How long does each jump last?

4. What do the constant terms 0.2 and 6.5 tell you about the frog and the basketball player? How is this information represented on the graph?

5. For each jumper, describe the pattern of change in the height over time. Explain how the pattern is reflected in the table and the graph.

B. A jewelry maker would like to increase his profit by raising the price of his jade earrings. However, he knows that if he raises the price too high, he won't sell as many earrings and his profit will decrease.

The jewelry maker's business consultant develops the equation $P = 50s - s^2$ to predict the monthly profit *P* for a sales price *s*.

1. Make a table and a graph for this equation.

2. What do the equation, table, and graph suggest about the relationship between sales price and profit?

3. What sales price will bring the greatest profit?

4. How does this equation compare with the equations in Question A? How does it compare with other equations in this unit?

ACE Homework starts on page 64.

- The average flea weighs 0.000001 pound and is 2 to 3 millimeters long. It can pull 160,000 times its own weight and can jump 150 times its own length. This is equivalent to a human being pulling 24 million pounds and jumping nearly 1,000 feet!

- There are 3,000 known species and subspecies of fleas. Fleas are found on all land masses, including Antarctica.

- Most fleas make their homes on bats, rats, squirrels, and mice.

- The bubonic plague, which killed a quarter of Europe's population in the fourteenth century, was spread by rat fleas.

- Flea circuses originated about 300 years ago and were popular in the United States a century ago.

 Go Online   **For:** Information about fleas
PHSchool.com **Web Code:** ape-9031

4.3 Putting It All Together

You have used equations to model a variety of quadratic functions. You may have noticed some common characteristics of these equations. You have also observed patterns in the graphs and tables of quadratic functions.

To understand a relationship, it helps to look at how the value of one variable changes each time the value of the other variable increases by a fixed amount. For a linear relationship, the y-value increases by a constant amount each time the x-value increases by 1.

Look at this table for the linear relationship $y = 3x + 1$. The "first differences" are the differences between consecutive y-values.

Because the y-value increases by 3 each time the x-value increases by 1, the first differences for $y = 3x + 1$ are all 3.

Now, you'll look at differences for quadratic relationships.

$y = 3x + 1$

x	y
0	1
1	4
2	7
3	10
4	13
5	16

First differences

$4 - 1 = 3$
$7 - 4 = 3$
$10 - 7 = 3$
$13 - 10 = 3$
$16 - 13 = 3$

Getting Ready for Problem 4.3

The simplest quadratic relationship is $y = x^2$, and it is the rule for generating square numbers. In fact, the word *quadratic* comes from the Latin word for "square."

The table below shows that the first differences for $y = x^2$ are not constant.

$y = x^2$

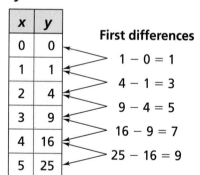

x	y
0	0
1	1
2	4
3	9
4	16
5	25

First differences

$1 - 0 = 1$
$4 - 1 = 3$
$9 - 4 = 5$
$16 - 9 = 7$
$25 - 16 = 9$

• What happens when you look at the "second differences" for $y = x^2$?

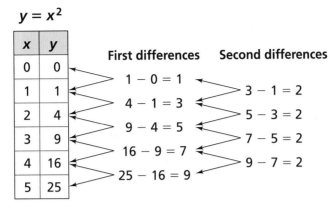

$y = x^2$

x	y
0	0
1	1
2	4
3	9
4	16
5	25

First differences
1 − 0 = 1
4 − 1 = 3
9 − 4 = 5
16 − 9 = 7
25 − 16 = 9

Second differences
3 − 1 = 2
5 − 3 = 2
7 − 5 = 2
9 − 7 = 2

• Study the pattern of first and second differences for $y = x^2$.
Do you think the tables for other quadratic functions will show a similar pattern?

Problem 4.3 Functions and Patterns of Change

A. 1. Make a table of values for each quadratic equation below. Include integer values of x from −5 to 5. Show the first and second differences as is done for the table above.

   a. $y = 2x(x + 3)$ **b.** $y = 3x - x^2$
   c. $y = (x - 2)^2$ **d.** $y = x^2 + 5x + 6$

   2. Consider the patterns of change in the values of y and in the first and second differences. In what ways are the patterns similar for the four tables? In what ways are they different?

   3. What patterns of change seem to occur for quadratic relationships?

B. 1. Make a table of (x, y) values for each equation below. Show the first and second differences.

   a. $y = x + 2$ **b.** $y = 2x$ **c.** $y = 2^x$ **d.** $y = x^2$

   2. Consider the patterns of change in the values of y and in the first and second differences. How are the patterns similar in all four tables? How are they different?

   3. How can you use the patterns of change in tables to identify the type of relationship?

ACE Homework starts on page 64.

Leon invents a puzzle. He makes a large cube from 1,000 centimeter cubes. He paints the faces of the large cube. When the paint dries, he separates the puzzle into the original centimeter cubes. The object of Leon's puzzle is to reassemble the cubes so that no unpainted faces are showing.

When Leon examines the centimeter cubes, he notices that some are painted on only one face, some on two faces, and some on three faces. Many aren't painted at all.

active math
online

For: Painted Cubes Activity
Visit: PHSchool.com
Web Code: apd-4401

Problem 4.4 Looking at Several Functions

In this problem, you will investigate smaller versions of Leon's puzzle.

A. 1. The cube at the right is made of centimeter cubes. The faces of this cube are painted. Suppose you broke the cube into centimeter cubes. How many centimeter cubes would be painted on

   a. three faces?

   b. two faces?

   c. one face?

   d. no faces?

2. Answer the questions from part (1) for cubes with edges with lengths of 3, 4, 5, and 6 centimeters.

Organize your data in a table like the one below.

Edge Length of Large Cube	Number of Centimeter Cubes	Number of Centimeter Cubes Painted On			
		3 faces	2 faces	1 face	0 faces
2					
3					
4					
5					
6					

B. Study the patterns in the table.

1. Describe the relationship between the edge length of the large cube and the total number of centimeter cubes.

2. Describe the relationship between the edge length of the large cube and the number of centimeter cubes painted on

   a. three faces   **b.** two faces

   c. one face   **d.** zero faces

3. Decide whether each relationship in parts (1) and (2) is linear, quadratic, exponential, or none of these.

C. 1. Write an equation for each relationship in parts (1) and (2) of Question B. Tell what the variables and numbers in each equation mean.

2. Sketch the graph of each equation. What shapes could you have predicted? Explain.

ACE Homework starts on page 64.

Applications

1. A signal flare is fired into the air from a boat. The height h of the flare in feet after t seconds is $h = -16t^2 + 160t$.

   a. How high will the flare travel? When will it reach this maximum height?

   b. When will the flare hit the water?

   c. Explain how you could use a table and a graph to answer the questions in parts (a) and (b).

2. A model rocket is launched from the top of a hill. The table shows how the rocket's height above ground level changes as it travels through the air.

   a. How high above ground level does the rocket travel? When does it reach this maximum height?

   b. From what height is the rocket launched?

   c. How long does it take the rocket to return to the top of the hill?

Height of Model Rocket

Time (seconds)	Height (feet)
0.00	84
0.25	99
0.50	112
0.75	123
1.00	132
1.25	139
1.50	144
1.75	147
2.00	148
2.25	147
2.50	144
2.75	139
3.00	132
3.25	123
3.50	112
3.75	99
4.00	84

3. A basketball player takes a shot. The graph shows the height of the ball, starting when it leaves the player's hands.

Basketball Throws

a. Estimate the height of the ball when the player releases it.

b. When does the ball reach its maximum height? What is the maximum height?

c. How long does it take the ball to reach the basket (a height of 10 feet)?

4. The highest dive in the Olympic Games is from a 10-meter platform. The height h in meters of a diver t seconds after leaving the platform can be estimated by the equation $h = 10 + 4.9t - 4.9t^2$.

Homework Help Online
PHSchool.com

For: Help with Exercise 4
Web Code: ape-4404

a. Make a table of the relationship between time and height.

b. Sketch a graph of the relationship between time and height.

c. When will the diver hit the water's surface? How can you find this answer by using your graph? How can you find this answer by using your table?

d. When will the diver be 5 meters above the water?

e. When is the diver falling at the fastest rate? How is this shown in the table? How is this shown in the graph?

5. Kelsey jumps from a diving board, springing up into the air and then dropping feet-first. The distance d in feet from her feet to the pool's surface t seconds after she jumps is $d = -16t^2 + 18t + 10$.

a. What is the maximum height of Kelsey's feet during this jump? When does the maximum height occur?

b. When do Kelsey's feet hit the water?

c. What does the constant term 10 in the equation tell you about Kelsey's jump?

6. The equation $h = -16t^2 + 48t + 8$ describes how the height h of a ball in feet changes over time t.

a. What is the maximum height reached by the ball? Explain how you could use a table and a graph to find the answer.

b. When does the ball hit the ground? Explain how you could use a table and a graph to find the answer.

c. Describe the pattern of change in the height of the ball over time. Explain how this pattern would appear in a table and a graph.

d. What does the constant term 8 mean in this context?

For Exercises 7–10, do parts (a)–(d) without a calculator.

a. Sketch a graph of the equation.

b. Find the x- and y-intercepts. Label these points on your graph.

c. Draw and label the line of symmetry.

d. Label the coordinates of the maximum or minimum point.

7. $y = 9 - x^2$ **8.** $y = 2x^2 - 4x$

9. $y = 6x - x^2$ **10.** $y = x^2 + 6x + 8$

11. a. How can you tell from a quadratic equation whether the graph will have a maximum point or a minimum point?

b. How are the x- and y-intercepts of the graph of a quadratic function related to its equation?

c. How are the x- and y-intercepts related to the line of symmetry?

For Exercises 12–17, predict the shape of the graph of the equation. Give the maximum or minimum point, the x-intercepts, and the line of symmetry. Use a graphing calculator to check your predictions.

12. $y = x^2$ **13.** $y = -x^2$ **14.** $y = x^2 + 1$

15. $y = x^2 + 6x + 9$ **16.** $y = x^2 - 2$ **17.** $y = x(4 - x)$

For Exercises 18–22, tell whether the table represents a quadratic relationship. If it does, tell whether the relationship has a maximum value or a minimum value.

Go Online
PHSchool.com
For: Multiple-Choice Skills Practice
Web Code: apa-4454

18.

x	−3	−2	−1	0	1	2	3	4	5
y	−4	1	4	5	4	1	−4	−11	−18

19.

x	0	1	2	3	4	5	6	7	8
y	2	3	6	11	18	27	38	51	66

20.

x	0	1	2	3	4	5	6	7	8
y	0	−4	−6	−6	−4	0	6	14	24

21.

x	−4	−3	−2	−1	0	1	2	3	4
y	5	4	3	2	1	2	3	4	5

22.

x	−4	−3	−2	−1	0	1	2	3	4
y	18	10	4	0	−2	−2	0	4	10

23. a. For each equation, investigate the pattern of change in the y-values. Describe the patterns you find.

$$y = 2x^2 \qquad y = 3x^2 \qquad y = \tfrac{1}{2}x^2 \qquad y = -2x^2$$

b. Use what you discovered in part (a) to predict the pattern of change for each of these equations.

$$y = 5x^2 \qquad y = -4x^2 \qquad y = \tfrac{1}{4}x^2 \qquad y = ax^2$$

c. Do your observations hold for $y = 2x^2 + 5$? Do they hold for $y = 2x^2 + 5x$?

24. a. Make a table of (x, y) values for the six points shown on the graph.

b. The graph shows a quadratic relationship. Extend the graph to show x-values from 5 to 10. Explain how you know your graph is correct.

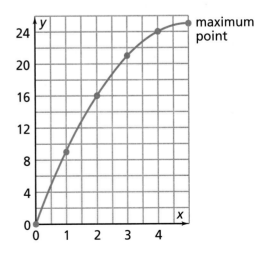

maximum point

Investigation 4 What Is a Quadratic Function? **67**

25. The graph shows a quadratic relationship. Extend the graph to show *x*-values from −4 to 0.

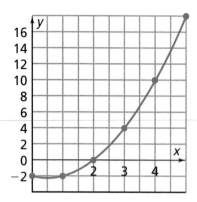

26. The table at the right shows a quadratic relationship. Extend the table to show *x*-values from 0 to −5. Explain how you know your table is correct.

27. A cube with edges of length 12 centimeters is built from centimeter cubes. The faces of the large cube are painted. How many centimeter cubes will have

a. three painted faces? **b.** two painted faces?

c. one painted face? **d.** no painted faces?

x	y
0	8
1	3
2	0
3	−1
4	0
5	3

28. Four large cubes are built from centimeter cubes. The faces of each large cube are painted. In parts (a)–(d), determine the size of the large cube.

a. For Cube A, 1,000 of the centimeter cubes have no painted faces.

b. For Cube B, 864 of the centimeter cubes have one painted face.

c. For Cube C, 132 of the centimeter cubes have two painted faces.

d. For Cube D, 8 of the centimeter cubes have three painted faces.

29. a. Copy and complete each table. Describe the pattern of change.

x	x
1	■
2	■
3	■
4	■
5	■

x	x^2
1	■
2	■
3	■
4	■
5	■

x	x^3
1	■
2	■
3	■
4	■
5	■

b. For each table, tell which column in the painted-cubes table in Problem 4.4 has a similar pattern. Explain.

30. Consider the relationships described by these equations. Are any of them similar to relationships in the painted-cubes situation? Explain.

$$y_1 = 2(x - 1) \qquad y_2 = (x - 1)^3 \qquad y_3 = 4(x - 1)^2$$

Connections

31. a. Describe the patterns of change in each table. (Look closely. You may find more than one.) Explain how you can use the patterns to find the missing entry.

Table 1

x	y
0	25
1	50
2	100
3	200
4	400
5	▧

Table 2

x	y
−3	3
−2	6
−1	9
0	12
1	15
2	▧

Table 3

x	y
2	6
3	12
4	20
5	30
6	42
7	▧

Table 4

x	y
−2	21
−1	24
0	25
1	24
2	21
3	▧

b. Tell which equation matches each table.

$$y_1 = x^2 - 12 \qquad y_2 = x(x + 1) \qquad y_3 = 25 - x^2$$
$$y_4 = (x)(x)(x) \qquad y_5 = 3(x + 4) \qquad y_6 = 25(2)^x$$

c. Which tables represent quadratic functions? Explain.

d. Do any of the tables include the maximum y-value for the relationship?

e. Do any of the tables include the minimum y-value for the relationship?

32. A potter wants to increase her profits by changing the price of a particular style of vase. Using past sales data, she writes these two equations relating income I to selling price p:

$$I = (100 - p)p \text{ and } I = 100p - p^2$$

a. Are the two equations equivalent? Explain.

b. Show that $I = 100 - p^2$ is not equivalent to the original equations.

c. It costs \$350 to rent a booth at a craft fair. The potter's profit for the fair will be her income minus the cost of the booth. Write an equation for the profit M as a function of the price p.

d. What price would give the maximum profit? What will the maximum profit be?

e. For what prices will there be a profit rather than a loss?

33. A square has sides of length x.

a. Write formulas for the area A and perimeter P of the square in terms of x.

b. Suppose the side lengths of the square are doubled. How do the area and perimeter change?

c. How do the area and perimeter change if the side lengths are tripled?

d. What is the perimeter of a square if its area is 36 square meters?

e. Make a table of side length, perimeter, and area values for squares with whole-number side lengths from 0 to 12.

f. Sketch graphs of the (*side length, area*) and (*side length, perimeter*) data from your table.

g. Tell whether the patterns of change in the tables and graphs suggest linear, quadratic, exponential relationships, or none of these. Explain.

34. Eggs are often sold by the dozen. When farmers send eggs to supermarkets, they often stack the eggs in bigger containers in blocks of 12 eggs $\times$ 12 eggs $\times$ 12 eggs.

a. How many eggs are in each layer of the container?

b. How many eggs are there in an entire container?

35. A cube has edges of length x.

    a. Write a formula for the volume V of the cube in terms of x.

    b. Suppose the edge lengths of the cube double. How does the volume change?

    c. How do the surface area and volume change if the edge lengths triple?

    d. Make a table for cubes with whole number edge lengths from 0 to 12. Title the columns "Side Length," "Surface Area," and "Volume."

    e. Sketch graphs of the (*edge length, surface area*) and (*edge length, volume*) data from your table.

    f. Tell whether the patterns of change in the tables and graphs suggest linear, quadratic, exponential relationships, or none of these.

36. Write each expression in expanded form.

    a. $-3x(2x - 1)$ **b.** $1.5x(6 - 2x)$

37. Write each expression in expanded form. Look for a pattern. Make a generalization about the expanded form of expressions of the form $(x + a)(x + a)$.

    a. $(x + 1)(x + 1)$ **b.** $(x + 5)(x + 5)$ **c.** $(x - 5)(x - 5)$

38. Write each expression in expanded form. Look for a pattern. Make a generalization about the expanded form of expressions of the form $(x + a)(x - a)$.

    a. $(x + 1)(x - 1)$ **b.** $(x + 5)(x - 5)$ **c.** $(x + 1.5)(x - 1.5)$

39. Use your generalizations from Exercises 37 and 38 to write each of these expressions in factored form.

    a. $x^2 + 6x + 9$ **b.** $x^2 - 6x + 9$ **c.** $x^2 - 9$ **d.** $x^2 - 16$

40. Write each expression in factored form.

    a. $2x^2 + 5x + 3$ **b.** $4x^2 - 9$ **c.** $4x^2 + 12x + 9$

41. a. Find the areas of these circles.

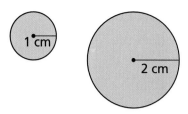

b. Copy and complete this table. Is the relationship between the area and the radius quadratic? Explain.

Radius (cm)	1	2	3	4	x
Area (cm²)	▨	▨	▨	▨	▨

c. Below are nets for two cylinders with heights of 2 meters. Find the surface areas of the cylinders.

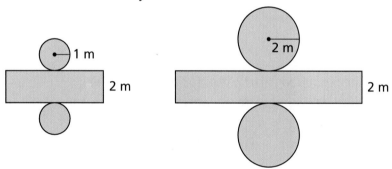

d. Copy and complete this table. Is the relationship between the surface area and the radius quadratic? Explain.

Radius (m)	1	2	3	4	x
Height (m)	2	2	2	2	2
Surface Area (m²)	▨	▨	▨	▨	▨

42. Multiple Choice The equation $h = 4 + 63t - 16t^2$ represents the height h of a baseball in feet t seconds after it is hit. After how many seconds will the ball hit the ground?

A. 2   **B.** 4   **C.** 5   **D.** 15

43. a. Complete the table to show surface areas of cylinders with equal radius and height. Use the nets shown.

Radius (ft)	1	2	3	4	x
Height (ft)	1	2	3	4	x
Surface Area (ft²)	▪	▪	▪	▪	▪

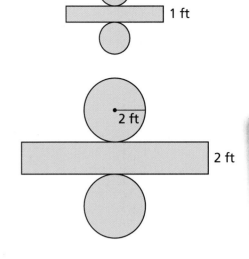

b. Is the relationship between surface area and radius quadratic? Explain.

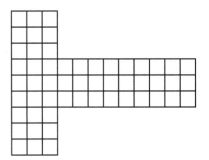

44. At the right is a net of a cube, divided into square units.

a. What is the edge length of the cube?

b. Find the surface area and volume of the cube.

c. Draw a net for a cube with a volume of 64 cubic units. What is the length of each edge of the cube? What is the surface area of the cube?

d. What formula relates the edge length of a cube to its volume? Is this relationship quadratic? Explain.

45. Silvio wants to gift wrap a cubic box that has edges measuring 16 inches. He has 10 square feet of wrapping paper. Is this enough to wrap the gift? Explain.

46. Multiple Choice Which table could represent a quadratic relationship?

F.

x	y
−3	−3
−2	−2
−1	−1
0	0
1	1
2	2
3	3

G.

x	y
−3	1
−2	2
−1	3
0	4
1	3
2	2
3	1

H.

x	y
1	0
2	2
3	6
4	12
5	20
6	30
7	42

J.

x	y
−1	10
0	7
1	4
2	1
3	4
4	7
5	10

47. Multiple Choice Suppose $y = x^2 - 4x$. If $y = 0$, what are all the possible values for x?

A. −4   **B.** 0   **C.** 4 or 0   **D.** −4 or 0

48. The cube buildings below are shown from the front right corner.

Building 1 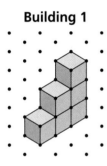   Building 2 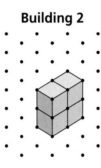   Building 3 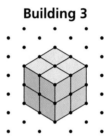   Building 4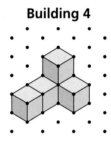

These drawings show the base outline, front view, and right view of Building 1. Draw these views for the other three buildings.

Base outline   Front view   Right view

49. Below are three views of a cube building. Draw a building that has all three views and has the greatest number of cubes possible. You may want to use isometric dot paper.

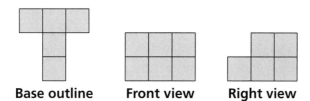

Base outline   **Front view**   **Right view**

50. Below are *base plans* for cube buildings. A base plan shows the shape of the building's base and the number of cubes in each stack.

Building 1

1	1	2
	3	1
	1	

Front

Building 2

1	1	2
1	3	
	1	

Front

Make a drawing of each building from the front right corner. You may want to use isometric dot paper.

Extensions

Use the following information for Exercises 51–53.

A soccer coach wants to take her 20-player team to the state capital for a tournament. A travel company is organizing the trip. The cost will be $125 per student. The coach thinks this is too expensive, so she decides to invite other students to go along. For each extra student, the cost of the trip will be reduced by $1 per student.

51. The travel company's expenses for the trip are $75 per student. The remaining money is profit. What will the company's profit be if the following numbers of students go on the trip?

    a. 20   b. 25   **c.** 60   **d.** 80

52. Let n represent the number of students who go on the trip. In parts (a)–(d), write an equation for the relationship described. It may help to make a table like the one shown here.

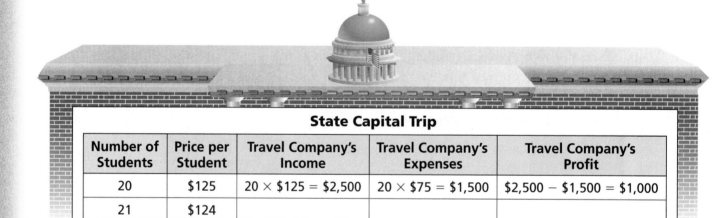

State Capital Trip

Number of Students	Price per Student	Travel Company's Income	Travel Company's Expenses	Travel Company's Profit
20	$125	20 × $125 = $2,500	20 × $75 = $1,500	$2,500 − $1,500 = $1,000
21	$124			

    a. the relationship between the *price per student* and n

    b. the relationship between the *travel company's income* and n

    c. the relationship between the *travel company's expenses* and n

    d. the relationship between the *travel company's profit* and n

53. Use a calculator to make a table and a graph of the equation for the travel company's profit. Study the pattern of change in the profit as the number of students increases from 25 to 75.

    a. What number of students gives the company the maximum profit?

b. What numbers of students guarantee the company will earn a profit?

c. What numbers of students will give the company a profit of at least $1,200?

54. A puzzle involves a strip of seven squares, three pennies, and three nickels. The starting setup is shown.

To solve the puzzle, you must switch the positions of the coins so the nickels are on the left and the pennies are on the right. You can move a coin to an empty square by sliding it or by jumping it over one coin. You can move pennies only to the right and nickels only to the left.

You can make variations of this puzzle by changing the numbers of coins and the length of the strip. Each puzzle should have the same number of each type of coin and one empty square.

a. Make drawings that show each move (slide or jump) required to solve puzzles with 1, 2, and 3 coins of each type. How many moves does it take to solve each puzzle?

b. A puzzle with n nickels and n pennies can be solved with $n^2 + 2n$ moves. Use this expression to calculate the number of moves required to solve puzzles with 1, 2, 3, 4, 5, 6, 7, 8, 9, and 10 of each type of coin.

c. Do your calculations for 1, 2, and 3 coins of each type from part (b) agree with the numbers you found in part (a)?

d. By calculating first and second differences in the data from part (b), verify that the relationship between the number of moves and the number of each type of coin is quadratic.

55. Complete parts (a) and (b) for each equation.

$y_1 = x + 1$ $\qquad\qquad$ $y_2 = (x + 1)(x + 2)$

$y_3 = (x + 1)(x + 2)(x + 3)$ $\qquad$ $y_4 = (x + 1)(x + 2)(x + 3)(x + 4)$

a. Describe the shape of the graph of the equation. Include any special features.

b. Describe the pattern of change between the variables.

56. The Terryton Tile Company makes floor tiles. One tile design uses grids of small, colored squares as in this 4 × 4 pattern.

a. Suppose you apply the same design rule to a 5 × 5 grid. How many small squares will be blue? How many will be yellow? How many will be orange?

b. How many small squares of each color will there be if you apply the rule to a 10 × 10 grid?

c. How many small squares of each color will there be if you apply the rule to an $n \times n$ grid?

d. What kinds of relationships do the expressions in part (c) describe? Explain.

57. This prism is made from centimeter cubes. After the prism was built, its faces were painted.

How many centimeter cubes have

a. no painted faces?   **b.** one painted face?

c. two painted faces?   **d.** three painted faces?

e. How many centimeter cubes are there in all?

Mathematical Reflections 4

In this investigation, you looked at the relationship between height and time for several situations. You also looked for common features in the tables, graphs, and equations for quadratic relationships. These questions will help you summarize what you have learned.

Think about your answers to these questions. Discuss your ideas with other students and your teacher. Then, write a summary of your findings in your notebook.

1. Describe three real-world situations that can be modeled by quadratic functions. For each situation, give examples of questions that quadratic representations help to answer.

2. How can you recognize a quadratic function from

   a. a table?

   b. a graph?

   c. an equation?

3. Compare the patterns of change for linear, exponential, and quadratic functions.

In this unit, you studied quadratic relationships. You learned to recognize quadratic patterns in graphs and tables and to write equations for those patterns. You answered questions about quadratic relationships by solving equations and by finding maximum and minimum points on graphs.

Go Online
PHSchool.com

For: Vocabulary Review Puzzle

Web Code: apj-4051

Use Your Understanding: Algebraic Reasoning

Test your understanding and skill in working with quadratic relationships by solving these problems about a carnival.

1. In the game pictured at the right, players hit the end of a lever with a mallet, propelling a weight upward. The player wins a prize if the weight hits the bell at the top.

   The height h of the weight in feet t seconds after the mallet strike is given by the equation $h = -16t^2 + bt$. The value of b depends on how hard the mallet hits the lever.

   a. Sketch the general shape of a graph of an equation of the form $h = -16t^2 + bt$.

   b. When Naomi plays, the weight rises 9 feet and falls back to the bottom in 1.5 seconds. Which table better matches this situation?

Table 1

Time (seconds)	0.0	0.25	0.5	0.75	1.0	1.25	1.5
Height (feet)	0	5	8	9	8	5	0

Table 2

Time (seconds)	0.0	0.25	0.5	0.75	1.0	1.25	1.5
Height (feet)	0	3	6	9	6	3	0

2. Wan's hit is hard enough to cause the weight to hit the bell. This situation is modeled by $h = -16t^2 + 32t$.

a. How high did the weight go?

b. How long did it take the weight to return to the starting position?

c. When was the weight 12 feet above the starting position?

3. The carnival is adding pony rides for young children. They have 180 feet of fence to build a rectangular pony corral.

a. Let x represent the length of the pony corral in feet. Write an expression for the width in terms of x.

b. Write an equation that shows how the area A of the corral is related to its length x.

c. What length and width will give an area of 2,000 square feet? Write and solve an equation whose solution is the required length.

d. What length and width will give the maximum area? Explain how you could use a table or graph to find this maximum area.

Explain Your Reasoning

To solve Problems 1–3, you had to use your knowledge of quadratic functions and of tables, graphs, and equations for quadratic situations.

4. Suppose the relationship between x and y is a quadratic function. What patterns would you expect to see

   a. in a table of (x, y) pairs?

   b. in a graph of (x, y) pairs?

   c. in an equation relating x and y?

5. How are the equations, tables, and graphs for quadratic relationships different from those for

   a. linear relationships?

   b. exponential relationships?

6. How can you tell whether the graph of a quadratic equation of the form $y = ax^2 + bx + c$ will have a maximum point or a minimum point?

7. What strategies can you use to solve quadratic equations such as $3x^2 - 5x + 3 = 0$ and $x^2 + 4x = 7$ by using

   a. a table of a quadratic function?

   b. a graph of a quadratic function?

Look Ahead

Quadratic functions are models for several important relationships between variables. They are also among the simplest examples of nonlinear relationships. You will encounter quadratic functions in future *Connected Mathematics* units and in future mathematics and science courses.

C

constant term A number in an algebraic expression that is not multiplied by a variable. In the expanded form of a quadratic expression, $ax^2 + bx + c$, the constant term is the number c. The constant term in the expression $-16t^2 + 64t + 7$ is 7. The constant term in the expression $x^2 - 4$ is -4.

término constante Un número en una expresión algebraica que no está multiplicado por una variable. En la forma desarrollada de una expresión cuadrática, $ax^2 + bx + c$, el término constante es el número c. El término constante en la expresión $-16t^2 + 64t + 7$ es 7. El término constante en la expresión $x^2 - 4$ es -4.

D

Distributive Property For any three numbers a, b, and c, $a(b + c) = ab + bc$.

propiedad distributiva Para cualesquiera tres números a, b y c, $a(b + c) = ab + bc$.

E

expanded form The form of an expression composed of sums and differences of terms, rather than products of factors. The expressions $x^2 + 7x - 12$ and $x^2 + 2x$ are in expanded form.

forma desarrollada La forma de una expresión compuesta de sumas o diferencias de términos, en vez de productos de factores. Las expresiones $x^2 + 7x - 12$ y $x^2 + 2x$ están representadas en forma desarrollada.

F

factored form The form of an expression composed of products of factors, rather than sums or differences of terms. The expressions $x(x - 2)$ and $(x + 3)(x + 4)$ are in factored form.

forma de factores La forma de una expresión compuesta de productos de factores, en vez de sumas o diferencias de términos. Las expresiones $x(x - 2)$ y $(x + 3)(x + 4)$ están representadas en forma de factores.

function A relationship between two variables in which the value of one variable depends on the value of the other. The relationship between length and area for rectangles with a fixed perimeter is a function; the area of the rectangle depends on, or is a *function* of, the length. If the variable y is a function of the variable x, then there is exactly one y-value for every x-value.

función Una relación entre dos variables en la cual el valor de una variable depende del valor de la otra variable. La relación entre la longitud y el área para rectángulos con un perímetro fijo puede considerarse como una función, donde el área del rectángulo depende de la longitud, o es una función de ésta. Si la variable y es una función de la variable x, entonces hay exactamente un valor de y para cada valor de x.

L

like terms Terms with the same variable raised to the same power. In the expression $4x^2 + 3x - 2x^2 - 2x + 1$, $3x$ and $-2x$ are like terms, and $4x^2$ and $-2x^2$ are like terms.

términos semejantes Términos con la misma variable elevada a la misma potencia. En la expresión $4x^2 + 3x - 2x^2 - 2x + 1$, $3x$ y $-2x$ son términos semejantes y $4x^2$ y $-2x^2$ son términos semejantes

line of symmetry A line that divides a graph or drawing into two halves that are mirror images of each other.

eje de simetría Una línea que divide una gráfica o un dibujo en dos mitades que son imágenes especulares entre sí.

linear term A part of an algebraic expression in expanded form in which the variable is raised to the first power. In the expression $4x^2 + 3x - 2x + 1$, $3x$ and $-2x$ are linear terms.

término lineal Una parte de una expresión algebraica en la que la variable está elevada a la primera potencia, especialmente en la forma desarrollada de una expresión. En la expresión $4x^2 + 3x - 2x + 1$, $3x$ y $-2x$ son términos lineales.

Ⓜ

maximum value The greatest y-value a function assumes. If y is the height of a thrown object, then the maximum value of the height is the greatest height the object reaches. If you throw a ball into the air, its height increases until it reaches the maximum height, and then its height decreases as it falls back to the ground. If y is the area of a rectangle with a fixed perimeter, then the maximum value of the area, or simply the maximum area, is the greatest area possible for a rectangle with that perimeter. In this unit, you found that the maximum area for a rectangle with a perimeter of 20 meters is 25 square meters.

valor máximo El mayor valor de y en una función. Si y es altura de un objeto lanzado, entonces el valor máximo de la altura, o simplemente la altura máxima, es la mayor altura que alcanza el objeto. Si lanzas una pelota al aire, su altura aumenta hasta que alcanza la altura máxima, y luego su altura disminuye a medida que vuelve a caer hacia la tierra. Si y es el área de un rectángulo con un perímetro fijo, entonces el valor máximo del área, o simplemente el área máxima, es la mayor área posible para un rectángulo con ese perímetro. En esta unidad, encontraste que el área máxima para un rectángulo con un perímetro de 20 metros es 25 metros cuadrados.

minimum value The least y-value a function assumes. If y is the cost of an item, then the minimum value of the cost, or simply the minimum cost, is the least cost possible for the item.

valor mínimo El valor más pequeño de y en una función. Si y es el costo de un artículo, entonces el valor mínimo del costo, o simplemente el costo mínimo, es el menor costo posible para ese artículo.

Ⓟ

parabola The graph of a quadratic function. A parabola has a line of symmetry that passes through the maximum point if the graph opens downward or through the minimum point if the graph opens upward.

parábola La gráfica de una función cuadrática. Una parábola tiene un eje de simetría que pasa por el punto máximo si la gráfica se abre hacia abajo, o por el punto mínimo si la gráfica se abre hacia arriba.

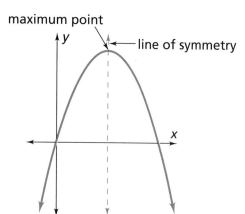

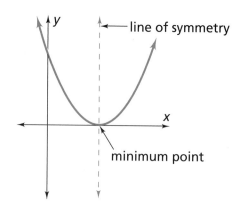

quadratic expression An expression that is equivalent to an expression of the form $ax^2 + bx + c$, where a, b, and c are numbers and $a \neq 0$. An expression in factored form is quadratic if it has exactly two linear factors, each with the variable raised to the first power. An expression in expanded form is quadratic if the highest power of the variable is 2. For example, $2x^2$, $3x^2 - 2x$, and $4x^2 + 2x - 7$ are all quadratic expressions. The expression $x(x - 2)$ is also a quadratic expression because $x(x - 2) = x^2 - 2x$. In this unit, you used quadratic expressions to represent the areas of rectangles for a fixed perimeter, the number of high fives between members of a team, and the path of a ball thrown into the air.

expresión cuadrática La expresión equivalente a una expresión de la forma $ax^2 + bx + c$, donde a, b, y c son números y $a \neq 0$. Una expresión en forma factorizada es cuadrática si tiene exactamente dos factores lineales, cada uno con la variable elevada a la primera potencia. Una expresión en forma desarrollada es cuadrática si la mayor potencia de la variable es 2. Por ejemplo, $2x^2$, $3x^2 - 2x$ y $4x^2 + 2x - 7$ son expresiones cuadráticas. La expresión $x(x - 2)$ también es una expresión cuadrática porque $x(x - 2) = x^2 - 2x$. En esta unidad, usaste expresiones cuadráticas para representar áreas de rectángulos para un perímetro fijo, el número de saludos entre los miembros de un equipo y el recorrido de una pelota lanzada al aire.

quadratic relationship A relationship between the independent and dependent variables such that, as the dependent values increase by a constant amount, the successive (first) differences between the dependent values change by a constant amount. For example, in $y = x^2$, as x increases by 1, the first differences for y increase by 3, 5, 7, 9, . . . and then the second differences increase by 2, 2, 2, ... The graphs of quadratic relationships have the shape of a U or upside down U with a line of symmetry through a maximum or minimum point on the graph that is perpendicular to the x-axis.

relación cuadrática Una relación entre las variables dependiente e independiente, de modo que, a medida aumentan los valores de la variable dependiente en una cantidad constante, las diferencias sucesivas (primera) entre los valores dependientes cambian en una cantidad constante. Por ejemplo, en $y = x^2$, a medida que x aumenta en 1, las primeras diferencias para y aumentan en 3, 5, 7, 9, . . . y luego las segundas diferencias aumentan en 2, 2, 2, ... Las gráficas de las relaciones cuadráticas tienen la forma de una U o una U invertida, con un eje de simetría que pasa por el punto máximo o mínimo de la gráfica perpendicular al eje de x.

quadratic term A part of an expression in expanded form in which the variable is raised to the second power. In the expression $4x^2 + 3x - 2x^2 - 2x + 1$, $4x^2$ and $-2x^2$ are quadratic terms.

término cuadrático Parte de una expresión en forma desarrollada, en la que la variable está elevada a la segunda potencia. En la expresión $4x^2 + 3x - 2x^2 - 2x + 1$, $4x^2$ y $-2x^2$ son términos cuadráticos.

term An expression that consists of either a number or a number multiplied by a variable raised to a power. In the expression $3x^2 - 2x + 10$, $3x^2$, $-2x$, and 10 are terms.

término Una expresión con números y/o variables multiplicados por una variable elevada a una potencia. En la expresión $3x^2 - 2x + 10$, $3x^2$, $-2x$, y 10 son términos.

triangular number A number that gives the total number of dots in a triangular pattern. The first four triangular numbers are 1, 3, 6, and 10, the numbers of dots in Figures 1 through 4 below.

número triangular Un número que da el número total de puntos en un patrón triangular. Los primeros cuatro números triangulares son 1, 3, 6 y 10, el número de puntos en las Figuras 1 a 4 de abajo.

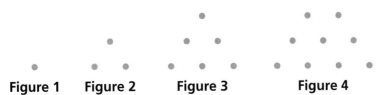

Figure 1   Figure 2   Figure 3   Figure 4

Index

Index

Acknowledgments

Team Credits

The people who made up the **Connected Mathematics 2** team —representing editorial, editorial services, design services, and production services— are listed below. Bold type denotes core team members.

Leora Adler, Judith Buice, Kerry Cashman, Patrick Culleton, Sheila DeFazio, Richard Heater, **Barbara Hollingdale, Jayne Holman,** Karen Holtzman, **Etta Jacobs,** Christine Lee, Carolyn Lock, Catherine Maglio, **Dotti Marshall,** Rich McMahon, Eve Melnechuk, Kristin Mingrone, Terri Mitchell, **Marsha Novak,** Irene Rubin, Donna Russo, Robin Samper, Siri Schwartzman, **Nancy Smith,** Emily Soltanoff, **Mark Tricca,** Paula Vergith, Roberta Warshaw, Helen Young

Additional Credits

Diana Bonfilio, Mairead Reddin, Michael Torocsik, nSight, Inc.

Technical Illustration

WestWords, Inc.

Cover Design

tom white.images

Connected Mathematics 2

Kaleidoscopes, Hubcaps, and Mirrors

Symmetry and Transformations

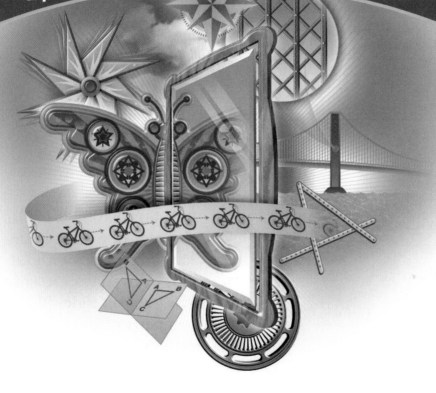

Glenda Lappan
James T. Fey
William M. Fitzgerald
Susan N. Friel
Elizabeth Difanis Phillips

PEARSON

Prentice
Hall

Boston, Massachusetts
Upper Saddle River, New Jersey

Kaleidoscopes, Hubcaps, and Mirrors

Symmetry and Transformations

If you rotated this wheel 72°, it would look exactly as it does in this picture. For what other rotations would the wheel look the same as it does here?

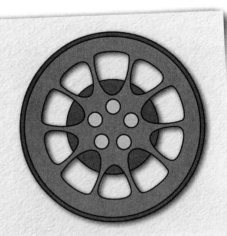

This tessellation is made of copies of a basic figure that fit together without gaps or overlaps. Describe how you can slide, flip, or turn parts of this design to fit exactly on top of other parts.

The drawing window of many geometry programs is like a coordinate grid. What happens to the coordinates of a point on a figure when you slide, flip, or turn the figure?

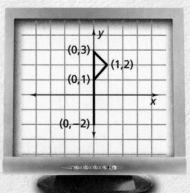

The kaleidoscope design, and quilts below may look very different, but all four illustrate an important property called symmetry. In each design, there is some part that is repeated to make a balanced pattern. In this unit, you will study the properties special to symmetric figures and the actions used to make them.

Mathematical Highlights

In *Kaleidoscopes, Hubcaps, and Mirrors* you will extend your knowledge of geometric shapes and ways to compare them.

You will learn how to

- Identify figures with different kinds of symmetry
- Describe types of symmetry in terms of the images made by applying reflections, rotations, and translations to points of the original figure.
- Use transformations to construct figures with different kinds of symmetry
- Use symmetry transformations to compare the size and shape of figures to see whether they are congruent
- Identify congruent triangles and quadrilaterals efficiently
- Use properties of congruent triangles to solve problems about shapes and measurements

As you work on problems in this unit, ask yourself questions about situations that involve geometric figures.

How can I use symmetry to describe the shapes and properties of figures in a design or a problem?

Which figures in a pattern are congruent?

What parts of a figure will be matched by a congruence transformation?

Three Types of Symmetry

When part of a design is repeated to make a balanced pattern, we say the design has **symmetry.** Artists use symmetry to make designs that are pleasing to the eye. Architects use symmetry to produce a sense of balance in their buildings. Symmetry is also a feature of animals, plants, and mechanical objects.

The butterfly, fan, and ribbon below illustrate three kinds of symmetry.

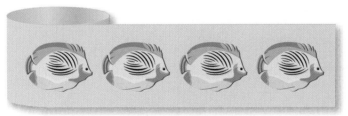

Getting Ready for Problem 1.1

- What part of each design is repeated to make a balanced pattern that allows us to say the three figures have symmetry?
- How do the figures suggest different kinds of symmetry?

You have probably made simple heart shapes by folding and cutting paper as shown below.

The resulting heart shape has **reflection symmetry,** which is sometimes called *mirror symmetry* or *line symmetry*. The fold shows the **line of symmetry.** A line of symmetry divides a figure into halves that are mirror images.

If you place a mirror on a line of symmetry, you will see half of the figure reflected in the mirror. The combination of the half-figure and its reflection will have the same size and shape as the original figure. You can use a mirror to check a design for symmetry and to locate the line of symmetry.

You can also use tracing paper to check for reflection symmetry. Trace the figure and the possible line of symmetry. Then reflect the tracing over the possible line of symmetry. If the reflected tracing fits exactly on the original figure, the figure has reflection symmetry.

What happens to the line of symmetry when you reflect the tracing and match it with the original figure? Does its location change?

Problem 1.1 Reflection Symmetry

Use a mirror, tracing paper, or other tools to find all lines of symmetry in each design or figure.

A.

B.

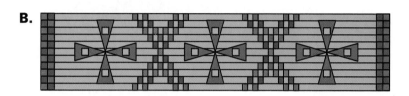

C.

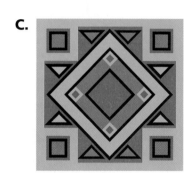

D.

E.

F.

G.

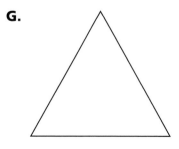

H.

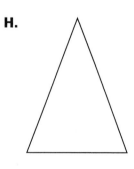

ACE Homework starts on page 15.

Rotation Symmetry

The pinwheel design at the right does not have reflection symmetry. However, it can be turned less than a full turn around its center point in a counterclockwise direction to positions in which it looks the same as it does in its original position. Figures with this property are said to have **rotation symmetry.**

The windmill, snowflake, and wagon wheel pictured below also have rotation symmetry.

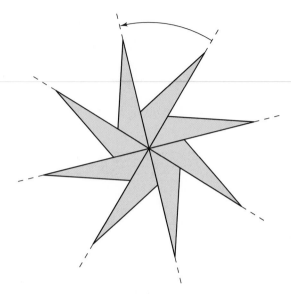

Which two of the three objects pictured above also have reflection symmetry?

To describe the rotation symmetry in a figure, you need to specify two things:

- The *center of rotation*. This is the fixed point about which you rotate the figure.

- The *angle of rotation*. This is the *smallest* angle through which you can turn the figure in a counterclockwise direction so that it looks the same as it does in its original position.

There are several rotation angles that move the pinwheel design above to a position where it looks like the original. In this problem, you will consider how these angles are related to the angle of rotation.

A. List all the turns of less than 360° that will rotate the pinwheel design to a position in which it looks the same as what is pictured. What is the angle of rotation for the pinwheel design?

B. In parts (1)–(3), list all the turns of less than 360° that will rotate the object to a position in which it looks the same as what is pictured. Then give the angle of rotation.

1. the windmill   **2.** the snowflake   **3.** the wagon wheel

C. Look at your answers for Questions A and B. For each object or figure, tell how the listed angles are related to the angle of rotation.

D. The hubcaps below have rotation symmetry. Complete parts (1) and (2) for each hubcap.

Hubcap 1

Hubcap 2

1. On a copy of the hubcap, mark the center of rotation. Then, find all the turns of less than 360° that will rotate the hubcap to a position in which it looks the same as what is pictured.

2. Tell whether the hubcap has reflection symmetry. If it does, draw all the lines of symmetry.

E. Draw a hubcap design that has rotation symmetry with a 90° angle of rotation but no reflection symmetry.

F. Draw a hubcap design that has rotation symmetry with a 60° angle of rotation and at least one line of symmetry.

G. Investigate whether rectangles and parallelograms have rotation symmetry. Make sketches. For the shape(s) with rotation symmetry, give the center and angle of rotation.

active math
online

For: Hubcap Maker
Visit: PHSchool.com
Web Code: apd-5102

ACE Homework starts on page 15.

A *kaleidoscope* (kuh ly duh skohp) is a tube containing colored beads or pieces of glass and carefully placed mirrors. When you hold a kaleidoscope up to your eye and turn the tube, you see colorful symmetric patterns.

The kaleidoscope was patented in 1817 by the Scottish scientist Sir David Brewster. Brewster was intrigued by the science of nature. He developed kaleidoscopes to simulate the designs he saw in the world around him.

Five of the designs below are called kaleidoscope *designs* because they are similar to designs you would see if you looked through a kaleidoscope.

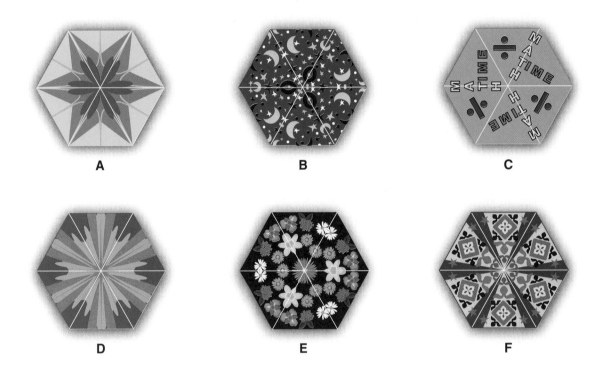

A   B   C

D   E   F

Use what you know about reflection and rotation symmetry to analyze the six designs.

A. Locate all the lines of symmetry in the designs.

B. Give the angles of rotation for the designs with rotation symmetry.

C. 1. Make a table showing the number of lines of symmetry and the angle of rotation for each design.

2. What relationship, if any, do you see between the number of lines of symmetry and the angle of rotation?

3. Analyze the kaleidoscope design below to see whether it confirms your relationship.

D. Each of the designs can be made by repeating a small piece of the design. We call this piece the **basic design element.** For each design, sketch or outline the basic design element.

E. One of the designs is *not* a kaleidoscope design. That is, it is not similar to a design you would see if you looked through a kaleidoscope. Which design do you think it is? Why?

ACE Homework starts on page 15.

The next three designs are examples of "strip patterns." You can draw a strip pattern by repeating a basic design element at regular intervals to the left and right of the original.

You can use a similar design strategy to make a "wallpaper pattern" like the one below.

Making a strip pattern or a wallpaper design requires a series of "draw and move" steps. You draw a basic design element. Then, you slide your pencil to a new position and repeat the element. You slide in the same way to a new position and repeat the element again, and so on. The slide movements from one position to the next are called **translations.**

Getting Ready for Problem

- Suppose the strip patterns on the previous page extend forever in both directions. Describe how you can move each infinite pattern so it looks exactly the same as it does in its original position.

- Suppose the wallpaper pattern on the previous page extends forever in all directions. Describe how you can move the infinite pattern so it looks exactly the same as it does in its original position.

A design has **translation symmetry** if you can slide the whole design to a position in which it looks exactly the same as it did in its original position.

To describe translation symmetry, you need to specify the distance and direction of the translation. You can do this by drawing an arrow indicating the slide that would move the design "onto itself."

Questions about translation symmetry are of two kinds.

- Given a basic design element, how can you use draw-and-slide operations to produce a pattern with translation symmetry?

- How can you tell whether a given design has translation symmetry?

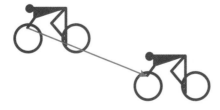

A. Cut a long strip of paper about one inch wide. Use the basic design element below to draw a strip pattern on the paper. The resulting strip pattern can be found in fabrics made by the Mayan people who live in Central America.

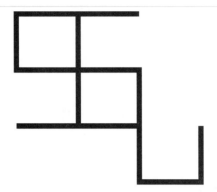

B. 1. Below is a part of a design that extends forever in all directions. Outline a basic design element that can be used to make the entire design using only translations.

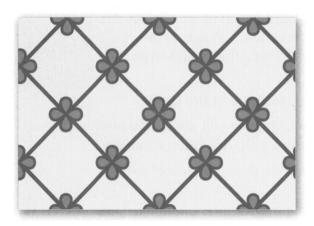

2. Describe precisely how the basic design element can be copied and translated to produce the pattern. Your description should include diagrams with arrows and measures of distances.

ACE Homework starts on page 15.

Applications

1. Which capital letters have reflection symmetry? For each one that does, describe all the lines of symmetry.

A B C D E F G H I J K L M N O P Q R S T U V W X Y Z

Tell whether the design has reflection symmetry. If it does, sketch the design and draw all the lines of symmetry.

Go Online
PHSchool.com
For: Multiple-Choice Skills Practice
Web Code: apa-5154

2.

3.

4.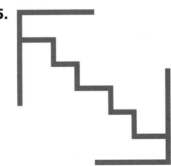

5.

For Exercises 6–9, tell whether the design has reflection symmetry. If it does, sketch the design and draw all the lines of symmetry.

6.

7.

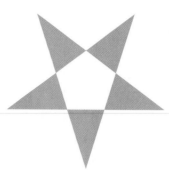

8.

9.

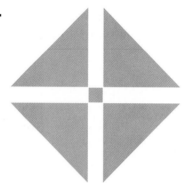

10. Which of the figures in Exercises 2–9 have rotation symmetry? For each one that does, find the angle of rotation and tell which multiples of this angle rotate the figure to a position in which it looks like the original.

Homework Help Online
PHSchool.com
For: Help with Exercise 10
Web Code: ape-5110

11. Which capital letters have rotation symmetry? For each one that does, give the angle of rotation.

A B C D E F G H I J K L M N O P Q R S T U V W X Y Z

For Exercises 12–14, use the flag shape at the right as a basic design element. Complete a design with rotation symmetry and give the angle of rotation.

12.

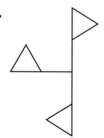

13.

14.

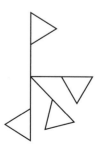

15. a. Give the angle of rotation for the hubcap at the right.

b. Copy the hubcap and draw the lines of symmetry.

16. Draw a hubcap design that has rotation symmetry with a 120° angle of rotation and at least one line of symmetry.

17. Multiple Choice Which figure does not have rotation symmetry?

A.   **B.**   **C.**   **D.**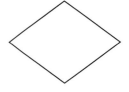

Describe the reflection and rotation symmetries for each traditional quilt design.

18.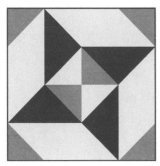

19.

For Exercises 20–23, copy the drawing. Then, draw a design with the given lines as lines of symmetry.

20.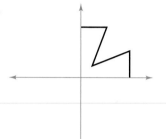

21.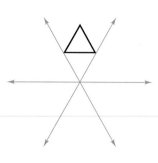

22.

23. 1 2 3 4 5 6 7 8 9 0

For Exercises 24 and 25, describe the rotation and reflection symmetries for the design.

24.

25.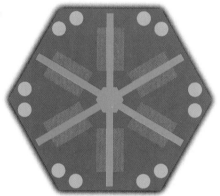

26. In parts (a) and (b), use a capital letter as the basic design element.

   a. Sketch a strip pattern with reflection symmetry only.

   b. Sketch a strip pattern with reflection symmetry and rotation symmetry.

27. a. Using the capital letter X as the basic design element, sketch part of a wallpaper pattern.

   b. Show, with arrows, all the translations that slide the design onto itself.

   c. Draw the lines of symmetry for your design.

   d. Describe the rotation symmetries in your design.

For Exercises 28–30, identify the basic design element for the wallpaper design. Then, describe how this basic design element can be copied and translated to produce the pattern. Include diagrams with arrows and measures of distance.

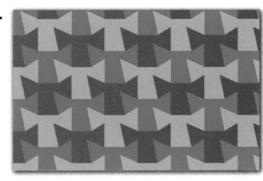

28.

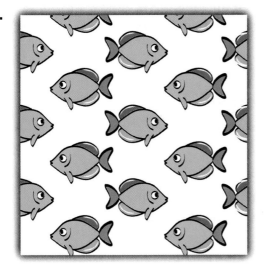

29.

30.

Connections

Consider state names written in capital letters (for example, ALABAMA or MICHIGAN).

31. Find a state name that has reflection symmetry when written horizontally.

32. Find a state name that has reflection symmetry when written vertically.

33. Write a word or phrase that has

    a. reflection symmetry when written horizontally

    b. reflection symmetry when written vertically

Draw an example of each type of polygon. Draw all the lines of symmetry. If the polygon has rotation symmetry, identify the center and angle of rotation.

34. square

35. non-square rectangle

36. non-rectangular parallelogram

37. isosceles triangle

38. equilateral triangle

39. non-square rhombus

40. isosceles trapezoid

The designs in Exercises 41–45 are actually first names. Describe the symmetries in each name. Then, write the name in standard lettering.

46. Copy the design below. Then use tracing paper to help you sketch a full kaleidoscope design from this basic design element.

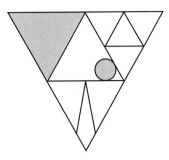

47. Prisms and cylinders each have two congruent faces one of which is the base. The drawings show a prism and a cylinder that are 4 centimeters high. Each is filled with a layer of centimeter cubes. The cubes in the bottom layer of the cylinder include some parts of cubes to make an exact covering of the base of the cylinder.

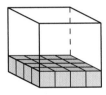

Rectangular Prism   Cylinder

   a. How many layers will it take to fill the prism?
   b What is the volume of the prism?
   c. What formula does this suggest for finding the volume of a prism?
   d. How many layers will it take to fill the cylinder?
   e. What is the volume of the cylinder?
   f. What formula does this suggest for finding the volume of a cylinder?
   g. How do the volumes of the prism and cylinder that are given compare?

48. At the right is a cylinder and below are three patterns that show the faces of that cylinder.

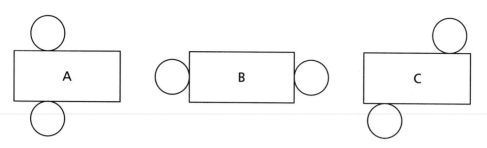

   a. Which pattern is not a flat pattern for a cylinder?

   b. Which patterns have reflection symmetry? Make sketches to show the lines of symmetry.

   c. Which patterns have rotation symmetry? Make sketches to show the centers of rotation.

   d. What measurements would you need to make to find the volume of a cylinder?

   e. How do your measurements connect to the formula for finding the volume?

   f. What is the volume of the cylinder if the base has a radius of 6 cm and the height is 15 cm?

49. Tyrone has been experimenting with cylinders and cones. He has made several paper cones and cylinders with the same height and base. He fills the cone with colored sand and pours it into the cylinder with the same base and height. To his surprise it always takes 3 cones of sand to exactly fill the cylinder.

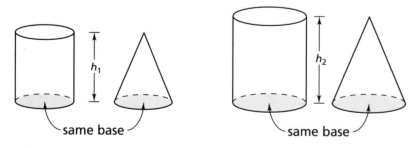

   a. The height of a cylinder is 8 cm and its base has a radius of 3 cm. What is the volume of the cone with the same base and height?

   b. What formula for the volume of a cone does Tyrone's experiments suggest?

   c. Tyrone makes some prisms and pyramids that are related. Each pair has the same base and height. He conducts the same experiment and finds that it always takes 3 pyramids to fill the matching prism exactly. What formula does this suggest for the volume of a pyramid?

d. If the base of a square pyramid is 7 cm on each edge and its height is 12 cm, what is its volume?

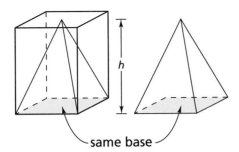

same base

These strip patterns are found in crafts in traditional cultures around the world. For each pattern, identify the basic design element and describe the lines of symmetry and center and angle of rotation. (Assume each design continues without bound to the left and right.)

50.

51.

52.

53.

Extensions

54. A regular hexagon can be enclosed by a circle as shown in the following sketch.

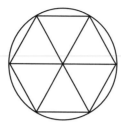

    a. Describe all the symmetries in the figure.

    b. What are the angle measures of the triangles in the figure? Explain how you know.

    c. Suppose you started with a circle with the center marked. How can you use the symmetries you observed in part (a) to construct

       • a regular triangle?

       • a regular hexagon?

    d. How are your answers to parts (a), (b), and (c) related to the symmetries in any kaleidoscope pattern?

55. In this investigation, you studied designs with reflection, rotation, and translation symmetries. The design below is a bit different from those you have seen.

    a. Trace a basic design element from which the rest of the pattern can be produced using only translations.

    b. Trace a smaller basic design element from which the rest of the pattern can be produced by using a translation followed by a reflection. Indicate the line of reflection and the length and direction of the translation.

    c. The movement required in part (b) to generate the pattern is called a *glide reflection*. What is the difference between a reflection and a glide reflection?

56. Using a capital letter as the basic design element, make a strip pattern using only glide reflections.

57. a. Make a sketch of the design below. Outline a basic design element that can be translated to produce the entire design.

b. Draw arrows to specify the distance and direction(s) you need to slide your basic element to make this design.

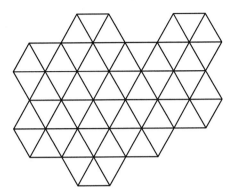

c. Can you translate a single triangle to make the design above? Explain.

Mathematical Reflections 1

In this investigation, you identified and made symmetric designs. These questions will help you summarize what you have learned.

Think about your answers to these questions. Discuss your ideas with other students and your teacher. Then, write a summary of your findings in your notebook.

1. How would you explain to someone what it means for a figure to have
   a. reflection symmetry?
   b. rotation symmetry?
   c. translation symmetry?

2. How can you use various drawing tools to test or draw figures with
   a. reflection symmetry?
   b. rotation symmetry?
   c. translation symmetry?

Investigation 2

Symmetry Transformations

You can make symmetric designs by copying a basic figure to produce a balanced pattern. For example, to construct a design with reflection symmetry, start with pentagon *ABCDE* and line *m* below.

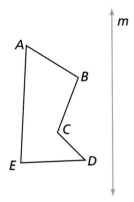

Reflect *ABCDE* in line *m* to get pentagon *A′B′C′D′E′*.

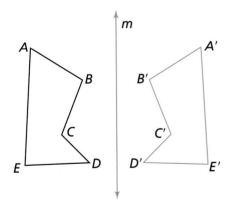

Reflecting a figure in a line is an example of a geometric operation called a **transformation.** A transformation produces a copy, or *image,* of an original figure in a new position.

In this investigation, you will explore the transformations associated with reflection, rotation, and translation symmetry.

2.1 Describing Line Reflections

Transformations that produce patterns with reflection symmetry are called **line reflections.**

Suppose you start with pentagon *ABCDE* and line *m* from the previous page.

How can you locate the reflection image A'B'C'D'E' without folding, tracing, or using a mirror?

Look for a precise way to describe a line reflection as you work through this problem.

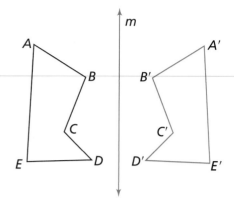

Problem 2.1 Describing Line Reflections

A. Copy pentagon *ABCDE*, its image, *A'B'C'D'E'*, and the line of reflection, *m*.

   1. Draw segments connecting each vertex of *ABCDE* to its image on *A'B'C'D'E'*. In other words, connect *A* to *A'*, *B* to *B'*, and so on.

   2. Use tools for measuring angles and lengths to see how the line of reflection is related to each segment you drew in part (1).

   3. Describe the patterns in your measurements from part (2).

B. 1. Copy quadrilateral *JKLM* and line *m* below. Use what you discovered in Question A to draw *J'K'L'M'*, the image of *JKLM* under a reflection in line *n*. Use only a pencil, a ruler, and an angle ruler or protractor. Explain how you located the image.

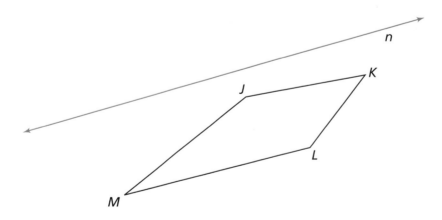

   2. Does *JKLM* have any symmetries? Explain.

   3. Does the figure made up of both *JKLM* and its reflection, *J'K'L'M'*, have any symmetries? Explain.

C. The design below has reflection symmetry. Copy the design. Use only a pencil, a ruler, and an angle ruler or protractor to locate the line of symmetry. Explain how you found the location of the line.

D. Complete this definition: A line reflection in a line *m* matches each point *X* on a figure to an image point *X′* so that . . .

E. Copy triangle *DEF* and line ℓ. Notice triangle *DEF* crosses the line.

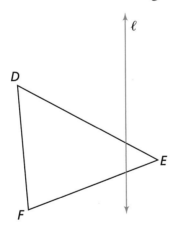

1. Does triangle *DEF* have reflection symmetry?

2. Draw the image of triangle *DEF* under a reflection in line ℓ.

3. Does the final figure, made of triangle *DEF* and its image, have reflection symmetry? Explain.

F. When you reflect a figure in a line, you can visualize reflecting the entire plane and taking the figure along for the ride. Are any points in the plane unmoved by a reflection? That is, are there any fixed points? Explain.

active math
online
For: The Transformation Tool
Visit: PHSchool.com
Web Code: apd-5201

ACE Homework starts on page 36.

2.2 Describing Rotations

The compass star shown at the right has rotation symmetry. You can turn it around its center point to a position in which it looks identical to the original figure. Such a turn matches each point in the original to an image point on the original figure.

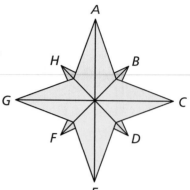

The transformation that turns a figure about a point, matching each point to an image point, is called a **rotation.**

In this problem, look for a way to describe the relationship between any point X and its image point X' under a rotation.

Problem 2.2 Describing Rotations

A. Copy the compass star above.

  1. What is the smallest counterclockwise turn (in degrees) that will rotate the star to a new position in which it looks identical to the original?

  2. Because the original figure has rotation symmetry, the image of each point on the original star is also a point on the rotated star. List the pairs of points and their images, matched by the rotation in part (1).

  3. Describe the paths the points of the original figure follow as they are "moved" to the positions of their images.

  4. How would you describe the relationship among any point X, its image, and the center of the compass star?

B. Copy the "flag" at the right.

  1. Does the flag have rotation symmetry? Explain.

  2. Draw the flag's image, $PQ'R'S'$, after a 60° counterclockwise rotation about point P. Use only tools for drawing and measuring segments and angles. Explain how you located the image points.

  3. Does the final figure, made up of the original flag and its image, have rotation symmetry?

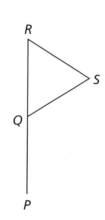

4. For which of these rotations about point P will the original flag and its image form a design with rotation symmetry?

12°   90°   40°   45°   180°

5. Can you make a design with rotation symmetry about P that consists of the original flag and more than one rotation image? If so, tell what rotations of the original are needed. If not, explain why.

C. 1. Point P is outside of rectangle $ABCD$. Copy the rectangle and point P. Draw the image of $ABCD$ after a 90° counterclockwise rotation about point P. Use only tools for drawing and measuring segments and angles.

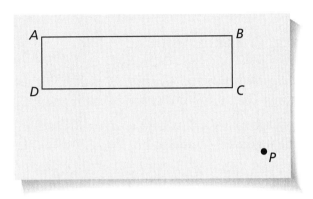

2. On your drawing in part (1), use a compass to draw a circle with center P and radius PB.

3. Describe the path the image of vertex B travels in a 90° rotation about point P. How is the movement of the image of vertex A similar? How is it different?

4. What can you say about segments PA and PA'? What can you say about segments PB and PB'?

5. Find the measures of angles APA', BPB', CPC', and DPD'. What can you conclude?

D. Complete this definition: A rotation of d degrees about a point P matches any point X with an image point X' so that . . .

E. When you rotate a figure about a point, you can visualize rotating the entire plane and taking the figure along for the ride. Are any points in the plane unmoved by a rotation? That is, are there any fixed points? Explain.

ACE Homework starts on page 36.

Strip patterns and wallpaper designs have translation symmetry. You can slide the designs to new positions where the overall pattern appears unchanged. The transformation that slides a figure, matching each point to an image point, is called a **translation.**

In this problem, look for a way to describe the relationship between any point X and its image point X' after a translation.

Problem 2.3 Describing Translations

A. Copy Diagrams 1 and 2, which show polygon $GHJKLM$ and its images under two different translations. Do the following for each diagram:

- Label the vertices of the image $G', H', J', K', L',$ and M' so that G' is the image of G, H' is the image of H, and so on.

- Draw line segments from each vertex of $GHJKLM$ to its image.

- Describe the pattern relating the segments GG', HH', etc.

Diagram 1

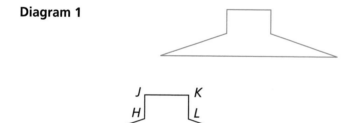

Diagram 2

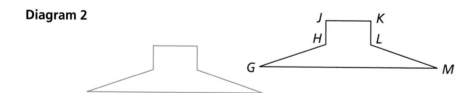

B. Will drew a polygon and then drew an arrow to specify a translation. Copy the polygon and the arrow. Draw the image of the polygon under the translation.

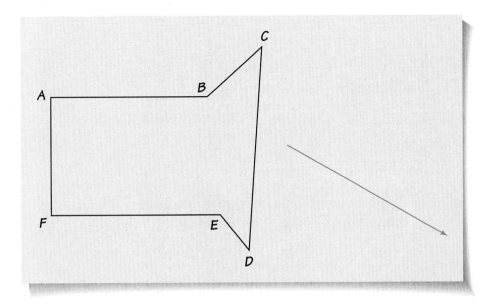

C. Complete this definition: A translation matches any two points X and Y with image points X' and Y' so that . . .

D. When you translate a figure, you can visualize translating the entire plane and taking the figure along for the ride. Are any points in the plane unmoved by a translation? That is, are there any fixed points? Explain.

 Homework starts on page 36.

2.4 Using Symmetry to Think About Tessellations

The design at the right is a **tessellation.** A tessellation is a design made from copies of a basic design element that cover a surface without gaps or overlaps.

Can you spot the basic design element that repeats over and over?

What types of symmetry do you see in the design as a whole?

To decide if a basic element will tessellate, you need to investigate transformations of the basic design element to see if some combination of transformations will cover the entire surface.

A. The design below is a tessellation.

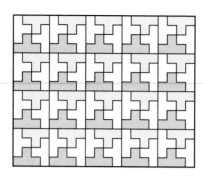

1. Sketch or outline the basic design element used to produce the tessellation. (**Hint:** Think about color as well as shape.)

2. Write directions or draw arrows to show how this basic element can be translated to produce other parts of the pattern.

3. Does the entire tessellation have reflection symmetry? Does it have rotation symmetry?

B. Rosslyn and Tevin both used the parallelogram at the right as a basic design element for a tessellation.

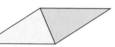

Rosslyn's Design

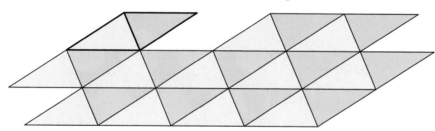

Tevin's Design

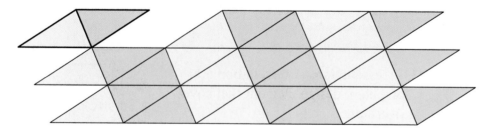

1. Does the basic design element have any symmetries? If so, describe them. If not, explain why.

2. Both Rosslyn and Tevin started their designs at the top left corner. Then, they made different moves to complete their tessellations. For each design, write detailed instructions explaining how to copy and move the highlighted element to fill the gap in the pattern. Is there more than one way to fill the gap?

3. Does either completed design have translation symmetry? Explain.

4. Does either completed design have reflection symmetry or rotation symmetry? Explain.

ACE Homework starts on page 36.

active math online

For: The interactive Escher-Like Maker
Web Code: apd-5204

Applications

1. Copy the diagram below. Draw the image of triangle *ABC* after a reflection in line *m*. Describe how the vertices of the image triangle relate to the vertices of the original triangle.

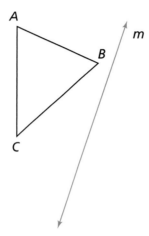

2. **a.** Copy the diagram at the right. Draw the reflection image of rectangle *JKLM* in line *ℓ*.

   b. Does the final drawing have reflection symmetry? Explain.

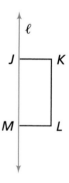

3. **a.** Copy the diagram below. Draw the reflection image of *PQRST* in the line *n*.

   b. Does the final drawing have reflection symmetry? Explain.

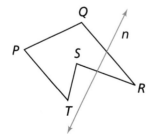

4. Quadrilateral $A'B'C'D'$ is a reflection image of quadrilateral $ABCD$.

Homework
Help **O**nline
——PHSchool.com
For: Help with Exercise 4
Web Code: ape-5204

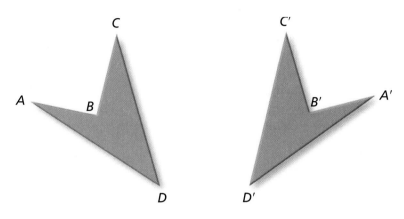

a. Copy the diagram and draw the line of reflection. Explain how you found it.

b. Describe the relationship between a point on the original figure and its image point on $A'B'C'D'$.

5. Shown below is a shape with reflection symmetry.

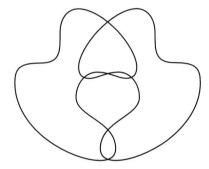

a. Copy the figure. Draw the line of reflection.

b. Label three points on the figure. Label the images of these points. Describe the relationship between each point and its image.

6. a. Copy triangle *XYZ*. Draw the image of the triangle after a 90° counterclockwise rotation about point *Z*. Describe how each vertex of the image triangle relates to the corresponding vertex on the original triangle.

b. Copy triangle *XYZ* and point *R*. Draw the image of the triangle after a 90° counterclockwise rotation about point *R*. Describe how each vertex of the image triangle relates to the corresponding vertex on the original triangle.

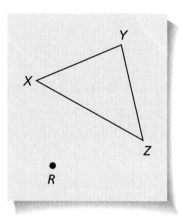

7. a. Copy polygon *FGHJK*. Draw the image of the polygon after a 180° counterclockwise rotation about point *K*. Describe how each vertex of the image polygon relates to the corresponding vertex on the original polygon.

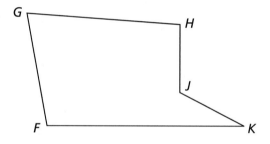

b. Copy polygon *FGHJK* and point *R*. Draw the image of the polygon after a 180° counterclockwise rotation about point *R*. Describe how each vertex of the image polygon relates to the corresponding vertex on the original polygon.

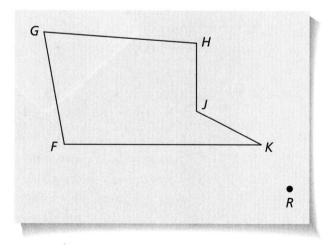

8. Copy triangle *PQR* and the arrow. Translate the triangle as indicated by the arrow. Describe how each vertex of the image triangle relates to the corresponding vertex on the original triangle.

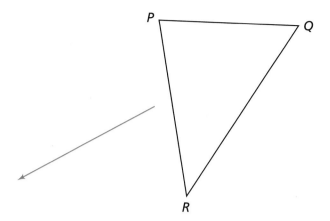

9. Use copies of the figure below for the drawings in parts (a)–(c).

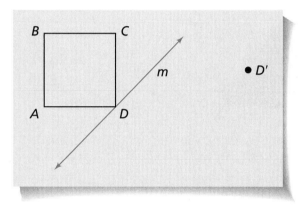

a. Draw the image of square ABCD under a reflection in line *m*.

b. Draw the image of square *ABCD* under a 45° rotation about point *A*.

c. Draw the image of square *ABCD* under the translation that slides point *D* to point *D′*.

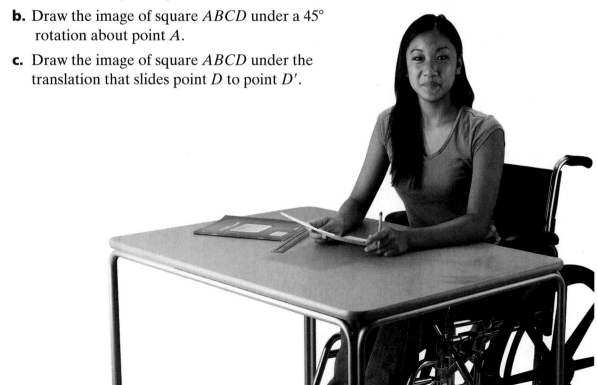

Exercises 10–13 each give a figure and its image under a transformation. Tell whether the transformation was a reflection, rotation, or translation. Then, indicate the line of reflection, the center and angle of rotation, or the direction and distance of translation.

Go Online
PHSchool.com
For: Multiple-Choice Skills
Practice
Web Code: apa-5254

10.

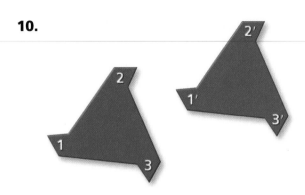

11.

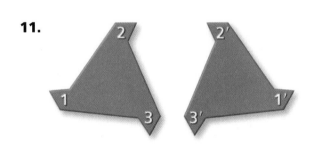

12. **13.**

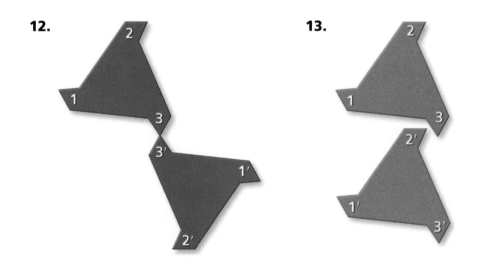

For Exercises 14 and 15, complete parts (a)–(c).

   a. Sketch a basic design element that can be used to produce the tessellation.

   b. Describe the types of symmetry in the tessellation. Assume the design continues without end in all directions.

   c. Describe the lines of symmetry, centers and angles of rotation, and directions and lengths of translations for the entire design.

14.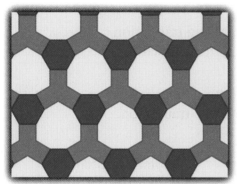

15.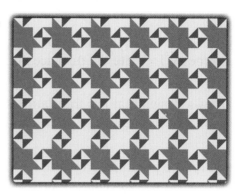

Connections

16. In the rectangle below, the lines of symmetry are shown. Explain how to use these lines of symmetry to find equal lengths in the figure.

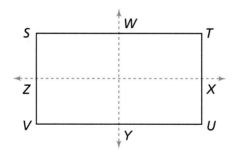

17. Draw a design that has both reflection symmetry and rotation symmetry. Explain how your design shows both types of symmetry.

18. What is the measure of each angle of a regular 10-sided polygon? Explain.

19. Draw a design that has reflection symmetry but no rotation symmetry. Show the line of symmetry.

20. Draw a design that has rotation symmetry but no reflection symmetry. What is the angle of reflection?

21. Can a regular pentagon and two regular hexagons meet at a vertex of a tessellation? Make a sketch to illustrate your answer.

22. Draw a design that has both reflection symmetry and translation symmetry. Indicate the distance and direction of the translation.

23. Draw a design that has translation symmetry but no reflection symmetry. Indicate the distance and direction of the translation.

24. a. Plot the points listed in the table on a coordinate grid, connecting them in order.

    b. What is the area of figure $ABCDE$?

    c. Apply the rule $(2x, 2y)$ to figure $ABCDE$ to obtain figure $A'B'C'D'E'$. Are the two figures similar? Explain.

    d. What is the area of figure $A'B'C'D'E'$?

    e. What rule can you apply to figure $ABCDE$ to obtain a smaller similar figure?

Point	Coordinates
A	(−2, −2)
B	(2, −2)
C	(2, 2)
D	(0, 5)
E	(−2, 2)
A	(−2, −2)

25. a. On a coordinate grid, draw a simple figure that has the x-axis as a line of symmetry.

    b. Apply the rule $(1.5x, 1.5y)$ to your figure. Is the new figure similar to the original?

    c. Apply the rule $(0.75x, 0.75y)$ to your original figure. Is the new figure similar to the original?

    d. Is the image in part (c) similar to the image in part (b)? Explain.

26. In *Stretching and Shrinking,* you used rubber bands to enlarge shapes. In the figure below, a rubber band was used to enlarge triangle *ABC.* The anchor point for the rubber band was at the origin. The knot traced around triangle *ABC* as the pencil drew triangle *DEF.*

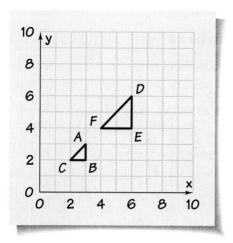

a. What is the scale factor from triangle *ABC* to triangle *DEF*?

b. On grid paper, sketch an enlargement of triangle *ABC* by a scale factor of 1.5 with the anchor point at the origin. Call this enlargement triangle *XYZ.*

c. How is triangle *XYZ* like or unlike a translation image of triangle *ABC*?

27. Multiple Choice This parallelogram has sides parallel to the line $y = x$. Which statement is true about the parallelogram?

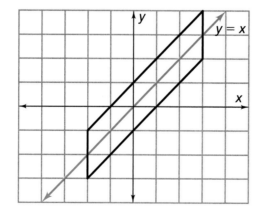

A. It has reflection symmetry in the line $y = x$.

B. It has rotation symmetry about the origin.

C. It has reflection symmetry in a vertical line that is not the *y*-axis.

D. It has rotation symmetry about a point that is not the origin.

28. a. Find the volume of a prism with the triangle at the right given as its base and with a height of 10 centimeters.

b. Find the volume of a pyramid with the same base and height.

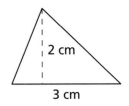

2 cm

3 cm

Extensions

29. Copy the figures below onto grid paper.

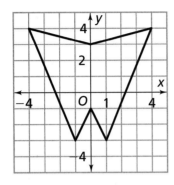 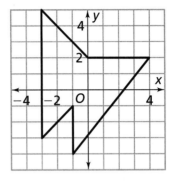

a. Which polygon has reflection symmetry about the *y*-axis?

b. Sketch images of each polygon under a line reflection in the *y*-axis.

c. How does the reflection image of the symmetric figure differ from the reflection image of the non-symmetric figure?

d. Will the difference you observed in part (c) occur for any pair of polygons in which one polygon has reflection symmetry and the other does not? Test your conjecture on several examples to see if you can find reasons for the patterns you observe.

30. Triangle *MBK* has its vertices on lines ℓ and *n*. Vertex *B* is the point of intersection of the lines.

a. Copy the figure at the right. Sketch the image of triangle *MBK* under a rotation of 180° about point *B*. Describe the locations of points M', B', and K'.

b. What angle in triangle $M'B'K'$ corresponds to angle *MBK* in the original triangle?

c. Make a conjecture about the angles formed when two lines intersect. Test your conjecture with several examples to see if you can find reasons for the patterns you observed.

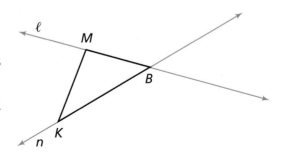

31. a. Copy the figure. Reflect triangle ABC in line ℓ. Label the image $A'B'C'$. Reflect triangle $A'B'C'$ in line m. Label the image $A''B''C''$.

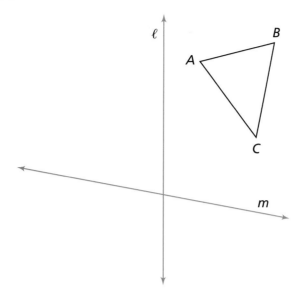

b. Can you relate triangle ABC to triangle $A''B''C''$ with a single transformation? If so, describe the transformation.

c. Practice reflecting figures in two intersecting lines. Make a conjecture based on your findings.

32. Copy the figures below onto grid paper.

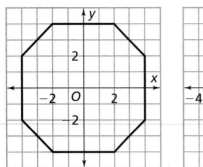 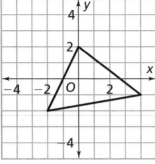

    a. Which polygon has rotation symmetry about the origin?

    b. Sketch the image of each polygon under a 90° counterclockwise rotation about the origin.

    c. How does the rotation image of the symmetric figure differ from the rotation image of the non-symmetric figure?

33. a. In the diagram below, lines *a* and *b* are parallel. Copy the diagram. Reflect triangle *EFG* in line *a*. Label the image *E′F′G′*. Reflect triangle *E′F′G′* in line *b*. Label the image *E″F″G″*.

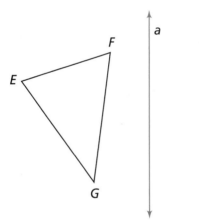 

    b. Can you move triangle *EFG* to triangle *E″F″G″* with a single transformation? If so, describe the transformation.

    c. Practice reflecting figures in two parallel lines. Make a conjecture based on your findings.

Mathematical Reflections 2

In this investigation, you identified properties of symmetry transformations. These questions will help you to summarize what you have learned.

Think about your answers to these questions. Discuss your ideas with other students and your teacher. Then, write a summary of your findings in your notebook.

1. In a line reflection,

    a. how are points and their images related to the line of reflection?

    b. how can you find the line of reflection if you know the images of some points?

2. In a rotation,

    a. how are points, their images, and the center of rotation related?

    b. how can you use the relationship between some points and their images to find the images of other points?

3. In a translation,

    a. how are points and their images related?

    b. how can you use the relationship between some points and their images to find the images of other points?

4. What is a basic design element in a tessellation? Explain and illustrate your answer.

Exploring Congruence

In *Stretching and Shrinking,* you learned that figures with the same shape are similar. Figures that have the same size, as well as the same shape, are said to be **congruent.**

In this investigation, you will learn some ways to compare the size and shape of figures. You will also use your knowledge about congruence to solve geometry problems.

3.1 Relating Symmetry and Congruence

You have learned about three kinds of transformations that relate a figure to an image that is the same size and shape. You can use this idea to think about congruence. Two figures are congruent if you can reflect, rotate, or translate one figure so the final image fits exactly on top of the other figure.

Getting Ready for Problem 3.1

All the turtles below are similar. The four small turtles are also congruent.

• What reflections, rotations, translations, and combinations of these transformations will relate each small turtle to the other congruent turtles?

The two quadrilaterals below are congruent.

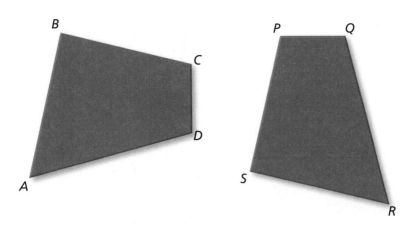

A. Suppose you copied *ABCD* and moved the copy so that it fit exactly on *PQRS*. Copy and complete these statements to show which vertices correspond. The arrow means "corresponds to."

$A \rightarrow$ ▨ $B \rightarrow$ ▨ $C \rightarrow$ ▨ $D \rightarrow$ ▨

B. The notation $\overline{AB}$ means "line segment *AB*." The symbol ≅ means "is congruent to." Copy and complete these statements to show which pairs of sides in the two quadrilaterals are congruent.

$\overline{AB} \cong$ ▨ $\overline{BC} \cong$ ▨ $\overline{CD} \cong$ ▨ $\overline{DA} \cong$ ▨

C. The notation ∠*A* means "angle *A*." Copy and complete these statements to show which angles are congruent.

$\angle A \cong$ ▨ $\angle B \cong$ ▨ $\angle C \cong$ ▨ $\angle D \cong$ ▨

D. Make a copy of *ABCD* on tracing paper. Investigate combinations of reflections, rotations, and translations that will move the copy of *ABCD* exactly on top of *PQRS*.

1. Is there a single reflection, rotation, or translation that matches each point of *ABCD* onto its corresponding point on *PQRS*?

2. What combination of reflections, rotations, and translations matches each point of *ABCD* onto its corresponding point on *PQRS*?

E. How could you rename *PQRS* so that the name shows how the vertices of *PQRS* correspond to those in *ABCD*?

ACE **Homework starts on page 56.**

Congruent polygons are often used to enhance the beauty and strength of buildings and other structures. This photograph of the George Washington Bridge in New York City shows congruent triangles in the bridge's towers.

If you look closely at the photograph, you can see that each tower is made up of rectangles. The diagonals of these rectangles form triangles.

Problem **3.2** Congruent Triangles

The figure at the right shows how the pieces of the bridge tower fit together.

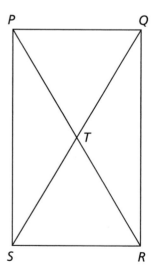

A. How many triangles can you find in the figure? Make a list using names such as $\triangle PTQ$, $\triangle PTS$, and so on. (The notation $\triangle PTQ$ means "triangle PTQ.")

B. Describe the symmetries of rectangle $PQRS$.

C. Make a list of the pairs of triangles that appear to be congruent.

D. For each pair you listed in Question C, describe a reflection, rotation, or translation that would match one triangle to its congruent partner.

E. Zoe writes $\triangle PTQ \cong \triangle RTS$. Is she correct? What information do you need to check her claim?

ACE Homework starts on page 56.

3.3 The Matching Game

The *Matching Game* will help you learn about properties of congruent polygons. The game is played by two teams of two players. The players can use only tools for drawing and measuring segments and angles.

- Each team has 15 points to "spend."

- One player on the first team is given a polygon with side and angle measures shown.

- The player gives his or her partner directions for drawing a congruent copy of the polygon, but does not show the polygon to his or her partner. For each side length or angle measure mentioned in the directions, the team must spend 1 point.

- The directions may include the words "triangle" or "quadrilateral" or "pentagon," but not any other clues such as "regular" or "right" or "square."

- When the drawer believes he or she has made a congruent copy, the players say "Done." The other team checks to see if the drawing is the same size and shape as the original.

- The teams take turns. The first team to spend all 15 of its points loses.

Getting Ready for Problem

How would you give directions to a partner for drawing a congruent copy of Figure 1?

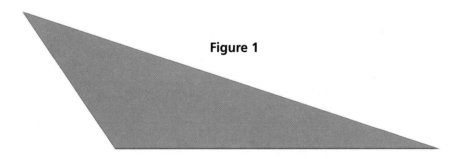

Figure 1

Use a set of *Matching Game* figures to play the game. Keep an eye out for winning strategies.

To play *The Matching Game* well, you need to think about this question:

How much information about two polygons will guarantee that they are congruent?

Problem 3.3 Congruent Triangles

A. 1. Suppose you are playing *The Matching Game*. Add steps to complete these drawing directions to make a figure congruent to Figure 1.

> **Step 1** Draw ∠*X* with a measure of 125°.
>
> **Step 2** On one side of ∠*X*, mark a point *Y* so that $\overline{XY}$ is 3.5 inches long.

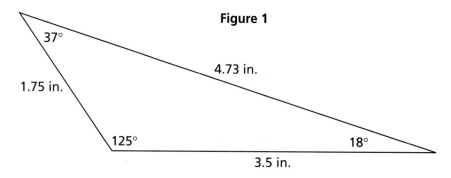

Figure 1

37°

4.73 in.

1.75 in.

125°   18°

3.5 in.

2. How many points would your team spend for all of your steps?

3. Find some other lists of directions that would work. Give the number of points for each possibility.

4. What are the fewest points your team would need to spend to make a congruent copy of Figure 1?

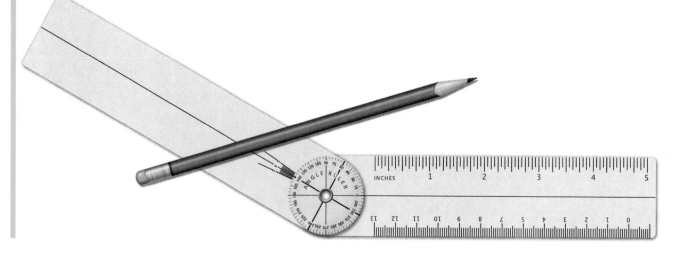

B. Tell whether you would be certain to draw a congruent copy of Figure 2 if you followed each set of directions.

Figure 2

Direction Set 1
Step 1 The figure is a triangle.
Step 2 Draw ∠A with a measure of 35°.
Step 3 Draw ∠B with a measure of 45°.
Step 4 Draw ∠C with a measure of 100°.

Direction Set 2
Step 1 The figure is a triangle.
Step 2 Draw ∠B with a measure of 45°.
Step 3 Draw $\overline{AB}$ with a length of 5 inches.
Step 4 Draw ∠C with a measure of 100°.

Direction Set 3
Step 1 The figure is a triangle.
Step 2 Draw ∠B with a measure of 45°.
Step 3 Draw $\overline{AB}$ with a length of 5 inches.
Step 4 Draw $\overline{AC}$ with a length of 3.6 inches.

Direction Set 4
Step 1 The figure is a triangle.
Step 2 Draw $\overline{AB}$ with a length of 5 inches.
Step 3 Draw $\overline{BC}$ with a length of 2.9 inches.
Step 4 Draw $\overline{CA}$ with a length of 3.6 inches.

C. Compare your results for Questions A and B with those of other students. Look for patterns that will help you answer this question:

What is the minimum information you need about the sides and angles of two triangles to be sure those triangles are congruent?

D. Identify a minimum set of angles and segments you could measure to give your partner enough information to draw a congruent copy of the pentagon. (You do not have to find the measures.)

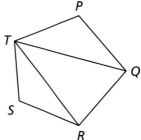

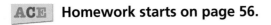
ACE Homework starts on page 56.

3.4 Polystrip Triangles and Quadrilaterals

In earlier geometry units, you used polystrips to build triangles, quadrilaterals, and other polygons. Building polystrip figures can help you study how side lengths affect the shapes of polygons.

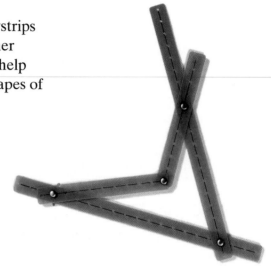

Problem 3.4 Side Lengths and Congruence

Use polystrips to explore the questions below. Make sketches to support your answers.

A. Tell how many different (non-congruent) triangles you can construct with each set of side lengths.

1. 20 cm, 20 cm, and 10 cm   **2.** 10 cm, 15 cm, and 20 cm

3. 20 cm, 5 cm, and 10 cm   **4.** 10 cm, 10 cm, and 10 cm

B. Tell how many different quadrilaterals you can construct with each set of side lengths in the given order.

1. 10 cm, 20 cm, 10 cm, 20 cm

2. 20 cm, 5 cm, 5 cm, and 5 cm

3. 10 cm, 10 cm, 20 cm, 20 cm

C. Compare your results for Questions A and B with those of other students. Look for patterns that will help you answer these questions.

1. What does knowing only the side lengths tell you about the size and shape of a triangle or a quadrilateral?

2. Suppose the corresponding sides of two triangles are the same length. Can you conclude that the triangles are congruent?

3. Suppose the corresponding sides of two quadrilaterals are the same length. Can you conclude that the quadrilaterals are congruent?

D. Figure 3 from *The Matching Game* is shown below. Write a set of drawing directions for the figure. How many points would you spend to give your directions?

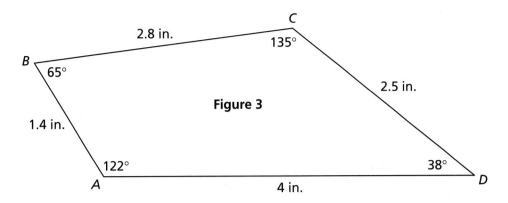

E. Figures 4 and 5 from *The Matching Game* are shown below. For each quadrilateral shape, write a set of drawing directions that would cost your team the minimum number of points. Do not use the name of the figure (rectangle or parallelogram) in your directions.

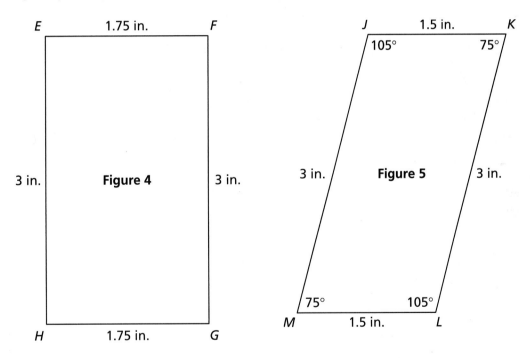

F. Compare your results for Questions D and E with those of other students. Look for patterns that will help you answer this question:

What is the minimum information you need about the sides and angles of two quadrilaterals to be sure those quadrilaterals are congruent?

ACE Homework starts on page 56.

Applications

Match each side and angle of the first shape in Exercises 1–4 with its congruent partner in the second shape.

1.

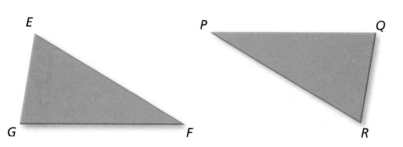

2.

3.

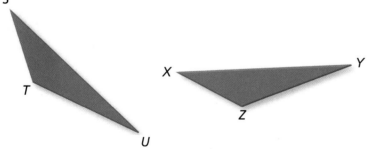

4.

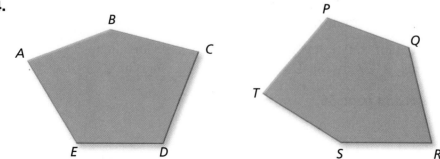

5. a. The figure below is a rectangle. Identify all the symmetries.

b. List all the sets of congruent triangles in this figure and give evidence for the congruence. Record your findings in a table with two columns. Label the columns "Sets of Congruent Triangles" and "Evidence for Congruence."

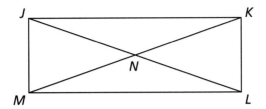

6. a. The figure below is a rhombus. Identify all the symmetries.

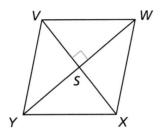

b. List all the sets of congruent triangles in the figure and give evidence for the congruence. Record your findings in a table like the one you made in Exercise 5.

In Exercises 7–10, you are given a triangle *ABC* and information about another triangle, *DEF*, which is shown below. Tell whether △*DEF* is *definitely congruent* to △*ABC*, *possibly congruent* to △*ABC*, or *definitely not congruent* to △*ABC*.

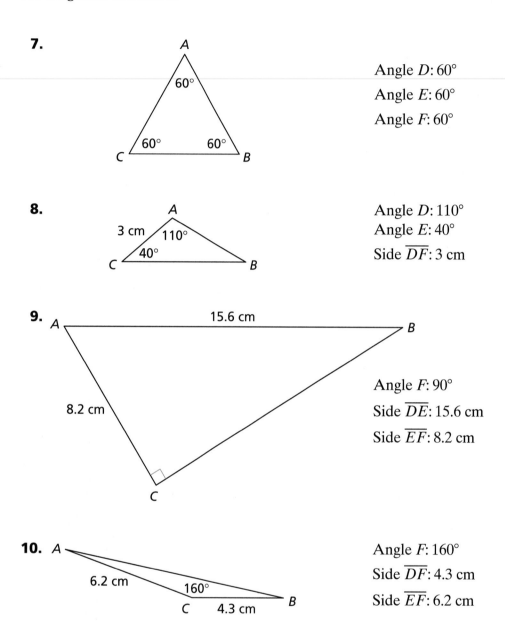

7.

Angle *D*: 60°

Angle *E*: 60°

Angle *F*: 60°

8.

Angle *D*: 110°

Angle *E*: 40°

Side $\overline{DF}$: 3 cm

9.

Angle *F*: 90°

Side $\overline{DE}$: 15.6 cm

Side $\overline{EF}$: 8.2 cm

10.

Angle *F*: 160°

Side $\overline{DF}$: 4.3 cm

Side $\overline{EF}$: 6.2 cm

For Exercises 11–13, write a set of drawing directions for the given figure. Include the fewest measurements possible. Figures shown are not drawn to actual size.

Homework Help Online
PHSchool.com
For: Help with Exercise 11
Web Code: ape-5311

11. Quadrilateral

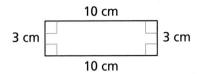

12. Quadrilateral

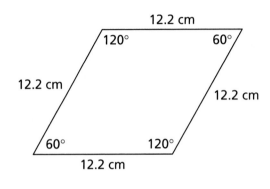

13. Triangle

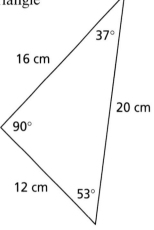

14. Multiple Choice Which set of directions ensure that you will make a congruent copy of the triangle below?

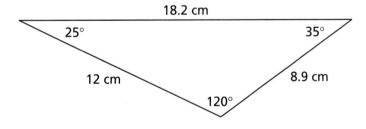

A. Draw a triangle with angle measures of 25°, 35°, and 120°.

B. Draw a triangle with one angle measuring 25°. Make a side next to that angle 12 cm long, and the side opposite that angle 8.9 cm long.

C. Make a triangle with side lengths of 8.9 cm and 12 cm.

D. Make a triangle with side lengths of 8.9 cm, 18.2 cm, and 12 cm.

15. a. Triangle *ABC* is shown below. Explain how you know that △*AOC* and △*AOB* are congruent.

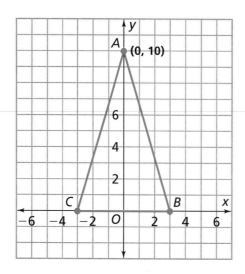

b. Use what you know about this figure to name equal lengths and congruent angles. Justify your statements.

16. a. Trapezoid *PQRS* is shown below. Explain how you know that sides *PS* and *QR* are congruent.

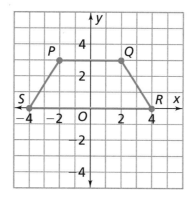

b. Use what you know about symmetry and congruence to show that the two base angles are congruent.

Connections

Tell whether the circles in each are congruent. Explain.

17.

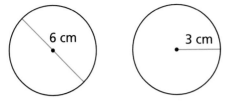

18. A circle with a radius of 4.2 cm and a circle with an area of 58.69 cm^2

For Exercises 19–21, find the perimeter and area of each figure. Then, tell whether the two figures are congruent.

19.

20.

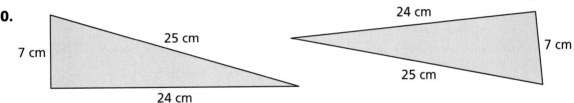

21.

22. If two shapes have equal perimeters, must the shapes be congruent? Give examples to support your answer.

23. If two shapes have equal areas, must the shapes be congruent? Give examples to support your answer.

24. a. What shape do you see if you slice through the center of a sphere and look at the new surface you created?

   b. Donna made several cylinders. For each cylinder, she made clay spheres so that the sphere fit exactly inside the cylinder. She squished the clay down to see how much of the cylinder it filled. Every time it filled the cylinder up to $\frac{2}{3}$ of its height. How could this help her to find the volume of the sphere?

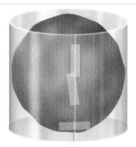 

   c. Use your ideas from part (b) to find the volume of a sphere that fits exactly inside a cylinder that is 11 inches high and has a base with radius 2.5 inches.

   d. Give a formula for the volume of a sphere.

25. In Problem 3.4, you discovered that knowing the side lengths of a triangle tells you exactly what its shape must be. You also found that the side lengths alone are not enough to tell you the shape of a quadrilateral.

How do these facts explain why braces are often used to help rectangular structures hold their shape?

brace

26. a. Plot the points listed in the table on a coordinate grid, connecting them in order.

b. What rule will transform figure *ABCDEF* into the figure below?

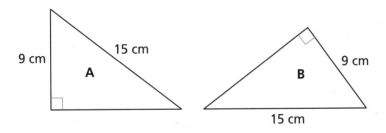

Point	Coordinates
A	(−1, −1)
B	(0, −2)
C	(1, −1)
D	(1, 1)
E	(0, 2)
F	(−1, 1)
A	(−1, −1)

c. Is the figure above similar to figure *ABCDEF*?

d. Apply the rule (2*x* + 1, 2*y*) to figure *ABCDEF*. Is the image similar to figure *ABCDEF*? Explain.

Extensions

27. a. Use what you know about side-length relationships in right triangles to find the length of the third side of each triangle.

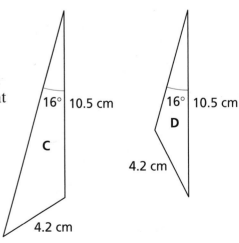

b. Are the triangles congruent? Explain.

28. Can you say for certain that the triangles at the right are congruent?

29. In Exercise 28, you are given 2 pairs of corresponding congruent sides and a pair of corresponding congruent angles, opposite a pair of given sides.

a. Is this the same arrangement of congruent sides and angles as in Exercise 27?

b. Why can we determine the triangles are congruent in one case but not in the other?

Mathematical Reflections 3

In this investigation, you discovered connections between symmetry and congruence. You learned how to determine whether two triangles are congruent without measuring all their sides and angles. You also learned to construct figures that are congruent to other figures. These questions will help you summarize what you have learned.

Think about your answers to these questions. Discuss your ideas with other students and your teacher. Then, write a summary of your findings in your notebook.

1. What does it mean to say that two geometric figures are congruent?

2. How can you use symmetry transformations to show that two figures are congruent?

3. Describe some ways that you can check, by measuring some sides and angles, whether two triangles are congruent.

Investigation 4

Applying Congruence and Symmetry

In Investigation 3, you explored two questions:

What does it mean to say that two geometric figures are congruent?

What information do you need to decide whether two triangles or two quadrilaterals are congruent?

You discovered that two triangles are congruent if any of the following are true:

- Two sides and the included angle of one triangle are congruent to two sides and the included angle of another.

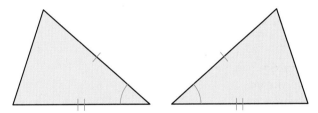

- Two angles and the common side in one triangle are congruent to two angles and the common side in another.

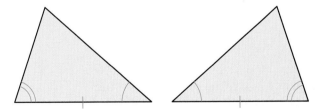

- Three sides of one triangle are congruent to three sides of another.

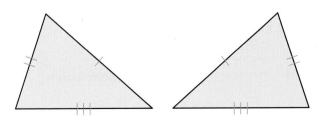

In this investigation, you will apply what you have learned about congruent polygons, symmetry, and symmetry transformations to solve problems.

 Finding Distances Without Measuring

An engineer is planning a footbridge across a river. Currently, there is an old cable bridge strung between two trees on opposite sides of the river (points *B* and *C*). The engineer wants the new bridge to start at one of the trees (point *B*) and span the shortest distance across the river (to point *A*). She needs to figure out how long the new bridge must be.

Her notebook includes the following sketch and instructions:

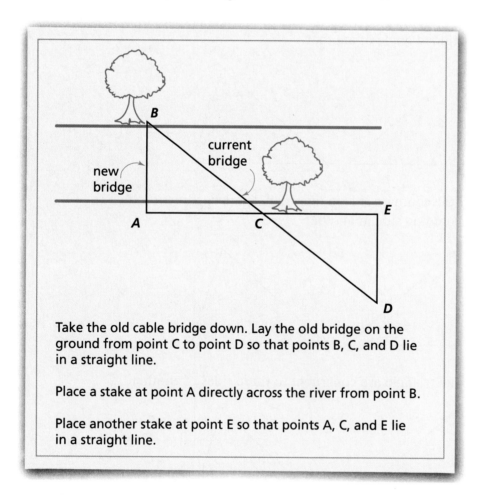

Take the old cable bridge down. Lay the old bridge on the ground from point C to point D so that points B, C, and D lie in a straight line.

Place a stake at point A directly across the river from point B.

Place another stake at point E so that points A, C, and E lie in a straight line.

Problem 4.1 Finding Distances Without Measuring

Use the engineer's sketch and notes to answer these questions.

A. In the two triangles, identify the sides and angles you know are congruent.

B. Do the engineer's notes provide enough information to conclude that the two triangles are congruent? If not, what additional information does she need?

C. Assume that the additional information you described in Question B is true. How could the engineer use the congruence of the triangles to find the distance across the river?

D. Which transformation or combination of transformations would match one of the triangles to the other?

ACE Homework starts on page 70.

You can sometimes use the symmetry in geometric figures to find information about sides and angles of these figures.

Problem 4.2 Using Symmetry to Find Properties of Shapes

A. $\overline{AM}$ is on a line of symmetry for $\triangle ABC$. Some lengths and angle measures are given. Find the other lengths and angle measures.

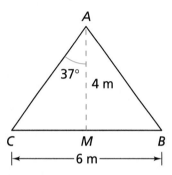

B. 1. In the circle below, two radii form the legs of a right triangle. The hypotenuse of the triangle is a dashed segment. What transformations of the hypotenuse would generate the quadrilateral formed by the dashed segments? Give more than one possibility if you can.

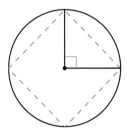

2. What shape is formed if the transformations you found in part (1) are applied to the full triangle? How do you know? Give reasons to support your answer.

C. 1. Quadrilateral *PQRS* has rotation symmetry about point *T*, the midpoint of $\overline{PR}$, with a 180° angle of rotation. Find the missing lengths and angle measures.

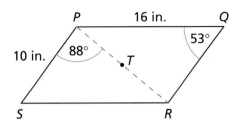

2. Use the given information and the information you found in part (1) to write a convincing argument that quadrilateral *PQRS* is a parallelogram.

D. Nathalie is trying to use transformations to show that the sum of the angle measures of a triangle is 180°. She starts with △*VWX* below (Triangle 1) and applies some transformations to make Triangle 2, then Triangle 3. Here's what she has done so far.

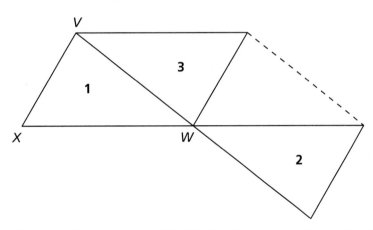

1. Which transformations might Nathalie have performed so far?

2. Will a copy of △*VWX* exactly fit the gap with the dashed line? How do you know?

3. How does the finished figure show that the sum of the angle measures of △*VWX* is 180°?

ACE Homework starts on page 70.

Applications

1. Determine whether $\triangle ABC$ and $\triangle DEC$ are congruent. Explain. Assume points B, C, and E are on the same line, as are points A, C, and D.

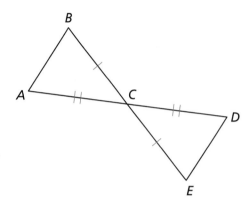

Decide whether you can tell for certain that the triangles in each are congruent based *only* on the given information.

Go Online
PHSchool.com

For: Multiple-Choice Skills Practice
Web Code: apa-5454

2.

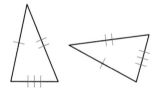

3.

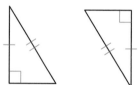

4.

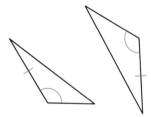

5.

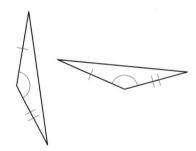

6.

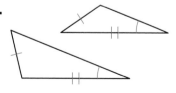

7.

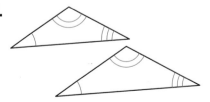

8. Suppose you want to prove that $\triangle KLN$ and $\triangle MLN$ are congruent. The diagram shows only $\overline{ML} = \overline{KL}$. What additional information do you need to show that the triangles are congruent because

  a. three pairs of corresponding sides are congruent?

  b. two sides and the included angle of one triangle are congruent to two sides and the included angle of the other?

  c. two angles and the common side of one triangle are congruent to two angles and the common side of the other?

9. In the diagram below, two cables extend in opposite directions from the top of a tower to the ground. Use what you know about congruent triangles to determine whether the cables are the same length.

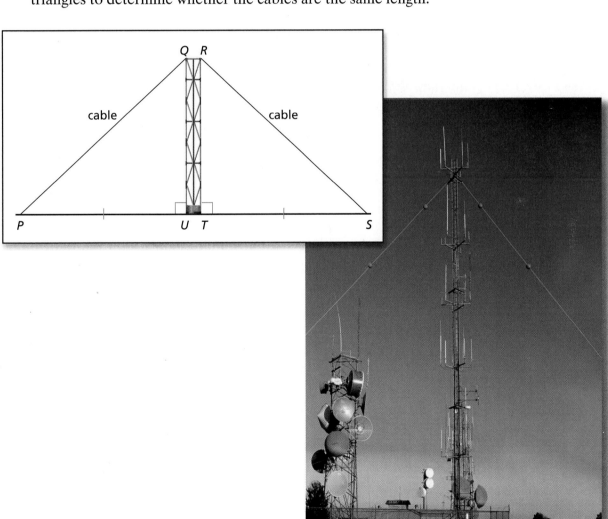

10. Alejandro wants to measure the distance directly across a pond from *A* to *B*. He uses string and some stakes to create the setup shown in the diagram below. None of his string can cross the pond. What information does Alejandro need to build into his setup to find the length of $\overline{AB}$?

Homework
Help Online
PHSchool.com
For: Help with Exercise 10
Web Code: ape-5410

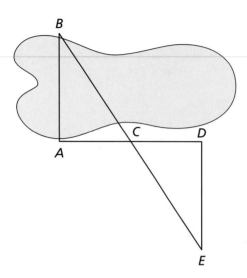

11. In △*FGH* at the right, $\overline{FM}$ and $\overline{GN}$ are on lines of symmetry. What does this symmetry tell you about

a. the angle measures in △*FGH*?

b. the side lengths of △*FGH*?

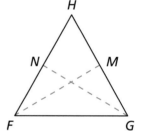

12. Pentagon *PQRST* at the right has rotational symmetry about point *C* with a 72° angle of rotation. What does this symmetry tell you about

a. the angle measures of *PQRST*?

b. the sides lengths of *PQRST*?

c. the segments from *C* to each of the vertices?

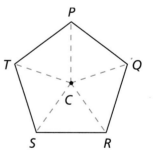

13. △*XYZ* was transformed several times. The quadrilateral below is formed from △*XYZ* and its images.

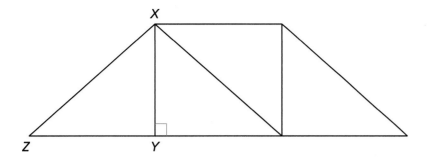

a. Tell which transformations might have been applied to △*XYZ* and in what order.

b. What type of quadrilateral resulted from the transformations? Explain.

14. Use what you know about congruent triangles to show that the diagonals of the square are congruent.

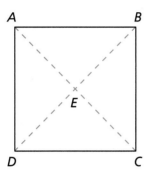

15. Multiple Choice Squares, rectangles, and rhombuses are all types of parallelograms. Which statement is true for all parallelograms?

A. The diagonals are congruent.

B. Each diagonal divides the other diagonal into two equal-sized pieces. (Another way to say this is that the diagonals bisect each other.)

C. The diagonals are perpendicular.

D. The diagonals bisect the angles at the vertices.

Connections

16. The engineer from Problem 4.1 decides to use similar triangles instead of congruent triangles to find the distance across the river. She makes the diagram below.

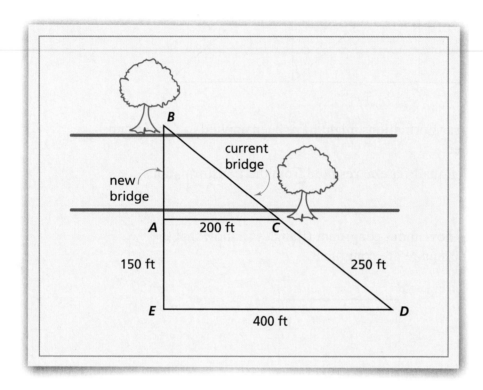

a. Which triangles appear to be similar? What must the engineer know about these triangles to conclude that they are similar?

b. Find the distance across the river from point *B* to point *A*. Explain how you found your answer.

17. To decide whether two polygons are congruent, you can divide them into triangles and compare the triangles. Are the pentagons below congruent? If not, which one has the greater area? Explain.

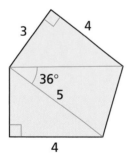

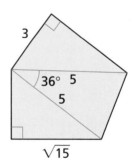

18. In the diagram below, line KB intersects $\overline{GT}$ at right angles and divides it into two congruent segments. Line KB is called the *perpendicular bisector* of $\overline{GT}$.

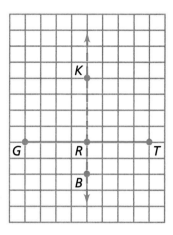

a. Is the distance from point K to point G the same as the distance from point K to point T? Explain.

b. Is the distance from point B to point G the same as the distance from point B to point T?

c. Are there any other points on line KB that are the same distance from point G and point T?

For Exercises 21–23, tell whether the triangles are congruent. Explain your reasoning.

19.

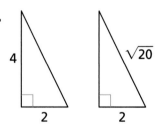

20.

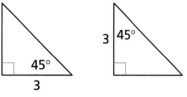

21.

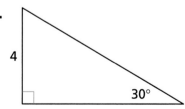

22. In the diagram below, line ℓ is parallel to line m. $\overline{DF}$ lies on line m, and point E lies on line ℓ. How can you use the diagram to show that the sum of the angles in triangle $\triangle DEF$ is 180°?

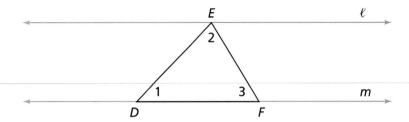

Extensions

23. In the figure below, $\overline{AB}$ is congruent to $\overline{DE}$ and $\angle BAD$ is congruent to $\angle EDA$. Use this information to show $\triangle ABC$ is congruent to $\triangle DEC$.

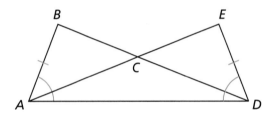

24. Point C is the center of the circle. $\overline{AE}$ and $\overline{BD}$ pass through point C. Show that $\triangle ABC$ is congruent to $\triangle DEC$.

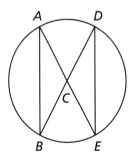

25. Show that the diagonals of the rhombus are perpendicular.

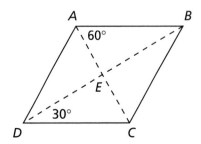

Mathematical Reflections 4

In this investigation, you applied what you have learned about symmetry and congruence. These questions will help you summarize what you have learned.

Think about your answers to these questions. Discuss your ideas with other students and your teacher. Then, write a summary of your findings in your notebook.

1. a. Describe what it means for two triangles to be congruent.

   b. Describe what it means for two triangles to be similar.

   c. Can two triangles be similar, but *not* congruent? Give examples to support your answer.

   d. Can two triangles be congruent, but *not* similar? Give examples to support your answer.

2. Give an example of how you could use symmetry to find side lengths and angle measures of a geometric figure.

Transforming Coordinates

The drawing window in many computer geometry programs is a coordinate grid. You make designs by specifying the endpoints of line segments. When you transform a design, the coordinates of its points change according to specific rules.

In this investigation, you will explore transformations of figures on coordinate grids. You will write rules for transforming a point (x, y) to its image under translations, rotations, and reflections. You will also look at the results of combining transformations. What you see and do visually is tracked and checked as a change in algebraic symbols.

5.1 Coordinate Rules for Reflections

The flag shape below consists of three segments. It was produced in a computer program, using the commands shown. The commands tell the computer to draw segments between the specified endpoints.

Draw:

Line [(0, −2), (0, 3)]

Line [(0, 3), (1, 2)]

Line [(1, 2), (0, 1)]

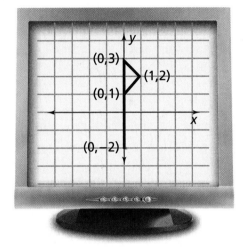

Getting Ready for Problem

- Is there a different set of commands that will produce the same flag as the one above?

- What commands will produce a square centered at the origin?

- What commands will produce a non-square rectangle?

Most geometry software allows you to reflect, rotate, and translate figures. These transformations change the coordinates of the figure.

In this problem, you will explore reflections of figures on coordinate grids. By looking for patterns in your results, you will be able to write algebraic rules for reflecting any point (x, y).

A. 1. Copy and complete these commands for drawing the flag.

Draw:

Line [(■, ■), (■, ■)]

Line [(■, ■), (■, ■)]

Line [(■, ■), (■, ■)]

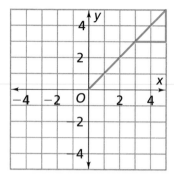

2. Write commands that will draw the image of the original flag under a reflection in the *y*-axis. Describe the pattern that relates each point (*x*, *y*) to its image. Which points remain unchanged?

3. Write commands that will draw the image of the original flag under a reflection in the *x*-axis. Describe the pattern that relates each point (*x*, *y*) to its image. Which points remain unchanged?

4. Write commands that will draw the image of the original flag under a reflection in the line *y* = *x*. Describe the pattern relating points (*x*, *y*) to their image. Which points remain unchanged?

Make copies of the diagram below as needed for Questions B–E.

B. List the coordinates of points *A–H*.

C. 1. List the coordinates of the images of points *A–H* under a reflection in the *y*-axis. Label the image points A'–H'.

    2. Compare the coordinates of each original point with the coordinates of its image. Use the patterns you see to complete this rule for finding the image of any point (x, y) under a reflection in the *y*-axis:

$$(x, y) \rightarrow (\blacksquare, \blacksquare)$$

D. 1. List the coordinates of the images of points *A–H* under a reflection in the *x*-axis. Label the image points A''–H''.

    2. Compare the coordinates of each original point with the coordinates of its image. Complete this rule for finding the image of any point (x, y) under a reflection in the *x*-axis:

$$(x, y) \rightarrow (\blacksquare, \blacksquare)$$

E. 1. List the coordinates of the images of points *A–H* under a reflection in the line $y = x$. Label the image points A'''–H'''.

    2. Compare the coordinates of each original point with the coordinates of its image. Complete this rule for finding the image of any point (x, y) under a reflection in the line $y = x$:

$$(x, y) \rightarrow (\blacksquare, \blacksquare)$$

ACE **Homework starts on page 88.**

5.2 **Coordinate Rules for Translations**

In this problem, you will explore how translating a figure affects its coordinates.

Problem 5.2 **Coordinate Rules for Translations**

A. In the design at the right, the left-most flag was made with the commands shown.

Draw:

Line [(−5, −4), (−5, 2)]

Line [(−5, 2), (−4, 1)]

Line [(−4, 1), (−5, 0)]

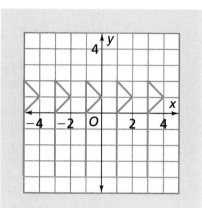

   1. Write commands for drawing the other four flags. Each set of commands should draw the segments in the same order as the commands for the original design.

   2. Compare the commands for the five flags. Describe a pattern that relates the coordinates of each flag to the coordinates of the flag to its right.

   3. Describe a pattern that relates the coordinates of each flag to the coordinates of the flag to its left.

B. 1. Write a set of commands for drawing the left-most flag in the design below. Then write commands for drawing the other four flags.

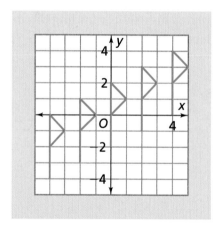

   2. Compare the commands for the five flags. Describe a pattern that relates the coordinates of each flag to the coordinates of the flag to its right.

3. Describe a pattern that relates the coordinates of each flag to the coordinates of the flag to its left.

C. 1. Copy the figure below. Experiment with translations of the figure. Try translations of different distances in directions parallel to the *x*-axis, *y*-axis, and the line $y = x$. In each case, tell what happens to the coordinates of a point on the original figure under the translation.

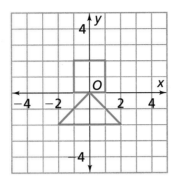

2. Complete each rule for finding the image of any point (x, y) under the given translation.

a. Horizontal translation by *b* units: $(x, y) \rightarrow (\blacksquare, \blacksquare)$

b. Vertical translation by *b* units: $(x, y) \rightarrow (\blacksquare, \blacksquare)$

c. Translation by *b* units in the direction of the line $y = x$:
$(x, y) \rightarrow (\blacksquare, \blacksquare)$

D. In parts (1)–(5), tell whether the rule describes a translation of any original figure.

1. $(x, y) \rightarrow (x + 2, y - 3)$

2. $(x, y) \rightarrow (2x, y)$

3. $(x, y) \rightarrow (x + 1, 3y)$

4. $(x, y) \rightarrow (x - 2, y + 1)$

5. For each rule that describes a translation, describe in words the image made by applying the translation to all points on the original figure.

ACE **Homework starts on page 88.**

5.3 Coordinate Rules for Rotations

You have explored rules for reflecting and translating a point (x, y). Writing rules for rotations is more difficult. In this problem, you will explore a few simple cases.

Getting Ready for Problem 5.3

Think of rotating the four flags in this diagram 90° counterclockwise about the origin (0, 0).

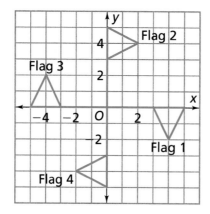

- How do the coordinates of a point on Flag 1 compare with their image points under the 90° rotation? Try some points to see. Record your results.

- How do the points on Flags 2, 3, and 4 compare with their image points under the same rotation? Test some points and record your results.

- Do you see a pattern that you could use to write a coordinate rule for a 90° rotation about the origin?

Problem 5.3

A. 1. Copy and complete these drawing commands for △ABC.

Draw:

Line [(■, ■), (■, ■)]

Line [(■, ■), (■, ■)]

Line [(■, ■), (■, ■)]

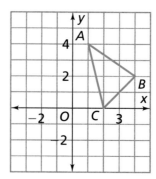

2. Write a set of commands that will draw the image of △ABC under each rotation about the origin.

    a. 90° counterclockwise rotation

    b. 180° rotation

    c. 270° counterclockwise rotation

    d. 360° rotation

B. 1. Organize your results from Question A as shown below.

Starting Point	90° Rotation	180° Rotation	270° Rotation	360° Rotation
A(1, 4)	(■, ■)	(■, ■)	(■, ■)	(■, ■)
B(4, 2)	(■, ■)	(■, ■)	(■, ■)	(■, ■)
C(2, 0)	(■, ■)	(■, ■)	(■, ■)	(■, ■)

2. Describe how the vertices of △ABC relate to the vertices of the image triangle.

3. Complete each rule for finding the image of any point (x, y) under the given rotation.

    a. 90° rotation about the origin: $(x, y) \rightarrow$ (■, ■)

    b. 180° rotation about the origin: $(x, y) \rightarrow$ (■, ■)

    c. 270° rotation about the origin: $(x, y) \rightarrow$ (■, ■)

    d. 360° rotation about the origin: $(x, y) \rightarrow$ (■, ■)

ACE Homework starts on page 88.

A 90° rotation puts the image of a point in an adjacent quadrant.

In some applications, like tessellations, an original shape may be transformed under a combination of transformations. In this problem you will explore how coordinate rules can track and check combinations of transformations.

Problem 5.4 Coordinate Rules for Transformation Combinations

A. 1. In the figure below, the distance between grid lines is 1 unit. Describe in words a transformation or a combination of transformations that will make images of the parallelogram as indicated.

    a. Parallelogram 1 → Parallelogram 2

    b. Parallelogram 1 → Parallelogram 3

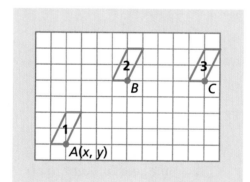

  2. In parts (a)–(b), refer to the rules for translations you wrote in Problem 5.2.

    a. Suppose point A is translated in the direction of the line $y = x$ to point B. Then, this image point is translated horizontally to point C. Complete this rule to show these translations algebraically:

$$A \rightarrow B \rightarrow C$$
$$(x, y) \rightarrow (\blacksquare, \blacksquare) \rightarrow (\blacksquare, \blacksquare)$$

b. Suppose the translations in part (a) are reversed. In other words, the horizontal translation is applied to *A* and then the diagonal translation is applied to the image point. Complete this rule to show these translations algebraically:

$$(x, y) \rightarrow (\blacksquare, \blacksquare) \rightarrow (\blacksquare, \blacksquare)$$

c. In parts (a) and (b), you did the same translations, but in different orders. Was the final image the same in both cases? Do you think reversing the order of any two translations will give the same results?

B. 1. You can probably think of more than one way to transform triangle 1 below to make images at positions 2 and 3.

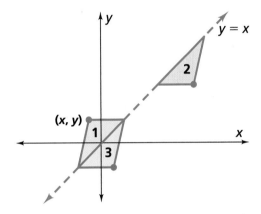

a. What coordinate rule rotates the point (x, y) by 180° about the origin?

b. What combination of coordinate rules first rotates the point (x, y) by 180° about the origin, and then translates the image diagonally in the direction of the line $y = x$ to position 2?

c. Suppose you reverse the order of the transformations in part (b). In other words, you first apply the translation and then apply the rotation. Is the image the same? Use coordinate rules to justify your answer.

2. Think about the two different orders of transformations you just applied to the triangle, a rotation then a translation or vice versa. Can you explain why the results are or are not the same by referring to the picture?

ACE **Homework starts on page 88.**

Applications

1. a. Write a set of computer commands for drawing the letter R shown at the right.

b. Write a set of commands for drawing the image of R under a reflection in the *y*-axis. Use your instructions to draw the image.

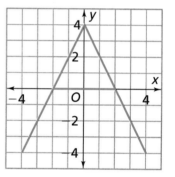

2. a. Write a set of computer commands for drawing the letter A shown at the right.

b. Write a set of commands for drawing the image of A under a reflection in the *x*-axis. Use your instructions to draw the image.

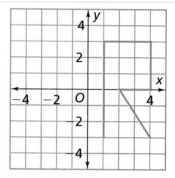

3. a. Write a set of computer commands for drawing the letter F shown at the right.

b. Write a set of commands for drawing the image of F under a reflection in the line $y = x$. Use your instructions to draw the image.

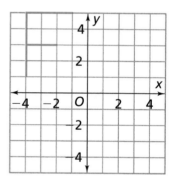

4. In Problem 5.2, you investigated how the images of the figure below are made by various translations. Copy this figure onto grid paper.

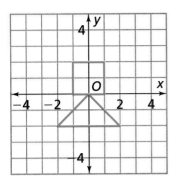

a. Draw two images made by translating the figure along the line $y = \frac{1}{2}x$. The three figures (the original and its images) should be equally spaced and should not overlap.

b. How do the coordinates change from one figure to the next?

c. Complete this rule for a translation of a point (x, y) along $y = \frac{1}{2}x$.
$(x, y) \rightarrow (\blacksquare, \blacksquare)$

Copy the figure at the right onto grid paper. Refer to the figure for Exercises 5–14.

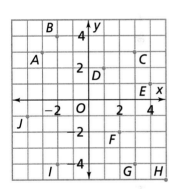

5. What are the coordinates of the image of point A under a translation in which $(2, 4)$ is the image of $(1, 2)$?

6. What are the coordinates of the image of point B under a translation in which $(3, -1)$ is the image of $(1, 2)$?

7. What are the coordinates of the image of point C under a translation in which $(-2, -3)$ is the image of $(1, 2)$?

8. What are the coordinates of the image of point D under a reflection in the y-axis?

9. What are the coordinates of the image of point E under a reflection in the x-axis?

For: Multiple-Choice Skills Practice
Web Code: apa-5554

10. What are the coordinates of the image of point F under a reflection in the line $y = x$?

11. What are the coordinates of the image of point G under a 90° counterclockwise rotation about the origin?

12. What are the coordinates of the image of point H under a 180° rotation about the origin?

13. What are the coordinates of the image of point *I* under a 270° counterclockwise rotation about the origin?

14. What are the coordinates of the final image of point *J* under a reflection in the *x*-axis followed by a reflection in the *y*-axis?

15. a. Copy the figure below onto grid paper. Draw the final image that results from rotating polygon *ABCD* 90° counterclockwise about the origin and then reflecting the image in the *x*-axis.

For: Help with Exercise 15
Web Code: ape-5515

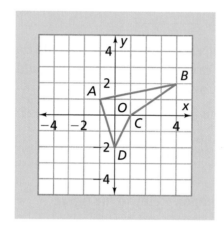

b. Make a new copy of the figure. Draw the final image that results from reflecting polygon *ABCD* in the *x*-axis and then rotating the image 90° counterclockwise about the origin.

c. Are the final images you found in parts (a) and (b) the same? Explain.

16. What single transformation is equivalent to a 90° counterclockwise rotation about the origin followed by a 270° counterclockwise rotation about the origin?

17. What single transformation is equivalent to a reflection in the *y*-axis followed by a reflection in the *x*-axis followed by another reflection in the *y*-axis?

18. Draw a figure on a coordinate grid. Perform one transformation on your original figure and a second transformation on its image. Is there a single transformation that will produce the same final result? Explain.

Connections

19. Diagonal *QS* divides parallelogram *PQRS* into congruent triangles.

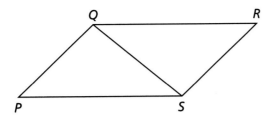

a. Suppose you made a copy of triangle *PQS* and fit it on top of the other triangle. Which vertices will correspond?

b. What single reflection, rotation, or translation would match one of the triangles exactly with the other?

c. Which pairs of sides and angles in the two triangles are congruent?

For Exercises 20–21, describe in detail the symmetries in the design.

20.

21.

22. The diagram at the right has rotation symmetry.

a. What center and angle of rotation will rotate each flag onto the other?

b. Compare the coordinates of key points on one flag with the coordinates of their images on the other flag. Describe the pattern you see.

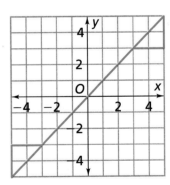

23. $\triangle PQR$ is scalene. The midpoint of $\overline{QR}$ is the origin $(0, 0)$. $\triangle PQR$ has been rotated $180°$ about the origin to produce the image shown by the dashed segments.

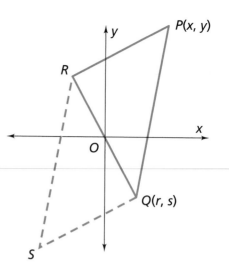

a. Tell which vertex of the image triangle matches with each vertex of $\triangle PQR$.

b. Which sides and angles in the two triangles are congruent?

c. What are the coordinates of points R and S?

d. What shape is $PQSR$? How do you know?

e. Sketch the result of reflecting the original triangle $\triangle PQR$ in the diagonal QR. Is the resulting diagram the same shape as $PQSR$?

24. Multiple Choice Which of these statements is *not* true about the figure below?

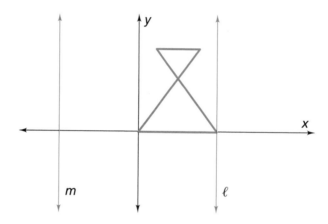

A. Reflecting the figure in the y-axis, and then reflecting the image in the x-axis, gives the same final image as rotating the figure $180°$ about the origin.

B. Reflecting the figure in line ℓ, and then reflecting the image in the y-axis, gives the same final image as reflecting the figure in line m.

C. Reflecting the figure in the y-axis and then rotating the image $180°$ about the origin gives the same final image as reflecting the figure in the x-axis.

D. Rotating the figure $90°$ counterclockwise about the origin and then rotating the image another $90°$ counterclockwise gives the same image as rotating the original image $180°$ about the origin.

Extensions

For Exercises 25–27, draw the figure on grid paper. Use symmetry transformations to draw a design with the given condition(s). Describe the transformations you used and the order in which you applied them.

25. a design that has at least two lines of symmetry

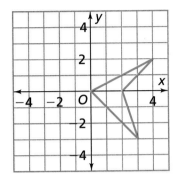

26. a design that has rotation symmetry

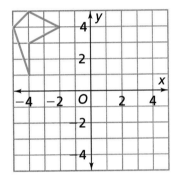

27. a design that has both reflection and rotation symmetry

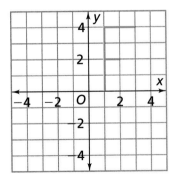

28. Investigate what happens when you rotate a figure 180° about a point and then rotate the image 180° about a different point. Is the combination of the two rotations equivalent to a single transformation? Test several cases, and make a conjecture about the result.

You might start your investigation with the figures below. Copy them onto grid paper. Rotate each polygon 180° about C_1 and then 180° about C_2.

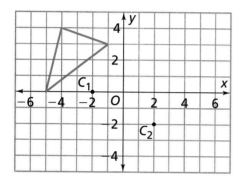 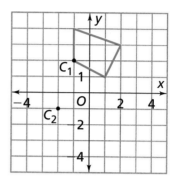

Mathematical Reflections 5

In this investigation, you looked at transformations of figures drawn on coordinate grids. You found that you could describe some symmetry transformations by telling what happens to a general point (x, y). These questions will help you summarize what you have learned.

Think about your answers to these questions. Discuss your ideas with other students and your teacher. Then, write a summary of your findings in your notebook.

What is the image of a point (x, y) under each transformation?

1. a reflection in the y-axis

2. a reflection in the x-axis

3. a reflection in the line $y = x$

4. a 90° counterclockwise rotation about the origin

5. a 180° counterclockwise rotation about the origin

6. a 270° counterclockwise rotation about the origin

7. a 360° counterclockwise rotation about the origin

8. a translation that slides $(1, 2)$ onto $(3, -2)$

9. a translation 6 units to the left followed by a translation 2 units down

10. a 90° counterclockwise rotation about the origin followed by a reflection in the y-axis

Unit Project

Making Tessellations

Materials:

grid paper, isometric dot paper, stiff paper, an angle ruler or protractor, transparent tape, and colored pencils or markers

Directions:

- Draw square *PQRS* on grid paper.
- Draw triangle 1 as shown.
- Draw triangle 1′, the image of triangle 1 under a 270° rotation about point *P*.
- Draw triangle 2 as shown.
- Draw triangle 2′, the image of triangle 2 under a 270° rotation about point *R*.

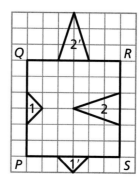

Now, you will start with a copy of square *PQRS* and perform the same rotations as before. However, this time, you will cut out triangles 1 and 2 and rotate the cut pieces.

- Copy square *PQRS* and triangles 1 and 2 onto a stiff sheet of paper. Cut out square *PQRS*.
- Cut out triangle 1, rotate it 270° about point *P*, and tape it in place.
- Cut out triangle 2, rotate it 270° about point *R*, and tape it in place.

Trace copies of your finished shape to make a tessellation. Recall that a *tessellation* is a design made by fitting together copies of a basic shape without gaps or overlaps. You can decorate the basic shapes to make your tessellation more interesting.

We say that the shape below *tessellates* because it can be used to make a tessellation.

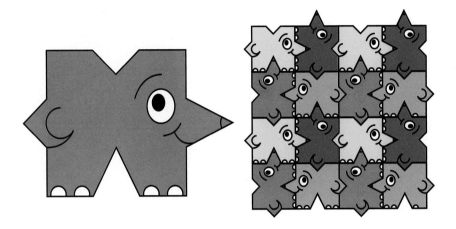

Starting with a square, try to make your own tessellating shape. Cut out pieces from the square, rotate them, and tape them in place. As you work, think about this question:

Will any cutout shape and any rotation turn a square into a shape that tessellates?

When you find a shape that tessellates, trace it several times to make a tessellation. Tape your basic shape to the paper.

Now, see if you can make a tessellating shape from a rhombus with angles of 60° and 120°. You may find it easier to make your design on isometric dot paper and then cut out a copy from stiff paper. As you work, think about this question:

Will any cutout shape and any rotation turn a rhombus with 60° and 120° angles into a shape that tessellates?

If you find a shape that tessellates, trace it several times to make a tessellation. Tape your basic shape to the paper. If you were unable to make a shape that tessellates, explain why you think your efforts were unsuccessful.

Unit Project

Making a Wreath and a Pinwheel

Origami is the Japanese art of paper folding. In this part of the project, you will make an Origami wreath and then transform your wreath into a pinwheel.

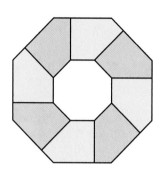  

Materials:

8 paper squares of the same size (4 paper squares in each of 2 colors gives a nice result)

Directions:

The wreath is made by connecting eight folded squares. Follow these instructions to fold each square:

● Fold a paper square to make the creases as shown.

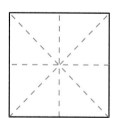

- Fold down the top corners of the square to make a "house." Then, fold the house in half so that the flaps are on the inside.

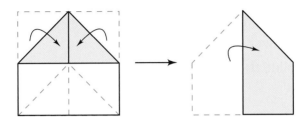

- Hold the "half-house" at its point, and push the bottom corner in along the folds to make a parallelogram.

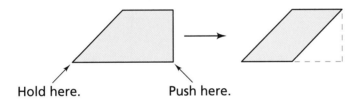

Hold here.   Push here.

Follow these steps to connect the eight pieces:

- Position two of the folded pieces as shown on the left below. (If you used different colors, use one piece of each color.) Slide the point of the right piece into the folded pocket of the left piece.

folded edge   folded edge

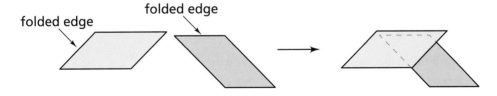

- Fold down the tips that extend over the inserted piece and tuck them into the valley formed by the folds of the inserted piece.

Fold these tips inward.   Tuck the tips into this pocket.

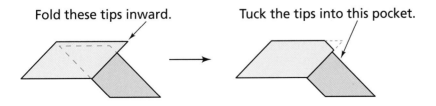

- Follow the steps above to attach the remaining folded pieces.
- Complete the wreath by connecting the last piece to the first piece, being careful to fold each flap over only one layer.
- To make a pinwheel, gently slide the sides of the wreath toward the center.

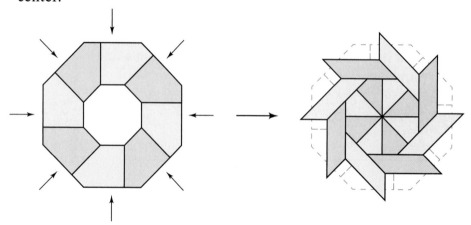

Study the drawings in the instructions for making the origami wreath and the pinwheel. Look for symmetries in the figures made at each stage.

1. Describe the reflection and rotation symmetries of each figure.
   a. the square b. the "house" c. the "half-house"
   d. the parallelogram e. the wreath f. the pinwheel

2. Slide your pinwheel back into a wreath shape. If you gently push on a pair of opposite sides, you will get a pinwheel with only two "wings." Describe the reflection and rotation symmetries of this figure.

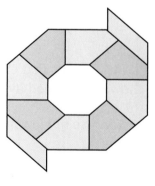

3. Slide your pinwheel back into a wreath shape. Gently push on opposite sides of the pinwheel to produce other shapes. Look at the shape of the center opening. What shapes can you make by pushing on the sides of the wreath?

Looking Back and Looking Ahead

Unit Review

In this unit, you learned how to describe symmetry in terms of reflections, rotations, and translations. You learned how to write rules describing the effects of a transformation on points and figures. You also discovered the connection between symmetry transformations and congruence.

Go Online
PHSchool.com
For: Vocabulary Review Puzzle
Web Code: apj-5051

Use Your Understanding: Geometric Reasoning

Test your understanding and skill with symmetry and transformations by solving these problems about a home improvement project.

1. The wallpaper design below has been selected for the kitchen.

   a. Describe the symmetries in the wallpaper pattern. Assume the design continues in the same way horizontally and vertically.

   b. The figure at the right is part of the wallpaper design. What is the smallest angle through which this figure can be rotated so that it looks the same as it does in its original position?

2. One of the square tiles for the kitchen floor is shown at the right.

    a. Describe all symmetries of the design on the tile.

    b. Identify the smallest basic design element that can be transformed to produce the entire design. Explain the transformation that will map that basic element onto all other parts of the design.

3. The living room rug has copies of the design at the right along its border. Here, the design is shown on a coordinate grid. Copy the figure onto grid paper. Draw the image of the design after each transformation.

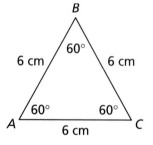

    a. a 90° counterclockwise rotation about the origin

    b. a reflection in the *y*-axis

    c. a translation with rule $(x, y) \rightarrow (x, y + 3)$

4. Consider triangle *ABC* at the right.

    a. What is the least number of measures needed to make a congruent copy of triangle *ABC*? Explain.

    b. Will the number of measures you specified guarantee a congruent copy no matter what those measures are? If so, explain why. If not, show an example that fails (a counter-example).

5. Line *k* is a line of symmetry for triangle *PQR*. What, if anything, does this tell you about each pair? Explain your answers.

    a. $\overline{PR}$ and $\overline{PQ}$

    b. $\angle Q$ and $\angle R$

    c. point *M* and $\overline{QR}$

    d. $\angle RPM$ and $\angle QPM$

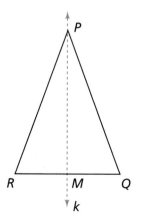

Explain Your Reasoning

Solving geometric problems requires using visual skills to see important patterns. However, you also need to be able to justify your conclusions.

6. How would you convince someone that a figure has the given symmetry?

   a. reflection symmetry
   b. rotation symmetry
   c. translation symmetry

7. Suppose you have a figure and its image under a rotation. How could you find the center and angle of rotation that produced the image?

8. Suppose you have a figure and its image under a reflection. How could you find the line of reflection that produced the image?

9. Give some combinations of congruent sides and angles that will guarantee that two triangles are congruent.

10. Give some combinations of congruent sides and angles that will *not* guarantee that two triangles are congruent.

Look Ahead

You will apply the geometric ideas and techniques that you learned in this unit and explore them in greater depth in future mathematics and science classes. You'll find them especially valuable in high school geometry and trigonometry. You might also use what you have learned to solve practical problems involving shapes and designs.

B

basic design element A part of a pattern or design that, when transformed using at least one type of symmetry transformation, will produce the entire design.

elemento de diseño básico Parte de un patrón o diseño que, cuando es transformado usando un tipo de simetría de transformación, producirá el diseño completo.

C

congruent figures Two figures are congruent if one is an image of the other under a translation, a reflection, a rotation, or some combination of these transformations. Put more simply, two figures are congruent if you can slide, flip, or turn one figure so that it fits exactly on the other. The polygons below are congruent.

figuras congruentes Dos figuras son congruentes si una es la imagen de la otra sometida a una traslación, una reflexión, una rotación o a alguna combinación de estas transformaciones. Expresado de manera más sencilla, dos figuras son congruentes si puedes deslizar, voltear o rotar una figura para que coincida exactamente con la otra. Los siguientes polígonos son congruentes.

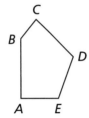 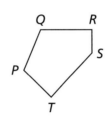

K

kaleidoscope A tube containing colored beads or pieces of glass and carefully placed mirrors. When a kaleidoscope is held to the eye and rotated, the viewer sees colorful, symmetric patterns.

caleidoscopio Tubo que contiene cuentas de colores o pedazos de vidrio y espejos ubicados cuidadosamente. Cuando alguien mira a través de un caleidoscopio y lo hace girar, puede ver patrones simétricos de gran colorido.

line of symmetry A line of symmetry divides a figure into halves that are mirror images. Lines *WY* and *ZX* below are lines of symmetry.

eje de simetría Un eje de simetría una figura en dos mitades que son imágenes reflejas. Las rectas *WY* y *ZX* de abajo en ejes de simetría.

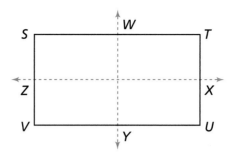

line reflection A transformation that maps each point of a figure to its mirror image, where a line acts as the mirror. Polygon $A'B'C'D'E'$ below is the image of polygon $ABCDE$ under a reflection over the line. If you drew a line segment from a point to its image, the segment would be perpendicular to, and bisected by, the line of reflection.

reflexión sobre un eje Una transformación en la que cada punto de una figura coincide con su imagen especular sobre un eje. El polígono $A'B'C'D'E'$ de abajo es la imagen del polígono $ABCDE$ sometido a una reflexión sobre un eje. Si dibujaras un segmento de recta desde un punto hasta su imagen, el segmento sería perpendicular al eje de reflexión y estaría bisecado por éste.

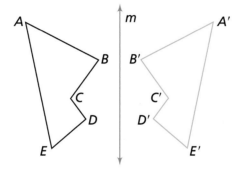

reflection symmetry A figure or design has reflection symmetry if you can draw a line that divides the figure into halves that are mirror images. The line that divides the figure into halves is called the *line of symmetry*. The figure below has reflection symmetry about a vertical line through its center. Reflection symmetry is sometimes referred to as *mirror symmetry* or *line symmetry*.

simetría de reflexión Una figura o diseño tiene simetría de reflexión si se puede dibujar una recta que divida la figura en dos mitades que sean imágenes especulares. La recta que divide la figura en dos mitades se llama *eje de simetría*. La siguiente figura tiene simetría de reflexión a ambos lados de una recta vertical que pasa por su centro.

rotation A transformation that turns a figure counterclockwise about a point. Polygon $A'B'C'D'$ below is the image of polygon $ABCD$ under a 60° rotation about point P. If you drew a segment from a point on polygon $ABCD$ to point P and another segment from the point's image to point P, the segments would be the same length and they would form a 60° angle.

rotación Una transformación por la que una figura gira alrededor de un punto en dirección contraria a las agujas del reloj. El siguiente polígono $A'B'C'D'$ es la imagen del polígono $ABCD$ sometido a una rotación de 60° alrededor el punto P. Si dibujaras un segmento desde un punto en el polígono $ABCD$ hasta el punto P y otro segmento desde la imagen del punto hasta el punto P, los segmentos tendrían la misma longitud y formarían un ángulo de 60°.

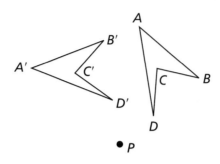

rotation symmetry A figure or design has rotation symmetry if it can be rotated less than a full turn about a point to a position in which it looks the same as the original. The hubcap design below has rotation symmetry with its center as the center of rotation and a 72° angle of rotation. This means that it can be rotated 72°, or any multiple of 72°, about its center point to produce an image that matches exactly with the original.

simetría de rotación Una figura o diseño tiene simetría de rotación si se puede rotar casi por completo alrededor de un punto hasta llegar a una posición en la que quede igual al dibujo original. El diseño de la siguiente cubierta tiene simetría de rotación: su centro es el centro de rotación y tiene un ángulo de rotación de 72°. Esto significa que se puede rotar 72°, o cualquier múltiplo de 72°, alrededor de su punto central para crear una imagen que coincida exactamente con la original.

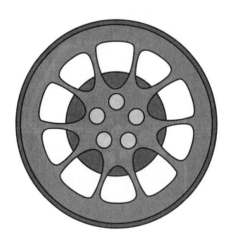

symmetry An object or design has symmetry if part of it is repeated to produce a balanced pattern. In this unit, you learned about three types of symmetry. The butterfly below has *reflection symmetry*, the fan has *rotation symmetry*, and the wallpaper design has *translation symmetry*.

simetría Un objeto o diseño tiene simetría si parte de dicho objeto se repite para crear un patrón equilibrado. En esta unidad, aprendiste tres tipos de simetría. La mariposa que ves a continuación tiene *simetría de reflexión*, el ventilador tiene *simetríade rotación* y el diseño del papel para empapelar tiene *simetríade traslación*.

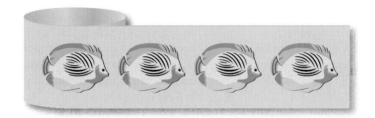

tessellation A design that covers a surface without gaps or overlaps and that consists entirely of copies of a basic design. Tessellations have translation symmetry. The designs below are tessellations.

teselado Un diseño realizado a partir de copias de un elemento básico de diseño con el que se cubre una superficie sin dejar huecos ni superponer elementos. Los teselados tienen simetría de traslación. El siguiente diseño es un teselado.

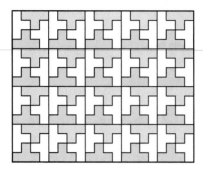

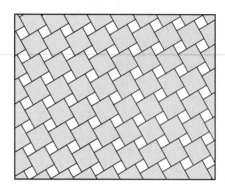

transformation A geometric operation that relates each point of a figure to an image point. The transformations you studied in this unit—reflections, rotations, and translations—are symmetry transformations. A symmetry transformation produces an image that is identical in size and shape to the original figure.

transformación Una operación geométrica en la que cada punto de una figura coincide con un punto de su imagen. Las transformaciones que estudiaste en la unidad—reflexiones, rotaciones y traslaciones—son transformaciones de simetría. Una transformación de simetría da como resultado una imagen con el mismo tamaño y la misma forma que la figura original.

translation A transformation that slides each point on a figure to an image point a given distance and direction from the original point. Polygon $A'B'C'D'E'$ below is the image of polygon $ABCDE$ under a translation. If you drew line segments from two points to their respective image points, the segments would be parallel and they would have the same length.

traslación Una transformación que desliza cada punto de una figura hacia un punto de su imagen a determinada distancia y dirección del punto original. El polígono $A'B'C'D'E'$ que se observa a continuación es la imagen del polígono $ABCDE$ sometido a una traslación. Si dibujaras segmentos de recta desde dos puntos hasta los puntos correspondientes en su imagen, los segmentos serían paralelos y tendrían la misma longitud.

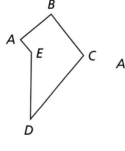
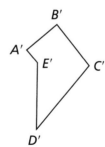

translation symmetry A design has translation symmetry if you can slide it to a position in which it looks exactly the same as it did in its original position. To describe translation symmetry, you need to specify the distance and direction of the translation. Below is part of a design that extends infinitely in all directions. This design has translation symmetry.

simetría de traslación Un diseño tiene simetría de traslación si se puede deslizar a una posición en la que se ve exactamente iqual que en la posición original. Para discribir la simetría de traslación se debe especificar la distancia y la dirección de la traslación. La figura de abajo es parte de un diseño que se extiende infinitamente en todas las direcciones. Este diseño tiene simetría de traslación.

Index

Index   **111**

Acknowledgments

Team Credits

The people who made up the **Connected Mathematics 2** team —representing editorial, editorial services, design services, and production services— are listed below. Bold type denotes core team members.

Leora Adler, Judith Buice, Kerry Cashman, Patrick Culleton, Sheila DeFazio, Richard Heater, **Barbara Hollingdale, Jayne Holman,** Karen Holtzman, **Etta Jacobs,** Christine Lee, Carolyn Lock, Catherine Maglio, **Dotti Marshall,** Rich McMahon, Eve Melnechuk, Kristin Mingrone, Terri Mitchell, **Marsha Novak,** Irene Rubin, Donna Russo, Robin Samper, Siri Schwartzman, **Nancy Smith,** Emily Soltanoff, **Mark Tricca,** Paula Vergith, Roberta Warshaw, Helen Young

Additional Credits

Diana Bonfilio, Mairead Reddin, Michael Torocsik, nSight, Inc.

Technical Illustration

WestWords, Inc.

Cover Design

tom white.images

Photos

2, Ryan McVay/PhotoDisc/Getty Images, Inc.; 3 t, Alfred Pasieka/Science Photo Library/Photo Researchers, Inc.; 3 b, Jeffrey Greenberg/Photo Researchers, Inc.; 8 l, Hans Georg Roth/Corbis; 8 m, Ted Kinsman/Photo Researchers, Inc.; 8 r, Pixoi Ltd/Alamy; 10, Cathy Melloan Resources/PhotoEdit; 11, Alfred Pasieka/Science Photo Library/Photo Researchers, Inc.; 13, BananaStock/SuperStock; 14, Bill Bachmann/Robertstock; 17, Ron Kimball/Ron Kimball Stock; 21 all, Copyright © 2005 Scott Kim, scottkim.com. All rights reserved.; 25, Richard Haynes; 35 both, Richard Haynes; 39, Richard Haynes; 45, Jeff Greenberg/Omni-Photo Communications, Inc.; 48, Hemera Technologies/Alamy; 50, R. Kord/Roberstock; 54, Russ Lappa; 57, Richard Haynes; 62, Peter Menzel/Stock Boston; 67, J. David Andrews/Masterfile; 71, Lars Howlett/Aurora Photos; 72, Terrance Klassen/SuperStock; 78, Novastock/Index Stock Imagery, Inc.; 79, Ryan McVay/PhotoDisc/Getty Images, Inc.; 80, Chuck Pefley/Alamy; 85, Richard Haynes; 98, Michael Newman/PhotoEdit

Connected Mathematics 2™

Say It With Symbols

Making Sense of Symbols

Glenda Lappan
James T. Fey
William M. Fitzgerald
Susan N. Friel
Elizabeth Difanis Phillips

PEARSON

Prentice
Hall

Boston, Massachusetts
Upper Saddle River, New Jersey

Say It With Symbols

Making Sense of Symbols

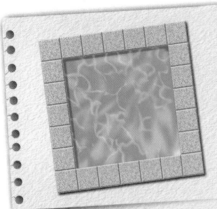

In-ground swimming pools are often surrounded by borders of tiles. How many border tiles *N* do you need to surround the square pool in the figure at the left?

The school choir is selling boxes of greeting cards to raise money for a trip.

How many boxes must the choir sell to make a $200 profit?

Perform the following operations on the first eight odd numbers.

- Pick an odd whole number.
- Square it.
- Subtract 1.

What patterns do you see in the resulting numbers?

You have used many powerful tools, including graphs, tables, and equations, to represent relationships among variables. Graphs allow you to see the shape of a relationship. They also help you identify intercepts and maximum and minimum points. Tables help you observe patterns of change in the values of the variables. Equations give you an efficient way to generalize relationships.

In *Say It With Symbols*, you will concentrate on symbolic expressions and equations. You will see that different ways of reasoning about a situation can lead to different but equivalent expressions. You will use mathematical properties to rewrite expressions, and you may discover that an equivalent expression allows you to think about a problem in a new way. And, you will learn new ways to solve equations. Pools are used as a context throughout this unit to introduce these ideas.

As you work through the unit, you will solve problems similar to those on the previous page.

Mathematical Highlights

Algebra provides ideas and symbols for expressing information about quantitative variables and relationships. In *Say It With Symbols,* you will solve problems designed to develop your understanding and skill in using symbolic expressions and equations in algebra.

You will learn how to

- Represent patterns and relationships in symbolic forms
- Determine when different symbolic expressions are mathematically equivalent
- Write algebraic expressions in useful equivalent forms
- Combine symbolic expressions using algebraic operations
- Analyze expressions or equations to determine the patterns of change in the tables and graphs that the equation represents
- Solve linear and quadratic equations using symbolic reasoning
- Use algebraic reasoning to validate generalizations and conjectures

As you work on problems in this unit, ask yourself questions about situations that involve symbolic expressions and equations.

What expression or equation represents the pattern or relationship in a context?

Can you write an equivalent expression for a given expression to provide new information about a relationship?

What operations can transform a given equation or expression into an equivalent form that can be used to answer a question?

How can symbolic reasoning help confirm a conjecture?

Investigation 1

Equivalent Expressions

When you want to communicate an idea in words, you can usually express it in many ways. All the statements below communicate the same information about Mika and Jim.

- Jim is older than Mika.
- Mika is younger than Jim.
- Jim was born before Mika.
- Mika was born after Jim.

Can you think of other ways to express the same idea?

Symbolic expressions, formulas, and equations are valuable tools in mathematics. The formula $P = 2L + 2W$ gives directions for calculating the perimeter of any rectangle with length L and width W.

$$W \begin{array}{c} \boxed{} \\ L \end{array}$$

Since you can usually think about a situation in more than one way, you can often express the situation in symbols in more than one way.

Getting Ready for Problem

Jim says the perimeter of the rectangle above is $P = 2(L + W)$. Mika says the perimeter is $P = 2L + 2W$.

- Why do you think Jim used parentheses in his equation?
- Are the expressions $2L + 2W$ and $2(L + W)$ *equivalent*? Do they produce the same perimeter for any given pair of lengths and widths? Explain your reasoning.

Since $2(L + W)$ and $2L + 2W$ represent the same quantity (the perimeter of a rectangle), they are **equivalent expressions.** This investigation explores situations in which a quantity is described with several different, but equivalent, expressions. The question is:

How can we determine if two expressions are equivalent?

Tiling Pools

In-ground pools are often surrounded by borders of tiles. The Custom Pool Company gets orders for square pools of different sizes. For example, the pool at the right has side lengths of 5 feet and is surrounded by square border tiles. All Custom Pool border tiles measure 1 foot on each side.

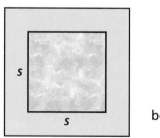

- How many border tiles do you need to surround a square pool?

Problem 1.1 Writing Equivalent Expressions

In order to calculate the number of tiles needed for a project, the Custom Pool manager wants an equation relating the number of border tiles to the size of the pool.

A. 1. Write an expression for the number of border tiles N based on the side length s of a square pool.

2. Write a different but equivalent expression for the number of tiles N needed to surround such a square pool.

3. Explain why your two expressions for the number of border tiles are equivalent.

B. 1. Use each expression in Question A to write an equation for the number of border tiles N. Make a table and a graph for each equation.

2. Based on your table and graph, are the two expressions for the number of border tiles in Question A equivalent? Explain.

C. Is the relationship between the side length of the pool and the number of border tiles linear, exponential, quadratic, or none of these? Explain.

ACE Homework starts on page 12.

1.2 Thinking in Different Ways

When Takashi reported his ideas about an equation relating N and s in Problem 1.1, he made the following sketch.

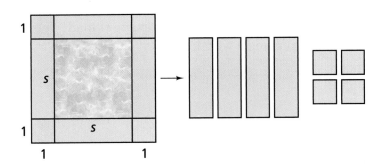

- What equation do you think Takashi wrote to relate N and s?

Problem 1.2 Determining Equivalence

A. Four students in Takashi's class came up with different equations for counting the number of border tiles. For each equation, make a sketch that shows how the student might have been thinking about the border of the pool.

1. Stella's equation: $N = 4(s + 1)$

2. Jeri's equation: $N = s + s + s + s + 4$

3. Hank's equation: $N = 4(s + 2)$

4. Sal's equation: $N = 2s + 2(s + 2)$

B. Use each equation in Question A to find the number of border tiles needed for a square pool with a side length of 10 feet. Can you conclude from your results that all the expressions for the number of tiles are equivalent? Explain your reasoning.

C. Which of the expressions for the number of border tiles in Question A are equivalent to Takashi's expression? Explain.

ACE Homework starts on page 12.

active math online

For: Algebra Tools Activity
Visit: PHSchool.com
Web Code: apd-6102

1.3 The Community Pool Problem

In this problem, we will interpret symbolic statements and use them to make predictions.

A community center is building a pool, part indoor and part outdoor. A diagram of the indoor part of the pool is shown. The indoor shape is made from a half-circle with radius x and a rectangle with length $4x$.

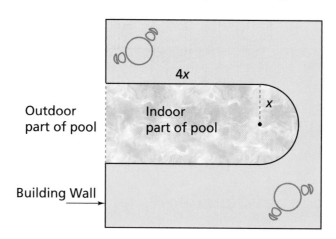

Problem 1.3 Interpreting Expressions

The exact dimensions of the community center pool are not available, but the area A of the whole pool is given by the equation:

$$A = x^2 + \frac{\pi x^2}{2} + 8x^2 + \frac{\pi x^2}{4}$$

A. Which part of the expression for area represents

    1. the area of the indoor part of the pool? Explain.

    2. the area of the outdoor part of the pool? Explain.

B. 1. Make a sketch of the outdoor part. Label the dimensions.

    2. If possible, draw another shape for the outdoor part of the pool. If not, explain why not.

C. Stella and Jeri each rewrote the expression for the area of the outdoor part of the pool to help them make a sketch.

$$\text{Stella:} \quad x^2 + \frac{\pi x^2}{8} + \frac{\pi x^2}{8}$$

$$\text{Jeri:} \quad \left(\frac{1}{2}x\right)\left(2x\right) + \frac{\pi x^2}{4}$$

1. Explain the reasoning each person may have used to write their expression.

2. Decide if these expressions are equivalent to the original expression in Question A, part (2). Explain your reasoning.

D. Does the equation for the area of the pool represent a linear, exponential, or quadratic relationship, or none of these? Explain.

ACE Homework starts on page 12.

1.4 Diving In

In the pool tile problems, you found patterns that could be represented by several different but equivalent symbolic expressions, such as:

$$4s + 4$$
$$4(s + 1)$$
$$s + s + s + s + 4$$
$$2s + 2(s + 2)$$

The equivalence of these expressions can be shown with arrangements of tiles. Equivalence also follows from properties of numbers and operations.

An important property is the **Distributive Property:**

For any real numbers $a, b,$ and c:

$$a(b + c) = ab + ac \quad \text{and} \quad a(b - c) = ab - ac$$

For example, this property guarantees that $4(s + 1) = 4s + 4$ for any s.

We say that $a(b + c)$ and $4(s + 1)$ are in *factored form* and $ab + ac$ and $4s + 4$ are in *expanded form*.

The next problem reviews the Distributive Property.

Swimming pools are sometimes divided into sections that are used for different purposes. A pool may have a section for swimming laps and a section for diving, or a section for experienced swimmers and a section for small children.

Below are diagrams of pools with swimming and diving sections. The dimensions are in meters.

1.

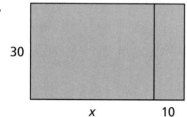

2.

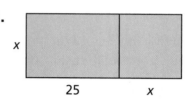

3.

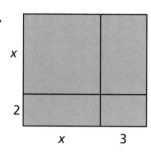

4.

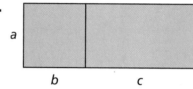

- For each pool, write two different but equivalent expressions for the total area.

- Explain how these diagrams and expressions illustrate the Distributive Property.

The Distributive Property, as well as the Commutative Property and other properties for numbers, are useful for writing equivalent expressions. The Commutative Property states that $a + b = b + a$ and $ab = ba$, where a and b are real numbers. These properties were discussed in previous units.

Problem 1.4 Revisiting the Distributive Property

A. Write each expression in expanded form.

   1. $3(x + 5)$ **2.** $2(3x - 10)$

   3. $2x(x + 5)$ **4.** $(x + 2)(x + 5)$

B. Write each expression in factored form.

   1. $12 + 24x$ **2.** $x + x + x + 6$

   3. $x^2 + 3x$ **4.** $x^2 + 4x + 3$

C. The following expressions all represent the number of border tiles N for a square pool with side length s.

$$4(s + 1)$$
$$s + s + s + s + 4$$
$$2s + 2(s + 2)$$
$$4(s + 2) - 4$$
$$(s + 2)^2 - s^2$$

Use the Distributive and Commutative properties to show that these expressions are equivalent.

D. Three of the following expressions are equivalent. Explain which expression is not equivalent to the other three.

   1. $2x - 12x + 10$ **2.** $12x - 2x + 10$

   3. $10 - 10x$ **4.** $10(1 - x)$

E. Copy each equation. Insert one set of parentheses in the expression to the left of the equal sign so that it is equivalent to the expression to the right of the equal sign.

   1. $6p + 2 - 2p = 4p + 12$

   2. $6p + 2 - 2p = 6p$

ACE Homework starts on page 12.

Applications

1. a. How many 1-foot-square border tiles do you need to surround a pool that is 10 feet long and 5 feet wide?

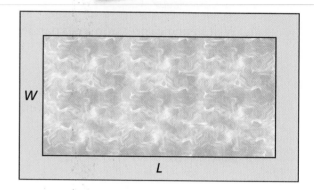

b. Write an equation for the number of border tiles needed to surround a pool *L* feet long and *W* feet wide.

c. Write a different but equivalent equation for the number of tiles needed in part (b). Explain why your equations are equivalent.

2. A square hot tub has sides of length *s* feet. A tiler creates a border by placing 1-foot-square tiles along the edges of the tub and triangular tiles at the corners, as shown. The tiler makes the triangular tiles by cutting the square tiles in half along a diagonal.

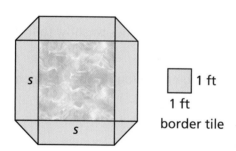

a. Suppose the hot tub has sides of length 7 feet. How many square tiles does the tiler need for the border?

b. Write an expression for the number of square tiles *N* needed to build this border for a square tub with sides of length *s* feet.

c. Write a different but equivalent expression for the number of tiles *N*. Explain why your expressions for the number of border tiles are equivalent.

d. Is the relationship between the number of tiles and side length linear, exponential, quadratic, or none of these? Explain.

3. A rectangular pool is L feet long and W feet wide. A tiler creates a border by placing 1-foot-square tiles along the edges of the pool and triangular tiles on the corners, as shown. The tiler makes the triangular tiles by cutting the square tiles in half along a diagonal.

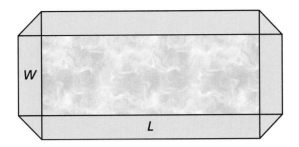

Homework Help Online
PHSchool.com
For: Help with Exercise 3
Web Code: ape-6103

a. Suppose the pool is 30 feet long and 20 feet wide. How many square tiles does the tiler need for the border?

b. Write two equations for the number of square tiles N needed to make this border for a pool L feet long and W feet wide.

c. Explain why your two equations are equivalent.

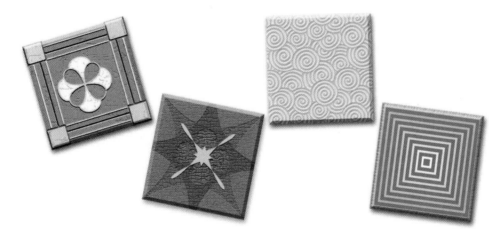

4. Below are three more expressions students wrote for the number of border tiles needed to surround the square pool in Problem 1.2.

$$4\left(\frac{s}{2} + \frac{s}{4}\right) + 4 \qquad 2\left(s + 0.5\right) + 2\left(s + 1.5\right) \qquad 4\left[\frac{s + (s + 2)}{2}\right]$$

a. Use each expression to find the number of border tiles N if $s = 0$.

b. Do you think the expressions are equivalent? Explain.

c. Use each expression to find the number of border tiles if $s = 12$. Has your answer to part (b) changed? Explain.

d. What can you say about testing specific values as a method for determining whether two or more expressions are equivalent?

5. A square surrounds a circle with a radius r. Each expression represents the area of part of this figure. Describe the shape or region each area represents.

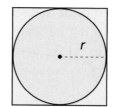

  a. $4r^2 - \pi r^2$ **b.** $4r^2 - \dfrac{\pi r^2}{4}$

6. The dimensions of a pool are shown below.

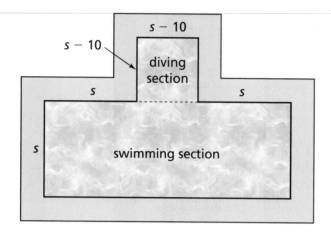

Each expression represents the surface area for part of the pool.

  i. $s(3s - 10)$ **ii.** $(s - 10)^2$

  iii. $2s^2 + s(s - 10)$ **iv.** $s^2 - 20s + 100$

a. Which expression(s) could represent the surface area of the diving section?

b. Which expression(s) could represent the surface area of the swimming section?

c. If you chose more than one expression for parts (a) and (b), show that they are equivalent.

d. Write an equation that represents the total surface area A of the pool.

e. What kind of relationship does the equation in part (d) represent?

For Exercises 7–9, complete parts (a)–(c).

    a. For each expression, write an equation of the form
       $y = expression$. Make a table and a graph of the two equations.
       Show x values from -5 to 5 on the graph.

    b. Based on your table and graph, tell whether you think the two
       expressions are equivalent.

    c. If you think the expressions are equivalent, use the properties you
       have learned in this investigation to verify their equivalence. If
       you think they are not equivalent, explain why.

7. $-3x + 6 + 5x$ and $6 + 2x$

8. $10 - 5x$ and $5x - 10$

9. $(3x + 4) + (2x - 3)$ and $5x + 1$

10. Use the Distributive Property to write each expression in expanded form.

    a. $3(x + 7)$ **b.** $5(5 - x)$ **c.** $2(4x - 8)$ **d.** $(x + 4)(x + 2)$

11. Use the Distributive Property to write each expression in factored form.

    a. $2x - 10x$ **b.** $2x + 6$ **c.** $14 - 7x$

12. Use the Distributive and Commutative properties to determine
    whether each pair of expressions is equivalent for all values of x.

    a. $3x + 7x$ and $10x$ **b.** $5x$ and $5x - 10x$

    c. $4(1 + 2x) - 3x$ and $5x + 4$ **d.** $5 - 3(2 - 4x)$ and $-1 + 12x$

13. Here is one way you might prove that $2(s + 2) + 2s$ is equivalent to
    $4s + 4$:

           (1) $2(s + 2) + 2s = 2s + 4 + 2s$

           (2) $= 2s + 2s + 4$

           (3) $= (2 + 2)s + 4$

           (4) $= 4s + 4$

    What properties of numbers and operations justify each step?

14. Find three equivalent expressions for $6x + 3$.

**For Exercises 15–17, copy the statement. Insert parentheses on the left side
of the equation, if necessary, to make the statement true for all values of p.**

15. $7 + 5p - p = 11p$

16. $7 + 5p - p = 7$

17. $7 + 5p - p = 7 + 4p$

Connections

In Exercises 18–23, each expression represents the area of a rectangle. Draw a divided rectangle for each expression. Label the lengths and areas. For Exercises 18–20, write an equivalent expression in expanded form. For Exercises 21–23, write an equivalent expression in factored form.

18. $x(x + 6)$ **19.** $x(x - 6)$ **20.** $x(5 + 1)$

21. $x^2 + 4x$ **22.** $x^2 - 2x$ **23.** $3x + 4x$

24. A circular pool with a radius of 4 feet has a 1-foot border.

    a. What is the surface area of the circular pool?

    b. What is the surface area of the border?

    c. Write an expression for the surface area of a circular pool with a radius of r feet.

    d. Write an expression for the area of a 1-foot border around a circular pool with a radius of r feet.

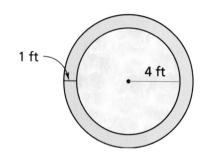

25. Multiple Choice Which of the following expressions is equivalent to $m + m + m + m + m$?

    A. $m + 5$ **B.** $5m$ **C.** m^5 **D.** $5(m + 1)$

26. Multiple Choice Which of the following expressions is equivalent to $a - b$, where a and b are any numbers?

    F. $b - a$ **G.** $a + b$ **H.** $-a + b$ **J.** $-b + a$

For Exercises 27–32, draw and label a rectangle whose area is represented by the expression. For Exercises 27–29, write an equivalent expression in expanded form. For Exercises 30–32, write an equivalent expression in factored form.

27. $(x + 1)(x + 4)$ **28.** $(x + 5)(x + 6)$ **29.** $3x(5 + 2)$

30. $x^2 + x + 2x + 2$ **31.** $x^2 + 7x + 10$ **32.** $x^2 + 14x + 49$

Find each sum or difference.

33. $\dfrac{5}{7} - \dfrac{1}{3}$ **34.** $\dfrac{5}{2} + \dfrac{1}{3}$

35. $\dfrac{1}{2}x + \dfrac{1}{2}x$ **36.** $\dfrac{2}{3}x - \dfrac{1}{2}x$

Go Online
PHSchool.com

For: Multiple-Choice Skills Practice
Web Code: apa-6154

Find each sum, difference, product, or quotient.

37. 2×14

38. $-2 - (-14)$

39. $-2 \div (-14)$

40. $-6 \times (-11)$

41. $-6 + 11$

42. $6 - 11$

43. $-18(3x)$

44. $\dfrac{-24x}{-8}$

45. $-18x \div 3$

Find the greatest common factor for each pair of numbers.

46. 35 and 40

47. 36 and 12

48. 100 and 25

49. 42 and 9

50. Below is a diagram of Otter Middle School's outdoor track. The shape of the interior region (shaded green) is a rectangle with two half circles at each end.

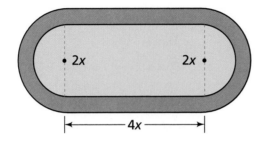

a. Find an expression that represents the area of the interior region.

b. Find the perimeter of the interior region as if you wanted to put a fence around it. Explain how you found your answer.

c. Write an expression equivalent to the one in part (b).

51. For Problem 1.2, Percy wrote the expression $8 + 4(s - 1)$ to represent the number of border tiles needed to surround a square pool with side length s.

    a. Is this expression equivalent to the other expressions? Explain.

    b. Four students used Percy's expression to calculate the number of border tiles needed for a pool with a side length of 6 feet. Which student performed the calculations correctly?

Stella

$8 + 4(6 - 1) = 8 + 24 - 1$
$= 31 \text{ tiles}$

Hank

$8 + 4(6 - 1) = 8 + 4(5)$
$= 8 + 20$
$= 28 \text{ tiles}$

Takashi

$8 + 4(6 - 1) = 12 + (6 - 1)$
$= 12 + 5$
$= 17 \text{ tiles}$

Jackie

$8 + 4(6 - 1) = 12(6 - 1)$
$= 12(5)$
$= 60 \text{ tiles}$

52. Lily invests D dollars in a money-market account that earns 10% interest per year. She does not plan on taking money out during the year. She writes the expression $D + 0.10D$ to represent the amount of money in the account at the end of one year.

    a. Explain why this expression is correct.

    b. Write an equivalent expression in factored form.

    c. Suppose Lily invested $1,500. How much money will she have in her account at the end of one year?

For Exercises 53 and 54, use this information: The ski club is planning a trip for winter break. They write the equation $C = 200 + 10N$ to estimate the cost in dollars C of the trip for N students.

53. Duncan and Corey both use the equation to estimate the cost for 50 students. Duncan says the cost is $10,500, and Corey says it is $700.

  a. Whose estimate is correct? Show your work.

  b. How do you think Duncan and Corey found such different estimates if they both used the same equation?

54. a. Suppose 20 students go on the trip. What is the cost per student?

  b. Write an equation for the cost per student S when N students go on the trip.

  c. Use your equation to find the cost per student when 40 students go on the trip.

55. The pyramid and rectangular prism have the same base and height.

  a. Find the volume of the pyramid.

  b. Draw a pyramid with a volume of $\left(\frac{1}{3}\right)\left(8\right)$ cubic units.

  Hint: You might find it easier to draw the related prism first.

  c. Draw a pyramid with a volume of $\left(\frac{1}{3}\right)\left(27\right)$ cubic units.

  d. Find a possible height of a pyramid whose volume is $9x^3$ cubic units.

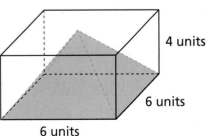

4 units

6 units

6 units

56. Below are two students' calculations for writing an equivalent expression for $10 - 4(x - 1) + 11 \times 3$.

a. Which student performed the calculations correctly?

b. What mistakes did the other student make?

Sarah

$$10 - 4(x - 1) + 11 \times 3 = 10 - 4x + 4 + 11 \times 3$$
$$= 10 - 4x + 4 + 33$$
$$= 10 - 4x + 37$$
$$= 10 + 37 - 4x$$
$$= 47 - 4x$$

Emily

$$10 - 4(x - 1) + 11 \times 3 = 10 - 4x + 4 + 11 \times 3$$
$$= 10 - 4x + 15 \times 3$$
$$= 25 - 4x \times 3$$
$$= 25 - 12x$$

Extensions

57. Percy wants to write an equation for the number of tiles needed to surround a square pool with sides of length s feet. He makes a table for pools with sides of length 1, 2, 3, 4, and 5 feet. Then he uses the patterns in his table to write the equation $N = 8 + 4(s - 1)$.

Border Tiles

Side Length	1	2	3	4	5
Number of Tiles	8	12	16	20	24

a. What patterns does Percy see in his table?

b. Is Percy's expression for the number of tiles equivalent to $4(s + 1)$, Stella's expression in Problem 1.2? Explain.

58. Two expressions for the number of border tiles for the pool at the right are given.

$$2(s + 0.5) + 2(s + 1.5)$$

$$4\left[\frac{s + (s + 2)}{2}\right]$$

Sketch a picture that illustrates each expression.

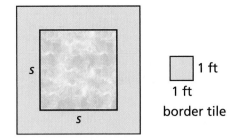

s

1 ft
1 ft
border tile

59. The *Expression Puzzles* below all start with the original expression $2n - 3 + 4n + 6n + 1$. Each one ends with a different expression.

a. Solve each puzzle by inserting one set of parentheses in the original expression so that it is equivalent to the desired result.

b. Show that your expression is equivalent to the desired result. Justify each step.

Expression Puzzles

Puzzle	Original Expression	Desired Result
1	$2n - 3 + 4n + 6n + 1$	$12n - 5$
2	$2n - 3 + 4n + 6n + 1$	$12n + 3$
3	$2n - 3 + 4n + 6n + 1$	$12n - 2$
4	$2n - 3 + 4n + 6n + 1$	$n + 1$

Mathematical Reflections 1

In this investigation, you found different but equivalent expressions to represent a quantity in a relationship. These questions will help you summarize what you have learned.

Think about your answers to these questions. Discuss your ideas with other students and your teacher. Then write a summary of your findings in your notebook.

1. What does it mean to say that two expressions are equivalent?

2. Explain how the Distributive and Commutative properties can be used to write equivalent expressions.

3. Explain how the Distributive and Commutative properties can be used to show that two or more expressions are equivalent.

Investigation 2

Combining Expressions

In the last investigation, you found several ways to write equivalent expressions to describe a quantity. You also learned several ways to show that two expressions are equivalent. We will continue to answer the questions:

- Are the expressions equivalent? Why?

- What information does each equivalent expression represent?

We will also look at ways to create new expressions and to answer the question:

- What are the advantages and disadvantages of using one equation rather than two or more equations to represent a situation?

2.1 Walking Together

In *Moving Straight Ahead*, Leanne, Gilberto, and Alana enter a walkathon as a team. This means that each person will walk the same number of kilometers. The walkathon organizers offer a prize to the three-person team that raises the most money.

- Leanne has walkathon pledges from 16 sponsors. All of her sponsors pledge $10 regardless of how far she walks.

- Gilberto has pledges from 7 sponsors. Each sponsor pledges $2 for each kilometer he walks.

- Alana has pledges from 11 sponsors. Each sponsor pledges $5 plus $0.50 for each kilometer she walks.

A. 1. Write equations to represent the money M that each student will raise for walking x kilometers.

   a. $M_{\text{Leanne}} = \blacksquare$

   b. $M_{\text{Gilberto}} = \blacksquare$

   c. $M_{\text{Alana}} = \blacksquare$

   2. Write an equation for the total money M_{total} raised by the three-person team for walking x kilometers.

B. 1. Write an expression that is equivalent to the expression for the total amount in Question A, part (2). Explain why it is equivalent.

   2. What information does this new expression represent about the situation?

   3. Suppose each person walks 10 kilometers. Explain which expression(s) you would use to calculate the total amount of money raised.

C. Are the relationships between kilometers walked and money raised linear, exponential, quadratic, or none of these? Explain.

ACE **Homework starts on page 28.**

2.2 Predicting Profit

The manager of the Water City amusement park uses data collected over the past several years to write equations that will help her make predictions about the daily operations of the park.

The daily concession-stand profit in dollars P depends on the number of visitors V. The manager writes the equation below to model this relationship.

$$P = 2.50V - 500$$

She uses the equation below to predict the number of visitors V based on the probability of rain R.

$$V = 600 - 500R$$

- What information might each of the numbers in the equations represent?

A. 1. Suppose the probability of rain is 25%. What profit can the concession stand expect? Explain.

    2. What was the probability of rain if the profit expected is $625? Explain your reasoning.

B. 1. Write an equation that can be used to predict the concession-stand profit P from the probability of rain R.

    2. Use this equation to predict the profit when the probability of rain is 25%. Compare your answer with your result in Question A, part (1).

C. 1. Write an equivalent expression for the profit in Question B. Explain why the two expressions are equivalent.

    2. Predict the probability of rain on a day when the concession-stand profit is $625. Compare your answer with the result you found in Question A, part (2).

    3. Predict the profit when the probability of rain is 0%. Does your answer make sense? Explain.

    4. Predict the profit when the probability of rain is 100%. Does your answer make sense?

D. Do the equations in Questions B and C represent a linear, exponential, or quadratic relationship, or none of these? Explain.

ACE Homework starts on page 28.

In the next problem, you will explore two familiar situations that have an interesting connection.

Tony and Paco will operate the water tube concession stand at Water City. Tony is responsible for designing the building that will store the rafts. Paco is responsible for deciding the rental fee for the tubes.

Problem 2.3 Using Equations

A. Every concession stand must have a rectangular floor space and a perimeter of 88 meters. Tony wants the greatest area possible.

   1. Write an equation for the area in terms of the length.

   2. What is the maximum area for the rectangular floor space?

B. Paco knows that on a typical day, the number of tube rentals n is related to the price to rent each tube p. Records from other water park locations suggest:

  • If the tubes are free (no price), there will be 54 rentals.

  • Each increase of $1 in the price will result in one less tube rented.

Paco uses this information to write the following equations:

  • Equation 1: $n = 54 - (1)p$

  • Equation 2: $I = np$, where I is the daily income

   1. Do these equations make sense? Explain.

   2. Write an equation for income in terms of the number of rentals n.

   3. The expenses for storage and maintenance of the rented tubes are $10 per day. Write an equation for daily profit D in terms of the number of rentals n.

4. Compare the equation in part (3) to the equation in Question A, part (1).

5. What number of rentals produces the maximum daily profit? What is the maximum profit? What rental price produces the maximum daily profit?

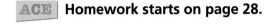 **Homework starts on page 28.**

The calculation of the quarterback rating in the National Football League (NFL™) uses a series of equations:

Completion Rating: $\text{CR} = 5\left(\dfrac{\text{completions}}{\text{attempts}}\right) - 1.5$

Yards Rating: $\text{YR} = \dfrac{\dfrac{\text{yards}}{\text{attempts}} - 3}{4}$

Touchdown Rating: $\text{TR} = 20\left(\dfrac{\text{touchdowns}}{\text{attempts}}\right)$

Interception Rating: $\text{IR} = 25\left(0.095 - \dfrac{\text{interceptions}}{\text{attempts}}\right)$

Overall Rating $= 100\left(\dfrac{\text{CR} + \text{YR} + \text{TR} + \text{IR}}{6}\right)$

Go Online
PHSchool.com **For:** Information about quarterback ratings
Web Code: ape-9031

Applications

1. The student council is organizing a T-shirt sale to raise money for a local charity. They make the following estimates of expenses and income:

   - Expense of $250 for advertising
   - Expense of $4.25 for each T-shirt
   - Income of $12 for each T-shirt
   - Income of $150 from a business sponsor

   a. Write an equation for the income I made for selling n T-shirts.

   b. Write an equation for the expenses E for selling n T-shirts.

   c. Suppose the student council sells 100 T-shirts. What is the profit?

   d. Write an equation for the profit P made for selling n T-shirts.

For Exercises 2–5, use the following information: In *Variables and Patterns,* **several students were planning a bike tour. They estimated the following expenses and incomes.**

   - $30 for each bike rental
   - $125 for cost of food and camp for each biker
   - $700 for van rental
   - $350 of income for each biker

2. **a.** Write an equation for the total expenses E for n bikers.

   b. Write an equation for the total income I for n bikers.

   c. Write an equation for the profit P for n bikers.

   d. Find the profit for 25 bikers.

   e. Suppose the profit is $1,055. How many bikers went on the trip?

   f. Does the profit equation represent a linear, quadratic, or exponential function, or none of these? Explain.

3. **Multiple Choice** Suppose someone donates a van at no charge. Which equation represents the total expenses?

   A. $E = 125 + 30$ **B.** $E = 125n + 30n$

   C. $E = 155$ **D.** $E = 155 + n$

4. Multiple Choice Suppose people supply their own bikes. Which equation represents the total expenses? (Assume they will rent a van.)

    F. $E = 125n + 700$ **G.** $E = 125 + 700 + n$

    H. $E = 825n$ **J.** $E = 350n + 125n + 700$

5. Multiple Choice Suppose people supply their own bikes. Which equation represents the profit? (Assume they will rent a van.)

    A. $P = 350 - (125 + 700 + n)$ **B.** $P = 350n - 125n + 700$

    C. $P = 350n - (125n + 700)$ **D.** $P = 350 - 125n - 700$

For Exercises 6–8, recall the equations from Problem 2.2
($P = 2.50V - 500$ and $V = 600 - 500R$).

6. Suppose the probability of rain is 50%. What profit can the concession stand expect to make?

7. What is the probability of rain if the profit expected is $100?

8. The manager estimates the daily employee-bonus fund B (in dollars) from the number of visitors V using the equation $B = 100 + 0.50V$.

    a. Suppose the probability of rain is 30%. What is the daily employee-bonus fund?

    b. Write an equation that relates the employee-bonus B to the probability of rain R.

    c. Suppose the probability of rain is 50%. Use your equation to calculate the employee-bonus fund.

    d. Suppose the daily employee-bonus fund is $375. What is the probability of rain?

Homework
Help **Online**
PHSchool.com
For: Help with Exercise 8
Web Code: ape-6208

Investigation 2 Combining Expressions   **29**

9. A manager of a park claims that the profit P for a concession stand depends on the number of visitors V, and that the number of visitors depends on the day's high temperature T (in Fahrenheit). The following equations represent the manager's claims:

$$P = 4.25V - 300 \qquad V = 50(T - 45)$$

a. Suppose 1,000 people visit the park one day. Predict that day's high temperature.

b. Write an equation for profit based on temperature.

c. Write an equation for profit that is equivalent to the equation in part (b). Explain what information the numbers and variables represent.

d. Find the profit if the temperature is 70°F.

10. A farmer has 240 meters of fence. The farmer wants to build a fence to enclose the greatest possible rectangular land area.

a. Write an equation for the fenced area A in terms of the length ℓ of the rectangular plot.

b. What are the dimensions of the rectangle with the greatest area?

c. Describe how you could find the information in part (b) from a graph of the equation.

d. Does the equation for area represent a linear, quadratic, or exponential function, or none of these? Explain.

11. In Exercise 10, suppose the farmer uses the 240 meters of fence to enclose a rectangular plot on only three sides and uses a creek as the boundary of the fourth side.

a. Write an equation for the fenced area A in terms of the length ℓ of the rectangular plot.

b. What are the dimensions of the rectangle with the greatest area?

c. Does the equation represent a linear, quadratic, or exponential function, or none of these? Explain.

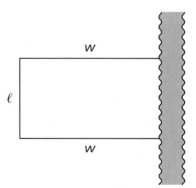

12. The math club is selling posters to advertise National Algebra day. The following equation represents the profits P they expect for selling n posters at x dollars.

$$P = xn - 6n$$

They also know that the number of posters n sold depends on the selling price x, which is represented by this equation:

$$n = 20 - x$$

a. Write an equation for profit in terms of the number of posters sold.
Hint: First solve the equation $n = 20 - x$ for x.

b. What is the profit for selling 10 posters?

c. What is the selling price of the posters in part (b)?

d. What is the greatest possible profit?

Connections

13. Multiple Choice Which statement is *false* when a, b, and c are different real numbers?

F. $(a + b) + c = a + (b + c)$ **G.** $ab = ba$

H. $(ab)c = a(bc)$ **J.** $a - b = b - a$

For Exercises 14–16, use the Distributive Property and sketch a rectangle to show the equivalence.

14. $x(x + 5)$ and $x^2 + 5x$

15. $(2 + x)(2 + 3x)$ and $4 + 8x + 3x^2$

16. $(x + 2)(2x + 3)$ and $2x^2 + 7x + 6$

Go Online
PHSchool.com
For: Multiple-Choice Skills Practice
Web Code: apa-6254

17. Some steps are missing in the solution to $11x - 12 = 30 + 5x$.

$$11x - 12 = 30 + 5x$$
$$11x = 42 + 5x$$
$$6x = 42$$
$$x = 7$$

a. Copy the steps above. Fill in the missing steps.

b. How can you check that $x = 7$ is the correct solution?

c. Explain how you could use a graph or a table to solve the original equation for x.

18. In the following graph, line ℓ_1 represents the income for selling *n* soccer balls. Line ℓ_2 represents the expenses of manufacturing *n* soccer balls.

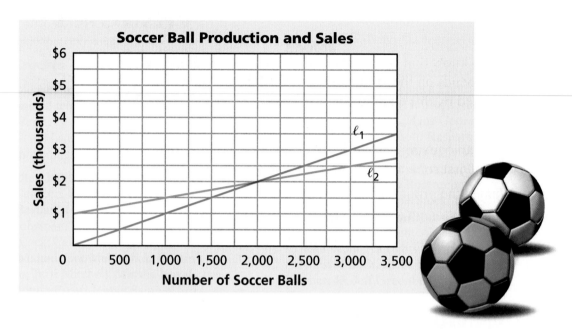

Soccer Ball Production and Sales

a. What is the start-up expense (the expense before any soccer balls are produced) for manufacturing the soccer balls? NOTE: The vertical axis is in *thousands* of dollars.

b. What are the expenses and income for producing and selling 500 balls? For 1,000 balls? For 3,000 balls? Explain.

c. What is the profit for producing and selling 500 balls? For 1,000 balls? For 3,000 balls? Explain.

d. What is the break-even point? Give the number of soccer balls and the expenses.

e. Write equations for the expenses, income, and profit. Explain what the numbers and variables in each equation represent.

f. Suppose the manufacturer produces and sells 1,750 soccer balls. Use the equations in part (e) to find the profit.

g. Suppose the profit is $10,000. Use the equations in part (e) to find the number of soccer balls produced and sold.

For Exercises 19–24, use properties of equality to solve the equation. Check your solution.

19. $7x + 15 = 12x + 5$

20. $7x + 15 = 5 + 12x$

21. $-3x + 5 = 2x - 10$

22. $14 - 3x = 1.5x + 5$

23. $9 - 4x = \dfrac{3 + x}{2}$

24. $-3(x + 5) = \dfrac{2x - 10}{3}$

25. The writing club wants to publish a book of students' short stories, poems, and essays. A member of the club contacts two local printers to get bids on the cost of printing the books.

   Bid 1:   cost = $100 + $4 × the number of books printed

   Bid 2:   cost = $25 + $7 × the number of books printed

   a. Make a table of (*number of books printed, cost*) values for each bid. Use your table to find the number of books for which the two bids are equal. Explain how you found your answer.

   b. Make a graph of the two equations. Use your graph to find the number of books for which the two bids are equal. Explain.

   c. For what numbers of books is Bid 1 less than Bid 2? Explain.

26. Use the information about printing costs from Exercise 25.

   a. For each bid, find the cost of printing 75 books.

   b. Suppose the cost cannot exceed $300. For each bid, find the greatest number of books that can be printed. Explain.

   The club decides to request bids from two more printers.

   Bid 3:   cost = $8 × the number of books printed

   Bid 4:   cost = $30 + $6 × the number of books printed

   c. For what number of books does Bid 3 equal Bid 4? Explain.

27. a. A soccer team has 21 players. Suppose each player shakes hands with each of the other players. How many handshakes will take place?

   b. Write an equation for the number of handshakes *h* among a team with *n* players.

   c. Write an equation for the number of handshakes that is equivalent to the equation in part (b).

28. a. Write an expression that is equivalent to $(x + 2)(x + 5)$.

b. Explain two methods for checking equivalence.

29. For the equation $y = (x + 2)(x + 5)$, find each of the following. Explain how you found each.

a. y-intercept

b. x-intercept(s)

c. maximum/minimum point

d. line of symmetry

For Exercises 30–35, find an equivalent expression.

30. $x^2 \cdot x^3$

31. $x \cdot x^0 \cdot x^5$

32. $\dfrac{x^2 \cdot x^3}{x}$

33. $\dfrac{x^8}{x^5}$

34. $\dfrac{x^5}{x^8}$

35. $\dfrac{4x^8}{2x^5}$

36. Mary's salary is $30,000 per year. What would be her new salary next year given each condition?

a. She gets a 15% raise.

b. Her salary grows by a factor of 1.12.

c. Her salary increases to 110% of what it is now.

37. Examine the three different cylinders.

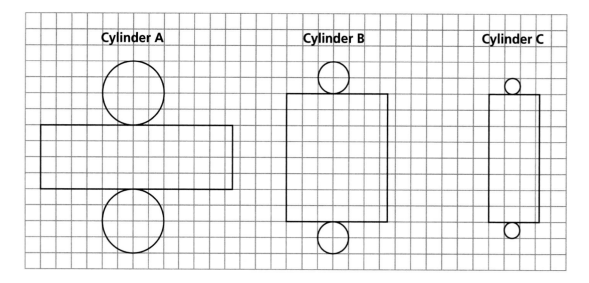

a. Compare the three cylinders.

b. Estimate the surface area of each cylinder. Which cylinder has the greatest surface area? Explain.

c. Which cylinder has the greatest volume? Explain.

Extensions

38. The Phillips Concert Hall estimates their concession-stand profits P_c and admission profits P_A with the following equations, where x is the number of people (in hundreds):

$$P_c = 15x - 500 \qquad P_A = 106x - x^2$$

The concession-stand profits include revenue from advertising and the sale of food and souvenirs. The admission profits are based on the difference between ticket sales and cost.

a. Write an equation for the total profit for P in terms of the number of people x (in hundreds).

b. What is the maximum profit? How many people must attend in order to achieve the maximum profit?

39. Recall the series of equations used to calculate a quarterback's rating in the *Did You Know?* after Problem 2.3. Tom Brady's statistics for 2004 are shown below. Use the equations and the statistics to find his overall rating that year.

Attempts: 474

Completions: 288

Yards: 3,692

Touchdowns: 28

Interceptions: 14

Mathematical Reflections 2

In this investigation, you combined expressions or substituted an equivalent expression for a quantity to make new expressions. You also used these expressions to make predictions. These questions will help you summarize what you have learned.

Think about your answers to these questions. Discuss your ideas with other students and your teacher. Then write a summary of your findings in your notebook.

1. Describe a situation in which it is helpful to add expressions to form a new expression. Explain how you can combine the expressions.

2. Describe a situation in which it is helpful to substitute an equivalent expression for a quantity in an equation.

3. What are the advantages and disadvantages of working with one equation rather than two or more equations in a given situation?

Investigation 3

Solving Equations

A problem often requires finding solutions to equations. In previous units, you developed strategies for solving linear and quadratic equations. In this investigation, you will use the properties of real numbers to extend these strategies.

3.1 Solving Linear Equations

How do you solve the following linear equation for x?

$$100 + 4x = 25 + 7x$$

Getting Ready for Problem 3.1

The steps below show one way to solve $100 + 4x = 25 + 7x$.

$$100 + 4x = 25 + 7x$$

$$(1) \quad 100 + 4x - 4x = 25 + 7x - 4x$$

$$100 = 25 + 3x$$

$$(2) \quad 100 - 25 = 25 + 3x - 25$$

$$75 = 3x$$

$$(3) \quad 75 \div 3 = 3x \div 3$$

$$25 = x$$

- Provide an explanation for each numbered step in the solution.
- The solution above begins by subtracting $4x$ from both sides of the equation. Could you begin with a different first step? Explain.
- How can you check that $x = 25$ is the correct solution?
- Describe another method for finding the solution to the equation.

The example in the Getting Ready uses the **properties of equality** that you learned in *Moving Straight Ahead*.

- You can add or subtract the same quantity to both sides of an equation to write an equivalent equation.

- You can multiply or divide both sides of an equation by the same non-zero number to write an equivalent equation.

You will continue to use these properties as well as the Distributive and Commutative properties to solve more equations.

Problem 3.1 Solving Linear Equations

A. A school choir is selling boxes of greeting cards to raise money for a trip.

The equation for the profit in dollars P in terms of the number of boxes sold s is:

$$P = 5s - (100 + 2s)$$

1. What information do the expressions $5s$ and $100 + 2s$ represent in the situation? What information do 100 and $2s$ represent?

2. Use the equation to find the number of boxes the choir must sell to make a $200 profit. Explain.

3. How many boxes must the choir sell to break even? Explain.

4. Write a simpler expression for profit. Explain what information the variables and numbers represent.

5. One of the choir members wrote the following expression for profit: $5s - 2(50 + s)$. Explain whether this expression is equivalent to the original expression for profit.

B. Describe how to solve an equation for s that has parentheses like $200 = 5s - (100 + 2s)$ without using a table or graph.

C. Solve each equation for x when $y = 0$. Check your solutions.

1. $y = 5 + 2(3 + 4x)$ 2. $y = 5 - 2(3 + 4x)$

3. $y = 5 + 2(3 - 4x)$ 4. $y = 5 - 2(3 - 4x)$

ACE Homework starts on page 45.

Ms. Lucero wants to install tiles around her square swimming pool. She receives two estimates:

- *Cover and Surround It* has a fixed charge of $1,000 for design and material delivery costs. They charge $25 per tile after the first 12 tiles.
- *Tile and Beyond* has a fixed charge of $740 for design and material delivery costs. They charge $32 per tile after the first 10 tiles.

The equations below show the estimated costs C (in dollars) of buying and installing N border tiles.

Cover and Surround It: $C_C = 1,000 + 25(N - 12)$

Tile and Beyond: $C_T = 740 + 32(N - 10)$

Recall that you can use *subscripts* to show different uses for a variable: C_C means cost for *Cover and Surround It*; C_T means cost for *Tile and Beyond*.

- Do the equations make sense given the description above for each company's charges?

Ms. Lucero wants to know when the costs of each company are the same.
How can Ms. Lucero use the equation $C_C = C_T$ to answer her question?

Problem 3.2 Solving More Linear Equations

A. 1. Without using a table or graph, find the number of tiles for which the two costs are equal.

   2. How can you check that your solution is correct?

   3. How can you use a graph or table to find the number of tiles for which the two costs are equal?

   4. For what numbers of tiles is *Tile and Beyond* cheaper than *Cover and Surround It* ($C_T < C_C$)? Explain your reasoning.

B. Use the techniques that you developed in Problem 3.1 and in Question A to solve each equation for x. Check your solutions.

   1. $3x = 5 + 2(3 + 4x)$ **2.** $10 + 3x = 2(3 + 4x) + 5$

   3. $3x = 5 - 2(3 + 4x)$ **4.** $7 + 3(1 - x) = 5 - 2(3 - 4x)$

ACE Homework starts on page 45.

Sometimes mathematical problems that appear to be different are actually the same. Finding the x-intercepts of $y = x^2 + 5x$ is the same as solving $x^2 + 5x = 0$ for x. The *solutions* to $x^2 + 5x = 0$ are also called the *roots* of the equation. In *Frogs, Fleas, and Painted Cubes* you found the solutions or roots by using a table or graph of $y = x^2 + 5x$ as shown.

x	y
−7	14
−6	6
−5	0
−4	−4
−3	−6
−2	−6
−1	−4
0	0
1	6
2	14
3	24

← *x*-intercept or solution (for −5, 0)

← *x*-intercept or solution (for 0, 0)

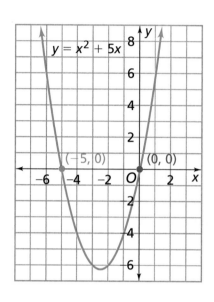

- What is the factored form of $x^2 + 5x$?
- What is the relationship between the factored form of $x^2 + 5x$ and the x-intercepts of the graph of $y = x^2 + 5x$?

Getting Ready for Problem 3.3

To factor the expression $x^2 + 5x + 6$, Trevor draws the area model at the right.

- Does the model match $x^2 + 5x + 6$?
- Find the factors of $x^2 + 5x + 6$.
- What are the x-intercepts of the graph of $y = x^2 + 5x + 6$?
- Describe the relationship between the x-intercepts of the graph of $y = x^2 + 5x + 6$ and the factored form of $x^2 + 5x + 6$.

Algebra provides tools, such as factoring, that can help solve quadratic equations like $x^2 + 5x = 0$ without using tables or graphs. Before using this tool, you need to review how to write quadratic expressions in factored form.

Problem 3.3 Factoring Quadratic Expressions

A. Jaime suggests the method below to factor $x^2 + 8x + 12$.

- Find factor pairs of 12 such as 1 and 12, 2 and 6, 3 and 4, −1 and −12, −2 and −6, and −3 and −4.
- Pick the factor pair whose sum is 8: $2 + 6 = 8$.
- Write the factored form: $(x + 2)(x + 6)$.

1. Use an area model to show why Jaime's method works for the expression $x^2 + 8x + 12$.

2. Could Jaime have used another factor pair, such as 1 and 12 or 3 and 4, to make an area model for $x^2 + 8x + 12$? Explain.

B. Use a method similar to Jaime's to write each expression in factored form. Show why each factored form is correct.

1. $x^2 + 5x + 4$ **2.** $x^2 - 5x + 4$

3. $x^2 - 3x - 4$ **4.** $x^2 + 4x + 4$

C. 1. Examine the following expressions. How are they similar to and different from those in Question B?

     a. $x^2 + 4x$ **b.** $4x^2 + 32x$

     c. $6x^2 - 4x$ **d.** $x^2 - 4$

2. Will Jaime's method for factoring work on these expressions? If so, use his method to write them in factored form. If not, find another way to write each in factored form.

D. 1. Examine the following expressions. How are they similar to and different from those in Question B?

     a. $2x^2 + 8x + 8$

     b. $4x^2 + 4x + 1$

     c. $2x^2 + 9x + 4$

2. Will Jaime's method work on these expressions? If so, write them in factored form. If not, find another way to write each in factored form. Explain why your expression is equivalent to the original expression.

ACE Homework starts on page 45.

3.4 Solving Quadratic Equations

In the last problem, you explored ways to write a quadratic expression in factored form. In this problem, you will use the factored form to find solutions to a quadratic equation.

If you know that the product of two numbers is zero, what can you say about the numbers?

Getting Ready for Problem 3.4

- How can you solve the equation $0 = x^2 + 8x + 12$ by factoring?

First write $x^2 + 8x + 12$ in factored form to get $(x + 2)(x + 6)$. This expression is the product of two linear factors.

- When $0 = (x + 2)(x + 6)$, what must be true about one of the linear factors?

- How can this information help you find the solutions to $0 = (x + 2)(x + 6)$?

- How can this information help you find the x-intercepts of $y = x^2 + 8x + 12$?

Problem 3.4 Solving Quadratic Equations

A. 1. Write $x^2 + 10x + 24$ in factored form.

    2. How can you use the factored form to solve $x^2 + 10x + 24 = 0$ for x?

    3. Explain how the solutions to $0 = x^2 + 10x + 24$ relate to the graph of $y = x^2 + 10x + 24$.

B. Solve each equation for x without making a table or graph.

    1. $0 = (x + 1)(2x + 7)$ **2.** $0 = (5 - x)(x - 2)$

    3. $0 = x^2 + 6x + 9$ **4.** $0 = x^2 - 16$

    5. $0 = x^2 + 10x + 16$ **6.** $0 = 2x^2 + 7x + 6$

    7. How can you check your solutions without using a table or graph?

C. Solve each equation for x without making a table or graph. Check your answers.

1. $0 = x(9 - x)$

2. $0 = -3x(2x + 5)$

3. $0 = 2x^2 + 32x$

4. $0 = 18x - 9x^2$

D. You can approximate the height h of a pole-vaulter from the ground after t seconds with the equation $h = 32t - 16t^2$.

1. Suppose the pole-vaulter writes the equation $0 = 32t - 16t^2$. What information is the pole-vaulter looking for?

2. The pole-vaulter wants to clear a height of 17.5 feet. Will the pole-vaulter clear the desired height? Explain.

ACE **Homework starts on page 45.**

You can find the solutions to many quadratic equations using tables or graphs. Sometimes, however, these methods will give only approximate answers. For example, the solutions to the equation $x^2 - 2 = 0$ are $x = \sqrt{2}$ and $x = -\sqrt{2}$. Using a table or graph, you only get an approximation for $\sqrt{2}$.

You can try a factoring method, but the probability of readily factoring any quadratic expression $ax^2 + bx + c$, where a, b, and c are real numbers is small.

We know that the Greeks used a geometric method to solve quadratic equations around 300 B.C. Mathematicians from India probably had methods for solving these equations around 500 B.C., but their methods remain unknown.

For years, mathematicians tried to find a general solution to $ax^2 + bx + c = 0$. In a book published in 1591, François Viète was the first person to develop a formula for finding the roots of a quadratic equation. It is called the *quadratic formula* and is given below.

$$x = \frac{-b \pm \sqrt{b^2 - 4ac}}{2a}$$

This formula can be used for any quadratic equation. You will learn more about this formula in later mathematics courses.

Go Online
PHSchool.com

For: Information about François Viète
Web Code: ape-9031

Applications

1. The organizers of a walkathon discuss expenses and income. They make the following estimates:

   - Expense for advertisement: $500
   - Expense for participant T-shirts: $6 per child, $8.50 per adult
   - Income from business sponsors: $1,000
   - Expense for emergency medical services: $250
   - Income from registration fees: $5 per child, $15 per adult

   a. Suppose 30 adults and 40 children participate in the walkathon. Find the total income, the total expenses, and the profit. Show your work.

   b. Write an equation showing the profit P in the form:

   $$P = \text{(expression for income)} - \text{(expression for expenses)}.$$

   c. Write another expression for profit that is equivalent to the one in part (b).

   d. Suppose 30 adults and 40 children participate. Use your equation from part (b) or part (c) to find the profit. Compare your answer to the profit you calculated in part (a).

   e. Suppose 100 children participate and the profit is $1,099. How many adults participated? Show your work.

2. Marcel and Kirsten each try to simplify the following equation:

$$P = (1{,}000 + 5c + 15a) - (500 + 6c + 8.50a + 250)$$

They are both incorrect. Study the steps in their reasoning and identify their mistakes.

a.

Marcel

$P = (1{,}000 + 5c + 15a) - (500 + 6c + 8.50a + 250)$
$= 1{,}000 + 5c + 15a - 500 + 6c + 8.50a + 250$
$= 1{,}000 - 500 + 250 + 5c + 6c + 15a + 8.50a$
$= 750 + 11c + 23.50a$ *incorrect answer*

b.

Kirsten

$P = (1{,}000 + 5c + 15a) - (500 + 6c + 8.50a + 250)$
$= 1{,}000 + 5c + 15a - 500 - 6c - 8.50a - 250$
$= 1{,}000 - 500 - 250 + 5c - 6c + 15a - 8.50a$
$= 250 + c + 6.50a$ *incorrect answer*

3. According to the equation $V = 200 + 50(T - 70)$, the number of visitors to a park depends on the day's high temperature T (in Fahrenheit). Suppose 1,000 people visited the park one day. Predict that day's high temperature.

Homework Help Online
PHSchool.com
For: Help with Exercise 3
Web Code: ape-6303

For Exercises 4–7, solve each equation for x using the techniques that you developed in Problem 3.1. Check your solutions.

4. $10 + 2(3 + 2x) = 0$

5. $10 - 2(3 + 2x) = 0$

6. $10 + 2(3 - 2x) = 0$

7. $10 - 2(3 - 2x) = 0$

8. The two companies from Problem 3.2 decide to lower their costs for a Fourth of July sale. The equations below show the lower estimated costs C (in dollars) of buying and installing N border tiles.

Cover and Surround It: $C_C = 750 + 22(N - 12)$

Tile and Beyond: $C_T = 650 + 30(N - 10)$

a. Without using a table or graph, find the number of tiles for which the cost estimates from the two companies are equal.

b. How can you check that your solution is correct?

c. Explain how a graph or table could be used to find the number of tiles for which the costs are equal.

d. For what numbers of tiles is *Tile and Beyond* cheaper than *Cover and Surround It*? Explain your reasoning.

e. Write another expression that is equivalent to the expression for *Tile and Beyond's* cost estimate (C_T). Explain what information the variables and numbers represent.

9. The school choir from Problem 3.1 has the profit plan $P = 5s - (100 + 2s)$. The school band also sells greeting cards. The equation for the band's profit is $P = 4s - 2(10 + s)$. Find the number of boxes that each group must sell to have equal profits.

For Exercises 10–17, solve each equation for *x* without using tables or graphs. Check your solutions.

10. $8x + 16 = 6x$

11. $8(x + 2) = 6x$

12. $6 + 8(x + 2) = 6x$

13. $4 + 5(x + 2) = 7x$

14. $2x - 3(x + 6) = -4(x - 1)$

15. $2 - 3(x + 4) = 9 - (3 + 2x)$

16. $2.75 - 7.75(5 - 2x) = 26$

17. $\frac{1}{2}x + 4 = \frac{2}{3}x$

18. Write each product in expanded form.

a. $(x - 2)(x + 2)$

b. $(x - 5)(x + 5)$

c. $(x - 4)(x + 4)$

d. $(x - 12)(x + 12)$

19. Write each of these quadratic expressions in equivalent factored form.

Go Online
PHSchool.com

For: Multiple-Choice Skills
Practice
Web Code: apa-6354

   a. $x^2 + 5x + 4$ **b.** $8 + x^2 + 6x$

   c. $x^2 - 7x + 10$ **d.** $x^2 + 7x$

   e. $x^2 - 6 + 5x$ **f.** $2x^2 - 5x - 12$

   g. $x^2 - 7x - 8$ **h.** $x^2 - 5x$

20. Write each of these expressions in factored form.

   a. $x^2 - 16$ **b.** $x^2 - 36$

   c. $x^2 - 49$ **d.** $x^2 - 400$

   e. $x^2 - 64$ **f.** $x^2 - 144$

For Exercises 21–23, solve each equation for x. Check your solutions by using calculator tables or graphs.

21. $x^2 + 1.5x = 0$ **22.** $x^2 + 6x + 8 = 0$ **23.** $8x - x^2 = 0$

24. The equation $H = -16t^2 + 8t$ describes the height of a flea (in feet) after t seconds during a jump.

   a. Is the flea's jump equation linear, quadratic, or exponential?

   b. Write an expression that is equivalent to $-16t^2 + 8t$.

   c. Without using a graph or a table, find the time when the flea lands on the ground. Explain how you found your answer.

25. Use an area model to factor each expression.

   a. $x^2 + 8x + 15$ **b.** $x^2 - 9$ **c.** $2x^2 + 5x + 3$

26. Use your answers to Exercise 25 to solve each equation.

   a. $x^2 + 8x + 15 = 0$ **b.** $x^2 - 9 = 0$ **c.** $2x^2 + 5x + 3 = 0$

In Exercises 27 and 28, each solution contains an error.

- Find the error, and correct the solution.
- How would you help a student who made this error?

27.

$6x^2 - x = 1$

Solution

$6x^2 - x - 1 = 0$

$(3x - 1)(2x + 1) = 0$

$3x - 1 = 0$ or $2x + 1 = 0$

$x = \dfrac{1}{3}$ or $x = -\dfrac{1}{2}$

incorrect answer

28.

$24n^2 - 16n = 0$

Solution

$24n^2 - 16n = 0$

$24n^2 = 16n$

$n = \dfrac{16}{24}$ or $n = \dfrac{2}{3}$

partially correct answer

Connections

29. In Problem 3.1, the equation for profit P in terms of the number of boxes sold s is $P = 5s - (100 + 2s)$. The number of boxes sold also depends on the number of choir members.

 a. Suppose each member sells 11 boxes. Write an equation that will predict profit from the number of choir members n.
 Hint: First find an expression for the number of boxes sold.

 b. Write an equivalent expression for profit in part (a). Explain what the variables and numbers represent.

 c. Suppose the choir has 47 members. What is the profit?

 d. Suppose the profit is $1,088. How many choir members are there?

 e. In part (d), how many boxes were sold?

30. The equations $N = 2s + 2(s + 2)$ and $N = 4(s + 2) - 4$ both represent the number of 1-foot square border tiles needed to surround a square pool with sides of length s in feet.

 a. Suppose $N = 48$. Solve $N = 2s + 2(s + 2)$ for s.

 b. Suppose $N = 48$. Solve $N = 4(s + 2) - 4$ for s.

 c. How do your answers for parts (a) and (b) compare? Explain.

31. Multiple Choice If $\frac{3}{4}(x - 4) = 12$, what is the value of x?

A. 6 **B.** 8 **C.** $18\frac{1}{3}$ **D.** 20

32. Multiple Choice What is the value of $x^2(7 - x) + 1$ when $x = 5$?

F. 201 **G.** 28 **H.** 51 **J.** 75

33. In Problem 3.2, you found the number of tiles for which the cost estimates for the two companies were equal. What is the side length of the largest square pool that can be surrounded by that number of tiles? Explain your reasoning.

For Exercises 34 and 35, use the Distributive and Commutative properties to simplify each expression. Check that the original expression and your simplified expression are equivalent by testing several x values in both expressions.

34. $2(9x + 15) - (8 + 2x)$ **35.** $(7x - 12) - 2(3x + 10)$

Each figure in Exercises 36–40 has an area of 24 square meters. Find each labeled dimension.

36.
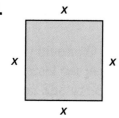

37.
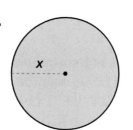

38.
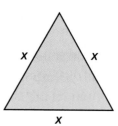

39.
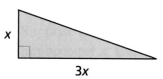

40.
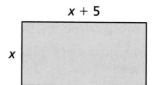

41. An oil company ships oil in spherical tanks that are 3 meters in diameter. The company now wants to ship oil in cylindrical tanks that are 4 meters high, but have the same volume as the spheres. What radius must the cylindrical tanks have?

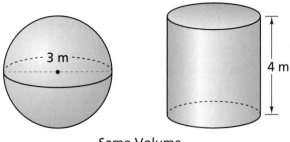

Same Volume
Not drawn to scale

42. Write a quadratic equation that has

   a. one solution (one x-intercept)

   b. two solutions (two x-intercepts)

43. John wants to know if he can bounce a superball over his house. You can approximate the height h of the superball on one bounce with the equation $h = 48t - 16t^2$, where t is the number of seconds after the ball hits the ground.

   a. How long is the ball in the air?

   b. Suppose his house is 30 feet tall. Will the ball make it over his house? Explain.

44. You can write quadratic expressions in factored and expanded forms. Which form would you use for each of the following? Explain.

   a. to determine whether a quadratic relationship has a maximum point or a minimum point

   b. to find the x- and y-intercepts of a quadratic relationship

   c. to find the line of symmetry for a quadratic relationship

   d. to find the coordinates of the maximum or minimum point for a quadratic relationship

45. Each team in a lacrosse league must play each of the other teams. The number of games g played in a league with n teams is $g = n^2 - n$. What are the x-intercepts for the graph of this equation? Explain what information they represent.

46. The height (in feet) of an arch above a point x feet from one of its bases is approximated by the equation $y = 0.2x(1,000 - x)$. What is the maximum height of the arch? Explain.

Extensions

For Exercises 47 and 48, find the value of c for which $x = 3$ is the solution to the equation.

47. $3x + c = 2x - 2c$ **48.** $3x + c = cx - 2$

49. Write two linear equations that have the solution $x = 3$. Are there more than two equations with a solution of $x = 3$? Explain.

50. Insert parentheses into the expression $13 = 3 + 5x - 2 - 2x + 5$ so that the solution to the equation is $x = 1$.

51. Write the following in expanded form.

a. $(x - 0.2)(x + 0.2)$

b. $(x - 12.5)(x + 12.5)$

c. $(x - \sqrt{5})(x + \sqrt{5})$

d. $(x - \sqrt{2})(x + \sqrt{2})$

52. Factor.

a. $x^2 - 100$

b. $x^2 - 1.44$

c. $x^2 - 7$

d. $x^2 - 24$

53. Below are the graphs of $y = 1.5x + 6$ and $y = -2x + 15$. The scale on the x-axis is 1, and the scale on the y-axis is 3.

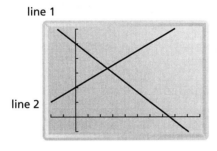

line 1

line 2

a. Is $y = 1.5x + 6$ or $y = -2x + 15$ the equation of line 1?

b. Find the coordinates of the point of intersection of the two lines.

c. How could you find the answer to part (b) without using a graph or a table?

d. What values of x satisfy the inequality $1.5x + 6 < -2x + 15$? How is your answer shown on the graph?

e. What values of x satisfy the inequality $1.5x + 6 > -2x + 15$? How is your answer shown on the graph?

54. Use the graph of $y = x^2 - 9x$ below. The scale on the x-axis is 1. The scale on the y-axis is 2.

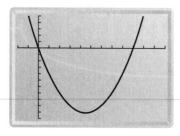

   a. What are the coordinates of the x-intercepts?

   b. How could you find the answer to part (a) without using a graph or a table?

   c. What values of x satisfy the inequality $x^2 - 9x < 0$? How is your answer shown on the graph?

   d. What values of x satisfy the inequality $x^2 - 9x > 0$? How is your answer shown on the graph?

   e. What is the minimum y-value? What x-value corresponds to this minimum y-value?

55. Use the quadratic formula from the *Did You Know?* after Problem 3.4 to solve each equation.

   a. $x^2 - 6x + 8 = 0$ **b.** $-x^2 - x + 6 = 0$

   c. $10 - 7x + x^2 = 0$ **d.** $4x^2 - x = 0$

   e. $2x^2 - 12x + 18 = 0$ **f.** $3x + x^2 - 4 = 0$

For Exercises 56 and 57, use what you have learned in this investigation to solve the equation. Show your work and check your solutions.

56. $x^2 + 5x + 7 = 1$ **57.** $x^2 + 6x + 15 = 6$

Mathematical Reflections 3

In this investigation, you learned methods for solving linear and quadratic equations. These questions will help you summarize what you have learned.

Think about your answers to these questions. Discuss your ideas with other students and your teacher. Then write a summary of your findings in your notebook.

1. Describe some general strategies for solving linear equations, including those with parentheses. Give examples that illustrate your strategies.

2. Describe some strategies for solving quadratic equations of the form $ax^2 + bx + c = 0$. Give examples.

3. How are the solutions of linear and quadratic equations related to graphs of equations?

Investigation 4

Looking Back at Functions

Throughout your work in algebra, you have identified patterns of change between variables as linear, exponential, and quadratic functions. You have used tables, graphs, and equations to represent and reason about these functions. In this unit, you have found that writing equivalent expressions for a quantity or variable can reveal new information about a situation. This investigation will help pull these ideas together.

 Pumping Water

Every winter, Magnolia Middle School empties their pool for cleaning. Ms. Theodora's math class decides to collect data on the amount of water in the pool and how long it takes to empty it. They write an equation to represent the amount of water w (in gallons) in the pool after t hours.

$$w = -250(t - 5)$$

Problem 4.1 Looking at Patterns of Change

A. Answer the following questions. Explain your reasoning.

1. How many gallons of water are pumped out each hour?

2. How long will it take to empty the pool?

3. How many gallons of water are in the pool at the start?

B. 1. Write an expression for the amount of water in the tank after t hours that is equivalent to the original expression.

2. What information does this new expression tell you about the amount of water in the tank?

3. Which expression is more useful in this situation? Explain.

C. 1. Describe the pattern of change in the relationship between the two variables w and t.

2. Without graphing the equation, describe the shape of the graph. Include as much information as you can.

D. Suppose the equation for the amount of water w (in gallons) in another pool after t hours is $w = -450(2t - 7)$.

1. How many gallons of water are pumped out each hour?

2. How long will it take to empty the pool?

3. How many gallons of water are in the pool at the start?

4. Write an expression that is equivalent to $-450(2t - 7)$. Which expression is more useful? Explain.

ACE **Homework starts on page 60.**

4.2 Generating Patterns

In this problem, you are given two data points for a linear, exponential, and quadratic relationship. You will use these points to find more data points. Then you will write an equation for each relationship.

A. The first two rows in a table of numbers are given below. Write four more numbers in each column to make a linear relationship, an exponential relationship, and a quadratic relationship.

Data Points

x	Linear y	Exponential y	Quadratic y
1	1	1	1
2	4	4	4
3	▨	▨	▨
4	▨	▨	▨
5	▨	▨	▨
6	▨	▨	▨

B. Explain why the pattern in each column is correct.

C. 1. Write an equation for each relationship. Explain what information the variables and numbers represent.

   2. Compare your equations with those of your classmates. Do you all have the same equations? Explain.

ACE **Homework starts on page 60.**

4.3 Sorting Functions

In the following problem, a set of equations relating x and y is given. Some of the expressions for y are in factored form, and some are in expanded form.

Which form is easier to use to determine whether a function is linear, exponential, quadratic, or none of these?

Which form is easier to use to determine the x- and y-intercepts, rates of change, and maximum or minimum points of the graph of the function?

Problem 4.3 Sorting Functions

Use the following equations for Questions A–C.

(1) $y = x^2 + 8x + 16$

(2) $y = \frac{1}{3}(3^x)$

(3) $y = 10 - 2x$

(4) $y = 2x^3 + 5$

(5) $y = (x^2 + 1)(x^2 + 3)$

(6) $y = 0.5^x$

(7) $y = 22 - 2x$

(8) $y = \frac{3}{x}$

(9) $y = (x + 4)(x + 4)$

(10) $y = (4x - 3)(x + 1)$

(11) $y = 20x - 4x^2$

(12) $y = x^2$

(13) $y = 3^{x-1}$

(14) $y = 16 - 2(x + 3)$

(15) $y = 4x^2 - x - 3$

(16) $y = x + \frac{1}{x}$

(17) $y = 4x(5 - x)$

(18) $y = 2(x - 3) + 6(1 - x)$

A. Which equations represent functions that are

   1. linear?   **2.** exponential?   **3.** quadratic?

B. 1. For each function in Question A, find those equations that represent the same function.

   2. Without graphing the equation, describe the shape of the graph of those equations in part (1). Give as much detail as possible, including patterns of change, intercepts, and maximum and minimum points.

C. Pick one linear, one quadratic, and one exponential equation. Describe a problem that could be represented by each equation.

ACE **Homework starts on page 60.**

Applications

1. A pump is used to empty a swimming pool. The equation $w = -275t + 1{,}925$ represents the gallons of water w that remain in the pool t hours after pumping starts.

   a. How many gallons of water are pumped out each hour?

   b. How much water is in the pool at the start of pumping?

   c. Suppose there are 1,100 gallons of water left in the pool. How long has the pump been running?

   d. After how many hours will the pool be empty?

   e. Write an equation that is equivalent to $w = -275t + 1{,}925$. What information does it tell you about the situation?

   f. Without graphing, describe the shape of the graph of the relationship between w and t.

2. A new pump is used to empty the pool in Exercise 1. The equation $w = -275(2t - 7)$ represents the gallons of water w that remain in the pool t hours after pumping starts.

   a. How many gallons of water are pumped out each hour?

   b. How much water is in the pool at the start of pumping?

   c. Suppose there are 1,000 gallons of water left in the pool. How long has the pump been running?

   d. After how many hours will the pool be empty?

   e. Write an equation that is equivalent to $w = -275(2t - 7)$. What information does it tell you about the situation?

3. A truck has a broken fuel gauge. Luckily, the driver keeps a record of mileage and gas consumption. The driver uses the data to write an equation for the relationship between the number of gallons of gas in the tank g and the number of miles driven m since the last fill-up.

$$g = 25 - \frac{1}{15}m$$

   a. How many gallons of gasoline are in a full tank? Explain.

   b. Suppose the driver travels 50 miles after filling the tank. How much gas is left?

c. After filling the tank, how many miles can the driver travel before 5 gallons remain?

d. After filling the tank, how many miles can the driver travel before the tank is empty?

e. How many miles does the driver have to travel in order to use 1 gallon of gas? Explain.

f. In the equation, what do the numbers 25 and $\frac{1}{15}$ tell you about the situation?

4. A middle school pays $2,500 to print 400 copies of the yearbook. They give some free copies to the yearbook advisor and staff and sell the rest to students. The equation below tells how close the school is to paying for the printing bill.

$$y = 2{,}500 - 15(N - 8)$$

Describe what information the numbers and variables represent in this situation.

Homework Help Online
PHSchool.com
For: Help with Exercise 4
Web Code: ape-6404

5. The Department of Natural Resources is collecting data on three different species of animals. They find that these species show different patterns of population growth. They write the equations below to represent the population P of each species after x years.

Species 1	**Species 2**	**Species 3**
$P_1 = 10{,}000 + 100x$	$P_2 = 10(3^x)$	$P_3 = 800 + 10x^2$

a. Describe what information the numbers and variables represent in each equation.

b. Describe the pattern of growth for each species. Explain how the patterns differ.

c. Pick any two species. After how many years will the populations of the two species be equal? Explain how you got your answer.

6. The tables below represent the projected growth of certain species of deer. Use the three tables to answer parts (a)–(c).

Table 1	
Year	**Deer**
2000	1,000
2001	1,030
2002	1,061
2003	1,093
2004	1,126

Table 2	
Year	**Deer**
2000	1,000
2001	1,030
2002	1,060
2003	1,090
2004	1,120

Table 3	
Year	**Deer**
2000	1,000
2001	3,000
2002	9,000
2003	27,000
2004	81,000

a. Describe the growth represented in each table. Are any of these patterns linear, exponential, or quadratic?

b. Write an equation for each linear, exponential, or quadratic pattern in part (a).

c. Does any table show a population of deer growing at a rate of 300% per year? Explain.

7. Suppose the figures shown are made with toothpicks.

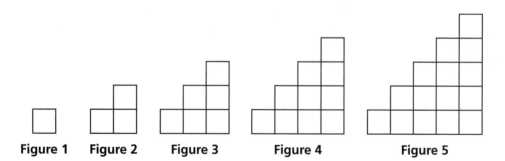

Figure 1 Figure 2 Figure 3 Figure 4 Figure 5

a. What patterns in the set of figures do you notice?

b. How many toothpicks do you need to make Figure 7?

c. Is the relationship between the perimeter and the figure number linear, quadratic, or exponential? Explain.

d. Is the relationship between the total number of toothpicks and the figure number linear, quadratic, or exponential?

e. Write an equation to represent the perimeter of Figure *N*. Explain your rule.

f. Write an equation to represent the total number of toothpicks needed to make Figure *N*. Explain your rule.

For Exercises 8–10, use the graphs below.

Graph 1

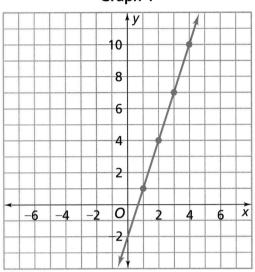

Graph 2

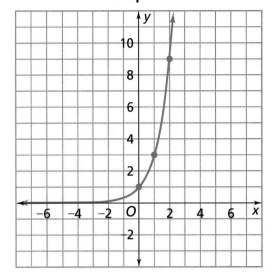

Graph 3

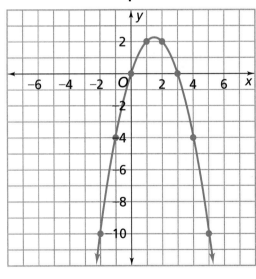

Graph 4

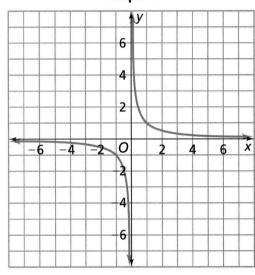

8. Which graphs represent linear, quadratic, or exponential functions?

9. Make a table of *y*-values for *x* = 1, 2, 3, . . . 6 for each linear, quadratic, or exponential function.

10. Write an equation for each linear, quadratic, or exponential function. Describe your strategy.

For Exercises 11–17, match each equation with one of the graphs below.

Graph A
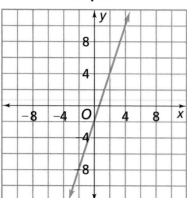

Graph B
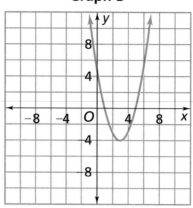

Graph C
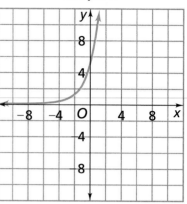

Graph D
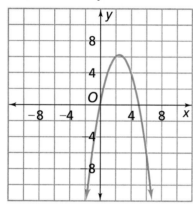

Graph E
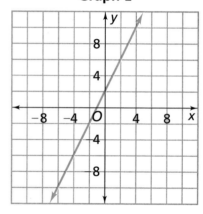

Graph F
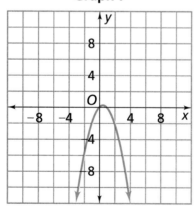

Graph G
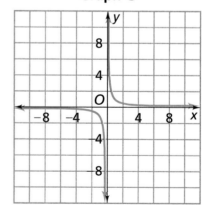

11. $y = \dfrac{1}{x}$

12. $y = x(5 - x)$

13. $y = (x - 1)(x - 5)$

14. $y = x(1 - x)$

15. $y = 2 + 2x$

16. $y = 5(2^x)$

17. $y = -2 + 3x$

18. For parts (a)–(c), use the set of equations below.

(1) $y = x^2 + 8x$ (4) $y = 2(x - 3) + 6$ (7) $y = 0.25^x$

(2) $y = 2x$ (5) $y = x(x + 8)$ (8) $y = 17 + x(x + 3)$

(3) $y = 4^{x-1}$ (6) $y = 0.25(4^x)$ (9) $y = (x + 1)(x + 17)$

a. Which equations represent linear, quadratic, or exponential functions?

b. Find any equations that represent the same function.

c. Without graphing the equation, describe the shape of the graph of each equation in part (b). Give as much detail as possible, including patterns of change, intercepts, and maximum and minimum points.

19. Pick a linear, quadratic, and exponential equation from Exercise 18. Describe a problem that can be represented by each equation.

Connections

20. Use the figure of the pool for parts (a)–(d). Drawing is not to scale.

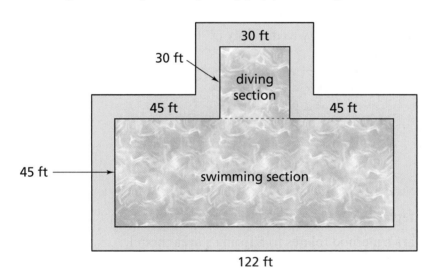

a. How many 1-foot square tiles do you need to build a border that is 1-tile wide around the pool?

b. What is the surface area of the water?

c. The swimming section is 4 feet deep. The diving section is 10 feet deep. What is the volume of the pool?

d. The pool is filled at a rate of 600 cubic feet per hour. How long does it take to fill the pool?

21. a. Give the formula for the circumference of a circle with radius r.

   b. Give the formula for the area of a circle with radius r.

   c. Give the formula for the volume of a cylinder with a height of h and radius of r.

   d. For parts (a)–(c), which equations are linear? Explain.

22. A line has a slope of 1.5 and goes through the point $(2, 5)$.

   a. Find the coordinates of three other points that lie on the line.

   b. Find the coordinates of the y-intercept.

   c. Find the y-coordinate of the point whose x-coordinate is -4.

   d. Write an equation for the line.

23. Sabrina uses an area model to find the product $(x + 2)(x + 3)$.

Tara uses the Distributive Property to multiply $(x + 2)(x + 3)$.

$$(x + 2)(x + 3) = (x + 2)x + (x + 2)3$$
$$= x^2 + 2x + 3x + 6$$
$$= x^2 + x(2 + 3) + 6$$
$$= x^2 + 5x + 6$$

   a. Explain each step in Tara's method.

   b. Explain how Tara's method relates to Sabrina's area model.

   c. Use the Distributive Property to find each product.

   i. $(x + 5)(x + 3)$ **ii.** $(x + 4)(x + 1)$ **iii.** $(x - 2)(x + 4)$

24. The equation $d = -16t^2 + 16t + 6.5$ represents the distance d in feet, from the ground to the top of a basketball player's head t seconds after the player jumps.

    a. Find the distance to the top of the player's head after 0.1 second.

    b. Find the distance to the top of the player's head after 0.3 second.

    c. Find the distance to the top of the player's head after 1 second.

    d. What operations did you perform to calculate your answers in parts (a)–(c)? In what order did you perform the operations?

25. A bacteria colony begins with 5,000 bacteria. The population doubles every hour. This pattern of exponential growth can be modeled by the equation $b = 5,000(2^t)$, where b is the number of bacteria and t is the number of hours.

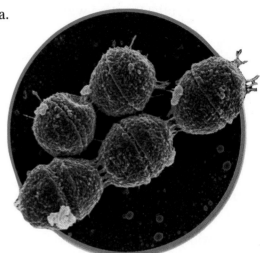

    a. What is the population of the colony after 3 hours? After 5 hours?

    b. What mathematical operations did you perform to calculate your answers in part (a)? In what order did you perform these operations?

Write an expression equivalent to the given expression.

26. $5 - 6(x + 10) - 4$

27. $-3(x - 4) - (x + 3)$

28. $x(x + 2) - 5x + 6$

29. $6x^2 + 5x(x - 10) + 10$

30. $\frac{1}{2}x^2 + \frac{1}{4}x^2 + x^2 + 3x$

31. $7x^2 - 3.5x + 0.75x - 8$

Go Online
PHSchool.com
For: Multiple-Choice Skills Practice
Web Code: apa-6454

32. Write an equation for

    a. y in terms of z given $y = 6x + 10$ and $x = 2z - 7$

    b. P in terms of n given $P = xn - 6n$, and $x = 12 - n$

    c. A in terms of w given $A = \ell w$ and $\ell = 15 - w$

For Exercises 33–35, give an equation for each function.

33. a parabola with x-intercepts $(-3, 0)$ and $(2, 0)$

34. a line with a slope of -4 and an x-intercept of $(2, 0)$

35. an exponential function with a growth factor of 1.25

36. a. Sketch each equation on the same coordinate grid.

$$y = 4x^2 \qquad y = -4x^2 \qquad y = \tfrac{1}{4}x^2 \qquad y = -\tfrac{1}{4}x^2$$

    b. What is the effect of the variable a in the equation $y = ax^2$?

37. a. Sketch each equation on the same coordinate grid.

$$y = 4x^2 + 5 \qquad y = 4x^2 - 5 \qquad y = 4x^2 + 3 \qquad y = 4x^2 - 3$$

    b. What is the effect of the variable c in the equation $y = 4x^2 + c$?

38. You want to tie the anchor wire of a flagpole to the ground at a distance that is half the height of the pole. What is the height of the tallest flagpole you can support with a 60-foot anchor wire?

39. The figures show cones inside cylinders with the same radius and height. Which cone has a volume of $3\pi x^2$ cubic units? Explain.

Cone 1   **Cone 2**

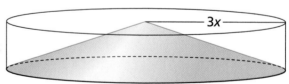

Extensions

40. Caley's cell phone company offers two different monthly billing options for local phone service.

Plan I: $25 for up to 100 minutes, plus $0.50 for each extra minute.

Plan II: $50 for an unlimited number of minutes.

a. Suppose Caley uses about 200 minutes each month. What is the best option for her? Explain.

b. For what number of minutes are the costs of the two plans equal? Explain.

c. Write an equation for each plan. Describe how the variables and numbers represent the growth patterns of the plans.

d. Graph each equation on the same coordinate grid. Describe how the graphs describe the growth patterns of the phone plans.

41. The equation below represents the space s in feet between cars that is considered safe given the average velocity v in feet per second on a busy street.

$$s = \frac{v^2}{32} + v + 18$$

a. Suppose a car travels at a rate of 44 feet per second. How far should it be from the car ahead of it in order to be safe?

b. What is 44 feet per second in miles per hour?

c. Suppose a taxi is 100 feet behind a car. At what velocity is it safe for the taxi to be traveling in feet per second? In miles per hour?

42. a. Graph $y = x^2 + 4$. Is it possible to find x when $y = 0$? Explain.

   b. Give two examples of a quadratic equation ($ax^2 + bx + c = 0$, where a, b, and c are real numbers) with no solution.

   c. Give two examples of a quadratic equation with 1 solution.

   d. Give two examples of a quadratic equation with 2 solutions.

43. Below is the graph of $y = (x + 2)(x - 1)(x - 5)$. The scale on the x-axis is 1. The scale on the y-axis is 5.

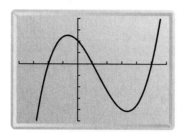

   a. What are the solutions to $(x + 2)(x - 1)(x - 5) = 0$? How are the solutions shown on the graph?

   b. What values of x satisfy the inequality $(x + 2)(x - 1)(x - 5) < 0$? How is your answer shown on the graph?

   c. How can you find the answer to part (b) without using the graph?

For part (c), use what you know about multiplying positive and negative numbers.

Mathematical Reflections 4

In this investigation, you studied equations that represent linear, exponential, or quadratic functions. You also used expanded or factored expressions for *y* to make predictions about the shape of the graph of these functions. These questions will help you summarize what you have learned.

Think about your answers to these questions. Discuss your ideas with other students and your teacher. Then write a summary of your findings in your notebook.

1. Describe how you can tell whether an equation is a linear, exponential, or quadratic function. Include the factored or expanded form of the expression for *y*.

2. Describe how you can determine specific features of the graph of a function from its equation. Include its shape, *x*- and *y*-intercepts, maximum and minimum points, and patterns of change.

Investigation 5

Reasoning With Symbols

You have looked at patterns and made conjectures and predictions. You have given informal arguments to support your conjectures. In this investigation, you will look at how algebra can help you further justify some of your conjectures by providing evidence or proof.

5.1 Using Algebra to Solve a Puzzle

People receive a lot of information by email. Some emails are useful, while others are for fun. A puzzle similar to the following appeared in several emails in 2003.

Problem 5.1 Using Algebra to Solve a Puzzle

On February 1, 2006, Elizabeth shared the following puzzle with her classmates.

> • Pick a number from 1 to 9.
>
> • Multiply this number by 2.
>
> • Add 5.
>
> • Multiply by 50.
>
> • If you already had your birthday this year, add 1,756. If not, add 1,755.
>
> • Subtract the four-digit year in which you were born.

A. 1. Suppose the year is 2006. Work through the steps using today's month and day.

   2. You should have a three-digit number. Look at the first digit and the last two digits. What information do these numbers represent?

B. Let n represent the number you choose in the first step. Repeat the steps with n. Use mathematical statements to explain why the puzzle works.

C. Will the puzzle work for the current year? If not, how can you change the steps to make it work?

ACE Homework starts on page 76.

5.2 Odd and Even Revisited

In *Prime Time,* you looked at factors and multiples. You explored several conjectures about even and odd whole numbers, including:

- The sum of two even whole numbers is even.
- The sum of an even whole number and odd whole number is odd.

How might you convince a friend that these conjectures are true?

Are these conjectures true for odd and even integers?

Getting Ready for Problem 5.2

Daphne claims that the algebraic expression $2n$, where n is any integer, will produce all even integers.

- Is Daphne correct? Explain.
- Write a symbolic expression that will produce all odd integers. Explain why it works.

Problem 5.2 Odd and Even Revisited

Rachel offers the following argument for showing that the sum of two even integers is even.

> - Let n and m represent any integer.
> - Then $2n$ and $2m$ are two even integers.
> - $2n + 2m$ is the sum of two even integers.
> - But $2n + 2m = 2(n + m)$.
> - $2(n + m)$ is an even integer.
> - So the sum of two even integers is even.

A. Study Rachel's argument. Provide reasons for each step. Does her argument prove the conjecture that the sum of any two even integers is an even integer? Explain.

B. Bianca offers the following argument:

- You can represent even numbers as a rectangular array with one dimension equal to 2. The following pictures represent the sum of two even numbers.

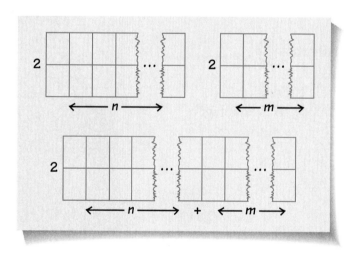

Does Bianca's argument prove the conjecture about the sum of two even numbers? Explain.

C. Use a method similar to those in Questions A and B to show that the following conjectures are true.

1. The sum of an odd integer and an even integer is an odd integer.

2. The product of an even and an odd integer is even.

ACE Homework starts on page 76.

5.3 Squaring Odd Numbers

In this problem, you will operate on odd numbers and look for patterns.

Problem 5.3 Squaring Odd Numbers

A. Perform the following operations on the first eight odd numbers. Record your information in a table.

- Pick an odd number.
- Square it.
- Subtract 1.

B. What patterns do you see in the resulting numbers?

C. Make conjectures about these numbers. Explain why your conjectures are true for any odd number.

ACE Homework starts on page 76.

Applications

Maria presents several number puzzles to her friends. She asks them to think of a number and to perform various operations on it. She then predicts the result. For Exercises 1 and 2, show why the puzzles work.

1.

> **Puzzle 1**
>
> • Pick a number.
> • Double it.
> • Add 6.
> • Divide by 2.
> • Subtract the number you thought of.

Maria claims the result is 3.

2.

> **Puzzle 2**
>
> • Think of a number.
> • Add 4.
> • Multiply by 2.
> • Subtract 6.
> • Divide by 2.
> • Subtract the number you thought of.

Maria claims the result is 1.

3. a. Design a puzzle similar to Maria's puzzles.

   b. Try it on a friend.

   c. Explain why your puzzle works.

For Exercises 4–6, show that the following conjectures are true.

4. The sum of two odd integers is even.

5. The product of two even integers is even.

6. The product of two odd integers is odd.

7. Look at the product of three consecutive whole numbers. For example:

$$1 \times 2 \times 3 \qquad 2 \times 3 \times 4 \qquad 3 \times 4 \times 5$$

Homework Help Online
PHSchool.com
For: Help with Exercise 7
Web Code: ape-6507

    a. What patterns do you observe?

    b. Make a conjecture about the product of three consecutive whole numbers. Explain why your conjecture is correct.

8. Look at the product of four consecutive whole numbers.

    a. What patterns do you observe?

    b. Make a conjecture about the product of four consecutive whole numbers. Explain why your conjecture is correct.

9. **a.** Are the following numbers divisible by 2? Explain.

            10,034   69,883

    b. What patterns among these numbers do you notice that can help you determine whether a number is divisible by 2?

    c. Explain your conclusion.

10. **a.** Look at several numbers that are divisible by 4.

    b. What patterns among these numbers do you notice that can help you determine whether a number is divisible by 4?

    c. Explain your conclusion.

11. **a.** Look at several numbers that are divisible by 5.

    b. What patterns among these numbers do you notice that can help you determine whether a number is divisible by 5?

    c. Explain your conclusion.

Connections

12. Study the sequence of cube buildings below.

- What pattern do you notice?
- Use the pattern to construct the next building in the sequence.
- Think about your steps as you construct your building. The labels below show one way you might think about the pattern.

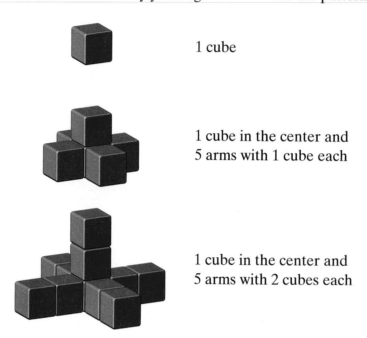

1 cube

1 cube in the center and 5 arms with 1 cube each

1 cube in the center and 5 arms with 2 cubes each

a. Describe a pattern you see in the cube buildings.

b. Use your pattern to write an expression for the number of cubes in the *n*th building, where *n* is an integer.

c. Use your expression to find the number of cubes in the fifth building.

d. Use the Distributive and Commutative properties to write an expression equivalent to the one in part (b). Does this expression suggest another pattern in the cube buildings? Explain.

e. Look for a different pattern in the buildings. Describe the pattern and use it to write a different expression for the number of cubes in the *n*th building.

For Exercises 13 and 14, suppose a chess tournament has *n* participants. Each participant plays each of the other participants twice.

13. a. Find the total number of games played for tournaments with 2, 3, 4, 5, and 6 participants.

   b. Look for a pattern in your data. Use the pattern to write an expression for the number of games played in a tournament with *n* participants.

14. Gina used a table to answer Exercise 13. Make a table like the one below to record wins (W) and losses (L) for a tournament with *n* participants.

Game 1

	P_1	P_2	P_3	...	P_n
P_1					
P_2					
P_3					
...					
P_n					

Game 2

   a. How many cells should your table have?

   b. How many cells in the table will not be used? Explain.

   c. Use your answers from parts (a) and (b) to write an expression for the total number of games played.

   d. Compare your expressions for the total number of games played in Exercises 13(b) and 14(c).

For Exercises 15–18, answer parts (a) and (b) below.

   a. Write an equation to represent each situation.

   b. Write a problem that can be solved by substituting a value into the equation. Then solve your problem.

15. Suppose you go on an 8-hour car trip. You travel at an average rate of r miles per hour for the first 6 hours on the highway and at an average rate of 30 mph slower for the last 2 hours in the city. Find the distance traveled.

16. Suppose a bag contains only dimes and quarters. The bag has 1,000 coins. Find the amount of money in the bag.

17. Suppose the length of a rectangular pool is 4 feet longer than twice the width. Find the area of the pool.

18. Suppose that for a concert, there are x reserved seats that cost $15 per seat and $(4,000 - x)$ unreserved seats that cost $9 per seat. The concert sells out. Find the amount of money collected for the concert.

Solve each equation for x without using a table or a graph.

19. $(x - 4)(x + 3) = 0$

20. $x^2 + 4x = 0$

21. $x^2 + 9x + 20 = 0$

22. $x^2 + 7x - 8 = 0$

23. $x^2 - 11x + 10 = 0$

24. $x^2 - 6x - 27 = 0$

25. $x^2 - 25 = 0$

26. $x^2 - 100 = 0$

27. $2x^2 + 3x + 1 = 0$

28. $3x^2 + 10x + 8 = 0$

Go Online
PHSchool.com

For: Multiple-Choice Skills Practice
Web Code: apa-6554

29. The height of a ball (in feet) t seconds after it is thrown is $h = -16t^2 + 48t$. Find each without using a table or graph.

    a. the height of the ball after 2 seconds

    b. the maximum height of the ball

    c. the total time the ball is in the air

    d. How could you use a table or graph to answer parts (a)–(c)? Explain.

For Exercises 30 and 31, write an equation of the form $y = $ *expression* for each expression. Show whether the two expressions are or are not equivalent

    (a) with a table and graph.

    (b) without a table or graph.

30. $9x - 5(x - 3) - 20$ and $5 - 4x$

31. $(10x - 5) - (4x + 2)$ and $10x - 5 - 4x + 2$

For Exercises 32–36, complete each table without using a calculator. Decide whether the relationship is linear, quadratic, exponential, or none of these.

32.

x	5	−5	−3	−7
$y = 4(x - 7) + 6$	▪	▪	▪	▪

33.

x	5	−5	−3	−7
$y = -3 - 7(x + 9)$	▪	▪	▪	▪

34.

x	5	−5	−3	−7
$y = 2(3)^x$	▪	▪	▪	▪

35.

x	5	−5	−3	−7
$y = 3x^2 - x - 1$	▪	▪	▪	▪

36.

x	5	−5	−3	−7
$y = 5(x - 2)(x + 3)$	▪	▪	▪	▪

37. For Exercises 32 and 33, write an equivalent expression for y that would make the calculations easier.

38. Study the pattern in each table. Write an equation for those that are linear, exponential, or quadratic. Otherwise, write *none of these*.

Table 1

x	y
−2	15
0	9
2	3
3	0
4	−3

Table 2

x	y
0	−16
1	−15
2	−12
3	−7
4	0

Table 3

x	y
−2	2
−1	1
0	0
1	1
2	2

Table 4

x	y
0	3
1	12
2	48
3	192
4	768

Table 5

x	y
1	4
2	2
3	$\frac{4}{3}$
4	1
5	$\frac{4}{5}$

Extensions

39. a. Find the next statement for the following pattern.

$$1^2 + 2^2 = 3^2 - 2^2$$
$$2^2 + 3^2 = 7^2 - 6^2$$
$$3^2 + 4^2 = 13^2 - 12^2$$
$$4^2 + 5^2 = 21^2 - 20^2$$

b. Make a conjecture about these statements.

c. Show that your conjecture is correct.

40. For many years, mathematicians have been looking for a way to generate prime numbers. One of their proposed rules follows.

$$P = n^2 - n + 41$$

The rule suggests that if *n* is a whole number, then $n^2 - n + 41$ is a prime number.

George claims the rule is not true because he tested it for several values of *n* and found one that did not yield a prime number.

a. Test the rule for several values of *n*. Is each result prime?

b. Is George correct? Explain.

41. a. Look at several numbers that are divisible by 3.

b. What patterns among these numbers do you notice that can help you determine whether a number is divisible by 3?

c. Explain why your method works.

42. a. Look at several numbers that are divisible by 6.

b. What patterns among these numbers do you notice that can help you determine whether a number is divisible by 6?

c. Explain why your method works.

43. Judy thinks she knows a quick way to square any number whose last digit is 5. (Example: 25)

- Look at the digit to the left of 5. Multiply it by the number that is one greater than this number. (Example: $2 \times 3 = 6$)

- Write the product followed by 25. This is the square of the number. (Example: 625 is the square of 25.)

a. Try this squaring method on two other numbers that end in 5.

b. Explain why this method works.

In this investigation, you made conjectures about patterns that you observed and represented these conjectures in symbolic statements. You also found ways to show that your conjectures were valid.

Think about your answers to this question. Discuss your ideas with other students and your teacher. Then write a summary of your findings in your notebook.

1. Describe how and why you could use symbolic statements to show relationships or generalizations.

2. Describe how you can show that your generalizations are correct.

Unit Project

Finding the Surface Area of Rod Stacks

In this unit project, you will find different ways to find the surface area of colored rod stacks.

Part 1: Staircase Stacks

1. Choose a rod length to use to make a staircase stack. Use one of the unit rods to determine the dimensions of your chosen rod.

2. Stack several rods of this length as shown. Each rod is one unit high and one unit wide and is staggered one unit.

Stacked Rods   **Unit Rod**

   Find the surface area of one rod, a stack of two rods, a stack of three rods, and so on. Describe a pattern that you see in the surface areas of the stacks you made.

3. Write an equation that shows the relationship between the surface area A and the number of rods n in the stack. Explain.

4. Repeat Exercises 1–3 for two other rod lengths.

5. Find a student who used rods of the same length for Exercises 1–3 and whose expression from Exercise 3 looks different from yours. Are your expressions equivalent? Explain.

6. a. Make a table with columns for rod length and surface area equation. Complete the table for rod lengths 2 through 10. You will need to find students who used rods that you didn't use.

   b. Do the equations in your table represent linear, quadratic, or exponential relationships? Explain.

   c. Write an equation for the surface area A of any stack of n rods of length ℓ.

   d. Use your equation from part (c) to find the surface area of a stack of 50 rods of length 10.

Part 2: Finding the Surface Area of a Rectangular Prism

Suppose rods of length 4 are stacked to form a rectangular prism as shown at the right.

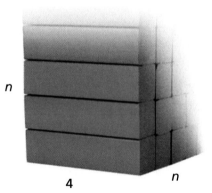

7. What are the dimensions of the prism?

8. Find an equation for the surface area of the prism.

9. Suppose the prism is 10 rods high and 10 rods wide. What is the surface area of the prism?

10. How would the equation change if the rod length were something other than 4?

11. Is the relationship between the surface area and the number of rods in a prism stack linear, quadratic, exponential, or none of these? Explain.

Write a report about the results you found for rod stacks and rod prisms. Explain how you found the equations for surface area in each case. Use diagrams to show what you did and what you found.

Looking Back and Looking Ahead

In this unit, you learned and practiced the standard rules for using symbolic expressions in algebra. You used properties of numbers and operations to write algebraic expressions in equivalent forms and to solve linear and quadratic equations with algebraic reasoning.

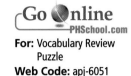

Go Online
PHSchool.com
For: Vocabulary Review Puzzle
Web Code: apj-6051

Use Your Understanding: Symbols

Test your understanding and skill in the use of algebraic notation and reasoning by solving these problems about managing a concert tour.

The promoter pays appearance fees to each group on the concert program. Some groups also get a portion of the ticket sales.

- The lead group earns $15,000, plus $5 for every ticket sold.
- Another group earns $1,500, plus $1.50 for every ticket sold.
- The third group earns a flat fee of $1,250.

1. For parts (a)–(c), use E for the promoter's expenses and t for the number of tickets sold.

 a. Write an equation to show payments to each separate group.

 b. Write an equation to show payment to the lead group and the combined payments to the other groups.

 c. Write an equivalent equation different from parts (a) and (b) to show the simplest calculation of the total amount paid to the performers.

2. Tickets cost $25, $30, and $40.

 a. Write an equation that shows how the promoter's income from ticket sales I depends on the number of each type of ticket sold x, y, and z.

 b. The promoter sells 5,000 tickets at $25, 3,000 tickets at $30, and 950 tickets at $40. Find the average income per ticket.

 c. Write an equation that shows how the average income per ticket sold V depends on the variables x, y, z, and t.

3. Square tiles were used to make the pattern below.

    a. Write an equation for the number of tiles T needed to make the nth figure. Explain.

    b. Find an equivalent expression for the number of tiles in part (a). Explain why they are equivalent.

    c. Write an equation for the perimeter P of the nth figure.

    d. Identify and describe the figure in this pattern that can be made with exactly 420 tiles.

    e. Describe the relationship represented by the equations in parts (a) and (c).

Explain Your Reasoning

When you solve problems by writing and operating on symbolic expressions, you should be able to explain your reasoning.

    4. How can writing two different equivalent expressions or equations for a situation be helpful?

    5. How can solving a linear or quadratic equation be helpful?

    6. How can a symbolic statement be helpful in expressing a general relationship or conjecture?

Look Ahead

The algebraic ideas and techniques you have used in this unit will be applied and extended in future mathematics courses and in science and business problems.

In later mathematics courses you will explore more techniques for solving quadratic and polynomial equations. You will also learn how to write equivalent expressions using more properties of real numbers.

English/Spanish Glossary

C

Commutative Property of Addition A mathematical property that states that the order in which quantities are added does not matter. It states that $a + b = b + a$ for any two real numbers a and b. For example, $5 + 7 = 7 + 5$ and $2x + 4 = 4 + 2x$.

propiedad conmutativa de la suma Una propiedad matemática que dice que el orden en que se suman las cantidades no tiene importancia. Para cualquieres números reales a y b, $a + b = b + a$. Por ejemplo, $5 + 7 = 7 + 5$ y $2x + 4 = 4 + 2x$.

Commutative Property of Multiplication A mathematical property that states that the order in which quantities are multiplied does not matter. It states that $ab = ba$ for any two real numbers a and b. For example, $5 \times 7 = 7 \times 5$ and $2x(4) = (4)2x$.

propiedad conmutativa de la multiplicación Una propiedad matemática que dice que el orden en que se multiplican los factores no tiene importancia. Para cualquieres números reales, $ab = ba$. Por ejemplo, $5 \times 7 = 7 \times 5$ y $2x(4) = (4)2x$.

D

Distributive Property A mathematical property used to rewrite expressions involving addition and multiplication. The Distributive Property states that for any three real numbers a, b, and c, $a(b + c) = ab + ac$. If an expression is written as a factor multiplied by a sum, you can use the Distributive Property to *multiply* the factor by each term in the sum.

$$4(5 + x) = 4(5) + 4(x) = 20 + 4x$$

If an expression is written as a sum of terms and the terms have a common factor, you can use the Distributive Property to rewrite the expression as the common factor multiplied by a sum. This process is called *factoring*.

$$20 + 4x = 4(5) + 4(x) = 4(5 + x)$$

propiedad distributiva Una propiedad matemática usada para reescribir expresiones que incluyen la suma y la multiplicación. La propiedad distributiva se establece para cualquieres números reales a, b, y c, $a(b + c) = ab + ac$. Si una expresión se escribe como la multiplicación de un factor por una suma, la propiedad distributiva puede usarse para multiplicar el factor por cada término de la suma.

$$4(5 + x) = 4(5) + 4(x) = 20 + 4x$$

Si una expresión se escribe como la suma de los términos y los términos tienen un factor común, la propiedad distributiva puede usarse para reescribir o descomponer en factores la expresión como la multiplicación del factor común por una suma.

$$20 + 4x = 4(5) + 4(x) = 4(5 + x)$$

equivalent expressions Expressions that represent the same quantity. For example, $2 + 5$, $3 + 4$, and 7 are equivalent expressions. You can apply the Distributive Property to $2(x + 3)$ to write the equivalent expression $2x + 6$. You can apply the Commutative Property to $2x + 6$ to write the equivalent expression $6 + 2x$.

expresiones equivalentes Expresiones que representan la misma cantidad, como por ejemplo $2 + 5$, $3 + 4$ y 7. Puedes aplicar la propiedad distributiva a $2(x + 3)$ para escribir la expresión equivalente $2x + 6$. Puedes aplicar la propiedad conmutativa a $2x + 6$ para escribir la expresión equivalente $6 + 2x$.

expanded form The form of an expression made up of sums or differences of terms rather than products of factors. The expressions $x^2 + 7x + 12$ and $x^2 + 2x$ are in expanded form.

forma desarrollada La forma de una expresión compuesta de sumas o diferencias de términos en vez de productos de factores. Las expresiones $x^2 + 7x + 12$ y $x^2 + 2x$ están representadas en forma desarrollada.

factored form The form of an expression made up of products of factors rather than sums or differences of terms. The expressions $(x + 3)(x + 4)$ and $x(x - 2)$ are in factored form.

forma de factores La forma de una expresión compuesta de productos de factores en vez de sumas o diferencias de términos. Las expresiones $(x + 3)(x + 4)$ y $x(x - 2)$ están representadas en forma de factores.

parabola The graph of a quadratic function. A parabola has a line of symmetry that passes through the maximum point if the graph opens downward or through the minimum point if the graph opens upward.

parábola La gráfica de una función cuadrática. Una parábola tiene un eje de simetría que pasa por el punto máximo si la gráfica se abre hacia abajo o por el punto mínimo si la gráfica se abre hacia arriba.

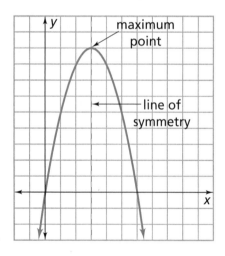

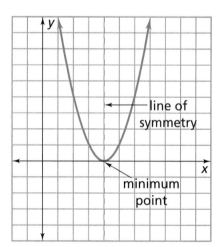

properties of equality The properties of equality state that if you add or subtract both sides of an equation by the same number, the two sides of the equation remain equal. If you multiply or divide both sides of an equation by the same non-zero number, the two sides of the equation remain equal.

propiedades de igualdad Las propiedades de igualdad establecen que si se suma o resta el mismo número a ambos lados de una ecuación, los dos lados de la ecuación se mantienen iguales. Si ambos lados de una ecuación se multiplican o dividen por el mismo número distinto de cero, los dos lados de la ecuación se mantienen iguales.

R

roots The roots of an equation are the values of x that make y equal 0. For example, the roots of $y = x^2 + 5x$ are -5 and 0 because $(-5)^2 + 5(-5) = 0$ and $0^2 + 5(0) = 0$. The roots of $y = x^2 + 5x$ are the solutions to the equation $0 = x^2 + 5x$. The roots of an equation are the x-intercepts of its graph.

raíces Las raíces de una ecuación son los valores de x que hacen que y equivalga a 0. Por ejemplo, las raíces de $y = x^2 + 5x$ son -5 y 0 porque $(-5)^2 + 5(-5) = 0$ y $0^2 + 5(0) = 0$. Las raíces de $y = x^2 + 5x$ son las soluciones de la ecuación $0 = x^2 + 5x$. Las raíces de una ecuación son los puntos de intersección del eje de las x de la gráfica de esa ecuación.

T

term An expression with numbers and/or variables multiplied together. In the expression $3x^2 - 2x + 10, 3x^2, -2x$, and 10 are terms.

término Una expresión con números y/o variables multiplicados entre sí. En la expresión $3x^2 - 2x + 10, 3x^2, -2x$, y 10 son términos.

Index

Acknowledgments

Team Credits

The people who made up the **Connected Mathematics 2** team —representing editorial, editorial services, design services, and production services— are listed below. Bold type denotes core team members.

Leora Adler, Judith Buice, Kerry Cashman, Patrick Culleton, Sheila DeFazio, Richard Heater, **Barbara Hollingdale, Jayne Holman,** Karen Holtzman, **Etta Jacobs,** Christine Lee, Carolyn Lock, Catherine Maglio, **Dotti Marshall,** Rich McMahon, Eve Melnechuk, Kristin Mingrone, Terri Mitchell, **Marsha Novak,** Irene Rubin, Donna Russo, Robin Samper, Siri Schwartzman, **Nancy Smith,** Emily Soltanoff, **Mark Tricca,** Paula Vergith, Roberta Warshaw, Helen Young

Additional Credits

Diana Bonfilio, Mairead Reddin, Michael Torocsik, nSight, Inc.

Technical Illustration

WestWords, Inc.

Cover Design

tom white.images

Photos

2, Tom Carter/PhotoEdit; **3,** Elio Ciol/Corbis; **5,** Ryan McVay/PictureQuest; **10,** Photodisc/Getty Images, Inc.; **14,** Tim Kiusalaas/Masterfile; **17,** Jeff Greenberg/AGE Fotostock; **19,** Jules Frazier/PictureQuest; **21,** Richard Haynes; **23,** Michael Mancuso/Omni-Photo Communications, Inc.; **26,** Jeff Greenberg/Omni-Photo Communications, Inc.; **27,** Photodisc/Getty Images, Inc.; **29,** Stephen Simpson/Getty Images, Inc.; **30,** Terry W. Eggers/Corbis; **33,** Syracuse Newspapers/The Image Works; **35,** Jeff Greenberg/The Image Works; **41,** Richard Haynes; **43,** Dennis MacDonald/PhotoEdit; **44,** Francois Viete (1540–1603) (engraving) (b/w photo), French School, (19th century)/Private Collection, Lauros/Giraudon/www.bridgeman.co.uk; **47,** Tom Carter/PhotoEdit; **52,** Syracuse Newspapers/Al Campanie/The Image Works; **58,** David Young-Wolff/PhotoEdit; **61,** Lester Lefkowitz/Getty Images, Inc.; **62,** Tom Brakefield/Corbis; **67,** Dr. Gary Gaugler/Photo Researchers, Inc.; **69,** Spencer Platt/Getty Images, Inc.; **73,** Richard Haynes; **79,** Esbin/Anderson/Omni-Photo Communications, Inc.; **83,** Richard Haynes; **85,** Russ Lappa; **86,** Russ Lappa

The Shapes of Algebra

Linear Systems and Inequalities

Glenda Lappan

James T. Fey

William M. Fitzgerald

Susan N. Friel

Elizabeth Difanis Phillips

PEARSON

Prentice
Hall

Boston, Massachusetts
Upper Saddle River, New Jersey

The Shapes of Algebra

How do you think you might use equations, graphs, and properties of geometric figures to make crop designs like those that have appeared over the past 20 years in farmer's fields?

Some eighth-graders hope to raise $600 with a fundraiser. They will earn a profit of $5 for every T-shirt sold and $10 for every cap. What are some ways they can exactly reach the goal of $600?

A family wants to drive their car and SUV no more than 1,000 miles a month. They also want to limit total CO_2 emissions to less than 600 pounds. The car emits 0.75 pounds of CO_2 per mile, and the SUV emits 1.25 pounds. What are some *(car miles, SUV miles)* pairs that meet these conditions?

In *The Shapes of Algebra*, you will apply and extend what you've learned about properties of polygons, symmetry, the Pythagorean Theorem, linear equations, slope, and solution methods for equations and inequalities.

You will connect geometry and algebra as you investigate geometric figures on coordinate grids and write equations and inequalities to describe the boundaries and interiors of those figures. You will write linear and quadratic equations whose solutions indicate coordinates of key points on quadrilaterals, triangles, and circles. You will also use inequalities to describe points in regions of the coordinate plane.

You will model problems like those on the previous page by writing systems of linear equations and inequalities. The methods for solving these systems combine geometric and algebraic reasoning.

Linear Systems and Inequalities

In *The Shapes of Algebra,* you will explore the relationship between algebra and geometry. Through this exploration, you will work with equations for lines and curves, and will develop an understanding of how systems of equations and inequalities can help you solve problems.

You will learn how to

- Write and use equations of circles
- Determine if lines are parallel or perpendicular by looking at patterns in their graphs, coordinates, and equations
- Find coordinates of points that divide line segments in various ratios
- Find solutions to inequalities represented by graphs or equations
- Write inequalities that fit given conditions
- Solve systems of linear equations by graphing, by substituting, and by combining equations
- Choose strategically the most efficient solution method for a given system of linear equations
- Graph linear inequalities and systems of inequalities
- Describe the points that lie in regions determined by linear inequalities and systems of inequalities
- Use systems of linear equations and inequalities to solve problems

As you work on problems in this unit, ask yourself questions like these:

What patterns relate the coordinates of points on lines and curves?

What patterns relate the points whose coordinates satisfy linear equations?

Does the problem involve an equation or an inequality?

Does the problem call for writing and/or solving a system of equations? If so, what method would be useful for solving the system?

Are there systematic methods that can be used to solve any systems of linear equations?

Investigation 1

Equations for Circles and Polygons

The photo below shows a "crop circle." Not all crop circles are made in crop fields, nor are they all circles. However, the term "crop circles" is often used to describe all such designs. Designs like these have appeared in fields around the world. At first, the origins of the crop circles were unknown. However, in many cases, the people who made them have come forward and taken credit for their work.

Getting Ready for Problem

Suppose you are planning to make a crop circle design like the one above.

- How can you outline the circle accurately?
- How can you locate sides and vertices of the other shapes in the design?
- How can you use equations and coordinate graphs to help plan your design?

You can outline the outer circle of a crop circle by using a rope. Anchor one end of the rope where you want the center of the circle. Hold the other end and, with the rope pulled taut, walk around the center point.

To plan the other parts of the design, it helps to draw the circle on a coordinate grid. In this problem, you will find an equation relating the coordinates of the points on a circle.

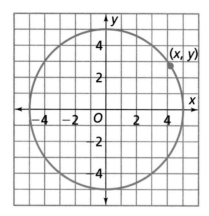

On the circle above, are there points for which it is easy to find the coordinates?

What mathematical ideas can help you find coordinates of other points on the circle?

Problem 1.1 Equations for Circles

A. 1. The circle above has a radius of 5 units and is centered at the origin. Estimate the missing coordinate for these points on the circle. If there is more than one possible point, give the missing coordinate for each possibility.

a. $(0, \blacksquare)$ **b.** $(\blacksquare, 0)$ **c.** $(3, \blacksquare)$

d. $(4, \blacksquare)$ **e.** $(\blacksquare, -3)$ **f.** $(\blacksquare, 4)$

g. $(-2, \blacksquare)$ **h.** $(\blacksquare, 2)$ **i.** $(\blacksquare, 5)$

2. Which of your coordinates from part (1) do you think are exactly correct? How do you know?

B. Think about a point (x, y) starting at $(5, 0)$ and moving counterclockwise, tracing around the circle.

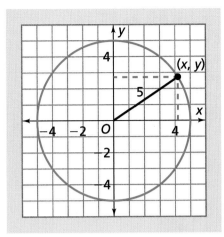

1. How does the y-coordinate of the point change as the x-coordinate approaches zero and then becomes negative?

2. The radius from the origin $(0, 0)$ to the point (x, y) has a length of 5 units. The diagram shows that you can make two right triangles with the radius as the hypotenuse. How do these triangles change as the point moves around the circle?

3. Use what you know about the relationship among the side lengths of a right triangle to write an equation relating x and y to the radius, 5.

4. Kaitlyn says that the relationship is $x + y = 5$ or $y = 5 - x$. Is she correct? Explain.

5. Does every point on the circle satisfy your equation? Explain.

C. These points are all on the circle. Check that they satisfy the equation you wrote in Question B part (3).

1. $(3, 4)$ 2. $(-4, 3)$ 3. $(\sqrt{13}, \sqrt{12})$ 4. $(0, -5)$

5. Does any point *not* on the circle satisfy the equation? Explain.

D. 1. Give the coordinates of three points in the interior of the circle. What can you say about the x- and y-coordinates of points inside the circle?

2. Use your equation from Question B to help you write an *inequality* that describes the points in the interior of the circle.

E. How can you change your equation from Question B to represent a circle with a radius of 1, 3, or 10 units?

ACE Homework starts on page 12.

1.2 Parallels and Perpendiculars

The design at the right is made from a circle and two overlapping rectangles. One way to make a crop circle with this design is to place stakes at key points and connect the stakes with string outlining the regions. However, you first need to find the location of these points. You can use what you know about coordinate geometry to analyze the design's key points and features.

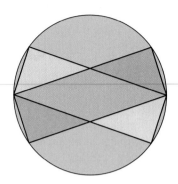

Problem 1.2 Parallels and Perpendiculars

This diagram shows some of the key points in the design. The design has reflection symmetry in both the *x*-axis and the *y*-axis. The radius is 5 units.

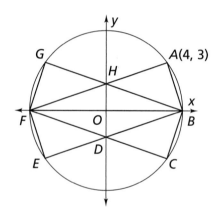

A. Find the coordinates of points *B, C, E, F,* and *G*.

B. List all pairs of parallel lines. How do the slopes of the lines in each pair compare? Explain why this makes sense.

C. List all pairs of perpendicular lines. How do the slopes of the lines in each pair compare? Explain why this makes sense.

D. Locate a new point *K*(2, *y*) on the circle. Draw a line segment from point *K* to the point (5, 0). Can you draw a rectangle with this segment as one side and all its vertices on the circle? If so, give the coordinates of the vertices.

E. 1. Kara was sketching on grid paper to try out some design ideas. She got interrupted! On a copy of Kara's diagram below, complete the polygons specified. (There may be more than one way to draw each one.) The polygons should all fit on the grid and should not overlap.

- Rectangle *ABCD*
- Parallelogram *EFGH*
- Parallelogram *PQRS*
- Rectangle *TUVW*

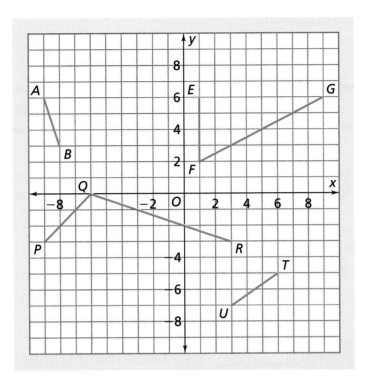

2. Give the coordinates of the vertex points for each figure.

3. Compare the slopes for all pairs of parallel sides. Describe the patterns you see. Are the patterns the same as you found in Question B?

4. Compare the slopes for all pairs of perpendicular sides. Describe the patterns you see. Are the patterns the same as you found in Question C?

5. What is true about the equations for a pair of parallel lines? What is true about the equations for a pair of perpendicular lines?

ACE Homework starts on page 12.

Dalton's class wants to design some interesting crop circles that are not circles. He starts with a diamond design.

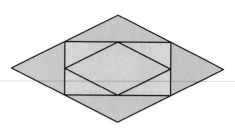

To draw this diamond design, you start with the outer rhombus. You connect the midpoints of its sides to form a rectangle, and then connect the midpoints of the rectangle's sides.

What would you need to check to know that the yellow shape is a rectangle?

How could you create this pattern by measuring and drawing or by folding paper and tracing creases?

Getting Ready for Problem 1.3

To make symmetric designs on a coordinate grid, it is helpful to have strategies for finding the coordinates of midpoints of line segments.

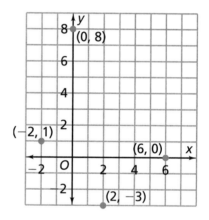

- How can you find the length of the line segment from $(0, 8)$ to $(6, 0)$ and from $(-2, 1)$ to $(2, -3)$?

- How can you estimate the coordinates of the midpoint of each segment?

Problem 1.3 Finding Midpoints

A. The figure at the right is a rhombus.

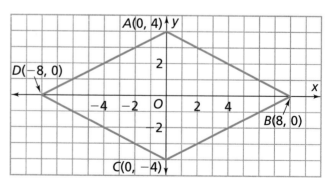

1. Estimate coordinates of P, the midpoint of side AB. Estimate the coordinates of S, the midpoint of side AD.

2. Explain why $\triangle APS$ is similar to $\triangle ABD$. What is the scale factor? How can you use these facts to check the coordinates of P and S? How can you use these facts to confirm that P and S are the midpoints?

3. Find the midpoints of sides BC and CD.

4. Check the midpoint coordinates by calculating the distance from each midpoint to the endpoints of the segments on which it is located. (Hint: Use symmetry to limit the calculations you do.)

B. Dalton tries a quadrilateral that is not symmetric.

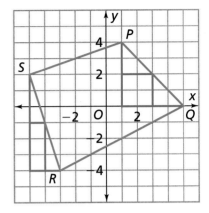

1. Dalton draws some lines on the quadrilateral to help him locate the midpoints of PQ and SR. Does this seem like a plan that would work no matter where P and Q or S and R are located? Explain.

2. Find coordinates of the midpoint of each side.

3. a. For each side, compare the coordinates of the endpoints to the coordinates of the midpoint. See if you can find a strategy for finding the coordinates of the midpoint of any line segment.

   b. Use your findings to complete this statement:

   The midpoint of the segment with endpoints (a, b) and (c, d) has coordinates . . .

C. Dalton connected the midpoints of the sides of $PQRS$ to form a quadrilateral.

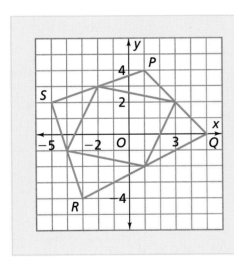

1. The quadrilateral appears to be a parallelogram. Verify this by finding the slopes of its sides.

2. Draw several quadrilaterals of your own. For each quadrilateral, find the midpoints of the sides (by measuring or paper folding), and connect those midpoints in order.

3. Describe the pattern in your results by completing this sentence:
When the midpoints of the sides of a quadrilateral are connected in order, the resulting figure is . . .

ACE Homework starts on page 12.

Applications

1. a. Write an equation that relates the coordinates x and y for points on the circle.

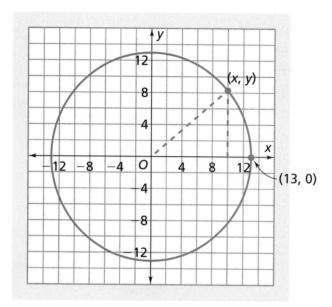

b. Find the missing coordinates for each of these points on the circle. If there is more than one possible point, give the missing coordinate for each possibility. Show that each ordered pair satisfies the equation.

$(0, \blacksquare)$ $\qquad$ $(5, \blacksquare)$ $\qquad$ $(-4, \blacksquare)$ $\qquad$ $(-8, \blacksquare)$

$(\blacksquare, 10)$ $\qquad$ $(\blacksquare, -6)$ $\qquad$ $(\blacksquare, 0)$ $\qquad$ $(\blacksquare, -2)$

c. Write an inequality that relates the coordinates x and y for points inside the circle.

d. Choose any point in the interior of the circle and confirm that this point is a solution for the inequality you wrote in part (c).

e. Choose any point outside the circle and check that it is not a solution for the inequality you wrote in part (c).

2. a. Write an equation that relates the coordinates x and y for points on the circle.

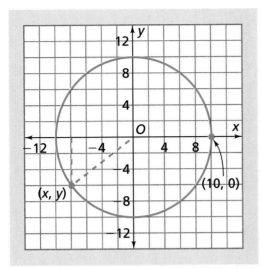

b. Find the missing coordinates for each of these points on the circle. If there is more than one possible point, give the missing coordinate for each possibility. Show that each ordered pair satisfies the equation.

(8, ■)   (3, ■)   (−4, ■)   (0, ■)

(■, −4)   (■, −6)   (■, 0)   (■, 2)

c. Write an inequality that describes the points in the interior of the circle.

d. Write an inequality that describes the points outside the circle.

e. Choose one point in the interior of the circle and one point outside the circle and confirm these are solutions for the appropriate inequalities.

active math
online

For: Algebra Tools
Visit: PHSchool.com
Web Code: apd-7102

3. On a copy of this diagram, draw quadrilaterals meeting the conditions in parts (a)–(d). Your figures should fit entirely on the grid and should not overlap.

Homework Help Online PHSchool.com
For: Help with Exercise 3
Web Code: ape-7103

a. Rectangle *ABCD* lies entirely in the second quadrant.

b. Rectangle *EFGH* lies entirely in the first quadrant.

c. Rectangle *PQRS* is not a square. It lies entirely in the third quadrant except for vertex *Q*.

d. Square *TUVW* lies entirely in the fourth quadrant.

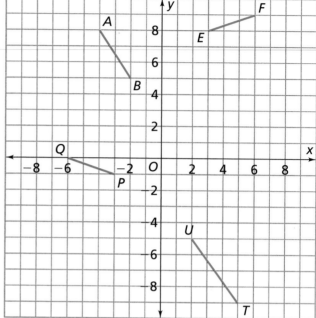

4. The quadrilaterals named in parts (a)–(d) are parallelograms formed on the diagram at the right. Give the coordinates for the fourth vertex. Then, calculate the slopes of the sides to show that the opposite sides are parallel.

a. *JKLM*

b. *NPQR*

c. *STUV*

d. *WYXZ*

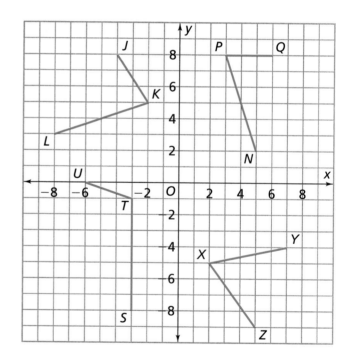

Find the equation of a line parallel to the given line.

5. $y = 2x + 3$

6. $y = -4x + 7$

7. $y = -3x + 5$

8. $y = \frac{1}{2}x - 12$

9. $y = -\frac{2}{3}x - 4$

10. $y = 6x - 9$

For Exercises 11–16, find the equation of a line perpendicular to the given line.

11. $y = 3x + 2$

12. $y = -\frac{3}{4}x - 2$

13. $y = -2x + 7$

14. $y = 5x - 1$

15. $y = \frac{1}{2}x + 3$

16. $y = -4x - 5$

17. a. The circle in this design is centered at the origin. Find coordinates for points J, K, and L.

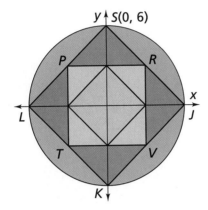

b. Points P, R, V, and T are the midpoints of the segments on which they lie. Find coordinates for each of these points.

c. Find coordinates of the vertices of the innermost quadrilateral. Is this quadrilateral a square? Explain.

Find the midpoint of the segment with the given endpoints.

18. $(0, 0)$ and $(4, 6)$

19. $(3, 2)$ and $(7, -4)$

20. $(1, 2)$ and $(8, 5)$

21. $(1, 2)$ and $(-5, 6)$

22. $(0, 0)$ and $(-4, -7)$

23. $(-1, -5)$ and $(-6, 2)$

Connections

Go Online
PHSchool.com

For: Multiple-Choice Skills Practice
Web Code: apa-7154

Use the Pythagorean Theorem to find the unknown side length.

24.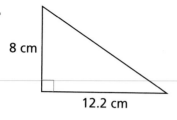
8 cm
12.2 cm

25.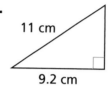
9.6 cm
21 cm

26.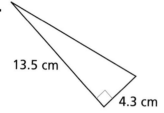
13.5 cm
4.3 cm

27.
11 cm
9.2 cm

Write an equation for the line with the given slope and *y*-intercept.

28. slope $\frac{1}{2}$, *y*-intercept $(0, 3)$

29. slope $-\frac{1}{3}$, *y*-intercept $(0, 5)$

30. slope 6, *y*-intercept $\left(0, \frac{1}{2}\right)$

Write an equation for the line with the given slope and that passes through the given point.

31. slope 2, point $(3, 1)$

32. slope -4, point $(-1, 7)$

33. slope $-\frac{5}{6}$, point $(0, 5)$

34. For each type of quadrilateral in the first column, identify all the properties from the second column that apply to that type of quadrilateral.

Quadrilateral Types

a. square

b. rectangle

c. rhombus

d. parallelogram

Properties

i. Two pairs of parallel sides

ii. Four right angles

iii. Two pairs of congruent sides

iv. Interior angle measures with a sum of 360°

v. Opposite angle measures with a sum of 180°

vi. Perpendicular diagonals

For Exercises 35–46, find the value of each expression.

35. $12 + (-18)$

36. $-9 + (-19)$

37. $-32 - 73$

38. $-23 - (-12)$

39. $90 - (-24)$

40. $34 - 76$

41. $-22 \times (-3)$

42. $5 \times (-13)$

43. -12×20

44. $-24 \div 6$

45. $-42 \div (-2)$

46. $84 \div (-4)$

47. Suppose you've drawn a design on a coordinate grid. Tell whether each coordinate rule will produce a similar design.

a. $(x, y) \rightarrow (x + 2, y + 3)$

b. $(x, y) \rightarrow (2x, 3y)$

c. $(x, y) \rightarrow (2.5x, 2.5y)$

d. $(x, y) \rightarrow (-2x, -2y)$

48. The radius of this crop design is 6 meters.

a. What is the area of the smaller square?

b. What is the area of the region between the smaller and larger squares?

c. What is the area of the region between the larger square and the circle?

d. Describe all the symmetries in the design.

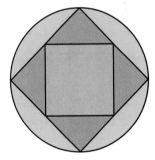

49. a. Consider the points $A(-2, 2), B(-1, -1), C(-1, 2), D(0, -3),$ $E(0, 2), F(1, 0), G(2, 0), H(4, -1), J(5, -1), K(6, -1.5)$. Without plotting points or drawing lines, find the slope of these lines.

line AB line CD line EF line GH line JK

b. Order the slopes in part (a) from least to greatest.

50. a. Suppose you connect the midpoints of the sides of a triangle as shown below to form a smaller triangle. How does the perimeter of the blue triangle compare to that of the original triangle?

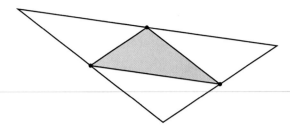

b. How does the area of the blue triangle compare to that of the original triangle?

51. Two students became intrigued by crop designs. They did a project comparing the occurrences of different shapes in three countries, A, B and C.

CROP CIRCLE OCCURRENCES

Boundary Type	Country A	Country B	Country C
Circle	12	12	6
Square	8	3	9

a. Make a circle graph to compare the total number of circular crop designs in three countries with the total number of square crop designs.

b. Make a bar graph to compare the crop designs from countries A, B, and C.

c. Make three statements summarizing the students' findings on crop designs in the three countries.

Find the equation of the line through the points.

52. $(2, 3)$ and $(0, 1)$

53. $(-1, 3)$ and $(2, -9)$

54. $(-1, -1)$ and $(3, 7)$

55. Kara started to find the midpoints of some segments, but she didn't finish. Her work is shown in parts (a)–(c). Finish her calculations to find the midpoint. Then give the coordinates of the segment's endpoints.

a. $\left(\dfrac{-3 + 9}{2}, \dfrac{-1 + 1}{2}\right)$

b. $\left(\dfrac{-3 - 4}{2}, \dfrac{-7 + 1}{2}\right)$

c. $\left(\dfrac{-3 + (-9)}{2}, \dfrac{-1 + (-1)}{2}\right)$

For Exercises 56–58, tell whether the lines intersect. If they do, find their intersection point both algebraically *and* graphically. If they don't intersect, explain how you know.

56. $y = x - 11$ and $y = 3x + 23$

57. $y = 2x + 10$ and $y = x + 20$

58. $y = 3x + 9$ and $y = 3(x + 10)$

59. Multiple Choice Which expression is equivalent to $3x + 10$?

A. $3(x + 10)$ **B.** $3x + 7x$

C. $5(x + 2) - 2x$ **D.** $2x - 5x + 10$

Extensions

60. This circle has radius 5 and center $(1, 2)$. Find or estimate the missing coordinates for these points on the circle. In each case, use the Pythagorean Theorem to check that the point is 5 units from the center.

a. $(\blacksquare, 6)$

b. $(5, \blacksquare)$

c. $(-3, \blacksquare)$

d. $(1, \blacksquare)$

e. $(\blacksquare, 2)$

f. $(4, \blacksquare)$

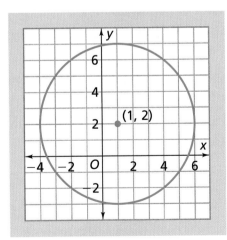

61. a. This circle has radius 5 and center (1, 2). $\overline{AC}$ is parallel to the x-axis. $\overline{BC}$ is parallel to the y-axis. What are the lengths of $\overline{AC}$, $\overline{BC}$, $\overline{AB}$ in terms of x and y?

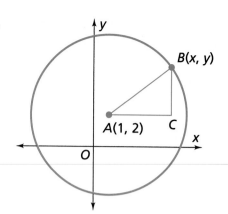

b. What equation shows how these side lengths are related?

c. Suppose you redraw the figure with $B(x, y)$ in a different position, but still on the circle. Would the coordinates of B still fit the equation you wrote in part (b)?

d. Based on this example, what do you think is the general equation for points on a circle with center (m, n) and radius r?

62. a. The vertices of the blue triangle are the midpoints of the sides of $\triangle FGH$. How are the sides of the blue triangle related to those of $\triangle FGH$? Use coordinates to check your ideas.

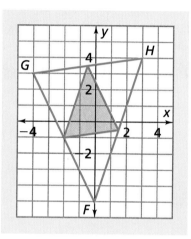

b. Draw several more triangles and connect their midpoints to form a smaller triangle. Record your observations.

63. Consider the points $O(0,0)$, $X(4, 5)$, $L(2, 3)$, and $M(6, 8)$.

a. Points U and V divide $\overline{OX}$ into three equal-length segments. Find the coordinates of points U and V.

b. Points W and Z divide $\overline{LM}$ into three equal-length segments. Find the coordinates of points W and Z.

c. $\overline{OX}$ can be translated to correspond with $\overline{LM}$. Describe the rule for this translation.

d. Check your coordinates for points W and Z by applying your translation rule to points U and V.

64. Use the diagram below. Record your answers to parts (a)–(c) in a copy of the table at the bottom of the page.

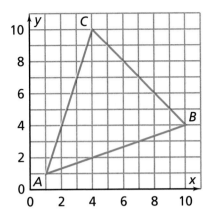

a. Find the coordinates of points X and Y that divide $\overline{AC}$ into three equal-length segments.

b. Find the coordinates of points M and N that divide $\overline{BC}$ into three equal-length segments.

c. Find the coordinates of points P and Q that divide $\overline{AB}$ into three equal-length segments.

d. Describe the pattern relating the coordinates of the endpoints to the coordinates of the two points that divide the segment into thirds.

e. How can you find the coordinates of the two points R and S that divide the segment joining points $G(x_1, y_1)$ and $H(x_2, y_2)$ into three equal-length segments?

Segment	Endpoint	Dividing Point	Dividing Point	Endpoint
$\overline{AC}$	A(■, ■)	X(■, ■)	Y(■, ■)	C(■, ■)
$\overline{BC}$	B(■, ■)	M(■, ■)	N(■, ■)	C(■, ■)
$\overline{AB}$	A(■, ■)	P(■, ■)	Q(■, ■)	B(■, ■)

65. Multiple Choice In triangle ABC, point D is on $\overline{AB}$ and point E is on $\overline{AC}$, such that $2AD = DB$ and $2AE = EC$. $2AD$ means twice the length of AD and $2AE$ means twice the length of AE. Which of the following statements is *not* true?

A. $\triangle ADE$ is similar to $\triangle ABC$

B. $BC = 3DE$

C. $\overline{DE}$ is parallel to $\overline{BC}$

D. area of $\triangle ABC = 3$(area of $\triangle ADE$)

66. In this diagram, the vertices of $PQRS$ are the midpoints of the sides of quadrilateral $WXYZ$. $\overline{WY}$ is twice as long as $\overline{SR}$.

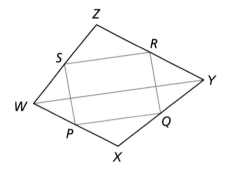

a. Explain why $\triangle WZY$ is similar to $\triangle SZR$.

b. How does the similarity of $\triangle WZY$ and $\triangle SZR$ imply that $\overline{SR}$ is parallel to $\overline{WY}$?

c. How could you show that $\overline{PQ}$ is parallel to $\overline{WY}$?

d. Why do the results of parts (b) and (c) imply that $\overline{SR}$ is parallel to $\overline{PQ}$?

e. How could you repeat the reasoning from parts (a)–(d) to show that $\overline{SP}$ is parallel to $\overline{RQ}$?

f. How does the reasoning from parts (a)–(e) show that $PQRS$ is a parallelogram?

Mathematical Reflections 1

The problems of this investigation challenged you to find patterns in the coordinates of points on line segments and circles. These questions will help you summarize what you have learned.

Think about your answers to these questions. Discuss your ideas with other students and your teacher. Then write a summary of your findings in your notebook.

Give specific examples to illustrate your answers to Questions 1–3.

1. What types of equations or inequalities describe points (x, y) that lie

   a. on a circle of radius r centered at the origin?

   b. in the interior of a circle of radius r centered at the origin?

2. The equations $y = mx + b$ and $y = nx + c$ represent two lines. How can you tell whether the lines are

   a. parallel?

   b. perpendicular?

3. How can you find the midpoint of the segment with endpoints (a, b) and (c, d)?

Investigation 2

Linear Equations and Inequalities

Connecting geometry and algebra can help you solve problems. In the last Investigation, you used algebra to describe and reason about geometric shapes in the coordinate plane. Now, you will use coordinate geometry to help you think about algebraic equations and inequalities.

Suppose the managers of a shopping center want to upgrade their security system. Two providers bid for the job.

- Super Locks will charge $3,975 to install the equipment and then $6.00 per day to monitor the system and respond to alerts.

- Fail Safe will charge $995 to install the equipment and then $17.95 per day to monitor the system and respond to alerts.

Both companies are reliable and capable, so the choice comes down to cost.

Getting Ready for Problem 2.1

- What kinds of equations will show how the costs for the two companies are a function of the number of days?

- What patterns do you expect to see in graphs of the equations?

- How can you use a graph to answer questions about which company offers the best price?

Graphs of Linear Systems

The cost of the security services from Super Locks and Fail Safe depends on the number of days the company provides service. The graph below shows the bids for both companies.

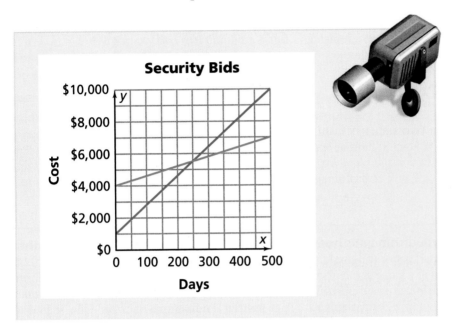

Security Bids

Cost / Days

Problem 2.1 Graphs of Linear Systems

A. Use the graphs to estimate the answers to these questions. Explain your reasoning in each case.

1. For what number of days will the costs for the two companies be the same? What is that cost?

2. For what numbers of days will Super Locks cost less than Fail Safe?

3. For what numbers of days will Super Locks cost less than $6,000?

4. What is the cost of one year of service from Fail Safe?

5. How can Fail Safe adjust its per-day charge to make its cost for 500 days of service cheaper than Super Locks' cost?

B. For each company, write an equation for the cost c for d days of security services.

C. For parts (1) and (4) of Question A, write an equation you can solve to answer the question. Then use symbolic methods to find the exact answers.

ACE | Homework starts on page 30.

2.2 Linear Inequalities

In Problem 2.1, you used graphic and symbolic methods to analyze a **system of linear equations.** The problem conditions could be expressed as two equations relating security costs and the number of days for the business contract. The coordinates of the intersection point of the graphs satisfied both equations in the system. This point is the *solution* of the system.

Getting Ready for Problem 2.2

The cost equations for the two security companies are a system of linear equations:

$$c = 3{,}975 + 6d \quad \text{(Super Locks)}$$
$$\text{and} \quad c = 995 + 17.95d \quad \text{(Fail Safe)}$$

In previous units, you learned some methods to solve this linear system to find the number of days for which the costs are the same for both companies. Here is one possible solution method:

$$3{,}975 + 6d = 995 + 17.95d \qquad (1)$$
$$2{,}980 = 11.95d \qquad (2)$$
$$249 \approx d \qquad (3)$$

- Give a reason for each step in the solution.
- What is the overall strategy that guides the solution process?
- What does the statement $d \approx 249$ tell you?
- How can the solution to this system help you answer this question: For what numbers of days will Super Locks cost less than Fail Safe?
- What does your answer to the previous question tell you about solutions to the inequality $3{,}975 + 6d < 995 + 17.95d$?

It is fairly easy to find some solutions to an inequality. However, sometimes it is useful to find all the solutions by solving the inequality symbolically. The following problems will help you develop strategies for solving inequalities.

Problem 2.2 Linear Inequalities

A. For each instruction in parts (1)–(6), start with $q < r$. Tell whether performing the operation on $q < r$ will give an inequality that is still true. If so, explain why. If not, give specific examples to show why the resulting inequality is false.

1. Add 23 to both sides.

2. Subtract 35 from both sides.

3. Multiply both sides by 14.

4. Multiply both sides by -6.

5. Divide both sides by 5.

6. Divide both sides by -3.

B. What do your results from Question A suggest about how working with inequalities is similar to and different from working with equations?

C. Solve these equations and inequalities.

1. $3x + 12 = 5x - 4$ **2.** $3w + 12 < 5w - 4$

3. $q - 5 = 6q + 10$ **4.** $r - 5 > 6r + 10$

ACE | Homework starts on page 30.

I need to end up with all the terms with variables on one side.

2.3 Solving Linear Inequalities

Many practical problems require solving linear inequalities. You can reason about inequalities, such as $2x - 4 < 5$ or $2x - 4 > -0.5x + 1$, using both symbolic and graphic methods. Solutions to inequalities with one variable are generally given in the form $x < a$, $x > a$, $x \leq a$, or $x \geq a$.

Getting Ready for Problem 2.3

- What are some values that satisfy the inequality $3x + 4 \leq 13$?
- Describe all the solutions of the inequality $3x + 4 \leq 13$.

All the solutions of $3x + 4 \leq 13$ can be displayed in a number-line graph. This graph represents $x \leq 3$, all x-values less than or equal to 3.

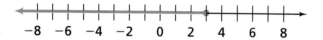

- Explain why the solutions of $3x + 4 < 13$ do *not* include the value 3.

The number-line graph below represents the solutions of $3x + 4 < 13$. It shows $x < 3$, all x-values strictly less than 3. The open circle shows that 3 is not a solution.

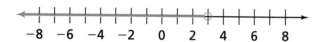

- Make a number-line graph showing the solutions of $2x - 4 < 5$.
- Explain in words what the graph tells about the solutions.

Problem 2.3 Solving Linear Inequalities

A. Use symbolic reasoning to solve each inequality. Then make a number-line graph of the solutions. Be prepared to justify your solution steps and to explain your graphs.

1. $3x + 17 < 47$

2. $43 < 8x - 9$

3. $-6x + 9 < 25$

4. $14x - 23 < 5x + 13$

5. $18 < -4x + 2$

6. $3,975 + 6d < 995 + 17.95d$

B. Luisa wants to use her graphing calculator to solve $2x - 3 \leq 1$. She graphs the linear functions $y = 2x - 3$ and $y = 1$. She uses an x- and a y-scale of 1.

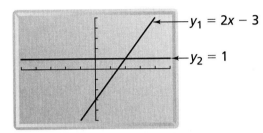

$y_1 = 2x - 3$

$y_2 = 1$

1. Luisa knows that the solution for $2x - 3 = 1$ is $x = 2$. How does this relate to the graphs of the lines she drew?

2. How do the graphs show that the solution of $2x - 3 \leq 1$ is $x \leq 2$?

3. How can you use the graph to find the solution of $2x - 3 > 1$? What is the solution?

4. For one of the inequalities in Question A, sketch a graph or use your graphing calculator to find the solution. Check that your solution agrees with the one you found by using symbolic reasoning.

ACE Homework starts on page 30.

Applications

1. a. Sam needs to rent a car for a one-week trip in Oregon. He is considering two companies. A+ Auto Rental charges $175 plus $0.10 per mile. Zippy Auto Rental charges $220 plus $0.05 per mile. Write an equation relating the rental cost for each company to the miles driven.

 b. Graph the equations.

 c. Under what circumstances is the rental cost the same for both companies? What is that cost?

 d. Under what circumstances is renting from Zippy cheaper than renting from A+?

 e. Suppose Sam rents a car from A+ and drives it 225 miles. What is his rental cost?

2. Maggie lives 1,250 meters from school. Ming lives 800 meters from school. Both girls leave for school at the same time. Maggie walks at an average speed of 70 meters per minute, while Ming walks at an average speed of 40 meters per minute. Maggie's route takes her past Ming's house.

For: Help with Exercise 2
Web Code: ape-7202

 a. Write equations that show Maggie and Ming's distances from school t minutes after they leave their homes.

Answer parts (b)–(d) by writing and solving equations or inequalities.

 b. When, if ever, will Maggie catch up with Ming?

 c. How long will Maggie remain behind Ming?

 d. At what times is the distance between the two girls less than 20 meters?

For Exercises 3–6, graph the system of equations and estimate the point of intersection. Then use symbolic reasoning to check whether your estimate is accurate.

3. $y = 2x + 4$ and $y = \frac{1}{2}x - 2$ **4.** $y = x + 5$ and $y = -3x + 3$

5. $y = 3$ and $y = 6x - 3$ **6.** $x = 2$ and $y = -\frac{2}{5}x + 4$

7. Suppose s and t are two numbers and that $s > t$. Decide whether each inequality must be true.

  a. $s + 15 > t + 15$ **b.** $s - (-22) > t - (-22)$

  c. $s \times 0 > t \times 0$ **d.** $\frac{s}{-6} > \frac{t}{-6}$

  e. $\frac{s}{6} > \frac{t}{6}$ **f.** $s \times -3 < t \times -4$

For Exercises 8–11, solve the inequality. Then, graph the solution on a number line.

8. $12 < 7x - 2$ **9.** $2x + 12 > 32$

10. $4x - 17 \leq 31$ **11.** $-16x - 12 > 14 - 10x$

Go **O**nline
PHSchool.com
For: Multiple-Choice Skills Practice
Web Code: apa-7254

12. Use these graphs to estimate solutions for the inequalities and equations in parts (a)–(f). Then, use symbolic reasoning to check your estimates.

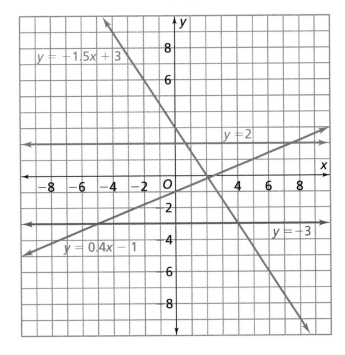

  a. $0.4x - 1 > 2$ **b.** $0.4x - 1 > -3$

  c. $-1.5x + 3 > 2$ **d.** $-1.5x + 3 < -3$

  e. $-1.5x + 3 = 0.4x - 1$ **f.** $-1.5x + 3 > 0.4x - 1$

Investigation 2 Linear Equations and Inequalities   **31**

Connections

Calculate the *y*-value for the given *x*-value.

13. $y = 3x + 2$ when $x = -2$ **14.** $y = -3x + 4$ when $x = 9$

15. $y = \frac{1}{2}x - 4$ when $x = 24$ **16.** $y = -5x - 7$ when $x = \frac{3}{15}$

17. $y = \frac{2}{3}x - 12$ when $x = -18$ **18.** $y = -\frac{1}{4}x - \frac{3}{4}$ when $x = -6$

Write an equation for the line satisfying the given conditions.

19. slope $= 2$, *y*-intercept $= -3$

20. slope $= -4$, passes through $(0, 1.5)$

21. passes through $(-2, 1)$ and $(4, -3)$

22. passes through $(4, 0)$ and $(0, 3)$

Identify the slope, *x*-intercept, and *y*-intercept of the line.

23. $y = 7x - 3$ **24.** $y = -3x + 4$ **25.** $y = \frac{2}{3}x + 12$

26. $y = -\frac{1}{4}x - 5$ **27.** $y = \frac{3}{4} - 17x$ **28.** $y = -\frac{3}{5}(x + 10)$

For Exercises 29–34, copy each pair of expressions. Insert <, >, or = to make a true statement.

29. $-18 \div -3$ ■ $-24 \div -4$

30. $1{,}750(-12)$ ■ $(1{,}749)(-12)$

31. $5(18 - 24)$ ■ $90 - (-120)$

32. $-8(-5)$ ■ $(-7)(-5)$

33. $4(-3 - (-7))$ ■ $4(-3) - 4(-7)$

34. $-5(-4)^2$ ■ $-4(-5)^2$

35. Write an equation or inequality that tells whether each point is inside, outside, or on the circle with a radius of 10 and centered at $(0, 0)$.

   a. $(6, 8)$ **b.** $(7, 7)$ **c.** $(-7, -7)$

   d. $(-6, 8)$ **e.** $(-7, 8)$ **f.** $(-7, -8)$

Copy each pair of fractions. Insert <, >, or = to make a true statement.

36. $\frac{6}{8}$ ■ $\frac{-18}{24}$ **37.** $\frac{6}{8}$ ■ $\frac{7}{9}$ **38.** $\frac{6}{8}$ ■ $\frac{-7}{9}$

39. $\frac{6}{8}$ ■ $\frac{-18}{-24}$ **40.** $\frac{6}{8}$ ■ $\frac{-7}{-9}$ **41.** $\frac{8}{6}$ ■ $\frac{-9}{-7}$

42. Use these figures for parts (a)–(f). Insert <, =, or > to make true statements.

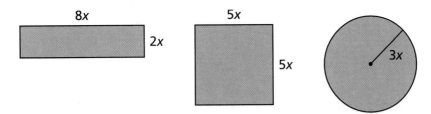

8x

2x

5x

5x

3x

- **a.** perimeter of square ▧ perimeter of rectangle
- **b.** area of square ▧ area of rectangle
- **c.** perimeter of square ▧ circumference of circle
- **d.** area of square ▧ area of circle
- **e.** perimeter of rectangle ▧ circumference of circle
- **f.** area of rectangle ▧ area of circle

43. The gender of a newborn child is nearly equally likely to be a boy or a girl. Consider the patterns likely to occur in a family with three children.

Copy parts (a)–(d). Insert <, =, or > to make true statements.

- **a.** P(all boys) ▧ P(all girls)
- **b.** P(exactly one boy) ▧ P(exactly 2 girls)
- **c.** P(BGB) ▧ P(BBG)
- **d.** P(two boys and one girl) ▧ P(all girls)

44. Multiple Choice If $w = 3x + c$, what is the value of x?

A. 3 **B.** $\dfrac{w - c}{3}$ **C.** $w - c$ **D.** $\dfrac{w + c}{3}$

45. Suppose $\dfrac{a}{b}$ and $\dfrac{c}{d}$ are two non-zero fractions and $\dfrac{a}{b} < \dfrac{c}{d}$.

a. Give an example of values of a, b, c, and d that satisfy $\dfrac{a}{b} < \dfrac{c}{d}$ and also $\dfrac{b}{a} < \dfrac{d}{c}$.

b. Give an example of values of a, b, c, and d that satisfy $\dfrac{a}{b} < \dfrac{c}{d}$ and also $\dfrac{b}{a} > \dfrac{d}{c}$.

46. Multiple Choice Which equation's graph is perpendicular to the graph of $y = 2.5x + 4$?

F. $y = 2.5x$ **G.** $y = 0.4x$ **H.** $y = -0.4x$ **J.** $y = -2.5x$

47. Multiple Choice For which set of points is one point the midpoint of the segment joining the other two points?

A. $(0, 0)$, $(5, 6)$, $(10, 3)$ **B.** $(0, 3)$, $(2, 6)$, $(-2, 0)$

C. $(4, 6)$, $(8, 12)$, $(16, 24)$ **D.** $(2, 0)$, $(2, 6)$, $(2, -3)$

48. Use a table or graph of $y = 5(2^x)$ to estimate the solution of the inequality $5(2^x) > 1,000$.

49. Use a table or graph of $y = x^2 - x - 6$ to estimate the solution of the inequality $x^2 - x - 6 < 0$.

For Exercises 50–55, write the equation in factored form. Then, use the equation to find the x- and y-intercepts for the graph of the equation.

50. $y = x^2 + 4x$ **51.** $y = x^2 + 4x + 4$ **52.** $y = x^2 + 3x - 10$

53. $y = x^2 - 8x + 16$ **54.** $y = x^2 - 4$ **55.** $y = x^2 + 4x + 3$

56. Multiple Choice Which expression is the factored form of $1x + 2x + 6$?

F. $3x + 6$ **G.** $2(x + 3)$ **H.** $3(x + 2)$ **J.** $3(x + 6)$

Extensions

57. In parts (a)–(d), find values of x that satisfy the given conditions. Then, graph the solution on a number line.

    a. $x + 7 < 4$ *or* $x + 3 > 9$ (That is, find the x-values that satisfy one inequality or the other or both.)

    b. $3x + 4 < 13$ *and* $12 < 6x$ (That is, find x-values that satisfy both inequalities.)

    c. $5x - 6 > 2x + 18$ *or* $-3x + 5 > 8x - 39$

    d. $-11x - 7 < -7x + 33$ *and* $9 + 2x > 11x$

58. Suppose m and n are positive whole numbers and $m < n$. Tell whether each statement is always true.

    a. $2^m < 2^n$ **b.** $m^2 < n^2$ **c.** $0.5^m < 0.5^n$ **d.** $\frac{1}{m} < \frac{1}{n}$

59. Solve these quadratic inequalities.

    a. $5x^2 + 7 \le 87$

    b. $5x^2 + 7 > 87$

60. Solve these exponential inequalities.

    a. $2(3^x) - 8 < 46$

    b. $2(3^x) - 8 > 10$

Hint:

Use a graph or table of $y = 5x^2 + 7$ for Exercise 59, and a graph or table of $y = 2x(3^x) - 8$ for Exercise 60, to estimate the solutions. Then adapt the reasoning used to solve linear inequalities to check the accuracy of your estimates.

Connections   Extensions

Mathematical Reflections 2

In this investigation, you learned graphic and symbolic methods for solving systems of linear equations and linear inequalities. These questions will help you summarize what you have learned.

Think about your answers to these questions. Discuss your ideas with other students and your teacher. Then write a summary of your findings in your notebook.

1. How can you use coordinate graphs to solve linear equations such as $ax + b = cx + d$ and linear inequalities such as $ax + b < cx + d$?

2. **a.** How can you use symbolic reasoning to solve inequalities such as $ax + b < c$?

   b. How can you use symbolic reasoning to solve inequalities such as $ax + b < cx + d$?

Investigation 3

Equations With Two or More Variables

You have done a lot of work with relationships involving two related variables. However, many real-world relationships involve three or more variables. For example, consider this situation:

The eighth-graders are selling T-shirts and caps to raise money for their end-of-year party. They earn a profit of $5 per shirt and $10 per cap.

This situation involves three variables: the *number of T-shirts sold*, the *number of caps sold,* and the *profit.* The profit for the fundraiser depends on the number of caps and the number of T-shirts sold.

Getting Ready for Problem 3.1

- What equation shows how the profit *p* is related to the number of shirts sold *s* and the number of caps sold *c*?

- Find the profit if the students sell

  30 shirts and 50 caps
  15 shirts and 10 caps
  12 shirts and 20 caps

- What do you think it means to *solve* an equation with three variables?

- What ideas do you have for finding solutions to the equation?

The equation relating *p, s,* and *c* represents every possible combination of T-shirts, caps, and profit values for the fundraiser. Suppose the class sets a profit goal of $P = \$600$. Finding combinations of T-shirt and cap sales that meet this goal requires solving an equation with only two variables, *s* and *c*.

Problem 3.1 Solving Equations With Two Variables

A. Find five pairs of numbers for shirt and cap sales that will allow the students to make a $600 profit exactly.

B. 1. Each answer for Question A can be expressed as an ordered pair (s, c). Plot these ordered pairs on a grid like the one below.

Fundraiser Sales

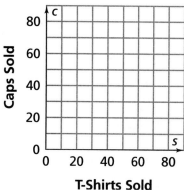

T-Shirts Sold

2. Is there a pattern in the points that suggests other solutions of the equation $600 = 5s + 10c$? Explain.

C. The equations in parts (1)–(4) are of the form $c = ax + by$ or $ax + by = c$. For each equation,

- find at least five solution pairs (x, y)

- plot the solutions

- find a pattern in the points and use the pattern to predict other solution pairs

1. $5 = x - y$ **2.** $10 = x + y$

3. $2x + y = 3$ **4.** $-3x + 2y = -4$

D. What does your work on Question C suggest about the graph of solutions for any equation of the form $ax + by = c$ or $c = ax + by$, where *a, b,* and *c* are fixed numbers?

ACE Homework starts on page 42.

There are two common forms of a linear equation.

- When the values of one variable depend on those of another, it is most natural to express the relationship as $y = mx + b$. Most of the linear equations you have seen have been in this *slope-intercept* form.

- When it is more natural to combine the values of two variables, the relationship can be expressed as $ax + by = c$. This is the *standard form* of a linear equation. The equations in Problem 3.1 were in standard form.

Getting Ready for Problem 3.2

It is easy to graph a linear equation of the form $y = mx + b$ on a calculator.

- Can you use a calculator to graph an equation of the form $ax + by = c$?
- Can you change an equation from $ax + by = c$ form to $y = mx + b$ form?
- How can rewriting the equation $600 = 5s + 10c$ (or $600 = 5x + 10y$) from Problem 3.1 in $y = mx + b$ form help you find solutions?

Problem 3.2 **Connecting** $y = mx + b$ **and** $ax + by = c$

A. Four students want to write $12x + 3y = 9$ in equivalent $y = mx + b$ form. Here are their explanations:

Jared

$$12x + 3y = 9$$
$$3y = -12x + 9 \quad (1)$$
$$y = -4x + 3 \quad (2)$$

Molly

$$12x + 3y = 9$$
$$3y = 9 - 12x \quad (1)$$
$$y = 3 - 12x \quad (2)$$

Ali

$$12x + 3y = 9$$
$$4x + y = 3 \quad (1)$$
$$y = -4x + 3 \quad (2)$$

Mia

$$12x + 3y = 9$$
$$3y = 9 - 12x \quad (1)$$
$$y = 3 - 4x \quad (2)$$
$$y = 4x - 3 \quad (3)$$

1. Did each student get an equation equivalent to the original? If so, explain the reasoning for each step. If not, tell what errors the student made.

2. What does it mean for two equations to be equivalent?

B. Write each equation in $y = mx + b$ form.

1. $x - y = 4$ **2.** $2x + y = 9$ **3.** $8x + 4y = -12$

4. $12 = 3x - 6y$ **5.** $x + y = 2.5$ **6.** $600 = 5x + 10y$

C. Suppose you are given an equation in $ax + by = c$ form. How can you predict the slope, y-intercept, and x-intercept of its graph?

D. Write each equation in $ax + by = c$ form.

1. $y = 5 - 3x$ **2.** $y = \frac{2}{3}x + \frac{1}{4}$ **3.** $x = 2y - 3$

4. $2x = y + \frac{1}{2}$ **5.** $y - 2 = \frac{1}{4}x + 1$ **6.** $3y + 3 = 6x - 15$

ACE Homework starts on page 42.

3.3 Intersections of Lines

At a school band concert, Christopher and Celine sell memberships for the band's booster club. An adult membership costs $10, and a student membership costs $5.

At the end of the evening, the students had sold 50 memberships for a total of $400. The club president wants to know how many of the new members are adults and how many are students.

Problem 3.3 Intersections of Lines

A. Let x stand for the number of $10 adult memberships and y for the number of $5 student memberships.

   1. What equation relates x and y to the $400 income?

   2. Give two solutions for your equation from part (1).

   3. What equation relates x and y to the total of 50 new members? Are the solutions you found in part (2) also solutions of this equation?

B. 1. Graph the two equations from Question A on a single coordinate grid like the one at the right.

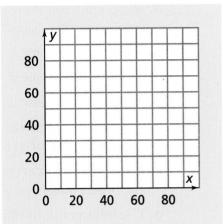

   2. Estimate the coordinates of the point where the graphs intersect. Explain what the coordinates tell you about the numbers of adult and student memberships sold.

   3. Consider the graph of the equation that relates x and y to the $400 income. Could a point that is *not* on this graph be a solution to the equation?

   4. Could there be a common solution for both of your equations that is *not* shown on your graph?

In Question A, you wrote a system of equations. One equation represents all (x, y) pairs that give a total income of $400, and the other represents all (x, y) pairs that give a total of 50 memberships. The coordinates of the intersection point satisfy both equations, or conditions. These coordinates are the *solution to the system*.

Many real-life problems can be represented by systems of equations. In Question C, you'll practice solving such systems graphically.

C. Use graphic methods to solve each system. In each case, substitute the solution values into the equations to see if your solution is exact or an estimate.

   1. $x + y = 4$ and $x - y = -2$

   2. $2x + y = -1$ and $x - 2y = 7$

   3. $2x + y = 3$ and $-x + 2y = 6$

ACE Homework starts on page 42.

Applications

1. For a fundraiser, students sell calendars for $3 each and posters for $2 each.

   a. What equation shows how the income I for the fundraiser depends on the number calendars c and posters p that are sold?

   b. What is the income if students sell 25 calendars and 18 posters?

   c. What is the income if students sell 12 calendars and 15 posters?

   d. What is the income if students sell 20 calendars and 12 posters?

   e. Find three combinations of calendar sales and poster sales that will give an income of exactly $100.

   f. Each answer in part (e) can be written as an ordered pair (c, p). Plot the ordered pairs on a coordinate grid.

   g. Use your graph to estimate three other (c, p) pairs that would meet the $100 goal.

2. Neema saves her quarters and dimes. She plans to exchange the coins for paper money when the total value equals $10.

   a. How many coins does she need to make $10 if all the coins are quarters? If all the coins are dimes?

   b. What equation relates the number of quarters x and dimes y to the goal of $10?

   c. Use the answers from part (a) to help you draw a graph showing all solutions to the equation.

   d. Use the graph to find five combinations of dimes and quarters that will allow Neema to reach her goal.

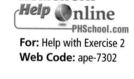

Homework
Help **O**nline
PHSchool.com
For: Help with Exercise 2
Web Code: ape-7302

3. Students in Eric's gym class must cover a distance of 1,600 meters by running or walking. Most students run part of the way and walk part of the way. Eric can run at an average speed of 200 meters per minute and walk at an average speed of 80 meters per minute.

   a. Suppose Eric runs for 4 minutes and walks for 8 minutes. How close is he to the 1,600-meter goal?

   b. Write an equation for the distance d Eric will cover if he runs for x minutes and walks for y minutes.

   c. Find three combinations of running and walking times for which Eric would cover 1,600 meters.

   d. Plot the ordered pairs for part (c) on a graph. Use the graph to estimate several other combinations of running and walking times for which Eric would cover 1,600 meters.

4. Kevin said that if you triple his age, the result will be 1 less than his mother's age.

   a. Which, if any, of these equations shows the relationship between Kevin's age x and his mother's age y? Choose all that are correct.
   $$3x - y = 1 \qquad y - 3x = 1 \qquad 3x + 1 = y \qquad 3x = 1 - y$$

   b. Find three pairs of (x, y) values that satisfy the equation relating Kevin's age and his mother's age. Plot these ordered pairs, and draw the line that matches the pattern.

   c. Use the graph to estimate three other ordered pairs that satisfy the equation. Use the equation to check the estimates.

   d. Which (x, y) pairs seem to be reasonable for Kevin's age and his mother's age?

Find three pairs of (x, y) values that satisfy each equation. Plot those points and use the pattern to find two more solution pairs.

   5. $6 = 3x - 2y$ (**Hint:** What is y if $x = 0$? What is x if $y = 0$?)

   6. $10 = x + 2y$

   7. $2x + y = 6$

   8. $-3x + 4y = -4$

9. Tell which line at the right is the graph of each equation in parts (a)–(d). Explain.

   a. $2x + 3y = 9$ **b.** $2x - 3y = 9$

   c. $x - 3y = 6$ **d.** $3x + 2y = 6$

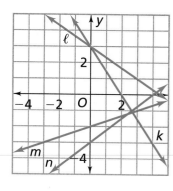

10. In Exercise 1, one equation relating the calendar and poster sales to the $600 goal is $3c + 2p = 600$. Suppose the company donating the calendars and posters said they would provide a total of 250 items.

   a. What equation relates c and p to the 250 items donated?

   b. Graph both equations on the same grid. Find the coordinates of the intersection point. Explain what these coordinates tell you about the fundraising situation.

11. In Exercise 2, one equation relating Neema's quarters and dimes to her goal of $10 (1,000 cents) is $25x + 10y = 1,000$. Suppose Neema collects 70 coins to reach her goal.

   a. What equation relates x and y to the number of coins Neema collected?

   b. Graph both equations on the same grid. Find the coordinates of the intersection point. Explain what these coordinates tell you about this situation.

12. In Exercise 3, one equation relating the times Eric spends running and walking to the goal of covering 1,600 meters is $200x + 80y = 1,600$. Suppose Eric runs and walks for a total of 12 minutes to reach his goal.

   a. What equation relates x and y to Eric's total time?

   b. Graph both equations on the same grid. Find the coordinates of the intersection point. Explain what these coordinates tell you about this situation.

13. In Exercise 4, one equation relating the ages of Kevin and his mother is $y - 3x = 1$. The sum of Kevin's age and his mother's age is 61 years.

a. What equation relates Kevin's and his mother's ages to their total age?

b. Graph both equations on the same grid. Find the coordinates of the intersection point. Explain what these coordinates tell you about the ages of Kevin and his mother.

14. Use graphing methods to solve each system of equations. [**Hint:** If you are using a graphing calculator, you can determine a good graphing window by first finding the x- and y-intercepts of each graph. For instance, find the x-intercept of $3x + 4y = 8$ by substituting 0 for y, and then find the y-intercept by substituting 0 for x.

If $y = 0$, then $3x + 4(0) = 8$, so $x = \frac{8}{3}$. The x-intercept is $(\frac{8}{3}, 0)$.

If $x = 0$, then $3(0) + 4y = 8$, so $y = 2$. The y-intercept is $(0, 2)$.]

a. $x - y = -4$ and $x + y = 6$

b. $-2x + y = 3$ and $x + 2y = -9$

c. $-2x + y = 1$ and $4x - 2y = 6$

Write the equation in $ax + by = c$ form. Identify the x-intercept, y-intercept, and slope.

15. $y = 4x - 2$ **16.** $y = -3x + 5$ **17.** $y = x - 7$

18. $y = 5x + 3$ **19.** $y = -8x - 12$ **20.** $y = -9x + 5$

For Exercises 21–26, write the equation in $y = mx + b$ form. Identify the x-intercept, y-intercept, and slope.

21. $-2x - y = -5$ **22.** $6x + 3y = -9$ **23.** $x - y = 4$

24. $3x + 4y = 12$ **25.** $-7x + 2y = -16$ **26.** $x - 5y = 55$

27. Look back over your work for Exercises 15–26. Look for patterns relating the standard form of the equation, $ax + by = c$, to the x-intercept, y-intercept, and slope.

a. Write a general formula for calculating the x-intercept from the values of a, b, and c.

b. Write a general formula for calculating the y-intercept from the values of a, b, and c.

c. Write a general formula for calculating the slope from the values of a, b, and c.

Connections

Solve the inequality and graph the solution on a number line.

28. $x + 3 < 5$

29. $x - 12 > -4$

30. $14 + x \leq -2$

31. $2x + 7 \geq -3$

32. $7x + 3 \leq -17 + 2x$

33. $-3 - 4x \geq 5x + 24$

34. $2x - 4 + 7x < -6x + 41$

35. $12x - 3 + 5 - 4x > 24 - 2x + 8$

Write an equation of a line parallel to the given line.

36. $y = 4x + 6$

37. $-6x + y = 3$

38. $x + y = 9$

39. $x + 4y = -20$

40. $y = -\frac{3}{4}x - 2$

41. $7x + y = -12$

For Exercises 42–47, write an equation of a line perpendicular to the given line.

42. $y = -4x + 2$

43. $y = -\frac{2}{3}x - 7$

44. $y = 6x + 12$

45. $-2x + y = -1$

46. $x - 4y = 20$

47. $2x + 3y = 8$

48. Tell whether each ordered pair is a solution of $3x - 5y = 15$. Show how you know.

    a. $(-2, -4)$

    b. $(0, -3)$

    c. $(-10, 9)$

    d. $(-5, -6)$

    e. $(-10, -9)$

    f. $(-4, -5.4)$

Go Online
PHSchool.com

For: Multiple-Choice Skills Practice
Web Code: apa-7354

49. The angle measures of the triangle below are x, y, and z.

    a. What equation shows how z depends on x and y?

    b. Find five combinations of values for x and y for which the value of z is 40.

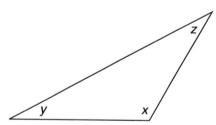

50. Multiple Choice Suppose k, m, and n are numbers and $k = m + n$. Which of the following statements must be true?

A. $k - m = n$ **B.** $m - k = n$

C. $2k = 2m + n$ **D.** $-n = k + m$

51. Multiple Choice Which equation is equivalent to $3x + 5y = 15$?

F. $3x = 5y + 15$ **G.** $x = -5y + 5$

H. $y = 0.6x + 3$ **J.** $y = -0.6x + 3$

52. Suppose you are given the linear equation $ax + by = c$.

a. What is the slope of every line parallel to this line?

b. What is the slope of every line perpendicular to this line?

53. You will need two sheets of grid paper and two different cans with paper labels (for example, tuna and soup cans). On grid paper, trace the top and bottom of each can. Cut these out. Now carefully remove the labels and trace these on grid paper.

a. Estimate and compare the surface areas of the cans (label + top + bottom or $A = \ell w + 2\pi r^2$).

b. After Joel removes his two labels, he notices that the labels are the exact same size and shape. Explain how this can happen.

54. Multiple Choice Which values are solutions of the quadratic equation $x^2 + 8x - 33 = 0$?

A. $x = -11$ and $x = -3$ **B.** $x = 11$ and $x = -3$

C. $x = -11$ and $x = 3$ **D.** $x = 11$ and $x = 3$

55. Use the graph of $y = x^2 + 8x - 33$ to find the solution of each inequality.

    a. $x^2 + 8x - 33 > 0$ **b.** $x^2 + 8x - 33 < 0$

56. a. What shape will this net make if it is cut out and folded?

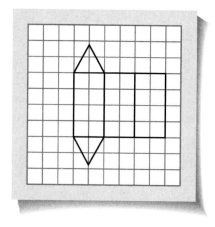

    b. Find the surface area of the shape.

    c. Find the volume of the shape.

57. Tell whether each line has a slope of $-\frac{1}{2}$.

    a. $y = \frac{-1}{-2}x + 3$ **b.** $y = \frac{-1}{2}x + 3$

    c. $y = \frac{1}{-2}x + 3$ **d.** $y = -\frac{1}{2}x + 3$

Without graphing, decide whether the lines are parallel, perpendicular, or neither.

58. $3x + 6y = 12$ and $y = 10 + \frac{-1}{2}x$

59. $y = -x + 5$ and $y = x + 5$

60. $y = 2 - 5x$ and $y = -5x + 2$

61. $y = -3 + 5x$ and $y = \frac{-x}{5} + 3$

62. $10x + 5y = 20$ and $y = 10x + 20$

Extensions

63. Jasmine wants to run a marathon. She knows she will have to walk some of the 26.2 miles, but she wants to finish in 5 hours. She plans to run 10-minute miles and walk 15-minute miles.

Let x stand for the number of minutes Jasmine runs. Let y stand for the number of minutes she walks.

   a. What equation relates x and y to the goal of completing the race in 5 hours?

   b. What equation relates x and y to the goal of covering 26.2 miles?

   c. For each equation, find several ordered-pair solutions (x, y). Then, plot the points with those coordinates and use the pattern to draw a graph of the equation. Graph both equations on the same axes.

   d. Use the graphs to estimate the combination of running and walking times that will allow Jasmine to complete the marathon in exactly 5 hours.

   e. Suppose Jasmine decides she wants to finish the marathon in less than 5 hours. Find five combinations of running and walking times that give a total time less than 5 hours.

   f. Express the condition that the total running and walking times must be less than 5 hours as an inequality.

   g. Make a graph of all the solutions of the inequality.

   h. Graph the linear equation from part (b) on the same axes as the inequality. Explain how the result shows Jasmine's options for running and walking times if she wants to finish the marathon in 5 hours or less.

64. a. Find coordinates of the midpoints of the sides of this triangle.

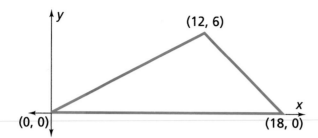

b. A segment from one vertex of a triangle to the midpoint of the opposite side is called a *median*. Find equations of the three medians of this triangle.

c. Use algebraic methods to find the coordinates of the point(s) where the median from the vertex $(12, 6)$ intersects the other medians.

d. The medians of any triangle intersect at a single point called the *centroid*. The centroid divides each median into two pieces that are related. Study the coordinates of the vertices, midpoints, and centroid of the triangle above. What is the special way in which the centroid splits each median?

e. Use the coordinates of the centroid and the vertices to calculate the lengths of the two segments that make up each median. Explain how the results confirm your answer to part (d) or how they suggest a revision of your original idea.

65. Your exploration in Exercise 64 focused on a single triangle. To test the patterns you observed, repeat the analysis from those problems with these other triangles.

a. A triangle with vertices $(0, 0)$, $(12, 0)$ and $(-6, 6)$

b. A triangle with vertices $(0, 0)$, $(12, 0)$ and $(4, 12)$

Mathematical Reflections 3

In this investigation, you used coordinate graphs to display solutions of linear equations of the form $ax + by = c$ and to find solutions of systems of linear equations. These questions will help you summarize what you have learned.

Think about your answers to these questions. Discuss your ideas with other students and your teacher. Then write a summary of your findings in your notebook.

Give specific examples to illustrate your answers to Questions 1–3.

1. What pattern will result from plotting all points (x, y) that satisfy an equation in the form $ax + by = c$?

2. How can you use a graph to find values of x and y that satisfy systems of two linear equations in the form $ax + by = c$?

3. How can you change linear equations of the form $ax + by = c$ to $y = mx + b$ form and vice versa?

Solving Systems of Linear Equations Symbolically

Every day of the year, thousands of airline flights crisscross the United States to connect large and small cities. Each flight follows a plan filed with air traffic control before take-off.

The flight paths of airplanes are not straight lines from take-off to landing. But parts of those paths are generally straight-line segments. At any hour of the day, the pattern of flight plans might look like the diagram below.

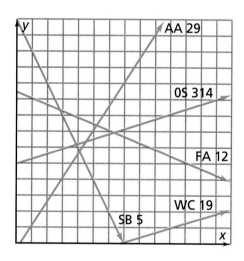

The diagram seems to show many potential mid-air collisions.

Why do you think such disasters almost never occur?

What information about flight paths is not shown on the diagram?

If planned flight paths are represented by equations, an air-traffic control system can calculate intersection points and warn of possible collisions. The equations for the flights in the diagram are shown in the table.

In this problem, you will explore a simplified air-traffic control system. You will ignore the height above the ground and time and consider only whether the flight paths of two planes intersect. These intersection points tell you which parts of the flight paths controllers need to examine more carefully to prevent collisions.

4.1 The $y = mx + b$ Case

The equations for the flight paths can be used to calculate the nine intersection points shown on the graph.

Getting Ready for Problem

A table of equations for the flight paths is at the right. To find the intersection of WC 19 and AA 29, you need to find the (x, y) pair that satisfies the system of linear equations below. (The bracket is a special notation used to indicate a system of equations.)

$$\begin{cases} y = 0.3x - 2 \\ y = 1.5x - 0.4 \end{cases}$$

Jeff writes the following to solve this system.

$$0.3x - 2 = 1.5x - 0.4$$
$$-1.2x = 1.6$$
$$x = \frac{1.6}{-1.2}$$
$$x = -\frac{4}{3}$$

Flight Paths

Airline/Flight	Equation
Apex Airlines Flight *AA 29*	$y = 1.5x - 0.4$
We-Care Air Flight *WC 19*	$y = 0.3x - 2$
Open Sky Airlines Flight *OS 314*	$y = 0.3x + 5$
Fly Away Airlines Flight *FA 12*	$y = -0.4x + 9.5$
Sky Bus Airlines Flight *SB 5*	$y = -2x + 14$

- Explain Jeff's reasoning.
- What does $x = -\frac{4}{3}$ tell you?
- How can you find the y-coordinate of the intersection point?

Problem 4.1 The $y = mx + b$ Case

A. Write and solve systems to find the intersections of these flight plans.

   1. WC 19 and SB 5   **2.** SB 5 and AA 29

   3. SB 5 and FA 12   **4.** FA 12 and AA 29

B. Study the work you did in Question A. Describe a strategy for solving any system of this form shown below.

$$\begin{cases} y = ax + b \\ y = cx + d \end{cases}$$

C. What could an air-traffic controller do if two flight plans intersect?

ACE Homework starts on page 59.

4.2 The $ax + by = c$ Case

When a system of linear equations is in $y = mx + b$ form, it is easy to write a single linear equation with the same solution as the system.

$$\begin{cases} y = ax + b \\ y = cx + d \end{cases} \text{ becomes } ax + b = cx + d.$$

The equations in a linear system are not always given in $y = mx + b$ form. In this problem, you'll consider systems of this form:

$$\begin{cases} ax + by = c \\ dx + ey = f \end{cases}$$

Getting Ready for Problem 4.2

Suppose the solution to a situation requires you to find values of x and y that satisfy the system:

$$\begin{cases} 3x - y = 30 \\ x + y = 14 \end{cases}$$

One useful strategy for solving a linear system is to rewrite the equations in familiar equivalent forms.

- Write each equation in $y = mx + b$ form. Then, find a solution using the method you learned in Problem 4.1.

- Write each equation in $x = ky + c$ form. Then, find a solution. Are the solutions the same?

- Why might you expect both methods to give the same solution?

Problem 4.2 Solving Systems by Writing Equivalent Forms

A. Decide whether it is easier to write each equation in equivalent $y = mx + b$ form or equivalent $x = ky + c$ form. Then, write each equation in the form you chose.

1. $x + y = 3$ **2.** $x - y = -5$

3. $2x + y = -1$ **4.** $x - 2y = 8$

5. $9x + 6y = 12$ **6.** $-x + 4y = 10$

7. In parts (1)–(6), how did you decide which form to use?

B. Solve each system by writing the equations in $y = mx + b$ or $x = ky + c$ form and then using the strategy from Problem 4.1.

1. $\begin{cases} x + y = 3 \\ x - y = -5 \end{cases}$ **2.** $\begin{cases} 3x - y = 30 \\ x + y = 14 \end{cases}$

3. $\begin{cases} x + 6y = 15 \\ -x + 4y = 5 \end{cases}$ **4.** $\begin{cases} x - y = -5 \\ -2x + 2y = 10 \end{cases}$

C. Look back over your work from Question B.

  1. What do you notice about the systems that makes this method a good one to use?

  2. Describe the steps needed in using this method to solve a system.

D. 1. What does it mean for two equations to be equivalent?

  2. What does it mean to solve a linear system?

ACE   **Homework starts on page 59.**

4.3   Solving Systems by Substitution

Writing the equations in a linear system in $y = mx + b$ or $x = ky + c$ form is not always easy. Sometimes the arithmetic becomes messy.

For example, consider how you would solve this system.

$$\begin{cases} 3x - y = 5 \\ 2x + 5y = -8 \end{cases}$$

Solve both equations for y to get $y = mx + b$ form.

$$3x - y = 5 \qquad\qquad 2x + 5y = -8$$
$$-y = 5 - 3x \qquad\qquad 5y = -8 - 2x$$
$$y = 3x - 5 \qquad\qquad y = -\frac{8}{5} - \frac{2}{5}x$$

Set the right sides of the equations equal.

$$3x - 5 = -\frac{8}{5} - \frac{2}{5}x$$
$$15x - 25 = -8 - 2x$$
$$17x = 17$$
$$x = 1$$

In this problem, you'll look at another solution method that is easier in many cases.

Check the reasoning in this method of solving a system of linear equations by *substitution* and see if you can explain why it works.

1. The system $\begin{cases} 3x - y = 5 \\ 2x + 5y = -8 \end{cases}$ is equivalent to the system $\begin{cases} y = 3x - 5 \\ 2x + 5y = -8. \end{cases}$

2. From that fact, any solution should satisfy $2x + 5(3x - 5) = -8$. Why is this equation an advantage over the two-equation system?

3. Solving this single equation for x, you get:

$$2x + 15x - 25 = -8$$
$$17x = 17$$
$$x = 1$$

4. Then $y = 3(1) - 5 = -2$.

5. The ordered pair $(1, -2)$ satisfies both equations in the original system:

$$3(1) - (-2) = 5 \qquad\qquad 2(1) + 5(-2) = -8$$

So $(1, -2)$ is the solution.

● Does this strategy produce the *only* solution for both equations in the original system? Why?

● Which solution strategy do you think is easier for this system, writing the equations in $y = ax + b$ form and setting them equal or using substitution? Why?

Problem 4.3 **Solving Systems by Substitution**

A. Use substitution to solve each system.

1. $\begin{cases} 2x + y = -1 \\ x - 2y = 12 \end{cases}$ **2.** $\begin{cases} 4x + 2y = 6 \\ -3x - 7y = 1 \end{cases}$ **3.** $\begin{cases} x - y = -5 \\ -x + 4y = 10 \end{cases}$

4. $\begin{cases} 3x + y = 4 \\ 6x + 2y = 7 \end{cases}$ **5.** $\begin{cases} 3x + 2y = 10 \\ -6x - 4y = -20 \end{cases}$ **6.** $\begin{cases} x + y = 13 \\ x - y = 2 \end{cases}$

B. You may have been puzzled by the solution to two of the systems in Question A. Complete parts (1) and (2) for each of these two systems.

1. Graph the two lines to see if you can make sense of the situation.

2. Write both equations in $y = mx + b$ form to see if this helps you understand the results.

C. 1. Decide whether writing in equivalent form or substituting would be easier for solving the system. Then, solve the system.

a. $\begin{cases} 4x + y = 6 \\ -3x + y = 1 \end{cases}$ b. $\begin{cases} 2x + y = 3 \\ -3x + 7y = 1 \end{cases}$

2. For each system, explain why you chose the solution method.

ACE Homework starts on page 59.

4.4 Solving Systems by Combination

You have already developed some useful strategies for solving a simple linear equation like $3x + 5 = 10$. You know that you can add or subtract the same quantity on both sides and preserve equality.

The same is true for multiplication or division. These ideas, called the *Properties of Equality,* can help you develop another method for solving linear equations. This method involves combining separate linear equations into one equation with only one variable.

Getting Ready for Problem

These steps show the *combination method* for solving $\begin{cases} x - y = 4 \\ x + y = 5. \end{cases}$

If $x - y = 4$ and $x + y = 5$, then	
$(x - y) + (x + y) = 4 + 5$	(1)
$2x = 9$	(2)
$x = 4.5$	(3)
$x + y = 5$	(4)
$4.5 + y = 5$	(5)
$y = 0.5$	(6)

- Give reasons for steps 1–5.
- Why is adding the two original equations an advantage?
- Would subtracting the two original equations work just as well?

A. Use the combination method to solve these linear systems.

1. $\begin{cases} -x + 4y = 3 \\ x + 2y = 5 \end{cases}$ **2.** $\begin{cases} 2x + 3y = 4 \\ 5x + 3y = -8 \end{cases}$ **3.** $\begin{cases} 2x - 3y = 4 \\ 5x - 3y = 7 \end{cases}$

B. 1. Explain why System B is equivalent to System A.

System A	System B
$\begin{cases} 3x + 2y = 10 \\ 4x - y = 6 \end{cases}$	$\begin{cases} 3x + 2y = 10 \\ 8x - 2y = 12 \end{cases}$

2. Rewriting System A as System B is a possible first step in solving the system by the combination method. Complete this solution process by combining the two equations in System B.

C. 1. Add the two equations in System A. Graph both equations in System A and the new equation you made by adding. What do the three equations have in common?

2. Graph System B and the new equation you made by adding. What do the three equations have in common?

3. Why does the graph you made with System B and the new equation help to solve the system?

D. In parts (1) and (2), write an equivalent system that is easy to solve by combining equations. Then find the solution. Check your work by solving the system with a different method.

1. $\begin{cases} 2x + 2y = 5 \\ 3x - 6y = 12 \end{cases}$ **2.** $\begin{cases} x + 3y = 4 \\ 3x + 4y = 2 \end{cases}$

E. 1. Decide whether equivalent form, substitution, or combination would be easiest for solving the system. Then, solve the system.

a. $\begin{cases} 2x + y = 5 \\ 3x - y = 15 \end{cases}$ **b.** $\begin{cases} x + 2y = 5 \\ x - 6y = 11 \end{cases}$ **c.** $\begin{cases} 2x + 6y = 7 \\ 3x - 2y = 5 \end{cases}$

d. $\begin{cases} 2x + y = 5 \\ -4x - 2y = -10 \end{cases}$ **e.** $\begin{cases} x + 2y = 5 \\ 3x + 6y = 15 \end{cases}$

2. For each system in part (1), explain how you decided which solution method to use.

F. Two of the systems in Question E did not have single solutions. How could you have predicted this before you started to solve them?

ACE Homework starts on page 59.

Applications

1. The diagram shows ferry routes between points surrounding a harbor. The distance between grid lines is 500 feet.

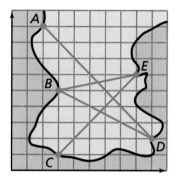

a. Call the bottom left corner on the grid the origin. Match each route with the equation that describes it.

Homework
Help **O**nline
PHSchool.com
For: Help with Exercise 1
Web Code: ape-7401

Route	Equation
A to D	$y = 0.2x + 2{,}200$
B to D	$y = x - 1{,}000$
B to E	$y = -x + 5{,}500$
C to E	$y = -0.5x + 3{,}250$

b. Find the coordinates of the intersection points of the four routes.

Solve each system.

2. $\begin{cases} y = 6x + 4 \\ y = 4x - 2 \end{cases}$
3. $\begin{cases} y = 3x + 7 \\ y = 5x - 7 \end{cases}$
4. $\begin{cases} y = -2x - 9 \\ y = 12x + 19 \end{cases}$

5. $\begin{cases} y = -x + 16 \\ y = -7x - 8 \end{cases}$
6. $\begin{cases} y = 17x - 6 \\ y = 12x + 44 \end{cases}$
7. $\begin{cases} y = -20x + 14 \\ y = -8x - 44 \end{cases}$

Go Online
PHSchool.com

For: Multiple-Choice Skills Practice
Web Code: apa-7454

For Exercises 8–13, write the equation in $y = mx + b$ form.

8. $4x + 6y + 12 = 0$

9. $-7x + 9y + 4 = 0$

10. $-4x - 2y - 6 = 0$

11. $-x + 4y = 0$

12. $2x - 2y + 2 = 0$

13. $25x + 5y - 15 = 0$

14. Write the equations in Exercises 8–13 in $x = ny + c$ form.

Solve the system by using substitution.

15. $\begin{cases} 3x + 4y = 9 \\ y = x - 3 \end{cases}$
16. $\begin{cases} 8x - 14y = 5 \\ x = 3y \end{cases}$
17. $\begin{cases} 12x + 4 = 8y \\ y = x - 7 \end{cases}$

18. $\begin{cases} y = 2x - 1 \\ 4x + 6y = 10 \end{cases}$
19. $\begin{cases} x = 7y - 10 \\ 3x - 2y = 8 \end{cases}$
20. $\begin{cases} 7x - 2y = 5 \\ x = y \end{cases}$

Solve the system by using the combination method.

21. $\begin{cases} 3x - 2y = 12 \\ -3x + 8y = -6 \end{cases}$
22. $\begin{cases} 4x + 9y = 7 \\ 4x - 9y = 9 \end{cases}$
23. $\begin{cases} 12x - 14y = -8 \\ -8x - 14y = 52 \end{cases}$

24. $\begin{cases} 5x + 15y = 10 \\ 5x - 10y = -40 \end{cases}$
25. $\begin{cases} -6x - 4y = 21 \\ -6x + 3y = 0 \end{cases}$
26. $\begin{cases} 2x - 3y = 14 \\ -x + 3y = -6 \end{cases}$

Connections

For Exercises 27–32, solve the equation. Check the solution.

27. $3x + 12 = 24$

28. $-7x - 13 = 15$

29. $8 - 2x = 30$

30. $-7 + 9x = 38$

31. $-4 - 6x = -22$

32. $8x + 17 = -15$

33. In parts (a)–(f), find the value of y when $x = -2$.

   a. $y = 3x - 7$ **b.** $3x - 2y = 10$ **c.** $7x - 4y = 12$

   d. $x = 4y - 2$ **e.** $3 = 2x - y$ **f.** $12 = -3x - 4y$

Write an equation for the line satisfying the given conditions.

34. slope $= -4$, y-intercept $= 3$

35. slope $= \frac{2}{3}$, passing through the point $(3, 4)$

36. slope $= -\frac{3}{4}$, y-intercept $= 2$

37. passes through the points $(5, 4)$ and $(1, 7)$

For Exercises 38–43, identify the slope and y-intercept of the line.

38. $3x + 2y = 4$ **39.** $4x - 8y = 12$ **40.** $x - y = 7$

41. $y = 4x - 8$ **42.** $2y = 4x + 6$ **43.** $y = 9$

44. Two lines can intersect at 0 points (if they are parallel), 1 point, or an infinite number of points (if they are the same). In parts (a)–(d), give all the possible numbers of intersection points for the two figures. Make sketches to illustrate the possibilities.

  a. a circle and a straight line   **b.** two circles

  c. a circle and a triangle   **d.** a circle and a rectangle

45. A chord is a line segment joining two points on a circle. Segment AC in the diagram at the right is a chord.

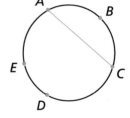

  a. How many chords can be drawn by joining the labeled points on this circle?

  b. How many points inside the circle are intersection points of two or more of the chords from part (a)?

  c. The chords cut the circle into several non-overlapping regions. How many regions are formed?

46. **Multiple Choice** Which point is *not* on the graph of $2x - 5y = 13$?

  A. $(9, 1)$ **B.** $(4, -1)$ **C.** $(0, 3.2)$ **D.** $(6.5, 0)$

47. The cylinder at the right represents an air conditioner unit with a radius of x feet and a height of 2 feet.

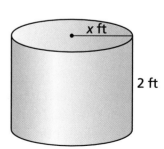

  a. Draw a net for a cover for the air conditioner. (The top and sides need to be covered, but not the bottom.)

  b. Which equation below represents the area of the cover? Which represents the volume? Justify your choices.

  $y = 2\pi x^2$ $y = \pi x^2 + 4\pi x$

  $y = 2x^3$ $y = \pi x(x + 4)$

48. Multiple Choice Kaya wants to fence off part of her yard for a garden. She has 150 feet of fencing. She wants a rectangular garden with a length 1.5 times its width. Which system represents these conditions?

F. $\begin{cases} 1.5w = \ell \\ w + \ell = 150 \end{cases}$ **G.** $\begin{cases} w = 1.5\ell \\ w + \ell = 150 \end{cases}$

H. $\begin{cases} 2w = 3\ell \\ w + \ell = 75 \end{cases}$ **J.** $\begin{cases} 3w = 2\ell \\ 2(w + \ell) = 150 \end{cases}$

49. Multiple Choice Which equation shows how to find one dimension of the garden described in Exercise 48?

A. $2.5w = 150$ **B.** $2.5\ell = 150$

C. $2w = 3(75 - w)$ **D.** $5w = 150$

50. This circle has a radius of 5 meters.

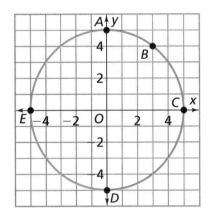

a. Copy and complete this table for the points on the circle.

	A	B	C	D	E
x	0	■	■	■	■
y	5	■	■	■	■

b. On grid paper, sketch the image of the circle after the rule $(x, y) \rightarrow (2x, 2y)$ is applied. Copy and complete this table for the images of points A, B, C, D, and E.

	A'	B'	C'	D'	E'
2x	0	■	■	■	■
2y	10	■	■	■	■

c. Sketch the image of the original circle after the rule $(x, y) \rightarrow (x + 2, y + 2)$ is applied. Copy and complete this table for the images of points A, B, C, D, and E.

	A'	B'	C'	D'	E'
$x + 2$	2	■	■	■	■
$y + 2$	7	■	■	■	■

d. Is the image in part (b) similar to or congruent to the original circle? What about the image in part (c)?

51. Without graphing, decide whether the graph of the equation is a line, a parabola, an exponential curve, an inverse variation curve, or a circle.

a. $2x - 3y = 10$

b. $x^2 + y^2 = 100$

c. $x^2 + x^2 = 100 - y$

d. $\frac{250}{x} = y$

e. $y = 2^x$

f. $y = x^2 - x^2 + x + 100$

g. $xy = 100$

h. $3x + 10 = y$

Tell whether the table represents a linear, quadratic, exponential, or inverse-variation relationship, and write an equation for the relationship.

52.

x	0	1	2	3	4	5	6	7
y	0	−3	−4	−3	0	5	12	21

53.

x	−1	0	1	2	3	4	5	6
y	$\frac{1}{3}$	1	3	9	27	81	243	729

54.

x	1	3	4	6	9	10	12	18
y	2	8	11	17	26	29	35	53

55.

x	1	2	3	4	6	8	10	12
y	12	6	4	3	2	1.5	1.2	1

56. Tell which graph matches the equation.

   a. $y = 2^{x-1}$ **b.** $y = -x^2 + 2x + 8$ **c.** $y = (x + 2)(x - 4)$

   d. $y = 2^x$ **e.** $y = 2x^2$ **f.** $25 = x^2 + y^2$

Graph 1

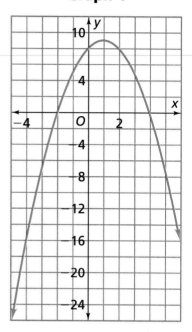

Graph 2

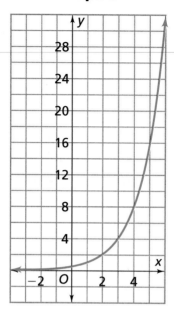

Graph 3

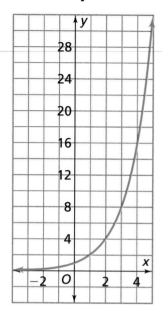

Graph 4

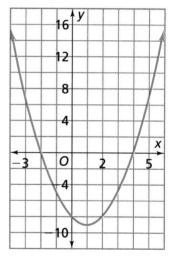

Graph 5

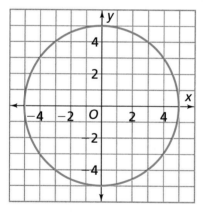

Graph 6

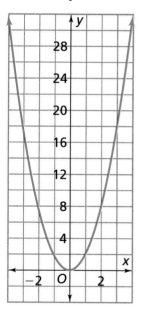

Solve each equation for x.

57. $5(x + 4) - 2x = 5 + 6x + 2x$ **58.** $2(x + 2) - 6x = 6x + 8 - 2x$

59. $x^2 - 7x + 12 = 0$ **60.** $x^2 + 5x - 6 = 0$

Extensions

61. Yolanda and Marissa both babysit. Yolanda charges $5.50 an hour. Marissa charges a base rate of $20, plus $0.50 an hour.

   a. For each girl, write an equation showing how the charge depends on babysitting time.

   b. For what times are Marissa's charges less than Yolanda's?

   c. Is there a time for which Yolanda and Marissa charge the same amount?

62. Raj's age is 1 year less than twice Sarah's age. Toni's age is 2 years less than three times Sarah's age.

   a. Suppose Sarah's age is s years. What is Raj's age in terms of s?

   b. How old is Toni in terms of s?

   c. How old are Raj, Sarah, and Toni if the sum of their ages is 21?

63. Melissa and Trevor sell candy bars to raise money for a class field trip. Trevor sells 1 more than five times as many as Melissa sells. Together they sell 49 candy bars.

   a. Let m be the number of candy bars Melissa sells. Let t be the number of candy bars Trevor sells. Write a linear system to represent this situation.

   b. Solve your system to find the number of candy bars each student sells.

64. Solve each system by using substitution or the combination method. You may get some strange results. In each case, graph the equations and explain what the puzzling results indicate about the solution.

a. $\begin{cases} x - 2y = 3 \\ -3x + 6y = -6 \end{cases}$

b. $\begin{cases} x - y = 4 \\ -x + y = -4 \end{cases}$

c. $\begin{cases} 2x - 3y = 4 \\ 4x - 6y = 7 \end{cases}$

d. $\begin{cases} 4x - 6y = 4 \\ -6x + 9y = -6 \end{cases}$

65. The equation of the line is $y = \frac{4}{3}x$. The equation of the circle is $x^2 + y^2 = 25$.

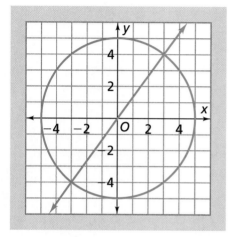

You can find the intersection points by solving the system below. Modify the substitution method to solve the system.

$$\begin{cases} y = \frac{4}{3}x \\ x^2 + y^2 = 25 \end{cases}$$

66. Write a system of the form $\begin{cases} ax + by = c \\ dx + ey = f \end{cases}$ that has the given solution.

a. $(3, 7)$

b. $(-2, 3)$

c. no solutions

67. Consider these equivalent systems.

$$\begin{cases} 2y - 3x = 0 \\ y + x = 75 \end{cases} \quad \text{and} \quad \begin{cases} 2y - 3x = 0 \\ 3y + 3x = 225 \end{cases}$$

a. Do the four equations in these two systems represent four different lines? Explain.

b. Adding the two equations in the second system gives $5y = 225$, or $y = 45$. Does $y = 45$ represent the same line as either equation in the system? Does it have anything in common with the lines in the system?

c. If you add the two equations in the first system, you get $3y - 2x = 75$. Does this equation represent the same line as either equation in the system? Does it have anything in common with the lines in the system?

d. What conjectures can you make about the results of adding any two linear equations? Consider the following questions:

- Will the result be a linear equation?

- Will the graph of the new equation have anything in common with the graphs of the original equation?

Mathematical Reflections 4

In this investigation, you learned several strategies for finding solutions of systems of linear equations. These questions will help you summarize what you have learned.

Think about your answers to these questions. Discuss your ideas with other students and your teacher. Then write a summary of your findings in your notebook.

1. What is the goal in solving a system of linear equations such as the ones below?

$$\begin{cases} y = -3x + 5 \\ y = 4x - 8 \end{cases} \qquad \begin{cases} 3x + y = 5 \\ 2x + 5y = -8 \end{cases}$$

2. Tell which solutions strategy would be most efficient for the system. Give reasons for your choice.

   a. $\begin{cases} y = 4x - 5 \\ y = 1.5x + 8 \end{cases}$

   b. $\begin{cases} x + 3y = 4 \\ x - 5y = 7 \end{cases}$

   c. $\begin{cases} 4x + 3y = 4 \\ x - 5y = 7 \end{cases}$

   d. $\begin{cases} 4x + 3y = 4 \\ 2x - 5y = 7 \end{cases}$

3. How can you check a possible solution of a system of linear equations?

Investigation 5

Linear Inequalities

You have studied many relationships that can be modeled by linear equations. The points that satisfy such relationships fall on a straight line. Points that do not satisfy a linear relationship (do not fall on a line) satisfy a *linear inequality*.

Graphing helps make sense of how solutions to inequalities are related to what you know about solutions to linear equations. The situations in this investigation can be modeled by linear inequalities.

5.1 Limiting Driving Miles

Vince reads that cars are a major source of air pollution. He decides to look at his family's driving habits. They have two vehicles, a car and an SUV. His parents estimate that the family drives about 1,200 miles each month. They decide to try to limit their driving to no more than 1,000 miles each month.

- Find ten possible (*car miles, SUV miles*) pairs that give a total of no more than 1,000 miles.

- One month the family drove the car 500 miles and the SUV 500 miles. Was the total for this month "no more than" 1,000 miles?

Problem 5.1 Graphing "No More Than" Situations

A. On a copy of the grid at the right, plot the ten points you found in the Getting Ready.

B. Look at the pattern of plotted points.

1. Are there other possible (*car miles, SUV miles*) pairs that give a total of no more than 1,000 miles?

2. We refer to a part of a graph or plane as a *region*. Describe where the points are located that represent a total of no more than 1,000 miles.

3. In what region are the points that do not meet this condition located? Give some examples of such points.

Monthly Mileage

C. Suppose Vince's family wants to limit their driving to at most 800 miles per month.

1. Draw a graph of (*car miles, SUV miles*) pairs that meet this condition.

2. Describe the region of the graph that includes all points that represent a total of no more than 800 miles.

D. Write inequalities to model the situations in Questions B and C.

ACE Homework starts on page 78.

5.2 Limiting Carbon Dioxide Emissions

Vince finds out that his family's car emits an average of 0.75 pounds of carbon dioxide (CO_2) per mile. The SUV emits an average of 1.25 pounds of CO_2 per mile.

Getting Ready for Problem 5.2

- Suppose Vince's family wants to limit CO_2 emissions from their car to at most 600 pounds per month. How many miles could they drive their car?

- Suppose Vince's family wants to limit CO_2 emissions from their SUV to at most 600 pounds per month. How many miles could they drive their SUV?

- Suppose they want to limit the total CO_2 emissions from *both* vehicles to at most 600 pounds per month. What are some (*car miles, SUV miles*) pairs that allow them to meet this condition?

Problem 5.2 Solving Linear Inequalities by Graphing

A. Suppose Vince's family wants their total CO_2 emissions to be *exactly* 600 pounds per month.

    1. Give six examples of (*car miles*, *SUV miles*) that give exactly 600 pounds of CO_2 emissions per month.

    2. Write an equation to model this condition.

    3. Graph your equation.

B. Suppose the family wants to limit their total CO_2 emissions to *at most* 600 pounds per month.

    1. Write an inequality that describes the possibilities for the miles they can drive their car if they do not drive their SUV at all.

    2. Write an inequality that describes the possibilities for the miles they can drive their SUV if they do not drive their car at all.

    3. Write an inequality that describes the possibilities for how many miles they can drive their car *and* their SUV.

    4. Draw a graph displaying (*car miles*, *SUV miles*) pairs that satisfy the inequality you wrote in Question B, part (3).

    5. Describe the region of the graph that includes all points that represent a total of no more than 600 pounds of CO_2 emissions.

C. Soo's family has a minivan and a hybrid car. The minivan emits 1.2 pounds of CO_2 per mile. The car emits 0.5 pounds of CO_2 per mile. The family wants to limit their total emissions to at most 500 pounds per month.

    1. The family plans to drive both vehicles. Write an inequality to describe the possibilities for how many miles they can drive each vehicle.

    2. Draw a graph displaying the (*car miles, minivan miles*) pairs that satisfy the inequality you wrote in Question C, part (1).

    3. Describe the region of the graph that includes all points that satisfy the condition.

ACE Homework starts on page 78.

5.3 Graphs of Linear Inequalities

In the last problem, you graphed the (*car miles, SUV miles*) pairs that limited CO_2 emissions to *at most* 600 pounds. To make a correct graph, you also had to consider the fact that the numbers of miles cannot be negative. In other words, all the points are in the first quadrant.

Getting Ready for Problem

- How would the graph of the inequality from Problem 5.2 be different if Vince's family wanted their CO_2 emissions to be *at least* 600 pounds per month?

- How would the graph be different if they wanted to limit their CO_2 emissions to be *less than* 600 pounds per month?

- Is $(-100, 540)$ a possible solution pair if they want to limit their CO_2 emissions to exactly 600 pounds per month? Why or why not?

The inequalities in the next problem are not limited to the first quadrant. As you work on the problem, think about general strategies for graphing inequalities. Notice that shading is used in the graphs to indicate the region in which the points satisfying the inequality lie.

A. Match each inequality with its graph.

1. $y - 3x \geq 6$ **2.** $x - 3y \geq 6$

3. $3x + y \leq 6$ **4.** $x + 3y \leq 6$

5. $y \geq -3x$ **6.** $y \leq -3x$

7. $x \geq -3$ **8.** $y \geq -3$

a.

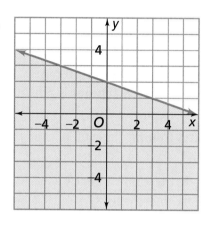

b.

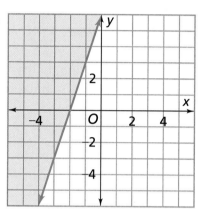

c.

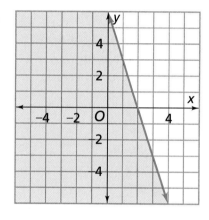

d.

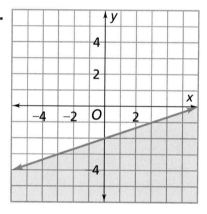

e.

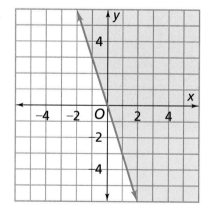

f.

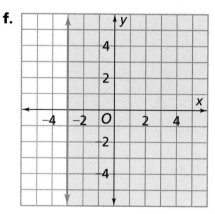

g.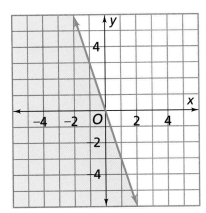

h.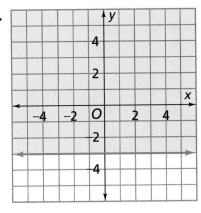

B. Describe your strategies for matching the graphs and inequalities.

C. 1. Rewrite the inequalities in parts (1)–(4) of Question A in either $y \le mx + b$ or $y \ge mx + b$ form.

  2. Compare this form of the inequalities with their graphs. How might this form help you determine which regions should be shaded?

D. Think about the inequality $y < 3x + 6$.

  1. Does the pair $(2, 12)$ satisfy the inequality? Explain.

  2. Below is the graph of $y < 3x + 6$. How is this graph different from the graphs in Question A? What is the reason for this difference?

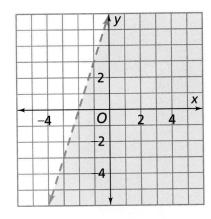

ACE Homework starts on page 78.

Vince's family determines that, on average, they drive their SUV more than twice as many miles as they drive their car. Vince writes

$$s > 2c$$

where s represents the number of miles they drive the SUV, and c represents the number of miles they drive the car.

Why does this inequality represent the situation?

The family agrees to limit the total CO_2 emissions to less than 600 pounds per month. Recalling that the car emits 0.75 pounds of CO_2 per mile and the SUV emits 1.25 pounds of CO_2 per mile, Vince writes

$$0.75c + 1.25s < 600$$

Together, the two inequalities form a **system of linear inequalities.**

$$\begin{cases} s > 2c \\ 0.75c + 1.25s < 600 \end{cases}$$

Why does this system of linear inequalities describe the situation?

How would the system change if Vince's family agrees to total emissions that are at most *600 pounds rather than* less than *600 pounds?*

Problem 5.4 Systems of Linear Inequalities

A. 1. Graph the inequality $0.75c + 1.25s < 600$. This graph shows the possible (*car miles, SUV miles*) pairs for which the total CO_2 emissions are less than 600 pounds per month.

  2. On the same axis, graph the inequality $s > 2c$. This graph shows the possible (*car miles, SUV miles*) pairs for which the number of SUV miles is more than twice the number of car miles.

  3. Where on the grid are the points that satisfy both conditions?

B. Nancy has a car and an SUV with the same emissions as Vince's family's vehicles. She will drive her car at least three times as much as her SUV. She wants to limit the total CO_2 emissions to at most 400 pounds per month. She draws the following graph.

Limiting CO$_2$ Emissions

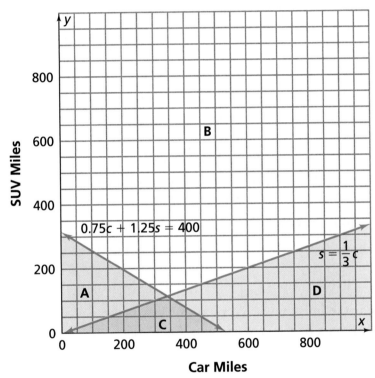

  1. Describe what information the points in each region represent in terms of the situation.

  2. In which region(s) are the points that satisfy both conditions?

ACE Homework starts on page 78.

Applications

1. Ana has a car and a motorcycle. She wants to limit the combined mileage of the two vehicles to at most 500 miles per month.

   a. Write an inequality to model this condition.

   b. Draw a graph of all the (*car miles, motorcycle miles*) pairs that satisfy this condition.

   c. What strategy did you use to draw your graph?

2. A developer plans to build housing for at least 50 families. He wants to build some single-family houses and some four-family apartment buildings.

   a. Write an inequality to model this situation.

   b. Draw a graph to display the possible pairs of numbers of single-family houses and apartments the developer can build.

3. The Simon family's car emits 0.75 pounds of CO_2 per mile. Their minivan emits 1.2 pounds of CO_2 per mile. The Simons want to limit their emissions to at most 400 pounds per month.

   a. Write an inequality to model this condition.

   b. Draw a graph of all the (*car miles, minivan miles*) pairs that satisfy this condition.

4. Math Club members are selling games and puzzles. They make a profit of $10 on a game and $8 on a puzzle. They would like to make at least $200.

   a. What are some possibilities for the number of games and puzzles the Math Club can sell to reach its goal?

   b. Write an inequality to model this situation.

   c. Draw a graph of all the (*number of games, number of puzzles*) pairs that meet the goal.

For Exercises 5–7, find three (*x, y*) pairs that satisfy the inequality and three (*x, y*) pairs that do not. Then, draw a graph showing all the solutions.

   5. $x - 4y \geq 8$ **6.** $4x - y \leq 8$ **7.** $x - 4y < 8$

8. In parts (a)–(d), graph the inequality.

    a. $x \geq 8 + 4y$ **b.** $x \geq 4$ **c.** $y < -2$ **d.** $2x - 4y \geq 8$

    e. What strategies did you use to draw the graphs?

9. Math Club members want to advertise their fundraiser each week in the school paper. They know that a front-page ad is more effective than an ad inside the paper. They have a $30 advertising budget. It costs $2 for each front-page ad and $1 for each inside-page ad. The club wants to advertise at least 20 times.

Homework Help Online
PHSchool.com
For: Help with Exercise 9
Web Code: ape-7509

    a. What are some possibilities for the numbers of front-page ads and inside-page ads the club can place?

    b. Write a system of linear inequalities to model this situation.

    c. Graph your system of inequalities. Be sure it is clear which region shows the solution.

10. The science club can spend at most $400 on a field trip to a dinosaur exhibit. It has enough chaperones to allow at most 100 students to go on the trip. The exhibit costs $3.00 for students 12 years and under and $6.00 for students over 12.

    a. How many students 12 years and under can go if no students over 12 go?

    b. How many students over 12 can go if no students 12 or under go?

    c. Write a system of linear inequalities to model this situation.

    d. Graph your system of inequalities. Be sure it is clear which region shows the solution.

Find three (x, y) pairs that satisfy the system of inequalities and three (x, y) pairs that do not. Then, draw a graph showing all the solutions.

11. $\begin{cases} 4x + 6y \leq 24 \\ x + 5y \leq 10 \end{cases}$ **12.** $\begin{cases} 2x - y \leq 4 \\ -x + y > -1 \end{cases}$

Connections

For Exercises 13 and 14, use a graph to solve the system of equations.

13. $\begin{cases} x + y = 18 \\ 3x - y = 10 \end{cases}$

14. $\begin{cases} 80x + 40y = 400 \\ 20x + 80y = 420 \end{cases}$

Go Online
PHSchool.com

For: Multiple-Choice Skills
Practice
Web Code: apa-7554

15. Multiple Choice What is the greatest whole-number value of x for which $4x < 14$?

A. 11   **B.** 3   **C.** 4   **D.** 14

16. The parks commission in the town of Euclid decides to build a triangular park with one side that is 400 feet long.

     a. What are some possibilities for the lengths of the other sides? Explain.

     b. The city planner writes these inequalities.

$$x + y > 400 \qquad x + 400 > y \qquad y + 400 > x$$

The variables x and y represent possible lengths for the other two sides of the triangle. Why do these inequalities make sense? Why does the planner need all three inequalities to describe the situation?

     c. Graph the three inequalities from part (b) on the same axes. Describe the region that represents the possible lengths for the other sides of the park.

     d. Give a pair of lengths for the other two sides of the park. Explain how to find this answer by using your graph in part (c).

     e. Give a possible pair of lengths that could not be the other two side lengths. Explain how to find this answer using your graph in part (c).

17. Robin wants to make a smoothie out of milk, strawberry yogurt, and ice. She finds this nutrition information:

- A cup of yogurt has 190 calories and 13 grams of protein.
- A cup of milk has 100 calories and 9 grams of protein.
- Ice has no calories and no protein.

Robin wants her smoothie to have about 335 calories and 24 grams of protein.

     a. Write a system of equations to model the conditions for Robin's smoothie.

b. Graph the equations from part (a).

c. How much yogurt and milk should Robin use to make her smoothie? Explain.

18. Kadian also wants a milk-and-yogurt smoothie. She wants her smoothie to have *at most* 400 calories and *at least* 20 grams of protein.

   a. Write a system of inequalities to model the conditions for Kadian's smoothie.

   b. Graph the system of inequalities. Be sure it is clear which region shows the solution.

   c. Use your graph for part (b) to describe some combinations of milk and yogurt amounts Kadian could use for her smoothie.

Extensions

19. Carolina wants to make a smoothie out of milk, strawberry yogurt, and ice. (See the protein and calorie information in Exercise 17.) She finds this additional information:

   ● A cup of milk has 306 milligrams of calcium.

   ● A cup of yogurt has 415 milligrams of calcium.

   ● Ice has no calcium.

   She wants her smoothie to have at most 400 calories, at least 20 grams of protein, and at least 700 mg of calcium.

   a. Write a system of inequalities to model the conditions for Carolina's smoothie.

   b. Graph the system of inequalities. Be sure it is clear which region shows the solution.

   c. What are some (*milk*, *yogurt*) combinations Carolina might choose?

20. Suppose you are making a smoothie. What nutrients are important to you? Would you like your smoothie to be a good source of vitamin C, calcium, fiber, protein, or calories? What ingredients would you like in your smoothie? Create guidelines for your smoothie. Using nutritional information about the ingredients, write a system of inequalities to help you decide how much of each item to include.

Mathematical Reflections 5

In this investigation, you explored situations that could be modeled with linear inequalities. You also solved systems of linear inequalities to find values that satisfied several conditions. These questions will help you to summarize what you have learned.

Think about your answers to these questions. Discuss your ideas with other students and your teacher. Then write a summary of your findings in your notebook.

1. Suppose you are given one linear inequality. How can you use a graph to find solutions to the inequality?

2. Suppose you are given a system of linear inequalities. How can you use graphs to find solutions to the system of inequalities?

Looking Back and Looking Ahead

In this unit, you extended your ability to use algebraic equations and inequalities to describe and reason about geometric shapes. You also learned how to use geometric patterns to reason about systems of linear equations and inequalities.

Go Online
PHSchool.com
For: Vocabulary Review Puzzle
Web Code: apj-7051

Use Your Understanding:
Connecting Geometry and Algebra

Demonstrate your understanding of the relationships between algebra and coordinate geometry by solving the following problems.

1. The equations for the two circles below are $(x + 3)^2 + y^2 = 25$ and $(x - 3)^2 + y^2 = 25$.

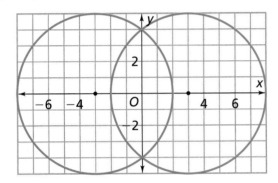

a. Tell which equation represents each circle. Explain.

b. Estimate the coordinates of the intersection points. Check by substituting the coordinates into the equations.

c. Show that $(-7, 3)$ is on the left circle in two ways:
  - Show that the coordinates satisfy the given equation.
  - Show geometrically that the point is 5 units from the center.

d. Show that $(-1, -3)$ is on the right circle in the two ways described in part (c).

e. Write an inequality describing the interior of each circle. Find two points in the interior of each circle and check that they satisfy the appropriate inequality.

2. The figure below is a rectangle.

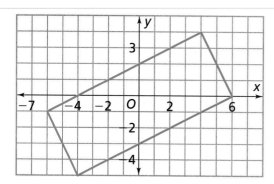

a. Use slopes to show that opposite sides are parallel.

b. Use slopes to show that adjacent sides are perpendicular.

c. Find the coordinates of the midpoints of the sides.

d. What kind of quadrilateral is formed when you connect the midpoints in order? Explain.

3. To encourage attendance to Talent Night, a school offers discounted tickets to students wearing school colors. Full-price tickets cost $9 and discounted tickets cost only $6. In all, 250 tickets are sold for a total of $2,100.

a. Let x represent the number of full-price tickets sold. Let y represent the number of discounted tickets sold. Write a system of equations to represent the information about the ticket sales.

b. Solve the system of equations in three ways.

- Use a graph to estimate.

- Use substitution.

- Use the combination method.

4. The Pep Club sells popcorn and juice at basketball games. The club earns $1.20 for each bag of popcorn and $0.80 for each cup of juice.

a. The club's goal is to earn at least $50 at each game. Let x represent the number of bags of popcorn sold, and let y represent the number of cups of juice sold. Write an inequality to represent the club's goal.

b. Find at least five (x, y) pairs that satisfy the inequality in part (a). Sketch a graph that represents all the solutions.

c. The club must buy supplies. They spend $0.15 for each bag and $0.20 for each cup. Suppose the club can spend at most $15 on supplies for each game. Write an inequality for this constraint.

d. Find at least five (x, y) pairs that satisfy the inequality in part (c). Sketch a graph of the inequality on the same axes you used in part (b). Label the region that shows the (x, y) pairs that satisfy both constraints.

Explain Your Reasoning

In this unit, you began by using algebraic equations and inequalities to describe key points on geometric figures.

5. Describe how you can write an equation or inequality that describes the coordinates of the points on each figure.

a. a circle of radius r centered at the origin $(0, 0)$

b. the interior of a circle of radius r centered at the origin $(0, 0)$

6. Describe how you can use the coordinates of the vertices of a quadrilateral to verify each of the following.

a. opposite sides are parallel

b. adjacent sides are perpendicular

7. Describe how to use coordinates of the endpoints of a segment to find the coordinates of the midpoint.

You also used graphs and algebraic reasoning to solve systems of linear equations and inequalities.

8. Consider systems of linear equations in the form $\begin{cases} ax + by = c \\ dx + ey = f. \end{cases}$

    a. What graph shape do you expect when the solutions of each equation are plotted separately?

    b. How will the solution to the system be shown when the two equations are graphed on the same axis?

    c. What numbers of solutions are possible for a system in this form? How are these possibilities shown by the graphs?

    d. How can you solve such a system by using substitution?

    e. How can you solve such a system by using the combination method?

    f. How can you check the solution of a system?

9. a. What will a graph of a linear inequality in the form $ax + by < c$ look like?

    b. What might a graph of a system of *two* linear inequalities of the form $ax + by < c$ look like?

Look Ahead

In future mathematical studies, you will extend your understanding and skill in working with algebraic equations that represent geometric shapes and their properties. You will also learn more ways to use graphs and drawings to illustrate conditions and solutions in algebraic problems.

C

chord A line segment with endpoints on a circle. Segments CD and AB in the diagram below are chords.

cuerda Segmento de recta cuyos extremos están sobre un círculo. Los segmentos CD y AB en el diagrama de abajo son cuerdas.

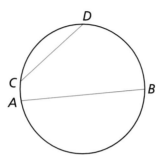

circle A geometric figure consisting of all points P that are a fixed distance r from a point C, called the center of the circle.

círculo Figura geométrica que consiste en que todos los puntos de P están a una distancia fija r del punto C, llamado centro del círculo.

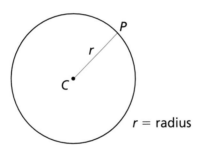

r = radius

L

linear equation in standard form The form $ax + by = c$ of a linear equation. Each side of the equation is a linear expression. The equation $6x + 3y = 12$ is in standard form. Although the slope-intercept form, $y = mx + b$, is common and useful, it is not generally considered the "standard form."

Ecuación lineal en forma general La forma $ax + by = c$ de una ecuación lineal. La ecuación $6x + 3y = 12$ está en forma general. Aunque la forma pendiente-intercepto, $y = mx + b$, es común y útil, por lo general no se considera "la forma general".

linear inequality A mathematical sentence, such as $ax + by + c < dx + ey + f$, which expresses a relationship of inequality between two quantities, each of which is a linear expression. For example, $y < -2x + 4$, and $6x + 3y \geq 12$ are linear inequalities, as are $x < 3$ and $2x + 3 < 7x$.

desigualdad lineal Enunciado matemático, como $3x + 22 < 8x + 7$ ó $3x + 4y \geq 12$ que expresa la relación de desigualdad entre dos cantidades, con cada cantidad como función lineal de una o más variables.

midpoint A point on a line segment that is equidistant from the endpoints of the segment. Point M is the midpoint of $\overline{AB}$.

punto medio Punto en un segmento de recta que es equidistante de los extremos del segmento. El punto M es el punto medio de $\overline{AB}$.

system of linear equations Two or more linear equations that represent constraints on the variables used. A solution of a system of equations is a pair of values that satisfies all the equations in the system. For example, the ordered pair $(1, 2)$ is the solution of the system because it satisfies both equations.

$$\begin{cases} 6x + 3y = 12 \\ -2x + y = 0 \end{cases}$$

sistema de ecuaciones lineales Combinación de dos o más ecuaciones lineales. Una solución de un sistema de ecuaciones es un par de valores que satisface todas las ecuaciones del sistema. Por ejemplo, el par ordenado $(1, 2)$ es la solución del sistema porque satisface ambas ecuaciones.

$$\begin{cases} 6x + 3y = 12 \\ -2x + y = 0 \end{cases}$$

system of linear inequalities Two or more linear inequalities that represent constraints on the variables used. A solution of a system of inequalities is a pair of values that satisfies all the inequalities in the system. The solution of the system

$$\begin{cases} 6x + 3y < 12 \\ -2x + y > 0 \end{cases}$$

is indicated by region A in the graph below. All the points in this region satisfy *both* inequalities. The points in region B satisfy $6x + 3y < 12$, but *not* $-2x + y > 0$. The points in region C satisfy $-2x + y > 0$, but *not* $6x + 3y < 12$. The points in the unshaded region do not satisfy either inequality.

sistema de desigualdades lineales Combinación de dos o más desigualdades. Una solución de un sistema de desigualdades es un par de valores que satisface todas las desigualdades en el sistema. La solución del sistema

$$\begin{cases} 6x + 3y < 12 \\ -2x + y > 0 \end{cases}$$

está indicada por la región A en la gráfica de abajo. Todos los puntos en esta región satisfacen *ambas* desigualdades. Los puntos en la región B satisfacen $6x + 3y < 12$, pero *no* $-2x + y > 0$. Los puntos en la región C satisfacen $-2x + y > 0$, pero *no* $6x + 3y < 12$. Los puntos en la región sin sombrear no satisfacen ninguna desigualdad.

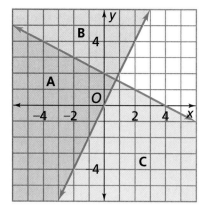

Index

Acting it out, 11, 47

Area model, 16, 33
 $ax + by = c$ form, 38–40, 45, 47, 51, 54, 87
 changing to $y = mx + b$ form, 39–40, 51

Bar graph, making, 18

Calculator, *see* **Graphing calculator**

Centroid, 50

Check answers, 7, 10, 29, 58, 68, 83, 86
 ACE, 12–13, 19–20, 31, 35, 43, 50, 60

Check for reasonableness, 7–8, 10, 29, 58, 68, 83, 86
 ACE, 12–13, 19–20, 31, 35, 43, 50, 60

Chord, 61, 87

Circle, 5–8, 23, 83, 85, 87
 ACE, 12–13, 15, 17–20, 32–33, 61–64, 66
 equation for, 6–8

Circle graph, making, 18

Combination method, solving with, 57–58, 60, 66, 84, 86

Concrete model, *see* **Model**

Coordinate graph, 5–7, 9–11, 24–25, 29, 36, 38, 51–52, 56, 58, 69–70, 72–75, 77, 82–86, 88
 ACE, 12–14, 19–21, 30–31, 34–35, 41–45, 48–49, 62, 64, 66–67, 78–81
 estimating with, 25, 31, 34, 42–43, 49, 83–84
 intersection points on, 52–53, 59, 66, 83
 making, 11, 14, 20, 29–31, 34–35, 38, 41–45, 48–49, 56, 58, 66, 70, 72, 77–81, 84–85

Coordinate grid, *see* **Coordinate graph**

Crop circle, *see* **Circle**

Diagram, 8, 10, 15, 17–18, 20, 22, 46, 50, 61–63, 87–88
 making, 61–63

Equation, *see also* **Linear equation**
 for circles, 6–8
 for polygons, 8–11
 writing, 7, 12–13, 16, 18, 25, 30, 32, 34, 39–46, 49–50, 53–54, 56, 58, 60–61, 63, 65–66, 70, 72, 75, 78–81, 83–85

Equivalent forms, solving with, 54–56, 57–58

Estimating, with a graph, 25, 31, 34, 42–43, 49, 83–84

Glossary, 87–88

Graph, *see also* **Coordinate graph**
 bar, 18
 circle, 18
 coordinate, *see* Coordinate graph
 of linear inequalities, 69–75
 of linear systems, 25

Graphing calculator, using, 29, 39, 45

Inequality, *see also* **Linear inequality,** 7

Interpreting data
 area model, 16, 33
 bar graph, 18
 circle graph, 18
 coordinate graph, 5–7, 9–14, 19–21, 24–25, 29–31, 34–36, 38, 41–45, 48–49, 51–52, 56, 58, 62, 64, 66–67, 69–70, 72–75, 77–86, 88
 diagram, 8, 10, 15, 17–18, 20, 22, 46, 50, 61–63, 87–88
 map, 59
 net, 48, 61
 number line, 28–29, 31, 35, 46
 picture, 5
 table, 18, 21, 34–35, 53, 62–63
 three–dimensional model, 61

Intersection points, 52–53, 59, 66, 83

Investigations
 Equations for Circles and Polygons, 5–23
 Equations With Two or More Variables, 37–51

Linear Equations and Inequalities, 24–36
Linear Inequalities, 69–82
Solving Systems of Linear Equations Symbolically, 52–68

Justify answer, 6–8, 23, 25, 27–29, 37–38, 41, 54, 56–58, 75, 83–86
 ACE, 12–13, 15, 19, 22, 44, 46, 49–50, 61, 66–67, 80–81

Justify method, 26, 29, 40, 53–58, 68, 75, 78–80

Linear equation, 4, 24–82
 ACE, 12–22, 30–35, 42–50, 59–67, 78–81
 changing between $y = mx + b$ and $ax + by = c$ form, 39–40, 51
 slope-intercept form of ($y = mx + b$), 39–40, 45, 51, 53–56, 60, 87
 standard form of ($ax + by = c$), 38–40, 45, 47, 51, 54, 87
 with two or more variables, 37–51
 $x = ky + c$ form, 54–55

Linear inequality, 4, 69–82, 87
 ACE, 78–81
 definition, 69, 87
 graph of, 69–75
 solving by graphing, 69–75

Linear system, *see* **System of linear equations**

Looking Back and Looking Ahead: Unit Review, 83–86

Manipulatives
 folding paper, 11
 tracing cans, 47

Map, 59

Mathematical Highlights, 4

Mathematical Reflections, 23, 36, 51, 68, 82

Median, 50

Midpoint, 10–11, 15, 18–20, 22, 23, 34, 50, 84–85, 88
 finding, 10–11, 23

Acknowledgments

Team Credits

The people who made up the **Connected Mathematics 2** team—representing editorial, editorial services, design services, and production services—are listed below. Bold type denotes core team members.

Leora Adler, Judith Buice, Kerry Cashman, Patrick Culleton, Sheila DeFazio, Richard Heater, **Barbara Hollingdale, Jayne Holman,** Karen Holtzman, **Etta Jacobs,** Christine Lee, Carolyn Lock, Catherine Maglio, **Dotti Marshall,** Rich McMahon, Eve Melnechuk, Kristin Mingrone, Terri Mitchell, **Marsha Novak,** Irene Rubin, Donna Russo, Robin Samper, Siri Schwartzman, **Nancy Smith,** Emily Soltanoff, **Mark Tricca,** Paula Vergith, Roberta Warshaw, Helen Young

Additional Credits

Diana Bonfilio, Mairead Reddin, Michael Torocsik, nSight, Inc.

Technical Illustration

WestWords, Inc.

Cover Design

tom white.images

Photos

2, Richard Haynes; **3,** Janet Foster/Masterfile; **5,** Topham/The Image Works; **7,** Richard Haynes; **11,** Richard Haynes; **16,** Richard Haynes; **24,** Spencer Ainsley/The Image Works; **27,** Richard Haynes; **33,** Arthur Tilley/Getty Images, Inc.; **37,** Richard Haynes; **40,** Jeff Greenberg/PhotoEdit; **42,** Siri Schwartzman; **49,** Yellow Dog Productions/Getty Images, Inc.; **52,** Bill Barley/SuperStock; **55,** Richard Haynes; **59,** Patrick Ben Luke Syder/Lonely Planet Images; **62,** David Grossman/The Image Works; **65,** Kwame Zikomo/SuperStock; **69,** Steve Craft/Masterfile; **73,** Peter Hvizdak/The Image Works; **76,** Chuck Savage/Corbis; **79,** Park Street/PhotoEdit; **84,** Dennis MacDonald/PhotoEdit

Connected Mathematics 2

Samples and Populations

Data and Statistics

Glenda Lappan

James T. Fey

William M. Fitzgerald

Susan N. Friel

Elizabeth Difanis Phillips

PEARSON

Prentice
Hall

Boston, Massachusetts
Upper Saddle River, New Jersey

Samples and Populations

Data and Statistics

A radio talk-show host asked her listeners to call in to express their opinions about a local election. Could the results of this survey be used to describe the opinions of all the show's listeners?

Yung-nan takes 150 beans from a jar of beans, marks them with a red dot, and mixes them with the unmarked beans. Then she scoops out a few beans and counts the number of marked ones. Will this method help her predict the total number of beans in the jar?

How is it possible to estimate the deer population of a state, or even of a small part of the state?

The United States Census attempts to gather information from every household in the United States. Gathering, organizing, and analyzing data from such a large population is expensive and time-consuming. In most studies of large populations, data are gathered from a *sample*, or portion, of the population. The data from the sample are then used to make predictions or to draw conclusions about the full population.

Sampling is an important tool in statistics and data analysis. Understanding how to select samples and use them to make predictions will help you answer questions like those on the previous page.

Mathematical Highlights

Data and Statistics

In *Samples and Populations,* you will explore ways of collecting and analyzing data.

You will learn how to

- Use the process of statistical investigation to explore problems
- Use information from samples to draw conclusions about populations
- Explore the influence of sample size on the variability of the distribution of sample means or medians
- Evaluate sampling plans
- Use probability to select random samples from populations
- Compare sample distributions using measures of center (mean, median), measures of variability (range, minimum and maximum data values, percentiles), and displays that group data (histograms, box-and-whisker plots)
- Explore relationships between paired values of numerical variables

As you work on the problems in this unit, ask yourself questions about situations that involve analyzing data using samples.

What is the population?

What is the sample?

What kinds of comparisons and relationships can I explore using data from the sample?

Can I use my results to make predictions or generalizations about the population?

Investigation 1

Comparing Data Sets

American shoppers have a great variety of products from which to choose. Many people turn to information in consumer surveys and product comparisons to help make decisions.

A consumer magazine rated 37 varieties of peanut butter. Each peanut butter was assigned a quality rating from 1 to 100 points. A panel of trained tasters made two general statements about quality:

- Peanut butters with higher quality ratings were smooth; had a sweet, nutty flavor; and were not overly dry or sticky.

- Peanut butters with lower quality ratings were not very nutty, had small bits of peanuts, or had a burnt or slightly rancid taste.

The article also gave the sodium content and price per 3-tablespoon serving for each type. Peanut butters were classified according to three attributes: natural or regular, creamy or chunky, and salted or unsalted. The data are presented in the table on the next page. A fourth attribute, name brand or store brand, has been added to the data.

Peanut Butter Comparison

	Peanut Butter	Quality Rating	Sodium per Serving (mg)	Price per Serving (cents)	Regular/ Natural	Creamy/ Chunky	Salted/ Unsalted	Name Brand/ Store Brand
1.	Smucker's Natural	71	15	27	natural	creamy	unsalted	name
2.	Deaf Smith Arrowhead	69	0	32	natural	creamy	unsalted	name
3.	Adams 100% Natural	60	0	26	natural	creamy	unsalted	name
4.	Adams	60	168	26	natural	creamy	salted	name
5.	Laura Scudder's All Natural	57	165	26	natural	creamy	salted	name
6.	Country Pure Brand	52	225	21	natural	creamy	salted	store
7.	Hollywood Natural	34	15	32	natural	creamy	unsalted	name
8.	Smucker's Natural	89	15	27	natural	chunky	unsalted	name
9.	Adams 100% Natural	69	0	26	natural	chunky	unsalted	name
10.	Deaf Smith Arrowhead	69	0	32	natural	chunky	unsalted	name
11.	Country Pure Brand	67	105	21	natural	chunky	salted	store
12.	Laura Scudder's All Natural	63	165	24	natural	chunky	salted	name
13.	Smucker's Natural	57	188	26	natural	chunky	salted	name
14.	Health Valley 100%	40	3	34	natural	chunky	unsalted	name
15.	Jif	76	220	22	regular	creamy	salted	name
16.	Skippy	60	225	19	regular	creamy	salted	name
17.	Kroger	54	240	14	regular	creamy	salted	store
18.	NuMade	43	187	20	regular	creamy	salted	store
19.	Peter Pan	40	225	21	regular	creamy	salted	name
20.	Peter Pan	35	3	22	regular	creamy	unsalted	name
21.	A & P	34	225	12	regular	creamy	salted	store
22.	Food Club	33	225	17	regular	creamy	salted	store
23.	Pathmark	31	255	9	regular	creamy	salted	store
24.	Lady Lee	23	225	16	regular	creamy	salted	store
25.	Albertsons	23	225	17	regular	creamy	salted	store
26.	ShurFine	11	225	16	regular	creamy	salted	store
27.	Jif	83	162	23	regular	chunky	salted	name
28.	Skippy	83	211	21	regular	chunky	salted	name
29.	Food Club	54	195	17	regular	chunky	salted	store
30.	Kroger	49	255	14	regular	chunky	salted	store
31.	A & P	46	225	11	regular	chunky	salted	store
32.	Peter Pan	45	180	22	regular	chunky	salted	name
33.	NuMade	40	208	21	regular	chunky	salted	store
34.	Lady Lee	34	225	16	regular	chunky	salted	store
35.	Albertsons	31	225	17	regular	chunky	salted	store
36.	Pathmark	29	210	9	regular	chunky	salted	store
37.	ShurFine	26	195	16	regular	chunky	salted	store

SOURCE: *Consumer Reports* and *Workshop Statistics: Student Activity Guide*

- Who might be interested in the results of this peanut butter study?
- What questions about peanut butter can be answered with these data?
- What questions about peanut butter cannot be answered with these data?

1.1 From Line Plots to Histograms

In this problem, you will look at the **distribution** of quality ratings for the regular peanut butters. You will use measures of center, minimum and maximum values, range, the shape of the data, and where the data cluster to describe the distribution. Locate quality ratings in the table.

Did You Know?

Arachibutyrophobia (uh rak ih byoo tih ruh FOH bee uh) is the fear of getting peanut butter stuck to the roof of your mouth!

A. Each dot on the line plot below represents the quality rating of one regular peanut butter from the table.

Regular Peanut Butter Quality Ratings

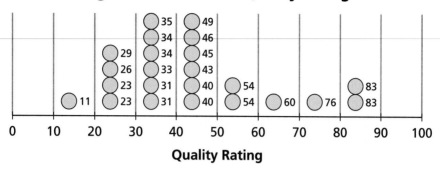

Quality Rating

1. Which interval (or intervals) includes the most quality ratings?

2. Look at the interval marked 40 to 50. What is the lowest rating in this interval? What is the highest rating in this interval?

3. Suppose you want to add a quality rating of 50 to the plot. In which interval would you put this value? Explain.

4. Suppose you want to add a quality rating of 59. In which interval would you put this value? Explain.

5. What do you think is the typical rating for regular peanut butters? Explain.

B. In the plot below, the collection of dots in the intervals have been used to make bars that show the number of data values in each interval.

Regular Peanut Butter Quality Ratings

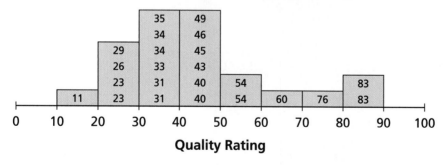

Quality Rating

1. To which interval would you add each of these quality ratings: 93, 69, 10, and 57?

2. How would you change the bar in an interval to show the addition of a new quality rating?

C. The **histogram** below shows the same distribution as the interval bars with numerical values in Question B. A frequency axis has been added to the side of the plot.

For: Stat Tools
Visit: PHSchool.com
Web Code: apd-8101

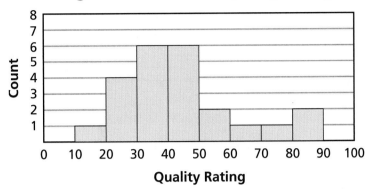

Regular Peanut Butter Quality Ratings

1. How is this histogram the same as the plot in Question B? How is it different?

2. Why is a scale on the vertical axis needed? What information does the scale provide?

3. To which interval would you add each of these quality ratings: 93, 69, 10, and 57? How would you change each bar to show a new quality rating?

D. Describe the distribution of quality ratings for the regular peanut butters. Use information from both the histogram and the table. Include the following in your description:

- the minimum and maximum values
- the range of the data and any outliers
- intervals where data cluster
- the shape of the distribution
- related statistics, such as the mean and median

ACE Homework starts on page 17.

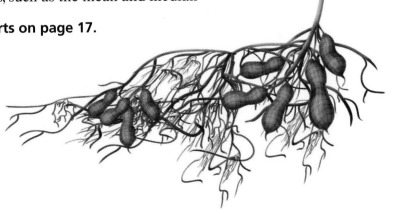

1.2 Using Histograms

In this problem, you will consider quality ratings for the natural peanut butters, which have no preservatives. By comparing histograms, you can decide whether natural or regular peanut butters have higher quality ratings.

Getting Ready for Problem 1.2

This list summarizes how to examine and describe a data distribution.

- *Read the data.* Identify individual values, the minimum and maximum data values, and the range.

- *Read between the data.* Identify intervals where the data cluster or there are gaps in the data.

- *Read beyond the data.* Describe the shape of the distribution. Identify statistics, such as the mean and median, and relate them to the shape of the distribution.

Look back at the way you described the distribution of quality ratings in Problem 1.1. Did you consider all the things mentioned above?

Problem 1.2 Using Histograms

A. 1. Make a histogram of the quality ratings for natural peanut butters. Use 10-point interval widths.

   2. Describe the distribution of quality ratings.

B. 1. The histogram in Problem 1.1 shows the quality ratings for the regular peanut butters. The interval width is 10 quality points. Make a new histogram of the quality ratings for regular peanut butters. This time, use interval widths of 5.

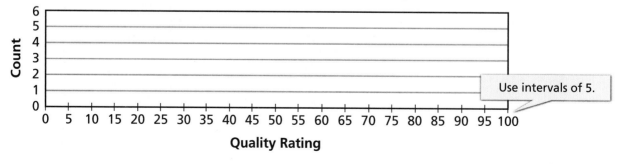

Regular Peanut Butter Quality Ratings

Use intervals of 5.

2. Make another histogram of the same data. Use interval widths of either 2 or 15.

3. a. Compare the histogram from Problem 1.1 and the histograms you made in parts (1) and (2). What is the same about the three histograms? What is different?

   b. What are the reasons for the differences in the histograms?

   c. Would your decision about what is a typical quality rating be affected by the histogram you used? Explain.

4. This rule of thumb can help you choose a good interval width for a histogram:

   If possible, use a width that gives 8–10 bars.

   Using this rule of thumb, which of the three histograms is best for representing the distribution of quality ratings for the regular peanut butters?

C. When the data sets you want to compare have different numbers of entries, you can change the vertical axis to show the percent of all values that lie in each interval. This is called a *relative frequency histogram*.

1. Make two new histograms like the one started below, one for natural peanut butters and one for regular peanut butters. Because 1 out of 14 of the natural peanut butters has a quality rating between 80 and 90 points, the relative frequency for this interval is 7%.

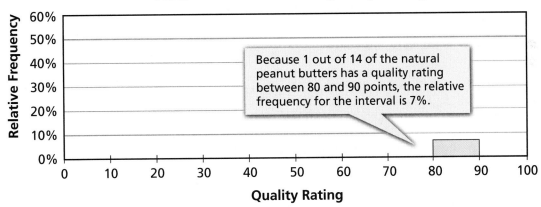

Natural Peanut Butter Quality Ratings

Because 1 out of 14 of the natural peanut butters has a quality rating between 80 and 90 points, the relative frequency for the interval is 7%.

2. Do natural peanut butters or regular peanut butters have higher quality ratings? Use the histograms and other relevant information to justify your choice.

ACE **Homework starts on page 17.**

Box-and-whisker plots, or *box plots*, are useful for showing the distribution of values in a data set. The box plot below is an example.

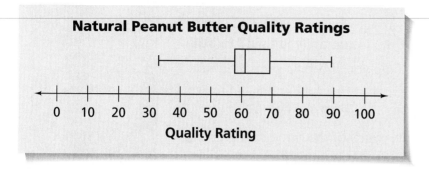

A box plot is constructed from the **five-number summary** of the data, which includes the minimum value, maximum value, median, lower quartile, and upper quartile.

When a set of data is ordered from least to greatest, the **lower quartile** is the median of the values to the left of the median. The **upper quartile** is the median of the values to the right of the median.

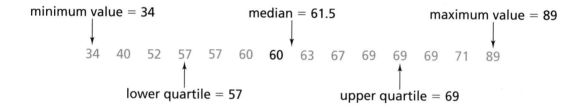

The box plot below shows how the five-number summary corresponds to the features of the box plot.

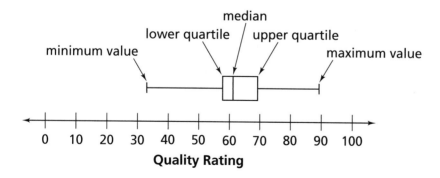

The five-number summary divides a data distribution into four parts.

About what percent of the data values fall in each of the following intervals?

- before the median
- after the median
- in the box (between the upper and lower quartiles)
- before the upper quartile
- after the upper quartile
- before the lower quartile
- after the lower quartile
- between the median and the upper quartile
- between the median and the lower quartile

What do you think the term *quartile* means?

You can compare distributions by displaying two or more box plots on the same scale.

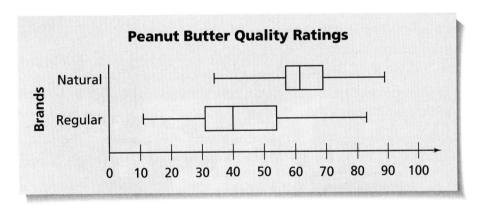

Many people consider *both* quality and price when deciding which products to buy. The box plots at the right show the distributions of per-serving prices for natural peanut butters and regular peanut butters.

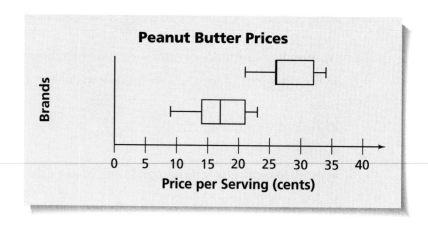

Peanut Butter Prices

Brands

Price per Serving (cents)

Problem 1.3 Box-and-Whisker Plots

In the Peanut Butter Comparisons table (before Problem 1.1), refer to the column that gives the price per serving.

A. 1. Calculate the five-number summary for the prices of the natural peanut butters.

    2. Calculate the five-number summary for the prices of the regular peanut butters.

    3. Which box plot above represents the distribution of prices for natural peanut butters and which represents the distribution of prices for regular peanut butters?

    4. How do the prices of the natural peanut butters compare with the prices of the regular peanut butters? Explain how you can make this comparison using box plots.

B. Refer to the plots below and the plots in Question A.

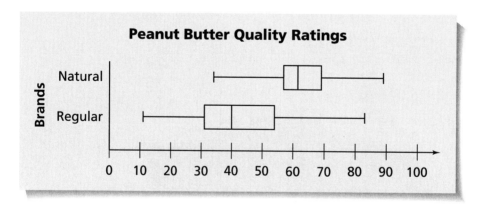

Peanut Butter Quality Ratings

Brands

Natural

Regular

    1. Suppose price is the only factor a buyer considers. Is natural peanut butter or regular peanut butter a better choice? Explain.

    2. Suppose quality is the only factor a buyer considers. Is natural peanut butter or regular peanut butter a better choice?

C. In a box plot, the length of the box represents the difference between the upper and lower quartiles. The difference is called the *interquartile range* (IQR).

1. What is the IQR for the quality ratings for natural peanut butters? What does it tell you?

2. What is the IQR for the quality ratings for regular peanut butters? What does it tell you?

D. Values in a data set that are much greater or much less than most of the other values are called *outliers*. To decide whether a value is an outlier, first find the IQR. Outliers are data values that are either

- greater than 1.5 times the IQR added to the upper quartile, or

- less than 1.5 times the IQR subtracted from the lower quartile

1. What are the outliers in the quality ratings for the natural peanut butters?

2. What are the outliers in the ratings for the regular peanut butters?

3. On a box plot, outliers are sometimes indicated with asterisks (*). The box plots in Question B and the box plots below show the same data distributions.

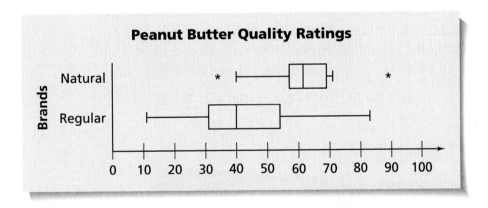

a. In the Question B plots, the whiskers extend to the minimum and maximum values. What values do the whiskers in the plots above extend to?

b. Describe how you would construct a box plot if you wanted to show the outliers in the distribution.

E. 1. Make a pair of box plots to compare the quality ratings for creamy and chunky peanut butters.

2. What is the IQR for each distribution? Use the IQR to determine whether there are any outliers.

3. Based on quality ratings, are creamy peanut butters or chunky peanut butters a better choice? Explain.

ACE Homework starts on page 17.

In this problem, you will use what you have learned to compare quality ratings for salted and unsalted peanut butters and for name brand and store brand peanut butters.

Problem 1.4 Analyzing Data

Justify your answers to the following questions with statistics and graphs, such as histograms and box plots.

A. Compare the quality ratings of salted peanut butters with the quality ratings of unsalted peanut butters. Based on quality ratings, are salted peanut butters or unsalted peanut butters a better choice?

B. Compare the quality ratings of name brands with the quality ratings of store brands. Based on quality ratings, are name brands or store brands a better choice?

C. Use your results from this and earlier problems to name the attributes of the type of peanut butter you would recommend to someone. Be sure to say whether the peanut butter would be natural or regular, creamy or chunky, salted or unsalted, and name brand or store brand.

D. Can you find at least one peanut butter in the table that has all the attributes you recommend?

ACE Homework starts on page 17.

Applications

1. The horizontal scale of a histogram begins at 40 and has interval widths of 10. In which intervals are the values 85 and 90 located?

2. **a.** Make two histograms, using the Peanut Butter Comparisons table before Problem 1.1, that allow you to compare the prices of natural peanut butters with the prices of regular peanut butters.

   b. What interval widths did you use? Why?

   c. Did you show counts or percents on the vertical axis? Why?

For Exercises 3–5, refer to the Peanut Butter Comparisons table. Use statistics and histograms to justify each answer.

3. Based on price, are creamy peanut butters or chunky peanut butters a better choice?

4. Based on price, are salted peanut butters or unsalted peanut butters a better choice?

5. Based on price, are name brands or store brands a better choice?

6. **a.** Suppose someone wants to choose a peanut butter based on price. Use your answers for Exercises 2–5 to list the four attributes— natural or regular, creamy or chunky, salted or unsalted, and name brand or store brand—you would recommend.

   b. Can you find at least one type of peanut butter that has all the attributes you recommend?

Sodium in Natural Peanut Butters

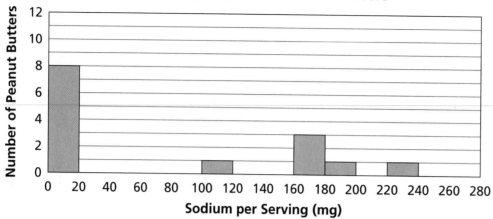

Sodium in Regular Peanut Butters

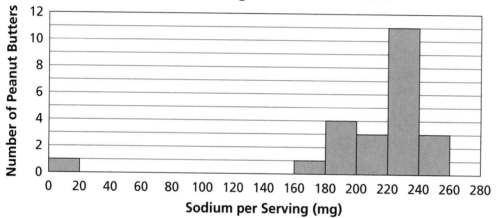

Box Plot A

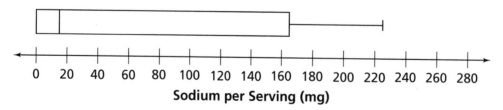

Box Plot B

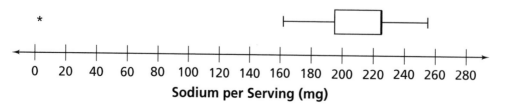

7. Which box plot shows the distribution of sodium values for the natural peanut butters? Explain.

8. Which box plot shows the distribution of sodium values for the regular peanut butters? Explain.

9. What is the median of the sodium values for the natural peanut butters? Explain what this tells you.

10. What is the median of the sodium values for the regular peanut butters? Explain what this tells you.

11. Where do the sodium values for natural peanut butters cluster?

12. Where do the sodium values for regular peanut butters cluster?

13. Suppose you are on a low sodium diet. Should you choose a regular or natural peanut butter? Explain.

For Exercises 14 and 15, fill in the blanks.

14. The sodium values for the natural peanut butters vary from __?__ to __?__. The range is __?__.

15. The sodium values for the regular peanut butters vary from __?__ to __?__. The range is __?__.

16. Box Plot A is missing a "whisker." Explain why.

17. Use the IQR to help you identify which data values are outliers in the sodium values for the regular peanut butters shown on Box Plot B.

18. Multiple Choice Which value is *not* needed to construct a box plot?

   A. upper quartile   **B.** minimum value

   C. median   **D.** mean

Investigation 1 Comparing Data Sets   **19**

Use the histograms below for Exercises 19–21. The means and medians are marked on each histogram.

Student Heights (Grades K–2)

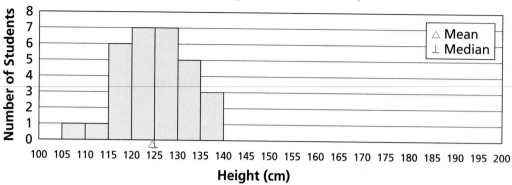

Student Heights (Grades 3–5)

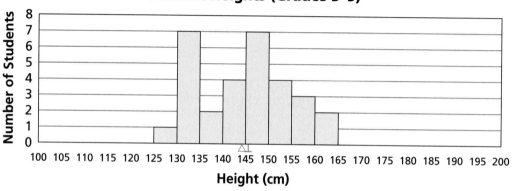

Student Heights (Grades 6–8)

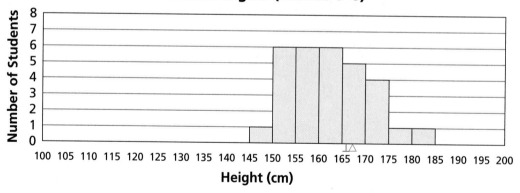

19. How much taller is a student in grades 6–8 than a student in grades K–2? Explain.

20. How much taller is a student in grades 6–8 than a student in grades 3–5?

21. The heights for the students in grades 3–5 cluster in a different way than those for students in grades K–2 and 6–8. What is different about the heights for the students in grades 3–5? Why do you think this might be so?

The graphs below compare prices (in U.S. dollars) of juice drinks sold in the United Kingdom. The titles and axis labels are missing. Use the graphs for Exercises 22–25.

Graph B

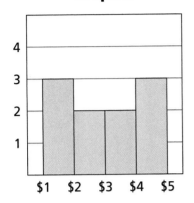

Graph A

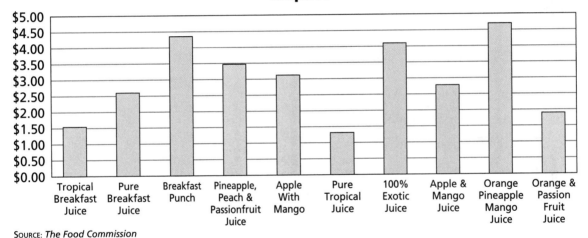

SOURCE: *The Food Commission*

22. Which graph could you use to identify the juice drinks with the greatest and least prices? Give the names of these drinks and their estimated prices.

23. What title and axis labels would be appropriate for each graph?

24. Suppose you were given only Graph A. Would you have enough information to make Graph B? Explain.

25. Suppose you were given only Graph B. Would you have enough information to make Graph A? Explain.

Investigation 1 Comparing Data Sets   **21**

26. Tim says TastiSnak raisins are a better deal than Harvest Time raisins because there are more raisins in each box. Kadisha says that, because a box of either type contains half an ounce, both brands give you the same amount for your money.

The students found the number of raisins and the mass for 50 boxes of each type. They made the plots below. Based on this information, which brand is a better deal? Explain.

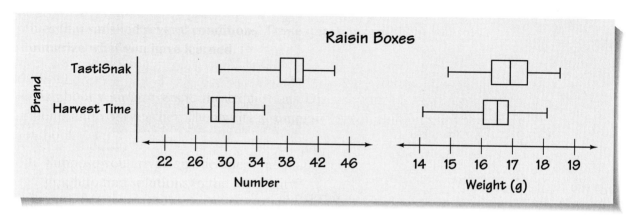

Connections

27. a. Make a data set with 20 values and a mean of 25.

   b. Do you think other students made the same data set as you? Explain.

   c. Does the median of the data set need to be close in value to the mean? Explain.

28. a. Some students were asked to randomly choose a number from 1 to 10. The results are shown. Make a circle graph of these data.

Go Online
PHSchool.com

For: Multiple-Choice Skills Practice
Web Code: apa-8154

Random Number Choosing

Number	1	2	3	4	5	6	7	8	9	10
Percent of Students Who Chose Number	1	5	12	11	10	12	30	9	7	3

   b. Make a bar graph of these data.

   c. What is the mode of the numbers selected?

   d. Based on the results, do you think the students actually chose the numbers at random?

   e. Nine students chose 5 as their number. How many students are in the seventh grade?

29. At a diving competition, Jeff's dive receives seven scores with a mean of 9.0. For his final score, the greatest and least scores are removed and the mean of the remaining scores is calculated. Jeff's final score for the dive is 9.1. What is the sum of the two removed scores? Explain.

30. Use the tables from National Basketball Association (NBA) teams below, statistics, and graphs to justify your answers to parts (a)–(c).

2004 Houston Rockets

Player	Age	Height (cm)
Baker	34	211
Barry	36	196
Bowen	30	206
Braggs	29	203
Howard	32	206
McGrady	26	203
Mutombo	39	218
Norris	32	185
Padgett	29	206
Sura	32	196
Ward	35	188
Weatherspoon	35	200
Wesley	35	185
Yao	25	229

Source: *www.nba.com*

2004 Chicago Bulls

Player	Age	Height (cm)
Chandler	23	216
Curry	23	211
Davis	37	206
Deng	20	203
Duhon	23	185
Gordon	22	191
Griffin	31	196
Harrington	31	206
Hinrich	24	191
Nocioni	26	200
Pargo	26	185
Piatowski	35	200
Reiner	23	211
Williams	25	191

Source: *www.nba.com*

a. Are the players on one team older than the players on the other team, or are they about the same age?

b. Are the players on one team taller than the players on the other team, or are they about the same height?

c. Based on these data, what estimates would you make for the age and height distributions of a typical professional men's basketball team? What cautions would you suggest in making generalizations from the given data?

31. Vicky has misplaced one of her algebra quizzes. The scores on the quizzes she has are 82, 71, 83, 91, and 78. She knows that the mean of all six quiz scores is 79.5. What is the score on the missing quiz?

32. Terrence's test scores in math class this semester are 98, 83, 72, 85, 91, 79, and 85. He thinks he can reasonably expect an 87 or better average for his semester grade. Without doing an exact computation, do you think he is correct? Explain.

Extensions

33. Bill and Joe are interested in baseball. The histogram below shows data they collected about the duration of baseball games. The title and axes labels are missing.

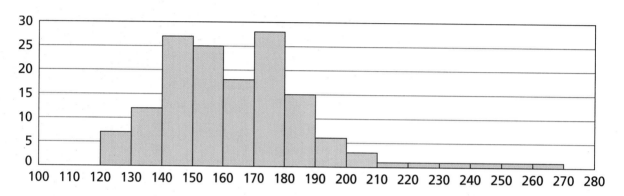

a. What title and axis labels are appropriate for this graph?

b. What does the shape of the graph tell you about the length of a typical baseball game?

c. About how many games are represented in the graph?

d. Estimate the lower quartile, median, and upper quartile for these data. What do these numbers tell you about the length of a typical baseball game?

Mathematical Reflections 1

In this investigation, you grouped data into intervals to make histograms, and you used the five-number summaries of data sets to make box plots. You used these graphs to analyze and compare data distributions. These questions will help you summarize what you have learned.

Think about your answers to these questions. Discuss your ideas with other students and your teacher. Then write a summary of your findings in your notebook.

1. **a.** Describe how to construct a histogram for a set of data.

   b. Describe how to construct a box plot for a set of data.

   c. In what ways are histograms and box plots alike? In what ways are they different?

2. **a.** How can you compare two data sets displayed in histograms?

   b. How can you compare two data sets displayed in box plots?

Choosing a Sample From a Population

Suppose you want to gather information about students in your class, such as their preferences for food, television, music, or sports. It would be fairly easy to conduct a survey. But collecting information about all the students in your school or all the people in your city, your state, or the entire country would be very difficult.

You can study a large population by collecting data from a small part, or **sample,** of that population. Depending on how the sample is selected from the population, it is possible to use data from the sample to help you *make predictions* or *draw conclusions* about the entire population. The challenge is to choose a sample that is likely to help you accurately predict information about a population.

Consider this information.

- Of children 9 to 13 years old, 59% say they get information about new clothing styles from friends, 58% say they get such information from television, 38% from school, and 31% from stores.

- The average child eats 1,500 peanut butter and jelly sandwiches before graduating from high school.

- Between grades 7 and 12, teenagers listen to about 10,500 hours of rock music. This is only 500 fewer hours than they spend in school over 12 years.

- The average American child watches 30,000 commercials each year.

How could the groups who reported these data know about the activities of all the children or teenagers in the United States?

Do you think each of these facts was gathered from a census (a survey of every person in the population) or from a sample?

Newspapers, magazines, radio and television programs, and Internet sites conduct surveys on a variety of subjects. Suppose a magazine with a national circulation asked its readers the five questions about honesty shown below. The magazine asks the readers to go to their Web site and enter their answers.

HONESTY SURVEY

1. **What would you do if you found someone's wallet on the street?**

a. Try to return it to the owner
b. Return it, but keep the money
c. Keep the wallet and the money

2. **What would you do if a cashier mistakenly gave you $10 extra in change?**

a. Tell the cashier about the error
b. Say nothing and keep the cash

3. **Would you cheat on an exam if you were sure you wouldn't get caught?**

a. Yes
b. No

4. **Would you download music from the Internet illegally instead of buying the CD?**

a. Yes
b. No

5. **Do you feel that you are an honest person in most situations?**

a. Yes
b. No

Problem 2.1 Using a Sample to Make Predictions

A. A *sampling plan* is a strategy for choosing a sample from a population. What is the population for the honesty survey? What is the sample? How is the sample chosen from the population?

B. Suppose 5,280 people complete the survey, and 4,224 of them answer "No" to Question 3. What percent of responders said they would not cheat on an exam?

C. Of the 5,280 responders, 1,584 answer yes to Question 4. What percent of responders said they would not download music illegally from the Internet?

D. Refer to the survey results given in Questions B and C. The United States population is about 300 million.

  1. Estimate how many people in the United States would say they would not cheat on an exam.

  2. Estimate how many people in the United States would say they would not download music illegally from the Internet.

E. List some reasons why predictions about all Americans based on this survey might be inaccurate.

F. How could you revise the sampling plan for this survey so you would be more confident that the results predict the percent of the United States population that is honest?

ACE Homework starts on page 36.

2.2 Selecting a Sample

Making accurate predictions about a population based on a sample can be complicated, even when you are interested in a relatively small population.

Suppose you are doing research on the lives of students at your school. You would like to answer these questions:

- How many hours of sleep do students get each night?
- How many movies do students watch each week?

If your school has a large student population, it might be difficult to gather and analyze data from every student.

How could you select a sample of your school population to survey?

Problem 2.2 Selecting a Sample

Ms. Ruiz's class wants to conduct this survey about hours spent sleeping and watching movies. They plan to survey students in their school. The class divides into four groups. Each group devises a plan for sampling the school population.

- Each member of Group 1 will survey the students who ride on his or her school bus.

- Group 2 will survey every fourth person in the cafeteria line.

- Group 3 will post a notice in the morning announcements asking for volunteers for their survey.

- Group 4 will randomly select 30 students for their survey from a list of three-digit student ID numbers. They will label the faces of a 10-sided solid with the numbers 0 through 9 and roll it three times to generate each number.

A. What are the advantages and disadvantages of each sampling plan?

B. Which plan do you think will lead to the most accurate predictions for students in the whole school? Explain.

C. The four sampling plans are examples of common sampling methods.

   1. Group 1's plan is an example of **convenience sampling.** What do you think convenience sampling is? Describe another plan that would use convenience sampling.

   2. Group 2's plan is an example of **systematic sampling.** What do you think systematic sampling is? Describe another plan that would use systematic sampling.

   3. Group 3's plan is an example of **voluntary-response sampling.** What do you think voluntary-response sampling is? Describe another plan that would use voluntary-response sampling.

   4. Group 4's plan is an example of **random sampling.** What do you think random sampling is? Describe another plan that would use random sampling.

D. Jahmal thinks Group 1's and Group 3's plans may not give samples that are likely to predict what is typical of the population. Do you agree or disagree? Explain.

ACE Homework starts on page 36.

2.3 Choosing Random Samples

In most cases, a good sampling plan is one that gives each sample selected from the population the same chance of being chosen. Sampling plans with this property are called random sampling plans. Samples chosen with a random sampling plan are called random samples.

To select a random sample from a population of 100 students, you could use spinners like these to generate pairs of random digits.

What two-digit numbers can you generate with these spinners?

How can you make sure student 100 has an equally likely chance of being included in your sample?

There are many other ways to select a random sample of students. For example, you could roll two 10-sided solids or generate random numbers with your calculator.

Getting Ready for Problem

Suppose you have two concert tickets. You want to choose one of your six best friends to go with you. Consider these possible strategies:

Strategy 1: Choose the first person who calls you tonight.

Strategy 2: Assign each friend a different whole number from 1 to 6. The number you roll on a six-sided number cube determines who goes.

Strategy 3: Tell each friend to meet you after school. Toss a coin to choose between the first two friends who arrive.

- You want to give each friend the same chance of being selected. Which strategy would accomplish this? Explain.

- Describe another strategy that would give each of your friends an equally likely chance of being selected.

The table on the next page shows data collected on a Monday in an eighth-grade class. The data include the number of hours of sleep each student got the previous night and the number of movies each student watched the previous week.

You can use statistics about a random sample of these data to make predictions about the entire population.

Problem 2.3 Choosing Random Samples

You are going to choose a sample and represent your sample with a line plot and a box plot. To make it easier to compare your sample's distribution with others, your class should decide on a scale before starting.

A. 1. Use spinners, 10-sided number cubes, a graphing calculator, or some other method to select a random sample of 30 students. (Your sample should contain 30 *different* students. If you select a student who is already in your sample, select another.)

2. For each student in your sample, record the number of movies watched and the number of hours slept.

B. 1. Make a line plot showing the distribution of the movie data from your sample.

2. Describe the variability in the number of movies watched by students in your sample.

3. Compare your distribution with those of other members of your class. Describe any similarities or differences.

4. What can you conclude about the movie-watching behavior of the population of 100 students based on all the samples? Explain.

C. 1. Make a box plot showing the distributions of the hours of sleep from your sample.

2. Describe the variability in the number of hours of sleep for students in your sample.

3. Compare your distribution with those of the other members of your class. Describe any similarities or differences.

4. What can you conclude about the hours of sleep of the population of 100 students based on the samples selected by members of your class? Explain.

 Homework starts on page 36.

Grade 8 Database

Student Number	Gender	Sleep (h)	Movies
01	boy	11.5	14
02	boy	2.0	8
03	girl	7.7	3
04	boy	9.3	1
05	boy	7.1	16
06	boy	7.5	1
07	boy	8.0	4
08	girl	7.8	1
09	girl	8.0	13
10	girl	8.0	15
11	boy	9.0	1
12	boy	9.2	10
13	boy	8.5	5
14	girl	6.0	15
15	boy	6.5	10
16	boy	8.3	2
17	girl	7.4	2
18	boy	11.2	3
19	girl	7.3	1
20	boy	8.0	0
21	girl	7.8	1
22	girl	7.8	1
23	boy	9.2	2
24	girl	7.5	0
25	boy	8.8	1
26	girl	8.5	0
27	girl	9.0	0
28	girl	8.5	0
29	boy	8.2	2
30	girl	7.8	2
31	girl	8.0	2
32	girl	7.3	8
33	boy	6.0	5
34	girl	7.5	5
35	boy	6.5	5
36	boy	9.3	1
37	girl	8.2	3
38	boy	7.3	3
39	girl	7.4	6
40	girl	8.5	7
41	boy	5.5	17
42	boy	6.5	3
43	boy	7.0	5
44	girl	8.5	2
45	girl	9.3	4
46	girl	8.0	15
47	boy	8.5	10
48	girl	6.2	11
49	girl	11.8	10
50	girl	9.0	4

Student Number	Gender	Sleep (h)	Movies
51	boy	5.0	4
52	boy	6.5	5
53	girl	8.5	2
54	boy	9.1	15
55	girl	7.5	2
56	girl	8.5	1
57	girl	8.0	2
58	girl	7.0	7
59	girl	8.4	10
60	girl	9.5	1
61	girl	7.3	5
62	girl	7.3	4
63	boy	8.5	3
64	boy	9.0	3
65	boy	9.0	4
66	girl	7.3	5
67	girl	5.7	0
68	girl	5.5	0
69	boy	10.5	7
70	girl	7.5	1
71	boy	7.8	0
72	girl	7.3	1
73	boy	9.3	2
74	boy	9.0	1
75	boy	8.7	1
76	boy	8.5	3
77	girl	9.0	1
78	boy	8.0	1
79	boy	8.0	4
80	boy	6.5	0
81	boy	8.0	0
82	girl	9.0	8
83	girl	8.0	0
84	boy	7.0	0
85	boy	9.0	6
86	boy	7.3	0
87	girl	9.0	3
88	girl	7.5	5
89	boy	8.0	0
90	girl	7.5	6
91	boy	8.0	4
92	boy	9.0	4
93	boy	7.0	0
94	boy	8.0	3
95	boy	8.3	3
96	boy	8.3	14
97	girl	7.8	5
98	girl	8.5	1
99	girl	8.3	3
100	boy	7.5	2

2.4 Choosing a Sample Size

In Problem 2.3, you used random samples to estimate the sleep and movie-viewing habits of 100 students.

Could you make good estimates with less work by selecting smaller samples?

In this problem, you will explore how the size of a sample affects the accuracy of statistical estimates.

Problem 2.4 Choosing a Sample Size

A. From the population of 100 students in Problem 2.3, select a random sample of 5 students and a random sample of 10 students. Record the number of movies watched and number of hours slept for each student. (The students *within* each sample should be different, but the same student may appear in both samples.)

B. 1. Use the samples in Question A and the sample of 30 students from Problem 2.3. For each sample, find the mean and median number of movies watched and the mean and median number of hours of sleep.

   2. Record the means and the medians in a class chart. This chart will contain means and medians from everyone's samples.

C. 1. Use the class data about the mean number of movies watched. For each sample size (samples of 5, 10, and 30 students), make a line plot of the distribution of the means. You will have three line plots. Compare the three distributions. Describe the variability in each distribution.

   2. The mean number of movies watched for the entire population of 100 students is about 4. Write a paragraph describing how well the means for samples of different sizes predict the mean for the population.

D. 1. Use the class data about the median number of movies watched. For each sample size, make a line plot of the distribution of the medians. You will have three line plots. Compare the three distributions. Describe the variability in each distribution.

   2. The median number of movies watched for all 100 students is 3. Write a paragraph describing how well the medians for samples of different sizes predict the median for the population.

E. For the entire population, the mean number of hours slept is 7.7, and the median is 10. Follow the procedures you used in Questions C and D to explore the distribution of means and medians for the samples of different sizes. Discuss how well samples of different sizes predict the mean and median for the entire population.

F. Suppose each student in your class chose a sample of 50 students and found the mean and median of the data for movies watched and hours slept. What would you expect line plots of these means and medians to look like? Explain.

ACE **Homework starts on page 36.**

Applications

For Exercises 1–4, describe the population and the sampling method.

1. A magazine for teenagers asks its readers to write in with information about how they solve personal problems.

2. An eighth-grade class wants to find out how much time middle school students spend on the telephone each day. Students in the class keep a record of the amount of time they spend on the phone each day for a week.

3. Ms. Darnell's class wants to estimate the number of soft drinks middle school students drink each day. They obtain a list of students in the school and write each name on a card. They put the cards in a box and select the names of 40 students to survey.

4. A survey found that 52% of American adults believe that global warming is a serious threat. The editors of the school paper want to find out how students in their school feel about this issue. They select 26 students for their survey—one whose name begins with A, one whose name begins with B, one whose name begins with C, and so on.

A middle school has 350 students. One math class wants to find out how many hours a typical student in the school spent doing homework last week. Several students suggest sampling plans. For Exercises 5–8, name the type of sampling method and tell whether you think it would give a sample that lets you make accurate predictions about the population.

5. Zak suggests surveying every third student on each homeroom class list.

6. Kwang-Hee suggests putting 320 white beans and 30 red beans in a bag. Each student would draw a bean as he or she enters the auditorium for tomorrow's assembly. The 30 students who draw red beans will be surveyed.

7. Ushio suggests that each student in the class survey everyone in his or her English class.

8. Kirby suggests putting surveys on a table at the entrance to the school and asking students to return completed questionnaires at the end of the day.

9. A radio host asked her listeners to call in to express their opinions about a local election. What kind of sampling method is she using? Do you think the results of this survey could be used to describe the opinions of all the show's listeners? Explain.

Manufacturers often conduct quality-control tests on samples of their products. For Exercises 10–13, describe a random sampling plan you would recommend to the company. Justify your recommendation.

10. A toy company produces 5,000 video-game systems each day.

11. A music company manufactures a total of 200,000 compact discs for about 100 recording artists each day.

12. A fireworks company produces more than 1,500 rockets each day.

13. A bottling company produces 25,000 bottles of spring water each day.

14. **a.** In Problem 2.3, suppose that, instead of choosing random samples of 30 students, you select the first 30 students for your sample, a second student selects the next 30 students for his sample, and so on. Is this procedure likely to result in samples that allow you to make accurate predictions about the population?

   b. Suppose you select students 1, 5, 9, 13, 17, 21, 25, . . . for your sample. Is this sample likely to allow you to make accurate predictions about the population?

For: Help with Exercise 14
Web Code: ape-8214

15. a. The homecoming committee wants to estimate how many students will attend the homecoming dance. However, they don't want to ask every student in the school. Describe a method the committee could use to select a sample of students to survey.

b. Describe how the committee could use the results of its survey to predict the number of students who will attend the dance.

For Exercises 16 and 17, use the graph below.

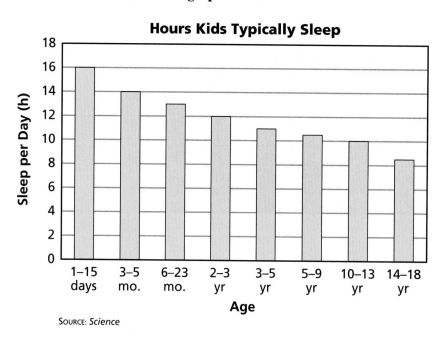

16. About how many more hours per day does a newborn sleep than a typical 10- to 13-year-old?

17. Suppose you want to survey a random sample of students in your school to find out how many hours they sleep each night. Which would be the best sample size: 5 students, 10 students, or 30 students? Explain.

Connections

18. Multiple Choice This stem-and-leaf plot shows Ella's diving scores from a recent competition. What was Ella's lowest score for the competition?

A. 0.03   **B.** 1.4

C. 8.0   **D.** None of these

Ella's Diving Scores

5	1 4
6	1
7	6
8	0 3

Key: 5 | 1 means 5.1

19. a. From age 5–18, the average student eats 1,500 peanut butter and jelly sandwiches. You can make about 15 sandwiches from an 18-ounce jar of peanut butter. How many jars of peanut butter would you need to make 1,500 sandwiches? Explain.

b. About how many jars of peanut butter does an average student eat each year from age 5 to age 18?

c. How many peanut butter sandwiches does a student need to eat each week to consume the number of jars per year from part (b)?

20. Multiple Choice Belissa is now 18 years old. An 18-ounce jar of Belissa's favorite peanut butter costs $2.29. She reasons that her mom has spent about $2,300 on peanut butter for her since she was 5 years old. Which best describes her estimate?

F. Less than the actual amount because she rounded the cost for a jar of peanut butter to the nearest dollar.

G. Less than the actual amount because she rounded the cost of a jar of peanut butter to the nearest tenth of a dollar.

H. More than the actual amount because she rounded the cost of a jar of peanut butter to the nearest dollar.

J. More than the actual amount because she rounded the cost of a jar of peanut butter to the nearest tenth of a dollar.

21. a. A geyser is a spring from which columns of boiling water and steam erupt. Using the graph, describe the overall relationship between the height of an eruption and the time since the previous eruption.

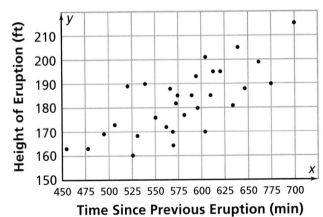

Geyser Eruption Data

b. The data above were collected for one particular geyser. What additional information would you need to decide whether the relationship in part (a) is true for most geysers?

Investigation 2 Choosing a Sample From a Population   **39**

This plot shows the number of hours students at a middle school spent doing homework one Monday. Use the plot for Exercises 22–24.

Minutes Spent on Homework

Grade 6		Grade 8
0 0 0 0 0 0	0	0
5 5 5 5 5 5	1	0 5 5
5 0 0	2	0 0 0 5 5 5
5 5 5	3	0 0 0 0 5 5 5
5 5 0	4	0 0 0 5 5 5
0 0	5	0 5
	6	0 5 5
0	7	5
5	8	0

Key: 5 | 3 | 0 means 35 minutes for Grade 6 and 30 minutes for Grade 8

22. Find the median homework time for each grade.

23. a. For each grade, describe the variability in the distribution of homework times.

   b. Use statistics to explain how the times for sixth-graders compare to the times for eighth-graders.

24. Could these data be used to describe what is typical of all school nights in each of the two grades? Explain.

25. Consider the following data set: 20, 22, 23, 23, 24, 24, and 25.

   a. Find the mean and the range of the values.

   b. Add three values to the data set so that the mean of the new data set is greater than the mean of the original data set. What is the range of the new data set?

   c. Add three values to the original data set so that the mean of the new data set is less than the mean of the original data set. What is the range of the new data set?

   d. How do the ranges of the three data sets compare? Why do you think this is so?

26. Multiple Choice You survey 30 students from a population of 150 eighth-graders. Which statement is *not* correct?

   F. The ratio of those sampled to those not sampled is 30 to 120.

   G. One out of every five people in the population was sampled.

   H. Twenty-five percent of the students in the population were sampled.

   K. One fifth of the students in the population were sampled.

27. There are 350 students in a school. Ms. Cabral's class surveys two random samples of students to find out how many went to camp last summer. Here are the results:

      Sample 1: 8 of 25 attended camp

      Sample 2: 7 of 28 attended camp

   a. Based on the results from Sample 1, what fraction of the students in the school would you predict attended camp? How many students is this?

   b. Based on the results from Sample 2, what fraction of the students in the school would you predict attended camp? How many students is this?

   c. Which sample predicts that the greater fraction of students attended camp?

   d. One of Ms. Cabral's students says, "We were careful to choose our samples randomly. Why did the two samples give us different predictions?" How would you answer the student's question?

Annie's teacher starts each class with the names of all his students in a container. He chooses students to present answers by pulling out names at random. Once a name is chosen, it is set aside. There are 12 girls and 6 boys in the class.

28. What is the probability Annie will be the first student chosen on Monday?

29. What is the probability Annie will be the first student chosen on Tuesday?

30. What is the probability Annie will be the first student chosen on both Monday and Tuesday?

31. What is the probability the first student chosen on a given day will be a girl?

32. Suppose Annie is chosen first. What is the probability that the next student selected will be another girl?

33. Suppose the teacher plans to choose six students during one class. Would you be surprised if only two girls were chosen? Explain.

Go Online
PHSchool.com
For: Multiple-Choice Skills Practice
Web Code: apa-8254

Alyssa wants to know what students think about replacing the candy in two vending machines in the cafeteria with more healthful snacks. There are 300 sixth-graders, 300 seventh-graders, and 200 eighth-graders. Half of the students in each grade are girls. Alyssa obtains a list of student names, grouped by grade, with the girls listed first in each grade. Use this information for Exercises 34 and 35.

34. Alyssa randomly chooses 3 *different* students from the list of 800 students.

   a. What are the chances the first choice is a girl? The second choice is a girl? The third choice is a girl?

   b. What are the chances that Alyssa chooses three girls?

35. Alyssa decides to choose one person *from each grade* at random.

    a. What are the chances that her sixth-grade choice is a girl?

    b. What are the chances that she chooses three girls?

Alyssa chooses one girl and one boy from each grade. She asks each, "Which would you prefer, a machine with healthful snacks or a machine with candy?" Base your answers to Exercises 36–39 on her results below.

Vending Machine Survey Results

	Grade 6	Grade 7	Grade 8
Girl	healthful snack	healthful snack	healthful snack
Boy	candy	candy	healthful snack

36. Predict how many sixth-grade students prefer a machine with healthful snacks.

37. Predict how many students in the whole school prefer a machine with healthful snacks.

38. What is the probability that a student chosen at random from the whole school is an eighth-grader who prefers machine with healthful snacks?

39. What advice would you give Alyssa's principal about Alyssa's data and the two vending machines? Explain.

40. Alyssa's principal polls all 800 students and finds that 600 prefer a machine with healthful snacks.

    a. What is the probability that a randomly selected student prefers a machine with healthful snacks?

    b. What is the probability that a randomly selected student is a girl who prefers a machine with healthful snacks?

    c. What is the probability that a randomly selected student is a boy who prefers a machine with healthful snacks?

    d. What advice would you give the principal about the data collected and the vending machines?

Extensions

41. Television stations, radio stations, and newspapers often use polls to predict the winners of elections long before the votes are cast. What factors might cause a pre-election poll to be inaccurate?

42. Political parties often conduct their own pre-election polls to find out what voters think about their campaign and their candidates. How might a political party bias such a poll?

43. Find out how a local television station, radio station, or newspaper takes pre-election polls. Do you think the method they use is sensible?

44. a. Polls conducted prior to presidential elections commonly use samples of about 1,000 eligible voters. There are at most 203 million eligible voters in the United States. About what percent of eligible voters are in a sample of 1,000?

    b. How do you think this small sample is chosen so that the results will predict the winner with reasonable accuracy?

45. Use the table on the next page for parts (a)–(f).

    a. Pick your favorite M&M's® color. From the table, select random samples of 5, 10, and 30 bags.

    b. For each bag in a sample, calculate the percent of your favorite color.

    c. For each sample size, make a line plot to display the distribution of the percent of your favorite color.

    d. Estimate the percent of your favorite color in all 100 bags.

    e. Predict the company's fixed percent of each color. Explain your reasoning.

Data From 100 Bags of Plain M&M's® Candies (pre-March 2004)

Bag	Green	Yellow	Orange	Blue	Brown	Red	Total
1	3	10	9	5	10	18	55
2	5	12	4	6	19	11	57
3	7	10	9	4	16	12	58
4	4	14	2	1	14	19	56
5	12	7	8	7	14	13	61
6	10	9	6	5	15	8	55
7	11	11	6	6	12	12	58
8	8	15	5	3	16	10	57
9	2	11	4	4	24	12	57
10	5	7	4	1	26	13	56
11	6	13	4	4	15	18	60
12	5	8	4	2	23	16	58
13	9	13	4	4	14	11	55
14	9	10	5	5	14	14	57
15	5	19	5	2	13	14	58
16	3	15	5	2	19	11	55
17	3	10	4	3	23	14	57
18	6	7	5	5	15	22	60
19	5	7	3	4	21	14	54
20	8	7	8	2	20	16	61
21	10	11	7	7	8	14	57
22	7	10	3	5	20	12	57
23	3	8	6	3	25	10	55
24	6	11	9	3	10	17	56
25	10	12	1	2	15	17	57
26	4	12	4	7	14	16	57
27	6	9	6	7	15	13	56
28	5	11	6	7	17	7	53
29	1	10	6	5	22	14	58
30	10	4	8	0	26	9	57
31	4	14	6	4	18	12	58
32	6	18	2	4	19	14	58
33	6	7	8	4	20	11	56
34	12	11	6	4	11	11	55
35	5	10	6	2	12	16	51
36	8	9	4	4	16	17	58
37	2	12	2	6	11	21	54
38	5	7	3	4	21	19	59
39	8	7	8	2	20	16	61
40	10	11	7	7	8	14	57
41	7	10	3	5	20	12	57
42	3	8	6	3	23	10	50
43	6	11	9	3	10	17	56
44	10	12	1	2	15	17	57
45	5	13	2	4	22	11	57
46	6	10	9	5	14	13	57
47	6	16	7	3	16	9	57
48	6	10	4	5	23	10	58
49	10	7	2	6	19	9	53
50	4	12	8	6	10	15	55

Bag	Green	Yellow	Orange	Blue	Brown	Red	Total
51	9	9	6	6	17	10	57
52	4	13	4	6	17	13	57
53	6	12	3	8	13	12	54
54	11	8	8	12	9	8	56
55	1	16	7	3	22	10	59
56	6	11	6	4	19	11	57
57	7	7	7	3	10	21	55
58	7	2	8	10	15	13	55
59	6	10	6	7	12	15	56
60	6	16	7	3	16	9	57
61	6	10	4	5	23	10	58
62	10	7	2	6	19	9	53
63	4	12	8	6	10	15	55
64	9	12	8	6	8	15	58
65	10	6	5	4	12	16	53
66	4	11	3	2	21	15	56
67	6	15	4	8	10	10	53
68	6	8	7	1	19	14	55
69	6	8	8	6	10	16	54
70	9	11	7	4	15	10	56
71	6	9	8	2	19	14	58
72	3	10	9	5	10	18	55
73	5	12	4	6	19	11	57
74	7	10	9	4	16	12	58
75	4	14	2	1	16	19	56
76	1	8	10	1	22	14	56
77	5	15	4	9	11	11	57
78	3	11	6	3	24	10	57
79	10	9	4	1	23	10	57
80	5	10	7	1	21	13	57
81	6	14	7	7	14	5	53
82	9	11	2	6	13	16	57
83	7	7	9	0	13	20	56
84	8	10	4	5	13	10	50
85	4	11	2	1	24	15	57
86	4	12	6	3	21	12	58
87	5	8	7	4	20	13	57
88	7	11	7	7	13	10	55
89	9	11	4	2	12	18	56
90	4	15	8	4	16	10	57
91	7	11	6	4	18	11	58
92	5	8	8	3	20	12	56
93	7	3	2	6	26	11	55
94	9	6	3	1	28	12	59
95	12	11	9	2	18	5	58
96	9	11	3	3	17	12	55
97	5	12	6	5	17	13	58
98	4	11	9	3	21	10	58
99	11	12	5	3	17	9	57
100	6	16	6	6	16	4	54

Mathematical Reflections 2

In this investigation, you learned about sampling techniques. You also made predictions about a population by examining data from random samples. The following questions will help you summarize what you have learned.

Think about your answers to these questions. Discuss your ideas with other students and your teacher. Then write a summary of your findings in your notebook.

1. Why are data often collected from a sample rather than from an entire population?

2. Describe several methods for selecting a sample from a population. Discuss the advantages and disadvantages of each method.

3. **a.** How are random samples different from convenience, self-selected, and systematic samples?

   b. Why is random sampling preferable to convenience, self-selected, or systematic sampling?

4. Describe three methods for selecting a random sample from a given population. What are the advantages and disadvantages of each method?

5. Suppose several random samples were selected from the same population. What similarities and differences would you expect to find in the medians, means, and ranges of the samples?

Investigation 3

Solving Real-World Problems

In this investigation, you will apply what you have learned about statistics to solve two real-world problems.

3.1 Solving an Archeological Mystery

Archeologists study past civilizations by excavating ancient settlements and examining the artifacts of the people who lived there.

On digs in southeastern Montana and north-central Wyoming, archeologists discovered the remains of two Native American settlements. They unearthed a number of arrowheads at both sites.

The tables below give the length, width, and neck width for each arrowhead the archeologists found. All measurements are in millimeters.

The archeologists hoped to use the arrowhead data to estimate the time period during which each site was inhabited.

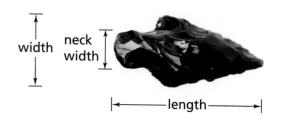

Site I: 15 Arrowheads

Length (mm)	Width (mm)	Neck Width (mm)
24	19	8
27	19	10
29	19	11
29	22	12
31	16	12
31	32	16
37	23	11
38	22	12
38	26	14
40	25	16
45	22	11
45	28	15
55	22	13
62	26	14
63	29	18

SOURCE: *Plains Anthropologist*

Site II: 37 Arrowheads

Length (mm)	Width (mm)	Neck Width (mm)
13	10	6
15	11	7
16	12	8
16	13	7
17	15	9
18	12	10
19	12	8
19	13	9
20	12	7
20	12	9
21	11	7
22	13	9
22	13	9
22	13	8
22	14	10
23	14	9
23	15	9
24	11	8
24	12	7

Length (mm)	Width (mm)	Neck Width (mm)
24	13	8
24	13	8
24	14	10
24	15	9
24	15	8
25	13	7
25	13	7
25	15	10
25	24	7
26	14	10
26	14	11
26	15	11
27	14	8
28	11	6
28	13	9
32	12	8
42	16	11
43	14	9

To help them with their work, the archeologists used arrowhead data from four other settlement sites. These data are given on the next page.

The archeologists knew the following:

- The Big Goose Creek and Wortham Shelter sites were settled between A.D. 500 and 1600.

- The Laddie Creek/Dead Indian Creek and Kobold/Buffalo Creek sites were settled between 4000 B.C. and A.D. 500.

How could you use these data to help you estimate the settlement periods for the new sites?

Big Goose Creek: 52 Arrowheads

Length (mm)	Width (mm)	Neck Width (mm)
16	13	9
16	14	10
17	13	8
17	13	10
18	12	7
18	12	8
18	13	7
18	13	8
18	15	11
19	11	8
20	11	6
20	12	8
21	11	7
21	12	7
21	12	9
22	12	9
22	13	8
22	13	10
23	13	8
23	13	9
23	14	9
24	14	9
24	14	11
25	13	7
25	13	8
25	14	8
26	11	8
26	12	12
26	14	9
26	16	10
27	13	9
27	13	9
27	14	9
27	14	9
27	17	13
28	10	5
28	13	7
28	15	9
29	15	8
30	11	7
30	13	8
30	14	8
30	14	8
30	14	9
30	15	11
31	12	8
33	13	7
33	15	9
34	15	9
35	14	10
39	18	12
40	14	8

SOURCE: *Plains Anthropologist*

Wortham Shelter: 45 Arrowheads

Length (mm)	Width (mm)	Neck Width (mm)
18	11	8
19	12	9
19	14	10
19	14	10
19	16	14
20	13	8
20	14	10
20	15	11
22	12	9
22	14	8
23	13	11
23	14	11
23	15	11
24	12	9
24	13	10
25	14	8
25	14	10
25	15	10
25	15	10
25	15	12
26	13	9
26	13	10
26	15	12
27	14	8
27	14	10
27	15	11
28	13	11
28	14	10
28	16	12
29	13	10
29	14	9
29	14	9
29	17	12
30	14	11
30	16	9
30	17	14
31	13	10
31	14	10
31	14	11
31	16	12
31	17	12
32	14	7
32	15	10
35	18	14
42	18	7

Laddie Creek/ Dead Indian Creek: 18 Arrowheads

Length (mm)	Width (mm)	Neck Width (mm)
25	18	13
27	20	13
27	20	14
29	14	11
29	20	13
30	23	13
31	18	11
32	16	10
32	19	10
35	20	15
37	17	13
38	17	14
39	18	15
40	18	11
41	15	11
42	22	12
44	18	13
52	21	16

Kobold/ Buffalo Creek: 52 Arrowheads

Length (mm)	Width (mm)	Neck Width (mm)
25	18	15
30	17	12
30	19	15
31	16	13
31	17	12
32	20	13
32	22	17
32	23	18
35	19	11
35	22	14
37	18	12
37	21	11
38	18	9
38	24	15
39	21	14
40	19	15
40	20	12
40	20	13
40	21	12
41	21	13
42	22	14
42	22	15
44	20	11
44	20	12
44	25	14
45	20	13
45	22	13
46	17	13
46	20	14
46	23	14
47	19	13
47	20	12
47	22	13
49	20	14
50	21	13
50	23	15
50	23	16
51	18	10
52	17	12
52	22	15
52	24	16
54	24	13
56	19	12
56	21	15
56	25	13
57	22	15
61	19	12
64	21	13
66	20	15
67	21	13
71	24	13
80	25	11

Problem 3.1 Comparing and Analyzing Data

The archeologists hypothesized that Native Americans inhabiting the same area of the country during the same time period would have fashioned similar tools.

A. Use box plots to compare the lengths of the arrowheads discovered at the new sites with the lengths of those from the known sites.

    1. Based on your comparisons, during which time period (4000 B.C. to A.D. 500, or A.D. 500 to 1600) do you think Site I was settled? Explain how your statistics and graphs support your answers.

    2. During which time period do you think Site II was settled? Explain how your statistics and graphs support your answers.

B. Use box plots to compare the widths of the arrowheads discovered at the new sites with the widths of those from the known sites. Do your findings support your answers from Question A? Explain.

C. Suppose the archeologists had collected only a few arrowheads from each new site. Might they have reached a different conclusion? Explain.

ACE Homework starts on page 54.

3.2 Simulating Cookies

Jeff and Ted operate the Custom Cookie Counter. Their advertising slogan is "Five giant chocolate chips in every cookie!"

One day, a customer complains when she finds only three chocolate chips in her cookie. Jeff thinks she must have miscounted because he mixes 60 chips into every batch of a dozen cookies.

Jeff and Ted examine a batch of cookies fresh from the oven. The drawing on the right shows what they find.

Getting Ready for Problem 3.2

- What is wrong with Jeff's reasoning about how many chocolate chips to add to each batch of cookie dough?

- What advice would you give to Jeff and Ted to help them solve their quality-control problem?

Ted wants to figure out how many chocolate chips they should add to each batch of dough to be fairly confident each cookie will have five chips. He comes up with an idea that involves random sampling. He explains his idea to Jeff.

"Think of a batch of dough as 12 cookies packed in a bowl. As we add chips to the dough, each chip lands in one of the cookies. There is an equally likely chance that a chip will land in any 1 of the 12 cookies."

"We can simulate adding the chips by generating random integers from 1 to 12. A 1 means a chip is added to cookie 1, a 2 means a chip is added to cookie 2, and so on.

"We can keep a tally of where the 'chips' land and stop when each 'cookie' contains at least five chips. The total number will be an estimate of the number of chips we need to add to each batch."

Jeff says, "If we only do this once, we might need only 60 chips. If we do it again, we might need 90. Some cookies might be loaded with chips before every cookie gets five chips. We need to repeat the experiment enough times to find a typical result."

Problem 3.2 Using a Simulation to Make a Decision

A. 1. Conduct the simulation Ted describes. Use a chart like the one at the right.

   2. Find the total number of chips in the entire batch.

B. 1. Make a histogram of the total number of chips from each student in your class.

   2. Describe what your histogram shows about the distribution of the results.

   3. Make a box plot of the total number of chips from each student in your class.

   4. Describe what your box plot shows about the distribution of the results.

C. Jeff and Ted want to be sure that most of the time there will be at least five chips in each cookie. However, they don't want to waste money by mixing in too many chips. Based on your class data and the two representations you made, how many chips would you advise them to use in each batch? Explain.

Cookie Number	Number of Chips per Cookie
1	
2	
3	
4	
5	
6	
7	
8	
9	
10	
11	
12	

D. 1. As a class, discuss students' recommendations from Question C. Choose a number the whole class can agree on.

   2. Conduct 30 simulations to randomly distribute the recommended number of chips among the 12 cookies. For each simulation, record whether each cookie has at least five chips. Organize your information in a table like the one at the right.

Simulation Trial Number	Did Each Cookie Have at Least Five Chips?
1	
2	
3	
4	
⋮	
30	

   3. What percent of the time did your simulation give at least five chips per cookie?

   4. Using the distribution of your simulation results, make a final recommendation to Jeff and Ted about how many chips to put in each batch. Justify your choice.

   5. Suggest what Jeff and Ted might say to promote their cookies in a more accurate way.

ACE Homework starts on page 54.

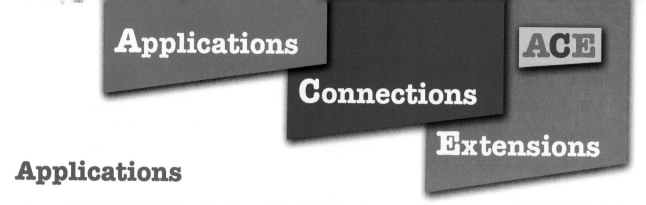
Applications

1. **a.** Refer to the arrowhead tables from Problem 3.1. These data include the neck width of each arrowhead. Calculate the five-number summaries of the neck-width data for all six sites (the two new sites and the four known sites).

neck width

   b. On the same scale, make a box plot of the neck-width data for each site.

   c. Based on your results from parts (a) and (b), during which time periods do you think Sites I and II were settled? Explain.

2. **a.** A baker makes raisin muffins in batches of four dozen. She pours a box of raisins into each batch. How could you use a sample from a batch of muffins to estimate the number of raisins in a box?

   b. There are 1,000 raisins in a box. How many raisins would you expect to find in a typical muffin? Explain.

3. Keisha opens a bag containing 60 chocolate chip cookies. She selects a sample of 20 cookies and counts the chips in each one. She records her data in the table shown.

   Estimate the number of chocolate chips in the bag. Explain.

Cookie	Chips
1	6
2	8
3	8
4	11
5	7
6	6
7	6
8	7
9	11
10	7

Cookie	Chips
11	8
12	7
13	9
14	9
15	8
16	6
17	8
18	10
19	10
20	8

4. Use Keisha's data from Exercise 3. Copy and complete each statement with the most appropriate fraction: $\frac{1}{4}, \frac{1}{6}$, or $\frac{1}{2}$.

More than ? of the cookies have at least 8 chips.

More than ? of the cookies have at least 9 chips.

More than ? of the cookies have at least 10 chips.

5. Yung-nan wants to estimate the number of beans in a large jar. She takes out 150 beans, marks each with a red dot, returns them to the jar, and mixes them with the unmarked beans. She then takes four samples from the jar.

Bean Samples

Sample	Total Beans	Beans With Red Dots
1	25	3
2	150	23
3	75	15
4	250	25

a. Which sample has the greatest percent of beans that are marked with red dots? Use this sample to predict the number of beans in the jar.

b. The shaded bars below are a visual way to think about making a prediction from Sample 3. Explain what the bars show and how they can be used to estimate the number of beans in the whole jar.

Sample 3
Beans in sample: 75

15, or 20% marked				

Whole Jar
Beans in entire jar: ?

150, or 20% marked				

c. Which sample has the least percent of beans that are marked with red dots? Use this sample to predict the number of beans in the jar.

d. What is your best guess for the total number of beans in the jar?

6. After testing many samples, an electric company determines that approximately 2 of every 1,000 light bulbs on the market are defective. Suppose Americans buy over a billion light bulbs every year. Estimate how many of these bulbs are defective.

7. Multiple Choice After testing many samples, a milk shipper determines that approximately 3 in every 100 cartons of milk leak. The company ships 200,000 cartons of milk every week. About how many of these cartons leak?

Go Online
PHSchool.com
For: Multiple-Choice Skills Practice
Web Code: apa-8354

    A. 3   **B.** 600   **C.** 2,000   **D.** 6,000

Connections

8. Multiple Choice The circle graph shows data for 1,585 students. Which is the best approximation of the number of students represented by the pink sector?

    F. 40   **G.** 160   **H.** 590   **J.** 58,650

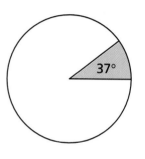

To monitor driving speeds, states set up radar checkpoints to measure the speeds of samples of drivers. Use this information for Exercises 9 and 10.

9. Suppose you want to show that drivers in your state generally obey speed limits. Where and when would you set up radar checkpoints?

10. Suppose you want to show that drivers in your state often exceed speed limits. Where and when would you set up radar checkpoints?

11. Sometimes graphs can be misleading. The graphs below all display the same data about the percent of newspapers recycled from 1993 to 2004.

Homework
Help Online
PHSchool.com
For: Help with Exercise 11
Web Code: ape-8311

a. Which graph do you think gives the clearest picture of the data pattern? Why?

b. Why are the other graphs misleading?

Number of Recycled Newspapers 1993–2004

Graph W

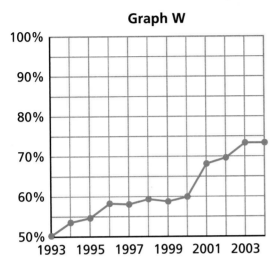

Graph X

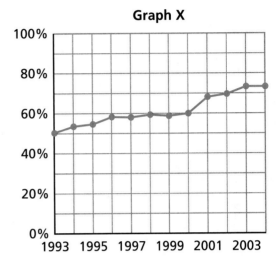

Graph Y

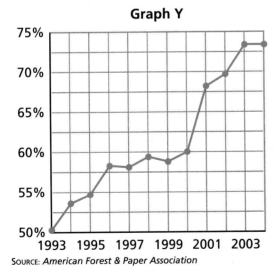

Graph Z

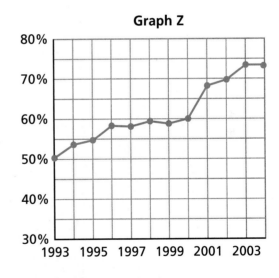

SOURCE: *American Forest & Paper Association*

Investigation 3 Solving Real-World Problems **57**

For Exercises 12–16, use these and other questions to analyze each survey.

- What is the goal of the survey?
- What is the population being studied?
- How is the sample chosen?
- How is the data analyzed and reported?
- Does the analysis support the conclusions?

12. In designing a remote control, representatives for a television manufacturer call 1,000 households with television sets. They find that remote-control users sit an average of 3 meters from their television sets. Based on this finding, the manufacturer designs the remote control to work well at distances of 2.5 meters to 3.5 meters from a television set.

13. A lightbulb manufacturer wants to know the "defect rate" for its product. One morning, the manager takes 10 boxes of 50 lightbulbs from the assembly line and tests them. All but five bulbs work. The manager concludes that production quality is acceptable.

14. A nutritionist wants to know what percent of Calories in a typical United States teenager's diet are from fat. She asks health teachers in Dallas, Texas, to have their students keep logs of what they eat on one school day. The nutritionist analyzes the logs and finds that the median intake was 500 fat Calories per day, which is the recommended daily allowance. She concludes that Calories from fat are not a problem in the diets of teenagers.

15. A cookie maker claims that there are over 1,000 chocolate chips in a bag of its cookies. A skeptical consumer calls the company and asks how they know this. A spokesperson says they chose a sample of bags of cookies, soaked each bag in cold water to remove all the dough, and weighed the chips that remained. In each case, the chips weighed more than a bag of 1,000 chocolate chips.

16. In the cafeteria line, Sam wrinkles his nose when he sees salami subs. When the cook asks what he would prefer, Sam replies, "I like bologna better." The cook surveys the next ten students. Seven students say they prefer bologna to salami. The cook decides to serve bologna subs instead of salami subs in the future.

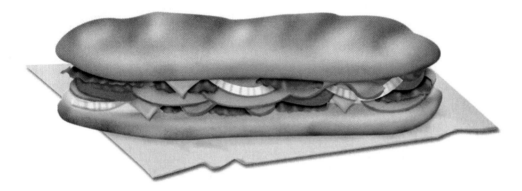

For Exercises 17–21, use the box plot below. Tell whether each statement is true. Explain.

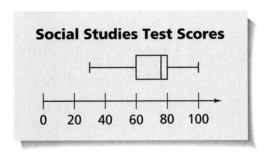

17. The class median is less than 80.

18. Half the class scored between 60 and 80.

19. At least one student earned a score of 100.

20. The class mean is probably less than the median.

21. If there are 30 students in the class, at least 10 scored above 80.

Extensions

22. A company produces pushpins in the percents shown in the table. The school secretary opens a large bag of pushpins. She puts the pins into small boxes to distribute to teachers. She puts 50 pins in each box.

Percent of Pushpins of Each Color

Color	Percent
white	15%
yellow	10%
red	15%
orange	20%
green	15%
blue	25%

   a. How many pushpins of each color do you expect to be in a box?

   b. How do you expect the number of pushpins of each color to vary across the samples?

   c. You can simulate filling the boxes by generating random integers from 1 to 20. Which numbers would you let represent each color? How many random numbers do you need to generate to simulate filling one box?

   d. Carry out the simulation described in part (c) three times. Compare the distributions of colors in your simulated samples with the expected distribution from part (a).

   e. Suppose the secretary selects a random sample of 1,000 pushpins from the bag. How closely would you expect the percent of each color in her sample to match the percent in the table?

23. You can use a simulation to help you answer this question:

If you select five students at random from your class, what is the probability that at least two will have the same birth month?

   a. Design a simulation to model this situation. Tell which month each simulation outcome represents.

   b. Use your birth-month simulation to produce at least 25 samples of five people. Use your results to estimate the probability that at least two people in a group of five will have the same birth month.

   c. Explain how you could revise your simulation to explore this question:

   What are the chances that at least two students in a class of 25 have the same birthday (month and day, but not year)?

Mathematical Reflections 3

In this investigation, you applied your knowledge of statistics and data displays to solve real-world problems. These questions will help you summarize what you have learned.

Think about your answers to these questions. Discuss your ideas with other students and your teacher. Then write a summary of your findings in your notebook.

1. How can you use statistics to

   a. compare samples?

   b. draw conclusions about the population from which each sample was selected?

2. In what ways can you expect the distribution of data values for a sample to be similar to and different from the distribution of data values for the entire population from which samples were selected?

Investigation 4

Relating Two Variables

Box plots and histograms allow you to look at one variable at a time. For example, you can use box plots to study the quality ratings of peanut butters. What if you wanted to study how the price of a peanut butter is related to its quality rating?

Finding the answer requires looking at how two variables are related. A **scatter plot** allows you to look at two variables at once. The scatter plot at the right shows (*quality rating, price*) pairs for each of the 37 types of peanut butter you studied in Investigation 1.

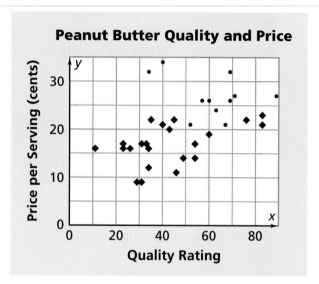

Peanut Butter Quality and Price

4.1 Are Quality Ratings and Prices Related?

Each point on the scatter plot gives you two pieces of information. For example, the point (60, 26) represents a peanut butter with a quality rating of 60 and a price of $0.26 per serving.

Problem 4.1 Interpreting Scatter Plots

A. Which symbol on the scatter plot represents data for the natural peanut butters? Which symbol is for the regular peanut butters?

B. What appears to be true about the prices of peanut butters with high quality ratings? With low quality ratings? Is there a relationship between quality rating and price? Explain.

C. Do any (*quality rating, price*) pairs appear to be unusual? Explain.

D. 1. How can you use the scatter plot to compare the quality ratings of natural with regular peanut butters?

　　2. How can you use the scatter plot to compare the prices of natural with regular peanut butters?

ACE **Homework starts on page 69.**

In *Data About Us*, a group of 54 sixth-grade students measured their arm spans and their heights. Their data are shown in the scatter plot.

Height and Arm Span

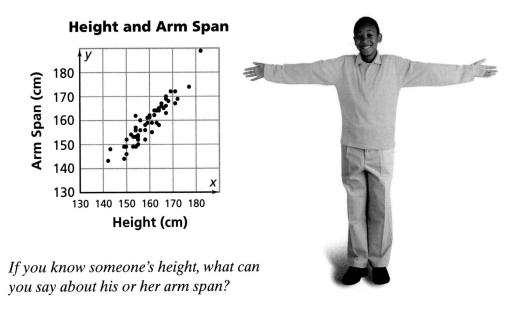

If you know someone's height, what can you say about his or her arm span?

Getting Ready for Problem

Find a line to model the trend in the data.

- Where does your line cross the *y*-axis?
- What is the *y*-coordinate of the point on the line with an *x*-coordinate of 190?
- What is the *x*-coordinate of the point with a *y*-coordinate of 175?

Problem 4.2 **Writing an Equation to Describe a Relationship**

A. Consider a line through (130, 130) and (190, 190).

1. How might you use this line to describe the relationship between height and arm span?

2. Write an equation for this line using *h* for height and *a* for arm span.

3. What is true about the relationship between height and arm span for the points on the line? For the points above the line? For the points below the line?

B. 1. Make a scatter plot of the (*body length, wingspan*) data from the table.

Airplane Comparisons

Plane	Engine Type	Body Length (m)	Wingspan (m)
Boeing 707	jet	46.6	44.4
Boeing 747	jet	70.7	59.6
Ilyushin IL-86	jet	59.5	48.1
McDonnell Douglas DC-8	jet	57.1	45.2
Antonov An-124	jet	69.1	73.3
British Aerospace 146	jet	28.6	26.3
Lockheed C-5 Galaxy	jet	75.5	67.9
Antonov An-225	jet	84.0	88.4
Airbus A300	jet	54.1	44.9
Airbus A310	jet	46.0	43.9
Airbus A320	jet	37.5	33.9
Boeing 737	jet	33.4	28.9
Boeing 757	jet	47.3	38.1
Boeing 767	jet	48.5	47.6
Lockheed Tristar L-1011	jet	54.2	47.3
McDonnell Douglas DC-10	jet	55.5	50.4
Aero/Boeing Spacelines Guppy	propeller	43.8	47.6
Douglas DC-4 C-54 Skymaster	propeller	28.6	35.8
Douglas DC-6	propeller	32.2	35.8
Lockheed L-188 Electra	propeller	31.8	30.2
Vickers Viscount	propeller	26.1	28.6
Antonov An-12	propeller	33.1	38.0
de Havilland DHC Dash-7	propeller	24.5	28.4
Lockheed C-130 Hercules/L-100	propeller	34.4	40.4
British Aerospace 748/ATP	propeller	26.0	30.6
Convair 240	propeller	24.1	32.1
Curtiss C-46 Commando	propeller	23.3	32.9
Douglas DC-3	propeller	19.7	29.0
Grumman Gulfstream I/I-C	propeller	19.4	23.9
Ilyushin IL-14	propeller	22.3	31.7
Martin 4-0-4	propeller	22.8	28.4
Saab 340	propeller	19.7	21.4

SOURCE: *Airport Airplanes*

2. Does your equation relating height and arm span from Question A also describe the relationship between body length and wingspan for airplanes? Explain.

3. Predict the wingspan of an airplane with a body length of 40 meters.

4. Predict the body length of an airplane with a wingspan of 60 meters.

C. 1. Use the scatter plot below. Does your equation relating height and arm span from Question A also describe the relationship between body length and wingspan for birds? Explain.

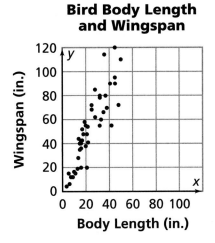

Bird Body Length and Wingspan

2. Find a line that fits the overall pattern of points. What is the equation of your line?

3. Predict the wingspan for a bird whose body length is 60 inches. Explain.

ACE Homework starts on page 69.

Human Development Index and Life Expectancies

The Human Development Index (HDI) is a number used to report how well a country is doing in overall human development. The HDI measures the average achievement in three basic dimensions of human development—a long and healthy life, access to education, and a decent standard of living.

Countries with an HDI of over 0.800 are part of the high human development group. Countries from 0.500 to 0.800 are part of the medium group. Countries below 0.500 are part of the low group.

Problem 4.3 Analyzing a Relationship

A. 1. Describe the variability in the data in the histogram.

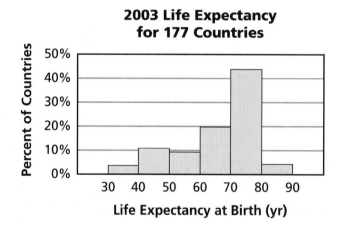

2. Estimate the percent of the countries with life expectancies of 60 years or greater.

3. Use the box plots. Describe how the life expectancies of the countries with upper and medium HDIs compare with the life expectancies of countries with low HDIs.

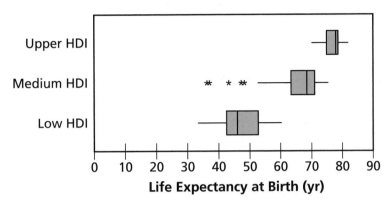

2003 Life Expectancy and HDI for 177 Countries

4. The medium HDI group has outliers. Using the table, identify which countries are the outliers. Explain.

2003 Life Expectancy and HDI

Country	Life Expectancy at Birth (yr)	HDI
Lao People's Dem. Rep.	54.7	0.545
Botswana	36.3	0.565
Zimbabwe	36.9	0.505
South Africa	48.4	0.658
Equatorial Guinea	43.3	0.655
India	63.3	0.602
Namibia	48.3	0.627
Uganda	47.3	0.508

SOURCE: *United Nations Development Programme*

B. Use a straightedge to locate the line $y = 0.01325x - 0.166$ on the scatter plot shown below. **Hint:** Use the equation to find two points, $(0, y_1)$ and $(80, y_2)$, on the line.

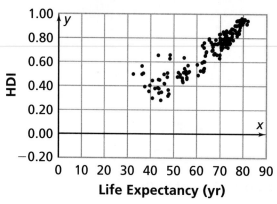

2003 Life Expectancy and HDI for 177 Countries

SOURCE: *United Nations Development Programme*

1. How well does this line model the relationship between life expectancy and HDI?

2. Use this line to estimate the HDI for $x = 90$ years.

3. Describe how you can use this line to estimate HDI when you know life expectancy.

ACE **Homework starts on page 69.**

Applications

1. a. Compare the values in the peanut butter comparison table in Problem 1.1 to the points on the scatter plot. Why are some points located on or very near the horizontal axis?

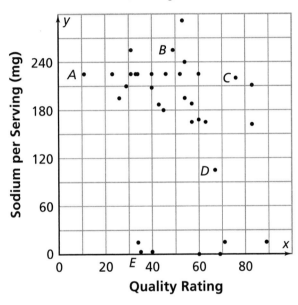

Peanut Butter Quality and Sodium Content

b. Give the approximate coordinates of each labeled point. Explain what the coordinates tell you about the peanut butter represented by the point.

c. Jeff says, "Most peanut butters, no matter what their quality rating, have between 160 and 240 milligrams of sodium per serving." Do you agree or disagree? Explain.

Nutrition Facts
Serving Size 2 Tbsp (32g)
Servings Per Container about 15

Amount Per Serving

Calories 190 Calories from Fat 140

	% Daily Value*
Total Fat 17g	**26%**
Saturated Fat 3.5g	**18%**
Cholesterol 0 mg	**0%**
Sodium 150mg	**6%**

	% Daily Value*
Total Carbohydrate 7g	**2%**
Dietary Fiber 2g	**8%**
Sugars 3g	
Protein 7g	

Vitamin A 0% • Vitamin C 0%
Calcium 0% • Iron 2% Niacin
20% Vitamin E 10%

*Percent Daily Values are based on a 2,000 calorie diet.

2. a. Plot the (*height, arm span*) data from the table below.

Homework Help Online
PHSchool.com
For: Help with Exercise 2
Web Code: ape-8402

Student Measurement Data

Gender	Height (cm)	Arm Span (cm)	Foot Length (cm)
F	160	158	25
M	111	113	15
F	160	160	23
F	152	155	23.5
F	146	144	24
F	157	156	24
M	136	135	21
F	143	142	23
M	147	145	20
M	133	133	20
F	153	151	25
M	148	149	23
M	125	123	20
F	150	149	20

b. Draw the line $y = x$ on your scatter plot.

c. Explain how this line can be used to describe the relationship between height and arm span.

d. Plot the (*height, foot length*) data.

e. Experiment with different lines to see if you can find one that fits the data. You might try $y = \frac{1}{2}x$ or $y = \frac{1}{3}y$. Give the equation of a line that "fits" the data.

3. This scatter plot shows (*length*, *width*) data for the arrowheads found at Kobold/Buffalo Creek (see Problem 3.1).

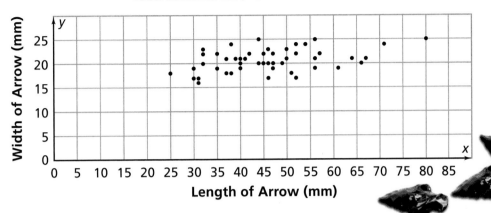

Kobold/Buffalo Creek Arrowheads

a. Estimate the range of the lengths.

b. Estimate the range of the widths.

c. Shannon drew the line $y = 20$. Do you think it gives a good estimate of the relationship between length and width? Explain.

d. Suppose you know the width of an arrowhead from the site that is not on the scatter plot. Can you predict its length? Explain.

Go Online
PHSchool.com
For: Multiple-Choice Skills
Practice
Web Code: apa-8454

Connections

For Exercises 4–6, use the graph below. There are two sections to the graph:

- The top section shows information about the world and about developing and least developed countries.

- The bottom section shows different continents.

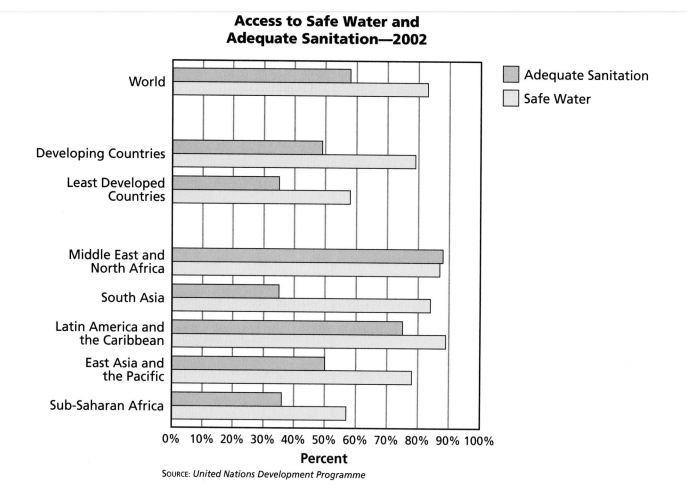

Access to Safe Water and Adequate Sanitation—2002

SOURCE: *United Nations Development Programme*

4. Write three comparison statements about the data.

5. Fill in the missing information to make a true statement.

With the exception of __?__ and __?__, at least 50% of the population of each region has access to adequate sanitation.

6. Multiple Choice Tell which fraction completes this statement:

In __?__ of the regions, less than 75% of the population has access to safe water.

A. $\frac{1}{5}$ **B.** $\frac{2}{5}$ **C.** $\frac{3}{5}$ **D.** $\frac{4}{5}$

7. A different type of scatter plot is shown at the right. Some of the peanut butters have the same price per serving and sodium content. When this happens, the "dots" are placed on top of each other so they slightly overlap. Suppose you know the price per serving for a peanut butter. Can you predict the amount of sodium in a serving? Explain.

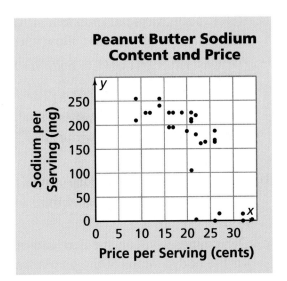

8. Using the data from the scatter plot in Exercise 7, tell which title matches each histogram below.

    Title 1: Distribution of Price per Serving

    Title 2: Distribution of Sodium per Serving

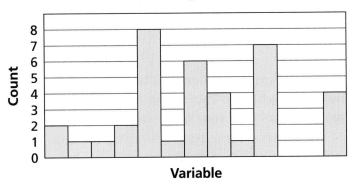

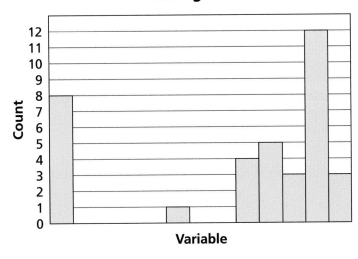

9. a. Refer to the Airplane Data from Problem 4.2. Make two histograms that allow you to compare the body lengths of propeller planes with those of jet planes. Experiment with interval widths of 5 or 10 meters. (Remember to use the same interval width on both graphs.)

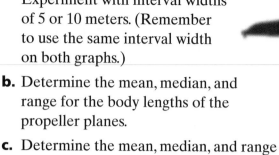

b. Determine the mean, median, and range for the body lengths of the propeller planes.

c. Determine the mean, median, and range for the body lengths of the jet planes.

d. Write three statements comparing the body lengths of propeller airplanes with the body lengths of jet airplanes.

For Exercises 10–13, write an equation for the line through the pair of points.

10. $(2, 3)$ and $(1, 6)$

11. $(0, 2)$ and $(-2, 7)$

12. $(-1, 0)$ and $(-2, -6)$

13. $(3, 7)$ and $(1, 8)$

Multiple Choice **Experts say that for every 20 pounds of body weight, you should carry only 3 pounds in a backpack. This means that your backpack should weigh no more than 15% of your body weight. Complete each sentence in Exercises 14–17 to make a true statement using the box plots on the facing page.**

14. At least ■ of students in seventh grade carry backpacks that are heavier than 15% of their body weight.

F. 25%   **G.** 50%   **H.** 75%   **J.** 100%

15. Over ■ of students in third grade carry backpacks that are in the acceptable weight range.

A. 25%   **B.** 50%   **C.** 75%   **D.** 100%

16. Between ■ of boys carry backpacks that are in the acceptable range.

F. 0 and 25%   **G.** 25% and 50%

H. 50% and 75%   **J.** 75% and 100%

17. Between ■ of girls carry backpacks that are not in the acceptable range.

A. 0 and 25%   **B.** 25% and 50%

C. 50% and 75%   **D.** 75% and 100%

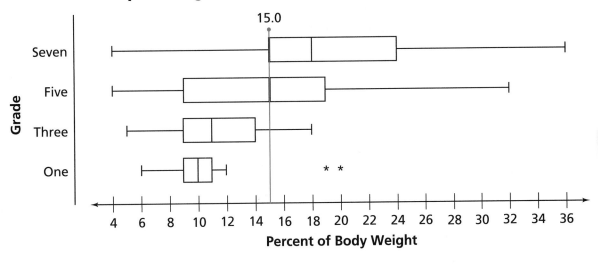

Backpack Weight as a Percent of Body Weight by Grade

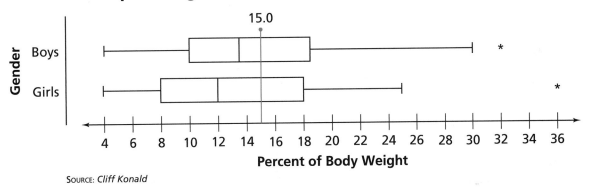

Backpack Weight as a Percent of Body Weight by Gender

Source: *Cliff Konald*

Tell whether each statement is true or false using the box plots above. Explain your reasoning.

18. Students in grades five and seven carry more backpack weight compared to body weight than do students in first or third grades.

19. Girls carry at least twice as much backpack weight compared to body weight as boys do.

20. The data for students in grade one has the most outliers.

21. The school Sam attends sells backpacks as a fundraiser. The school needs to sell $3,600 to earn enough to have a dance. Grade 6 collected $736.25. Grade 7 collected $1,211.25. Grade 8 collected $1,591.25. Sam says they have raised enough for the dance. He rounded the three totals to $800, $1,200, and $1,600 to get exactly $3,600. Is his estimate a good one? Why or why not?

22. **Multiple Choice** Sam's school bought some new technology equipment. They spent $2,089.98 on graphing calculators, $398.75 on motion detectors for experiments, and $4,456.20 on computers. The school will pay the bill in 12 equal installments. What is a reasonable amount for each payment?

F. $100

G. $500

H. $600

J. $1,000

For Exercises 23–25, use the box plot to choose one of the following numbers to make a correct statement: 75, 99, 106, 127, 151. Give evidence from the box plot to support each answer.

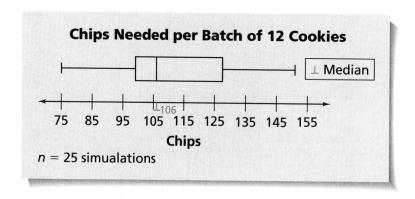

23. Half of all successful batches use fewer than __?__ chips.

24. You should add at least __?__ chips if you want to make a successful batch at least 75% of the time.

25. You should add at least __?__ chips if you want to make a successful batch at least 25% of the time.

26. **Multiple Choice** Which equation best fits the data in the graph?

A. $y = x$

B. $y = 7x$

C. $y = \dfrac{x}{7}$

D. There is too little information to know.

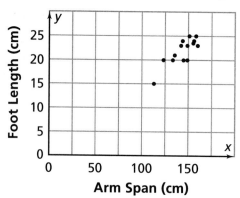

For a class project, students collect data about the number of boys or girls in the families of their classmates. Use the table below to answer Exercises 27–30.

Name	Number of Boys in the Family	Number of Girls in the Family
Anya	0	2
Brian	8	0
Charlie	1	2
Diane	0	1
Elisha	1	1
Felix	2	0
Gloria	0	2
Han	1	2
Ivan	1	1
Jorge	4	1

27. Anya wants to make a Venn diagram with the groups "Has Boys in the Family" and "Has Girls in the Family." She begins by placing herself on the diagram. Copy and complete her diagram below.

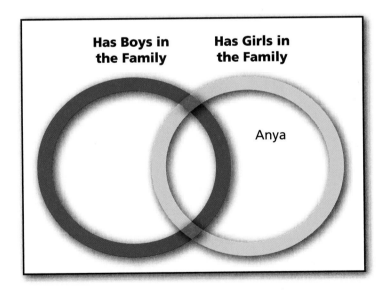

28. Make a bar graph that shows that the usual number of children in the family is two and that Brian's family is unusual.

29. Charlie wants to make a circle graph. What could the parts of the circle be labeled?

30. Make a graph to see if there is any relationship between the number of boys in a family and the number of girls in a family.

An Honor Society shovels snow for senior citizens on weekends. Some students can shovel only on Fridays, some can shovel only on Saturdays, some can shovel only on Sundays, some can shovel two out of three days, and some can shovel all three days. Justin is organizing this project and must report on it at the end of the school year.

For Exercises 31–35, decide which of these five representations Justin should choose. Explain why.

box plot	Venn diagram	circle graph
value bar graph	back-to-back stem-and-leaf plot	

31. Justin wants to know whom he can call on any snowy weekend day.

32. At the end of a month, Justin wants to show how many hours each person shoveled snow.

33. The Honor Society worked on the same project last year. Justin wants to compare the hours members spent shoveling snow this year with the hours spent shoveling snow last year.

34. The Honor Society performs four other service projects in addition to shoveling snow. Justin wants to report how the total hours spent on all the projects was divided among the five projects.

35. Some members contribute a lot of time and other just a little. Justin wants to make a graph that shows what is a typical time commitment, what is an outstanding time commitment, and what is an unusually low time commitment. He does not want to show individual names.

Extensions

36. a. The graph below models the relationship between a pumpkin's circumference and its weight. Suppose that, instead of being modeled by this curve, the relationship was modeled by the line $y = x$. What would this indicate about how the weight of a pumpkin changes as the circumference increases?

Pumpkin Measurements

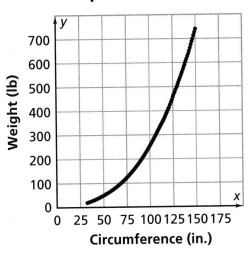

b. Describe what the actual curve indicates about how the weight of a pumpkin changes as the circumference increases.

Mathematical Reflections 4

In this investigation, you made scatter plots to look for relationships between pairs of variables. Where possible, you drew a line to fit the pattern in the points, and used the line to predict the value of one variable given the value of the other. These questions will help you summarize what you have learned.

Think about your answers to these questions. Discuss your ideas with other students and your teacher. Then write a summary of your findings in your notebook.

1. Describe some situations you explored in which the values of two variables are related in a predictable way. For example, you saw that you can estimate a person's arm span if you know his or her height.

2. Describe some situations you explored in which the values of two variables are not related in a predictable way. For example, as the lengths of the arrowheads increase, the widths do not increase in a regular pattern.

3. What does it mean to say one variable *is related to* another variable? Think about your answers to Questions 1 and 2.

Unit Project

Estimating a Deer Population

The statewide deer population in Michigan is estimated to be about 1.7 million.

How is it possible to estimate the deer population of a state, or even of a small part of a state?

The *capture-tag-recapture* method is one way of estimating a deer population. Biologists capture deer in a targeted area, tag them, and then release them. Later, they capture deer and count the number with tags to estimate the population of deer in the targeted area.

You can simulate the *capture-tag-recapture* method by using a container filled with white beans. Think of each bean as a deer in the upper peninsula of Michigan. Your job is to estimate the number of deer without actually counting them all.

Work with your group to perform the experiment described below.

Materials

a container with a lid

a package of white beans (about two cups)

a marker

Collect the Data

- Remove 100 beans from the container and mark them with a pen or marker.

- Put the marked beans back into the container and mix them with the unmarked beans.

- Without looking at the beans, one person should scoop out 25 beans from the jar. Record the number of marked and unmarked beans in this sample. Then, return the beans to the jar and mix the beans. Repeat this until everyone in your group has chosen a sample.

- Repeat the scoop-and-count procedure for samples of 50, 75, and 100 beans. For each sample, record the number of marked and unmarked beans.

Analyze and Summarize the Data

1. Find the percent of "deer" in each of your group's samples. Make one or more representations of these data.

2. Use tables, graphs, and statistics to analyze the data you collected.

3. Use your analysis to estimate the number of "deer" in your container.

4. Prepare a report about your experiment and findings. Be sure to include the following:

   - A discussion of how you investigated the problem

   - An analysis and summary of the data you collected, including tables, graphs, and statistics

   - An estimate of the number of "deer" in your container and an explanation of how you made this estimate

   You might also do Internet research on the following topics and include your findings in your report:

   - Other methods used to count deer

   - Methods used to count whales, salmon, prairie dogs, or other animals

Looking Back and Looking Ahead

Unit Review

In this unit, you collected, organized, and displayed sample data. You learned how to choose samples and how to compare samples in order to draw conclusions about the population from which they were taken. You also looked at the ways two attributes of a sample might be related.

For: Vocabulary Review Puzzle
Web Code: apj-8051

Use Your Understanding: Statistical Reasoning

Test your understanding and skill in the use of samples to describe populations by solving these problems that arose during a nutrition discussion in a health class.

1. One student claims that stores promote sales of cereals with high sugar content by putting them on low shelves, where children can see them.

   To test this claim, the class collects data for 77 different cereals. For each cereal, they record the sugar content and calories per serving and whether the cereal is on the top, middle, or bottom shelf.

   These plots show the sugar content of the cereals on each shelf.

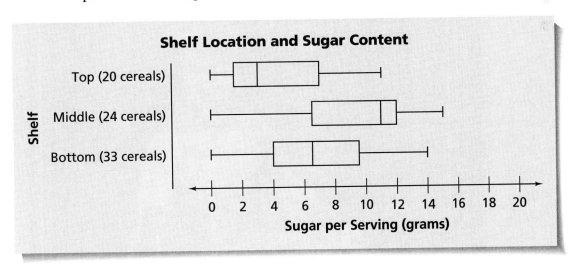

a. What is the range of sugar content for cereals on the top shelf? For cereals on the middle shelf? For cereals on the bottom shelf?

b. Estimate the median sugar content for the cereals on each shelf.

c. How many of the 20 top-shelf cereals have a sugar content greater than or equal to the upper quartile?

d. What percent of the 33 bottom-shelf cereals have a sugar content at least as great as the lower quartile but no greater than the upper quartile?

e. Does there seem to be a pattern relating sugar content and shelf placement for cereals?

f. The top shelf, middle shelf, and bottom shelf have different numbers of cereals. How does using a box plot make it easy to compare the three distributions?

g. Suppose you collected data from a sample of cereals in a supermarket near you. What do you think you would find out about the sugar content in cereals on different shelves?

2. Jerome wants to make a scatter plot to see if there is a relationship between sugar content and calories for the cereals. Instead of looking at data for all 77 cereals, he decides to choose a sample of 25. He considers three ways of selecting a sample.

- Method 1: List the 77 cereals in alphabetical order. Include every third cereal in the sample.

- Method 2: Choose the first eight cereals from each shelf.

- Method 3: Number the cereals from 1 to 77. Use two spinners with equal sections numbered 0–9 to produce 25 different two-digit numbers. Choose the cereals corresponding to these numbers.

a. Which method is an example of convenience sampling?

b. Which method is an example of random sampling?

c. Which method is an example of systematic sampling?

d. Which method would you recommend? Explain.

3. The health class randomly selects 50 of the 600 students in their school. They ask these students the following questions:

- Question 1: On how many school days last week did you eat cereal for breakfast?

- Question 2: Do you prefer sweetened or unsweetened cereal?

a. Of the students in the sample, 14 give answers of 4 or 5 to the first question. How many students in the entire school would you predict ate cereal on 4 or 5 days last week?

b. Of the students in the sample, 32 say they prefer sweetened cereal. How many students in the school would you expect to prefer sweetened cereal?

Explain Your Reasoning

When you compare data sets, read graphs, choose samples, and use samples to make predictions, you should be able to justify your procedures and conclusions.

4. In what types of situations are box plots useful tools?

5. In what types of situations are scatter plots useful tools?

6. When does it make sense to use data from a sample to study a population?

7. Describe three kinds of sampling methods and their strengths and weaknesses.

8. How could you choose a random sample?

Statistical techniques for collecting and displaying data and drawing conclusions are used in nearly every branch of science, business, and government work. You will extend and use your statistical understanding and skills in your classes, in your future jobs, and in your everyday life.

English/Spanish Glossary

B

box-and-whisker plot (or box plot) A display that shows the distribution of values in a data set separated into four equal-size groups. A box plot is constructed from the five-number summary of the data. The box plot below shows the distribution of quality ratings for natural brands of peanut butter.

gráfica de caja y brazos (o diagrama de caja) Una representación que muestra la distribución de valores de un conjunto de datos separada en cuatro grupos de igual tamaño. Una gráfica de caja y brazos se construye con el resumen de cinco números del conjunto de datos. La siguiente gráfica de caja y brazos representa la distribución de las calificaciones según la calidad de distintas marcas de mantequillas de maní.

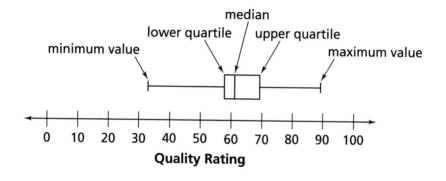

C

convenience sampling Choosing a sample because it is convenient. If you survey everyone on your soccer team who attends tonight's practice, you are surveying a convenience sample.

muestra de conveniencia Una muestra seleccionada porque es conveniente. Si entrevistaras a todos los integrantes de tu equipo de fútbol que asistan a la práctica esta noche, estarás encuestando una muestra de conveniencia.

D

distribution The arrangement of values in a data set.

distribución La disposición de valores en un conjunto de datos.

F

five-number summary The minimum value, lower quartile, median, upper quartile, and maximum value for a data set. These five values give a summary of the shape of the distribution and are used to make box plots. The five-number summary for the quality ratings for regular brands of peanut butter is as follows:

minimum value = 11
lower quartile = 31
median = 40
upper quartile = 54
maximum value = 83

resumen de cinco números El valor mínimo, el cuartil inferior, la mediana, el cuartil superior y el valor máximo de un conjunto de datos. Estos cinco valores dan un resumen de la forma de una distribución y se usan para hacer diagramas de caja. El resumen de cinco números para la calificación de calidad de las marcas de mantequilla de maní común es el siguiente:

valor mínimo = 11
cuartil inferior = 31
mediana = 40
cuartil superior = 54
valor máximo = 83

histogram A display that shows the distribution of numeric data. The range of data values, divided into intervals, is displayed on the horizontal axis. The vertical axis shows frequency in numbers or in percents. The height of the bar over each interval indicates the count or percent of data values in that interval. The histogram below shows quality ratings for regular brands of peanut butter. The height of the bar over the interval from 20 to 30 is 4. This indicates that four brands of peanut butter have quality ratings between 20 and 30.

histograma Una representación que muestra la distribución de datos numéricos. El rango de valores de los datos, dividido en intervalos, se representa en el eje horizontal. El eje vertical muestra la frecuencia en número o en porcentajes. La altura de la barra sobre cada intervalo indica el número, o porcentaje, de valores de datos en ese intervalo. El siguiente histograma representa la calificación por calidad de las marcas de mantequilla de maní común. La altura de la barra sobre el intervalo de 20 a 30 es 4. Esto indica que cuatro marcas de mantequilla de maní tienen una calificación entre 20 y 30.

Quality of Regular Brands

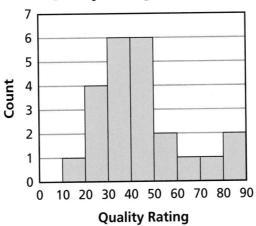

lower quartile The median of the data values to the left of the median (assuming the values are listed from least to greatest). For example, consider an odd number of data values:

1, 2, 5, 6, 7, 8, 8, 10, 12, 15, 20

There are 11 data values. The median of the data set is 8. (Six values are at or above 8 and six are at or below 8.) The median of the values to the left of the median (1, 2, 5, 6, 7) is 5. So, the lower quartile is 5.

Consider an even number of data values:
2, 3, 4, 5, 6, 6, 8, 8

There are eight data values. The median of the data set is 5.5, the average of 5 and 6. The data values to the left of the median are 2, 3, 4, and 5. The median of these values is 3.5. So, the lower quartile is 3.5.

cuartil inferior La mediana del valor de los datos a la izquierda de la mediana (asumiendo que los valores indicados van de menor a mayor). Por ejemplo, consideremos un número impar de valores de datos:

1, 2, 5, 6, 7, 8, 8, 10, 12, 15, 20

Hay 11 valores de datos. La mediana del conjunto de datos es 8. (Seis valores están en o sobre 8 y seis están en o bajo 8.) La mediana de los valores a la izquierda de la mediana es (1, 2, 5, 6, 7) es 5. De modo que el cuartil inferior es 5.

Consideremos un número par de valores de datos:
2, 3, 4, 5, 6, 6, 8, 8

Hay ocho valores de datos. La mediana del conjunto de datos es 5.5, el promedio de 5 y 6. Los valores de los datos a la izquierda de la mediana son 2, 3, 4 y 5. La mediana de estos valores es 3.5. De modo que el cuartil inferior es 3.5.

population The entire collection of people or objects you are studying.

población Un conjunto entero de personas u objetos en estudio.

random sampling Choosing a sample in a way that gives every sample from a population an equally likely chance of being selected.

muestra aleatoria Elegir una muestra de manera que se dé a cada miembro de una población la misma posibilidad de ser elegido.

sample A group of people or objects selected from a population.

muestra Un grupo de personas u objetos seleccionados de una población.

sampling distribution The distribution of the means (or medians) of a set of same-size samples selected randomly from the same population.

distribución de muestra Distribución de las medias (o medianas) de un conjunto de muestras del mismo tomaño, seleccionadas al azar de la misma población.

scatter plot A graph used to explore the relationship between two variables. The graph below is a scatter plot of (*quality rating, price per serving*) for several peanut butters. Each point represents the quality rating and price per serving for one peanut butter.

diagrama de dispersión Una gráfica usada para explorar la relación entre dos variables. El siguiente es un diagrama de dispersión (*clasificación de calidad, precio por porción*) para varias mantequillas de cacahuate. Cada punto representa la clasificación de calidad y el precio por porción de una mantequilla de cacahuate.

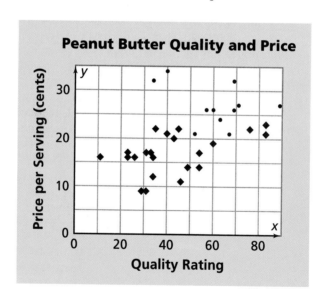

stem-and-leaf plot (or stem plot) A display that shows the distribution of values in a data set. Unlike a box plot or a histogram, a stem plot allows you to see the individual values in the data set. The stem plot below shows the distribution of quality ratings for regular brands of peanut butter. In this plot, the stems are a vertical list of the tens digits of the ratings. Attached to each stem are the corresponding leaves, in this case the ones digits. The leaves 3, 3, 6, and 9 next to the stem 2 indicate that the data set includes the values 23, 23, 26, and 29.

diagrama de tallo y hojas Una representación que muestra la distribución de valores en un conjunto de datos. A diferencia de una gráfica de caja y brazos o un histograma, un diagrama de tallo y hojas permite ver los valores individuales de un conjunto de datos. El diagrama de tallo y hojas siguiente muestra la distribución de la calificación por calidad de las marcas de mantequilla de maní común. En este diagrama, los tallos son una lista vertical de los dígitos de las decenas de las calificaciones. Unidas a cada tallo están las hojas correspondientes, en este caso, los dígitos de las unidades. Las hojas 3, 3, 6 y 9 al lado del tallo 2, indican que el conjunto de datos incluye los valores 23, 23, 26, y 29.

**Quality Ratings
of Regular
Peanut Butters**

Stem	Leaves
0	
1	1
2	3 3 6 9
3	1 1 3 4 4 5
4	0 0 3 5 6 9
5	4 4
6	0
7	6
8	3 3
9	

Key: 2 | 6 means 26

systematic sampling Choosing a sample in a methodical way. If you survey every tenth person on an alphabetical list of names, you are surveying a systematic sample.

muestra sistemática Una muestra seleccionada de una manera metódica. Si entrevistaras a cada décima persona en una lista de nombres en orden alfabético, estarías encuestando una muestra sistemática.

upper quartile The median of the data values to the right of the median (assuming the values are listed from least to greatest). For example, consider an odd number of data values:

1, 2, 5, 6, 7, 8, 8, 10, 12, 15, 20

There are 11 data values. The median of the data set is 8. The median of the values to the right of the median (8, 10, 12, 15, and 20) is 12. So, the upper quartile is 12.

Consider an even number of data values:
2, 3, 4, 5, 6, 6, 8, 8

There are eight data values. The median of the data set is 5.5, the average of 5 and 6. The data values to the right of the median are 6, 6, 8, 8. The median of these values is 7. So, the upper quartile is 7.

cuartil superior La mediana de los valores de los datos a la derecha de la mediana (asumiendo que los valores están indicados de menor a mayor). Por ejemplo, consideremos un número impar de valores de datos:

1, 2, 5, 6, 7, 8, 8, 10, 12, 15, 20

Hay 11 valores de datos. La mediana del conjunto de datos es 8. La mediana de los valores a la derecha de la mediana (8, 10, 12, 15, y 20) es 12. De modo que el cuartil superior es 12.

Consideremos un número par de valores de datos:
2, 3, 4, 5, 6, 6, 8, 8

Hay ocho valores de datos. La mediana del conjunto de datos es 5.5, el promedio de 5 y 6. Los valores de los datos a la derecha de la mediana son 6, 6, 8, 8. La mediana de estos valores es 7. De modo que el cuartil superior es 7.

voluntary-response sample A sample that selects itself. If you put an ad in the school paper asking for volunteers to take a survey, the students who respond will be a voluntary-response sample.

muestra de respuesta voluntaria Una muestra que se selecciona a sí misma. Si pones un anuncio en el periódico escolar pidiendo voluntarios para participar en una encuesta, los estudiantes que respondan serán una muestra de respuestas voluntarias.

Index

Index

Acknowledgments

Team Credits

The people who made up the **Connected Mathematics 2** team—representing editorial, editorial services, design services, and production services—are listed below. Bold type denotes core team members.

Leora Adler, Judith Buice, Kerry Cashman, Patrick Culleton, Sheila DeFazio, Richard Heater, **Barbara Hollingdale, Jayne Holman,** Karen Holtzman, **Etta Jacobs,** Christine Lee, Carolyn Lock, Catherine Maglio, **Dotti Marshall,** Rich McMahon, Eve Melnechuk, Kristin Mingrone, Terri Mitchell, **Marsha Novak,** Irene Rubin, Donna Russo, Robin Samper, Siri Schwartzman, **Nancy Smith,** Emily Soltanoff, **Mark Tricca,** Paula Vergith, Roberta Warshaw, Helen Young

Additional Credits

Diana Bonfilio, Mairead Reddin, Michael Torocsik, nSight, Inc.

Photos

2 t, Design Pics Inc./Alamy; **2 b,** eStock Photo/Peter Miller; **3,** Fritz Polking/The Image Works; **5,** Burke/Triolo Productions/FoodPix/PictureQuest; **7,** Michael Newman/PhotoEdit; **16,** Nicole Katano/AGE Fotostock; **21,** SW Productions/Getty Images, Inc.; **24,** Kim Karpeles/Alamy; **26,** Spencer Grant/PhotoEdit; **27,** Rob Melnychuk/Getty Images, Inc.; **30,** Richard Haynes; **35,** Max Oppenheim/Getty Images, Inc.; **37,** Design Pics Inc./Alamy; **39,** image100/SuperStock; **43,** Bob Johns/expresspictures.co.uk/Alamy; **47,** Louie Psihoyos/Corbis; **48,** Hemera Technologies/Alamy; **50,** SuperStock/AGE Fotostock; **51,** Gary Conner/Index Stock Imagery, Inc.; **54,** Hemera Technologies/Alamy; **56,** Peter Casolino/Alamy; **58,** David Mendelsohn/Masterfile; **63,** Richard Haynes; **65,** Brakefield Photo/PictureQuest; **70,** Richard Haynes; **71 all,** Hemera Technologies/Alamy; **72,** © Airbus—photo by exm company—P. Masclet; **79,** altrendo nature/Getty Images, Inc.; **81,** eStock Photo/Peter Miller

Technical Illustration

WestWords, Inc.

Cover Design

tom white.images

Data Sources

The peanut butter data on page 6 are from Consumer Reports®, September, 1990. Copyright © 1990–2006 Consumers Union of U.S., Inc.

The juice data on page 21 are from "Parents Beware: Juice in juice drinks costs up to £34 per litre!" in Food Magazine, April 30, 2004. Copyright © 2004 The Food Commission.

The team rosters on page 23 are from www.nba.com Copyright © 2004–2006 NBA Media Ventures, LLC.

The information in the third bullet on page 27 is reprinted with permission of the Institute of General Semantics, Fort Worth, TX.

The arrowhead data on pages 48, 49, and 71 are from "A Mathematical Technique for Dating Projectile Points Common to the Northwestern Plains" by George C. Knight and James D. Keyser in Plains Anthropologist #28 Volume 101. Copyright © 1983 Plains Anthropological Society.

The data for the graphs on page 57 are from The Recovered Paper Statistical Highlights, 2005 Edition, by the American Forest and Paper Association. Copyright © 2005 by the American Forest and Paper Association, Inc. Used by permission.

The airplane data on page 64 are from *Guide to Airport Airplanes* by William and Frank Berk. Copyright © 1993 Plymouth Press, Ltd.